James Lorimer

The Institutes of the Law of Nations

A Treatise of the Jural Relations of Separate Political Communities: Vol. I.

James Lorimer

The Institutes of the Law of Nations

A Treatise of the Jural Relations of Separate Political Communities: Vol. I.

ISBN/EAN: 9783337072025

Printed in Europe, USA, Canada, Australia, Japan

Cover: Foto ©Suzi / pixelio.de

More available books at **www.hansebooks.com**

THE INSTITUTES

OF

THE LAW OF NATIONS

A TREATISE OF THE

JURAL RELATIONS OF SEPARATE
POLITICAL COMMUNITIES

BY

JAMES LORIMER, LL.D.

ADVOCATE, REGIUS PROFESSOR OF PUBLIC LAW AND OF THE LAW OF NATURE AND
NATIONS IN THE UNIVERSITY OF EDINBURGH, MEMBER OF THE INSTITUTE
OF INTERNATIONAL LAW, CORRESPONDING MEMBER OF THE
ACADEMY OF JURISPRUDENCE OF MADRID, ETC.

IN TWO VOLUMES

VOL. I.

WILLIAM BLACKWOOD AND SONS
EDINBURGH AND LONDON
MDCCCLXXXIII

TO

HIS COLLEAGUES AND FRIENDS,

THE MEMBERS AND ASSOCIATES OF THE INSTITUTE
OF INTERNATIONAL LAW,

THIS ATTEMPT

TO DISCOVER THE JURAL RELATIONS OF

SEPARATE POLITICAL COMMUNITIES,

IS RESPECTFULLY AND

AFFECTIONATELY DEDICATED

BY

THE AUTHOR.

PREFATORY NOTE.

IN the volume which I now present to the public, I have endeavoured to determine the characteristics of national existence on which the right to international recognition depends, and to trace the specific rights which such recognition confers and the duties which it imposes, under normal conditions.

In the second volume, which I hope soon to publish, I shall take account of the action of those disturbing elements which appear to be inseparable from international life, and shall strive to fix the jural objects, and to determine the jural limits of war and neutrality.

My anxiety to place International Law on deeper and more stable foundations than comity or convention, and to vindicate for international jurisprudence the character of a science of nature which I have elsewhere claimed for jurisprudence as a whole, has led me to depart, to a considerable extent, from the lines which are followed in the ordinary text-books. More prominence has been given to the ethical element, and the conception of the interdependence of States has been substituted for that of their independence. Should it appear to those who do me the honour to criticise this work, that any justification of this course is desirable, beyond what is supplied by the book itself, I shall endeavour to furnish it in the second volume.

In the meantime, I have only to thank my colleagues of the Institute, Mr Westlake and M. Nys—and my former pupils, Mr Forrest and Mr Orr, Advocates—for their valuable suggestions and kind assistance in correcting the press.

CONTENTS.

INTRODUCTION.

CHAPTER I.—PRELIMINARY DEFINITIONS AND DIVISIONS, . . 1

Definitions—The law of nations is :
- (*A*) The law of nature realised in the relations of separate nations, . 1
- (*B*) The realisation of the freedom of separate nations, . . 2
- (*C*) The realisation of the freedom of separate nations by the reciprocal assertion and recognition of their real powers, . . . 3

Divisions—
I. In relation to its objects, the Law of Nations, or International Law, divides itself into three leading doctrines :
- (*A*) The doctrine of recognition, ... 3
- (*B*) The doctrine of the normal relations that result from the doctrine of recognition, ... 3
- (*C*) The doctrine of the abnormal relations that result from the doctrine of recognition, ... 4
  - 1st, The fundamental doctrine of recognition, as the doctrine of international existence *de facto*, or of State life for international purposes, corresponds to that fundamental doctrine of natural law which teaches that all rights and duties have their origin in, and are limited by, the facts of natural life, . 4
    - (*a*) Absolute recognition, or recognition that there is a State, 4
    - (*b*) Relative recognition, or recognition that there is such a State, ... 4

II. In relation to the spheres which it covers, or the interests which it embraces, International Law divides itself into :

(A) Public, ... 4
(B) Public and private, ... 5
(C) Private, ... 5

CHAPTER II.—OF THE NORMAL AND ABNORMAL RELATIONS OF STATES, 5

1st, Of the normal relations, ... 5
2d, Of the abnormal relations, ... 6
   (a) As between belligerents, ... 6
   (b) As between belligerents and neutrals, ... 6
   (c) As between neutrals, ... 6

CHAPTER III.—OF THE NATIONAL AND COSMOPOLITAN SCHOOLS OF INTERNATIONAL JURISPRUDENCE, ... 9

CHAPTER IV.—OF THE GENERAL CHARACTERISTICS OF THE LAW OF NATIONS, ... 11

(A) The law of nations is coeval with the existence of nations, . . 11
(B) The law of nations is coextensive with national development, . 12
(C) Only in so far as the conditions of its existence arise from the voluntary activity or inactivity of nations, can the positive law of nations be said to be voluntary, ... 13
(D) The object of the law of nations in each separate relation may be deduced from its general object—liberty, ... 15

BOOK I.

OF THE SOURCES OF THE LAW OF NATIONS.

CHAPTER I.—OF THE LAW OF NATURE AS DETERMINING THE OBJECTS OF THE LAW OF NATIONS, ... 19

CHAPTER II.—OF INTERNATIONAL CUSTOMS AS UNCONSCIOUS INTERPRETERS OF THE LAW OF NATURE IN INTERNATIONAL RELATIONS, ... 27

Of bad customs, ... 31
   (a) Those which are bad essentially, on the ground that they violate permanent natural laws, ... 32
   (b) Those which, continuing after the circumstances in which they arose have changed, no longer generate law, . . . 32
   (c) Those which have sprung out of reactionary tendencies, . . 33

CHAPTER III.—OF TREATIES, ... 37
1st, Those which determine an isolated fact in dispute between two nations, in accordance with a recognised principle, . . 43
2d, Those which define or determine a principle in dispute, by which it is intended that, as between the parties, a certain course of action shall in future be regulated, ... 43
3d, Those which profess to declare the absolute law of nations, and to which the parties not only bind themselves, but which they urge on the acceptance of other nations, ... 44

CHAPTER IV.—OF PRECEDENTS, . . . 51

CHAPTER V.—OF SCIENTIFIC OR CONSCIOUS INTERPRETATION OF THE NATURAL LAWS OF INTERNATIONAL RELATIONS, . . 54

Agencies by which the intellectual processes to which we must look for our systematic knowledge of the law of nations may be performed, ... 55
I. Sovereigns and their ministers, and in constitutional countries the legislative assemblies which act as the advisers of the executive, ... 55
II. Scientific jurists acting in conjunction, whether in their private capacity, or together with the constituted authorities of one or more States, ... 57
III. Scientific jurists acting in isolation, ... 58

CHAPTER VI.—OF CONTEMPORARY PUBLIC OPINION, . 87

BOOK II.

OF THE RECOGNITION OF STATE-EXISTENCE AS THE FUNDAMENTAL DOCTRINE OF THE LAW OF NATIONS.

CHAPTER I.—OF THE DISTINCTION BETWEEN INTERNATIONAL RECOGNITION AND INTERETHNICAL RECOGNITION, . . 93

CHAPTER II.—OF INTERNATIONAL RECOGNITION IN GENERAL, . 101

CHAPTER III.—OF PLENARY POLITICAL RECOGNITION, . . 104

Plenary political recognition may be defined as a formal declaration of the result of an inductive process, by which one separate political entity has satisfied itself that another entity, phenomenally presented to it, possesses a separate political existence, . . 104

CHAPTER IV.—OF THE RIGHT TO DETERMINE THE FACT OF JURAL STATE EXISTENCE, ... 105

The right to determine the fact of the jural existence or non-existence of a claimant for recognition rests with the State, or States, from which recognition is claimed, ... 105

CHAPTER V.—OF THE FUNCTION OF SCIENCE IN DETERMINING THE FACT OF JURAL STATE-EXISTENCE, . . . 108

The conditions which, if satisfied, imply a right to plenary political recognition, may be determined scientifically, and enunciated as permanent maxims of international law, ... 108

CHAPTER VI.—ON THE PRESUMPTION OF RECIPROCATING WILL, 109

CHAPTER VII.—OF RELIGIOUS CREEDS WHICH EXCLUDE THE PRESUMPTION OF RECIPROCATING WILL, . . . 113

CHAPTER VIII.—OF SECULAR CREEDS WHICH EXCLUDE THE PRESUMPTION OF RECIPROCATING WILL, . . . 126

1. Of intolerant monarchies, ... 127
2. Of intolerant republics, ... 131
3. Of intolerant anarchies, ... 132

CHAPTER IX.—OF THE PRESUMPTION OF RECIPROCATING POWER, 133

CHAPTER X.—OF THE SIZE OF THE STATE, ... 136

CHAPTER XI.—OF THE EXTERNAL FREEDOM, OR, AS IT IS COMMONLY CALLED, THE "INDEPENDENCE" OF THE STATE, . 139

1st, The recognition of the inchoate State as a jural claimant for separate recognition, ... 141
2d, Recognition for neutral purposes not directly connected with war, . 151

3d, Formal and public recognition, by which all the rights and privileges of an adult political community are acknowledged to reside in the new-born State, ... 152

CHAPTER XII.—OF THE INTERNAL FREEDOM OF THE STATE, . 155

CHAPTER XIII.— OF COMMUNITIES THAT ARE DEPRIVED OF INTERNAL FREEDOM, ON THE GROUND THAT THEY ARE INCAPABLE OF EXPRESSING OR REALISING THEIR RECIPROCATING WILL UNDER ANY FORM OF INTERNAL GOVERNMENT, . . 156

1st, Nonage, ... 157
2d, Imbecility, ... 157
  (*a*) Congenital imbecility, ... 157
  (*b*) Superinduced imbecility, ... 158
3d, Criminality, ... 160

CHAPTER XIV.—OF COMMUNITIES THAT ARE CUT OFF FROM RECOGNITION, ON THE GROUND THAT THE FORMS OF INTERNAL GOVERNMENT UNDER WHICH THEY PROFESS TO LIVE INCAPACITATE THEM FOR EITHER EXPRESSING OR REALISING RECIPROCATING WILL, ... 162

1st, Personal governments, whether hereditary or elective, and whether professing to be founded on divine or on human will, . . 163
2d, Class governments, or governments which rest on the assumption either of the absolute equality or permanent inequality of individuals or of classes, ... 165

CHAPTER XV.—OF THE NECESSITY OF ASCERTAINING THE RELATIVE VALUE OF STATES, ... 168

CHAPTER XVI.— OF THE MEANS OF ASCERTAINING THE RELATIVE VALUE OF STATES, ... 182

1st, The extent of the State as an element in determining its relative claim to recognition, ... 182
2d, The content of the State or the quality of the materials of which it is composed, ... 184
  (*a*) Material wealth, ... 185
  (*b*) Moral and intellectual qualities, ... 185

3d, The form of the State,	188
(*a*) Simple States,	191
(*b*) Composite States,	194
4th, The form of government, or the manner in which the materials of the State are brought into action,	203
(*a*) Constitutional monarchies, in which the constitution embraces the whole population, individuals being classified, and counted not as equally but as relatively or proportionally endowed with rational will,	208
(*b*) Constitutional republics, where the constitution res·s on the rational will of the community,	210
(*c*) Constitutional States, where the constitution embraces the rational will only to a partial extent,	211
(*d*) Non-constitutional States, where the general will finds expression only through the organic structure of society,	211
(*e*) Pseudo-despotic and pseudo-democratic States,	212
(*f*) Of the power by which the relative value of the State is to be determined and its international position assigned to it,	212
CHAPTER XVII.—OF PARTIAL RECOGNITION,	216

BOOK III.

OF THE NORMAL RELATIONS OF STATES.

CHAPTER I.— OF THE DISTINCTION BETWEEN NORMAL AND ABNORMAL RELATIONS; AND BETWEEN ABNORMAL RELATIONS WHICH ARE JURAL AND THOSE WHICH ARE ANTI-JURAL,	223
(*A*) Normal jural relations,	223
1st, Normal relations by the law of nature, between communities within and without the pale of recognition,	223
(*a*) Relations of mutual forbearance,	224
(*b*) Relations of pupilarity and guardianship,	224
2d, Normal relations by the law of nations between communities within the pale of recognition,	224
(*a*) Relations of mutual confidence,	224
(*b*) Relations of mutual aid,	224
(*B*) Abnormal jural relations,	224
1st, Abnormal jural relations by the law of nature between communities within and without the pale of recognition,	225

CONTENTS.

2d, Abnormal jural relations by the law of nations between communities within the pale of recognition, . . . 225
    (a) Active, ... 225
    (b) Passive, ... 225
(C) Abnormal anti-jural relations, ... 225
    1st, Abnormal anti-jural relations by the law of nature between communities within and without the pale of recognition, . 225
    2d, Abnormal anti-jural relations by the law of nations between communities within the pale of recognition, . . . 226
        (a) Violation of objective freedom, ... 226
        (b) Voluntary failure to maintain subjective freedom, . . 226
        (c) Voluntary failure to defend subjective freedom, . . 226
        (d) Voluntary neutrality, or failure to intervene in behalf of objective freedom, ... 226

CHAPTER II.—OF THE NORMAL RELATIONS BY THE LAW OF NATURE BETWEEN COMMUNITIES WITHIN AND WITHOUT THE PALE OF RECOGNITION, ... 226

1st, Negative, ... 227
2d, Positive, ... 227

CHAPTER III.—NORMAL RELATIONS BY THE LAW OF NATIONS BETWEEN COMMUNITIES WITHIN THE PALE OF RECOGNITION, 230

Of the relations of mutual confidence in general, . . . 230

CHAPTER IV.—OF POLITICAL INTERCOURSE—OF LEGATION, . 236

1st, Legation results from recognition, ... 236
2d, Legation is measured by recognition, ... 237
3d, A public minister represents the sovereignty of the State which sends him, as a whole, and not any separate branch or function of that sovereignty, ... 240
4th, Of the ranking of international agents, ... 241
    Regulations annexed to the Vienna Congress Treaty of June 9, 1815, 244
    Protocol of Conference of the Five Powers at Aix-la-Chapelle, November 21, 1818, ... 245
5th, The right of legation involves the conditions of its exercise, . 245
    (a) The right of passage through intermediate States, . . 246
    (b). The right of holding personal intercourse with the representative of sovereignty in the State to which he is sent, . . 247

(c) The rights of exterritoriality and inviolability, . . . 248
(d) Exterritoriality of ships, ... 252
(e) Exterritoriality of foreign armies, ... 260

CHAPTER V.—OF POLITICAL INTERCOURSE—*continued*, . . 260

Of the negotiation and ratification of treaties, ... 260

CHAPTER VI.—OF POLITICAL INTERCOURSE—*continued*, . . 269

The literature of legation, ... 269

CHAPTER VII.—OF MERCANTILE INTERCOURSE, . . . 287

The consular office, ... 287
The consular service of this country consists of five classes—
  1. Agents and consul-generals, ... 298
  2. Consul-generals, ... 298
  3. Consuls, ... 298
  4. Vice-consuls, ... 298
  5. Consular agents, ... 298
General instructions for her Majesty's consuls, issued by the Secretary
  of State for the Foreign Department, ... 300
With reference to the *exequatur*, or authority from the foreign State to
  act within its jurisdiction, ... 300
With reference to the advice and assistance to be given to British subjects, ... 302
Correspondence, public and private, ... 303
With reference to protection on board of British ships, . . . 304
The commercial report, &c., ... 305
Interference of foreign courts of justice, ... 308
With reference to naval courts, ... 310
Consular treaty between France and Italy, ... 316

CHAPTER VIII.—OF THE RECIPROCAL RECOGNITION OF PUBLIC
  MUNICIPAL LAW BY SEPARATE STATES, . . . 325

1st, Of the legislative capacity of the State, ... 325
2d, Of the distinction between legislation which has reference to public,
  and legislation which has reference to private, relations, . . 326
3d, Of the judicial capacity of the State, ... 328
4th, Of the executive capacity of the State, ... 330
5th, Of the *forum* of foreigners, ... 331

CONTENTS. xvii

6th, Of the exceptional position of criminal judgments, . . . 332
  (1st) The diversity of punishments arising from the necessity of adapting them to the special conditions of each people, or to the opinions with reference to these conditions which locally prevail, ... 338
  (2d) The difficulty of throwing criminal courts open to foreign prosecutors, as civil courts are thrown open to civil pursuers, . 339
7th, Of extradition treaties, ... 339
8th, Of the *droit de renvoi*, ... 344
Note—Resolutions of the Institute on the subject of "Extradition," . 345

CHAPTER IX.—OF THE RECIPROCAL RECOGNITION OF PRIVATE MUNICIPAL LAW BY SEPARATE STATES, . . . 348

1st, Introductory remarks, ... 348
  I. Of the relation in which private international law stands to the doctrine of international recognition, ... 350
  II. Of the objects of private international law, . . . 351
  III. Private international law being a doctrine of rights and duties, logically deducible from the doctrine of recognition, is a branch of the science of nature, ... 357
  IV. The fundamental propositions of private international law, . 370
  V. Of the temporary and partial exclusion of recognition necessitated by conflicting interpretations of natural law, and the consequent call for assimilation of municipal systems, . . . 371
  VI. Of the permanent exclusion of assimilation by diversity of circumstances, and the consequent call for the reciprocal recognition of conflicting municipal laws, ... 373
  VII. Diversity of circumstances does not always exclude assimilation of legal systems, ... 377
  VIII. The law-merchant, ... 379
  IX. Private international law is not a separate system of positive law, and in this respect it differs both from public international law and from municipal law public and private, . . 385
  X. The rules of private international law necessarily form part of every municipal system, and may consequently be enforced by the municipal executive, ... 390
  XI. Of treaties for the adoption of uniform rules of private international law, ... 392
  XII. The determination of the temporal limits of rules of law belongs to municipal, not to international, jurisprudence, . . 393
  XIII. Of the means of localising legal relations, . . . 396

(a) Of the classification of legal relations, ... 396
(b) Appreciation of the statutory theory, ... 404
(c) Modern significance of the statutory theory, . . . 407
(d) Of the localisation of the rights and obligations which result to persons from the possession of immovables, . . . 409
(e) Of the localisation of the personal rights and duties which result from the possession of movables, ... 416
(f) Of the localisation of the person, ... 422
(g) Of the localisation of jural acts, ... 438
(h) Of the rule, *locis regit actum*, ... 441
(i) Of the *lex fori*, ... 443

CHAPTER X.—RELATIONS OF MUTUAL AID, . . . 445

(A) Pacific co-operation in behalf of freedom, . . . 445
(B) Warlike co-operation in behalf of freedom, . . . 448

THE

INSTITUTES OF THE LAW OF NATIONS.

INTRODUCTION.

CHAPTER I.

PRELIMINARY DEFINITIONS AND DIVISIONS.

Definitions.

THOUGH I am not forgetful of the warning that *omnis definitio in jure periculosa est*, it seems to me desirable, for reasons similar to those which I stated at the outset of the 'Institutes of Law,'[1] that we should enter on the study of the Law of Nations, if not with a scientific definition, at all events with a definite statement of the object of our search. With this view, then, I shall venture to define the Law of Nations as:

(*A*) *The law of nature realised in the relations of separate nations.*

But we have seen[2] that the perfect relation of all separate rational entities, when realised, is freedom — liberty to be, and to develop themselves in accordance with their

[1] P. 1.   [2] *Ib.*, pp. 355, 356.

A

idea, or, in other words, with the special character which their nature has assigned to them. Assuming this to be so, the Law of Nations may be farther and more specifically defined as :

(*B*) *The realisation of the freedom of separate nations.*

Lastly: we discovered the arrangements of nature to be such that no created entity can realise its freedom in isolation. Freedom and independence, though so often confounded, are so far from being identical, that, in human relations, they are not even reconcilable;[1] whilst, in the relations of the human to the divine, freedom identifies itself with voluntary dependence.[2] Creaturely freedom is thus a position not only of absolute dependence on creative power, but of relative dependence on other created powers; and this relative dependence in the last analysis will be found to include all created powers. The greater, the more real, or, to use what we found[3] to be an equivalent expression, the more reasonable the power, the less, in one sense, is its dependence on other created powers. But power, as the measure of rights, all of which may be summed up in the right to liberty,[4] we farther discovered[5] to be the measure of responsibility, and that the discharge of this responsibility is involved in the exercise of the power to which it corresponds. Power thus necessarily becomes the source of another form of dependence. Real power cannot be "selfish" without ceasing to be real. It becomes phenomenal merely, and in the end self-contradictory and suicidal. But the more real it is, the more does its self-

---

[1] *Institutes of Law*, p. 371.   [2] *Ib.*, p. 368.   [3] *Ib.*, pp. 426, 427.
[4] *Ib.*, p. 235.   [5] *Ib.*, p. 238.

assertion involve the recognition, and, if need be, the vindication, of the powers which are centred in other entities. Subjective powers rest upon and are measured by objective powers, just as subjective rights and duties rest upon and are measured by objective rights and duties.

By keeping in view this law of what we may call ethical or jural gravitation, which, at bottom, is nothing more than "the golden rule," the universal recognition of which by humanity in all ages we have already pointed out,[1] and the validity of which in this particular branch of positive law will become apparent in all directions as we proceed, we arrive by anticipation at what, if I am not mistaken, we shall accept as the ultimate definition of the law of nations—namely this :

(*C*) *The law of nations is the realisation of the freedom of separate nations by the reciprocal assertion and recognition of their real powers.*

Accepting this, in the meantime, then, as the definition of our subject, let us inquire into its natural or scientific divisions, as regards the spheres which it covers, and the relations which these spheres embrace.

Divisions.

I. In relation to its objects, the Law of Nations, or as it is now more commonly called International Law, divides itself into three leading doctrines.

(*A*) The doctrine of recognition.

(*B*) The doctrine of the normal relations that result from the doctrine of recognition.

[1] *Institutes of Law*, p. 44.

(*C*) The doctrine of the abnormal relations that result from the doctrine of recognition.

1*st*, The fundamental doctrine of recognition, as the doctrine of international existence *de facto*, or of State life for international purposes, corresponds to that fundamental doctrine of natural law which teaches that all rights and duties have their origin in, and are limited by, the facts of natural life.[1] As the doctrine which carries it back to nature, the general doctrine of recognition is thus the fundamental doctrine of the Science of International Law—the doctrine in virtue of which it is a science. The general doctrine of recognition divides itself into :

(*a*) Absolute recognition, or recognition that there is a State.

(*b*) Relative recognition, or recognition that there is such a State.

II. In relation to the spheres which it covers, or the interests which it embraces, International Law divides itself into :

(*A*) *Public.*—*Where two States are its subjects.*

Here it is public on both sides.

As examples may be mentioned the laws of recognition, intervention, neutrality, &c.

Formally, though scarcely really, there belongs to this division the case in which one State becomes a claimant against another State on behalf of a private citizen, or a private company ; as—*e.g.*, under the twelfth article of the Treaty of Washington of May 8, 1871.

[1] *Institutes of Law*, pp. 57, 58, 260.

view to the attainment of their freedom as separate political entities.

If mankind were perfectly wise and virtuous, the doctrine of the normal relations of States would exhaust the science of International Law; and progress in the development of international relations consists in such a modification of the conditions of the realisation of Natural Law in the concrete, as shall render this doctrine more and more exhaustive. It is with a view to this progress that the abnormal relations of States, in so far as they are necessary or inevitable, receive jural recognition as transitory facts, which involve corresponding rights.

2d, *Of the Abnormal Relations.*—The doctrine of the abnormal relations of States rests on the recognition of conflict, or, as it is technically called, " belligerency," as an existing relation in point of fact, which, like all other recognised facts, involves rights and duties; and it seeks so to define these rights and duties as to determine the conditions, and consequent positive laws of their realisation in the concrete.

(*a*) As between belligerents;

(*b*) As between belligerents and neutrals;

(*c*) As between neutrals.

At first sight it appears as if to the two classes of Normal and Abnormal Relations a third class of mixed relations ought to be added, to which the relations of intervention and neutrality would fall to be relegated. But, on further consideration, it is obvious that, as there is no intermediate region of indifference between justice and injustice,[1] so there can be no jural

---

[1] *Institutes of Law*, pp. 319, 320.

(*B*) *Public and Private.*—Where a State and the citizen of another State are its subjects.

Here it is public on one side, and private on the other. Such is the law administered by Prize Courts, where the neutral State interposes, if at all, only diplomatically. On the ground that criminal law, even when dealing with private persons, involves public interests, the law of extradition seems to fall under this category.

(*C*) *Private.*—Where relations arising out of or dependent on the municipal laws of one State, fall to be realised by the municipal laws of another State.

Here it is private on both sides. Two private citizens sue each other before a municipal judge, with no appeal to any international tribunal.

CHAPTER II.

OF THE NORMAL AND ABNORMAL RELATIONS OF STATES.

The relations of States further divide themselves into those which are normal and those which are abnormal.

1*st*, *Of the Normal Relations.*

The doctrine of the normal relations of States, in its various subdivisions, seeks to define the reciprocal rights and duties of States living in peace and amity, and to define the positive laws by which, at the stage of civilisation which they have reached, their intercourse may best be conducted with a

relations which are partly normal and partly abnormal. Indifference between related entities is a contradiction in terms —an attitude which is not abnormal alone, but anti-jural— which carries us out of jurisprudence altogether. In accepting war and neutrality as inevitable, we accept them, not as indifferent, but as right—as jural, notwithstanding their abnormality. In consequence of their abnormality, however, they are right relatively only, not absolutely—temporarily only, not permanently. They are right only in relation to conditions that are wrong, because not wholly independent of human volition. If the conditions which generate belligerency or neutrality were as involuntary as the relations of belligerency or neutrality themselves, belligerency and neutrality would be normal relations. But these conditions are not natural phenomena, either ordinary, like the changes of the seasons, the alternations of day and night, and the processes of growth and decay; or extraordinary, like earthquakes and thunderstorms. They are aberrations from the natural life of man — unnatural phenomena, like preventible disease — the existence of which, and of their consequences, can be jurally recognised only with a view to their removal. A system of jurisprudence which rests on the assumption of the fundamental rectitude of human nature,[1] thus admits the laws of belligerency and neutrality only conditionally, and under protest. It makes no permanent provision for them, as it does for peaceful intercourse, rivalry, and trade. They are, we must hope, vanishing quantities; but for the present they are jural factors of international life, which we must be con-

[1] *Institutes of Law*, p. 59.

tent to regulate and control, but the present action of which we must not seek to weaken or impede. Whilst sin endures, it would be sinful to proclaim perpetual peace; but it is only those who believe in eternal sin and punishment, who are bound to believe in perpetual war.

From the natural law which declares rights and duties to be reciprocal and coextensive,[1] it follows that every doctrine of international law may be logically stated either as a doctrine of rights or as a doctrine of duties; and that an exhaustive doctrine of either would embrace both. The only reason for starting from rights, as is the custom in this and all other departments of jurisprudence, rather than from duties, is, that rights are the primary and duties the secondary consequences of existence.[2] Till we have a right to exist ourselves, no duty of recognising other existences can be incumbent on us. But this right, we have seen, is coincident with the fact of existence; and we have no right to continue to exist alongside of other existences, unless, longer than, or farther than we recognise that their right to existence corresponds to our own. Priority of fact, moreover, involves priority of phenomenon. Rights present themselves to consciousness before duties, and hence the convenience of adopting them as jural starting-points.

Lastly: it follows from the solidarity of rational coexistence, that interests are throughout coincident with rights and duties. A system of jurisprudence which took perfect cognisance of the interests of any single individual, or of any single State, provided the whole range of such interests were embraced

[1] *Institutes of Law*, p. 142.   [2] *Ib.*, p. 210.

SCHOOLS OF INTERNATIONAL JURISPRUDENCE. 9

by it, would logically result in the recognition not only of its rights and its duties, but of the rights and duties of every other created entity. But such a starting-point is unattainable by human insight. Our rights and our duties we may approximately determine, but the real, permanent, and ultimate interests of any creature are known to the Creator only. It is from accepting a limited insight into their own interests, as the guide of their actions, that most of the errors both of individuals and of States are committed. It is in the region of expediency that we fall into errors of policy, as it is in the region of conventionality that we fall into errors of taste.

CHAPTER III.

OF THE NATIONAL AND COSMOPOLITAN SCHOOLS OF
INTERNATIONAL JURISPRUDENCE.

To any one acquainted with the present tendencies of international thought and feeling, it must be obvious that two schools of international jurisprudence, giving prominence respectively to the principles of neutrality and intervention, tend to develop themselves, often to the extent of mutual exclusion. These two schools, corresponding to the negative and positive schools of general jurisprudence[1] in their broadest sense, may be characterised as the national and the

[1] *Institutes of Law*, p. 281.

cosmopolitan, or the patriotic and the philanthropic schools of international law. If carried out to their logical results in isolation, both are suicidal, because both lead to a denial of the existence of international relations, and, as a consequence, of the possibility of international law.

The negative or national school, setting out from the conception of national rights, and asserting the absolute independence of States, results in the isolation of separate States. International rights and duties thus equally cease, and international law, having no relations to declare, loses the object of its existence. Law, on this hypothesis, is bounded in its empire by the frontiers of each individual State, and beyond these frontiers Hobbes's terrible conception of universal war is realised. Till individual States had attained to a stage of moral and intellectual development, which humanity has as yet given no token of its ability to reach, the rule of the Leviathan would be the only refuge against anarchy, and universal Cæsarism the only hope of peace.

The cosmopolitan or positive school, on the other hand, recognising the necessary interdependence of States, but losing sight of their rights as separate communities, sacrifices the very subjects of international law. International law thus loses its function, for if there are no separate rights, there can be no relations between them—if there are no rights, there can be no duties. The logical result of the aspirations of this school would be the realisation of Dante's dream of a universal empire—of the Leviathan again, though of a nobler Leviathan, with higher aims than the mere suppression of internecine war. Its effect in international law would be

CHARACTERISTICS OF THE LAW OF NATIONS. 11

precisely analogous to the effect of pantheism in natural law. Separate freedom and separate responsibility would cease with separate existence. Both schools profess to be advocates of peace, which the negative school hopes to realise by the principle of absolute non-intervention; the positive school by the principle of international organisation carried to the extent of regulating national as well as international legislation; whilst the " peace party," rushing from the one extreme to the other, attempts to draw water at both wells. But whilst hopelessly conflicting in isolation, these two schools, when combined, become complementary; and it is their reconciliation, by the vindication of national freedom of action, not apart from, but in and through the recognition of international dependence, which constitutes the still very imperfectly solved problem of international law.

CHAPTER IV.

OF THE GENERAL CHARACTERISTICS OF THE LAW OF NATIONS.

(A) *The law of nations is coeval with the existence of nations.*
When contrasted with other branches of jurisprudence, there are several points of view in which the law of nations may be regarded as modern. There were not only men and families, but there were unions of families into clans and tribes, bound together by ties of blood (ὁμογάλακτες) and neighbourhood, before there were those greater ethnological and geographical combinations which we call nations.

As contrasted with the laws which govern individual and domestic relations, with the laws of status and even with the laws of contract, the law of nations is thus modern in the conditions of its existence; and priority of fact naturally led to prior discovery and definition by means of positive laws. The law of nations, however, is as old as the subjects which it governs, for these, as moral entities, had, inherent in them from the first, both rights and duties, however little they may have been known or enforced.

Nor could human communities, simply as such, ever have been wholly ignorant of or wholly indifferent to the laws which determined their relations to each other. Moral consciousness is an attribute of humanity; and the necessary character which we have elsewhere seen to belong to natural law, as a consequence of human existence, is thus a guarantee for the coincidence of International Law and International Existence. Till there were two nations international law could not have been; when there were two nations, it could not but have been, and even been known and acted upon, however imperfectly and irregularly.

(B) *The law of nations is coextensive with national development.*

Bare existence is by no means the only source of Positive Law. On the contrary, in historical times it is continually growing, not only as a science, or thing known, but as a fact or thing to be known. Human activity is a factor in its growth as well as human reason. As the life of individuals or nations progresses, as they increase in refinement, wealth, and power, new relations are developed, and new sources of positive law spring up. There was always, as we have seen, a natural law of the relations of separate communities, and this was more or less consciously recognised as the tide of reason, and consequent civilisation flowed or ebbed. In this conscious recognition of the natural laws which governed the conditions of coexistence, such as they were, there was thus always the germ even of a positive law of nations. But the positive law of nations, as it exists in our day, did not exist, and consequently could not be known, to the earlier races of mankind. Even now the same rights and duties do not belong to savages and civilised men; and, consequently, it is not ignorance alone which prevents the former from discovering the laws by which the rights and duties of the latter are defined. Even amongst civilised men, positive laws are not only differenced by differing circumstances, but there are periods of history which do not generate the laws at all which, at others, exercise the greatest influence. And this is true even of nations which have attained to degrees of civilisation not greatly dissimilar. It was not from the imperfection of their scientific insight that the Romans were ignorant of International Law. In accordance with the theory of universal dominion which governed their political development, there were no international relations to see, and they were logically shut out from the international doctrines to which, by the theory of separate dominion, we are logically conducted.

(*C*) *Only in so far as the conditions of its existence arise from the voluntary activity or inactivity of nations, can the positive law of nations be said to be voluntary.*

I have elsewhere pointed out the necessary character of positive law. In all its branches it is merely declaratory.[1] But this remark, as we have farther seen,[2] applies to its conditions only in so far as these are beyond the reach of human control. The laws which regulate the relations of author and publisher are just as necessary as those which regulate the relations of husband and wife. But it is not as necessary that there should be authors and publishers as that there should be husbands and wives. Even as regards husbands and wives—inasmuch as all men and women are not compelled to marry, the conditions are not wholly inevitable. For the single, the laws which govern the relations of husband and wife have no existence. Some conditions, again, such as that of coexistence itself, set human will wholly at defiance; and, as regards these, there is always a residuum even of positive law which is inevitable. To a considerable extent, however, the element of volition which is excluded from the law may modify the forms of its manifestation. And this applies to the law of nations just as it does to any other branch of positive law. Communities must coexist, but they may progress and retrograde, and thus form or abandon the conditions of positive law which, for the time being, regulate their coexistence. But whilst these conditions exist, the rights and duties which they involve are beyond human control. Men may make their bed, but they must lie on it as they have made it, till they make it again. Perhaps the most conspicuous forms in which the consequences of the forgetfulness of this primary characteristic of international,

[1] *Institutes of Law*, p. 255.   [2] *Ib.*, pp. 257, 258, and note.

as of all positive law, have manifested themselves, have been in the attempt to establish a *status quo*, and in the recognition in barbarous and semi-civilised races of the rights and the imposition on them of the obligations of European nations.

As the result of the preceding observations, the law of nations may be characterised as existing in three aspects.

1*st*, As a fact, whether known or unknown, and whether jurally enforceable or non-enforceable.

2*d*, As a fact, to some extent inevitably known to all men, and, to that extent, jurally enforceable even upon barbarous and semi-barbarous communities, whether by each other or by more advanced communities.

3*d*, As a fact, presumed to be known to those communities which hold each other to possess the characteristics of States or nations, as these characteristics have been mutually determined by themselves, and, to this extent, enforceable by them on each other.

It is in this latter sense alone, that the law of nations is regarded as positive International Law, and that it forms the subject of this treatise.

(*D*) *The object of the law of nations in each separate relation may be deduced from its general object—liberty; and a permanent science of ends may thus be reached. Recognition, intervention, and neutrality, with their subsidiary doctrines, may be defined. But a permanent science of means is conceivable only to the extent to which the conditions of international coexistence are unchangeable; and a permanent code of international law, embracing the variable conditions of coexistence, is as unattainable as a permanent code of national law.*

The necessary character which belongs to all true positive law, on the ground that there can no more be two positive laws governing the same relation than there can be two straight lines between the same points, belongs, of course, to the positive law of nations. Each of its genuine utterances, remounting to nature, may thus claim the authority of science; and, in the absence of international organisation, this is often the only authority which it can claim. But these utterances possess validity only in so far as the conditions of coexistence of which they take cognisance are unchanged; and they possess permanent validity only in so far as they are unchangeable. On this ground, it is obvious that, however important codification may be for temporary purposes, it can do nothing to advance the science of jurisprudence either in this or any other department. It simply stereotypes it at the stage which it has reached. Every step in advance is a departure from the code, as even Justinian discovered to his cost; and it can be made with safety only when we have a clearer perception than our predecessors of the object which we seek, of the ideal which we are striving to realise. In order to be of any permanent value, all codes, whether national or international, must contain, *in gremio*, provisions for their perpetual readjustment.[1]

---

[1] Field's *Outlines of an International Code*, p. 371, § 538.

BOOK I.

OF THE SOURCES OF THE LAW OF NATIONS

CHAPTER I.

OF THE LAW OF NATURE AS DETERMINING THE OBJECTS OF
THE LAW OF NATIONS.

OF the law of nature, and of positive law in general, of their sources, and of the relation in which they stand to each other, I have spoken with sufficient fulness in the 'Institutes of Law.' As the law of nature is of universal validity, there is nothing exceptional in the relation in which it stands to the branch of positive law which we call the law of nations;[1] and there is, consequently, no occasion for my recurring to the subject from a general point of view, farther than to repeat that *the law of nations is the law of nature, realised in the relations of separate political communities.*

But there are historical reasons which led to, and there are practical reasons which still maintain, the custom of combining the study of natural law with that of international law, which do not apply, with equal force, when other branches of positive law are in question. Of these it is necessary that we should form a clear conception.

In speaking of the general characteristics of the law of

[1] *Institutes of Law,* p. 12.

nations, I have said that, as compared with the other branches of positive law, the law of nations is new, both as a fact and as a science. From this circumstance, as well as from the indefinite character of the subjects with which it deals, arising in a great measure out of the conflicting opinions which still exist with reference to many questions of public law within the State, it is the least developed branch of the whole science of jurisprudence. Its history, consequently, as yet, affords no basis for dogmatism, even with reference to its objects. The experience of mankind has scarcely yet been sufficient to enable them to determine, with any degree of precision, what, as separate communities, they ought to seek, far less what they may hope to obtain. The moment we descend from the ultimate objects which are common to it with the science of ethics, or, at all events, with jurisprudence as a whole, and inquire into its proximate or separate objects, we find that these objects—the very ends which it seeks, or ought to seek, as a system by itself—are not only imperfectly determined, but are often vehemently disputed.

It is this aimless character, this want of a definite and proximate *terminus ad quem*, which is really the cause of the slow and faltering progress of international law. If its objects, and the necessary character of the corresponding doctrines, were admitted, it is obvious that so soon as the contingent circumstances of separate communities became known, the necessary but still general doctrines could be converted into special doctrines, or, in other words, into a system of definite rules of international conduct. These definite rules would not be invariable certainly, but they would be variable only to the

These considerations explain to us the exceptional dependence of the law of nations on the law of nature. In dealing with the law of nations, the jurist has always a preliminary function to perform, and as it is natural law that determines the objects of positive law in all its departments, the function is one which he can perform only by keeping it steadily in view.

Analogous instances of the consequences of indefiniteness of aim might be given from other departments of jurisprudence. What is it, for example, but the indefiniteness of our conceptions of its object or objects, which gives rise to the diversity both of our theories and our practice of punishment? When it is asked, Why do we punish? what is punishment to effect? half-a-dozen theorists rush to their ink-bottles or spring to their feet, each with a different answer. First comes the absolute theory: That it is the "wages of sin," having no curative object, or object of any kind more specific than to avenge outraged justice—whatever that may mean. As this theory logically results from the dogma of eternal damnation, it is usually maintained not on political, but on theological grounds. Then there are all the relative or therapeutic theories: "It is to protect society against the criminal by rendering him innoxious;" "it is to protect society against crime by making an example of him;" "it is to protect the criminal from his evil companions"—"from himself;" "it is to teach him;" "to terrify him;" "to elevate him;" "to humiliate him:" "it is to appeal to his head," "to his heart," "to his hide." The existence of these apparently conflicting and probably quite irreconcilable opinions, far from proving that we must abandon all theories of punishment, and betake ourselves to the practice of

extent to which circumstances varied. We should then have a law of nations subdivided into various departments, in the sense in which we have municipal law subdivided into a law of status, a law of contract, a law of guardianship, and the like.

In the absence of an international judicature and executive, the means of its enforcement might still be a matter of exceptional difficulty; but for its confident dogmatic statement, as it ought to be enforced, or, in other words, as a branch of the science of positive law, care and industry on the part of those whose duty it was to ascertain the special circumstances of the individual case would suffice. Natural law, in this, as in the other departments of positive law, would then retreat into the arsenal or the armoury of jurisprudence, and the jurist would not be called upon to wield it in his daily work, but only when, in the higher capacity of a scientific discoverer, he sought to indicate what was amiss, or as a legislator to supply what was defective in the positive system which it was his business to expound, to administer, or to reform.

But the case is very different where the object of the law is itself indefinite or disputed, where its general doctrines have as yet no fixed and recognised meaning, and where the questions which arise are not questions of means but questions of ends. Here, unless practice be contented to wait indefinitely on the terrible and often unintelligible teaching of experience, it must still invoke the aid of theory: the positive international jurist has no firm standing-ground of his own: there is no progressive or consistent history to record, and the day for dogmatism has not yet arrived.

—we know not what, proves just the reverse. It proves that theory has not yet done its work—that the theory of punishment requires further investigation;[1] and it tells us that till *it* is more mature, our practice must continue to be vacillating and inefficient. It explains to us that the reason why coddling, and schooling, and starving, and whipping, succeed each other alternately; and why one generation, or one decade, sets up the gallows, which the former generation or decade pulled down, is, that we have not yet made up our minds what we are to effect either by coddling, or schooling, or starving, or whipping, or hanging. We talk of observing and comparing the results of different punishments; but till we know what ultimate result we want, by what standard are we to measure the proximate results which we obtain? Suppose, when the results of whipping and of imprisonment, with a view to the protection of person or of property are compared, we find that whipping is the more effectual. Will that result satisfy the man who holds that it is not the protection of person or of property that is the object, or an object of punishment at all, but the elevation of the criminal in the social scale by the development of his feelings of self-respect?

The results of the utilitarian are worthless to the philanthropist, and equally so those of the philanthropist to the utilitarian, till they are reciprocally brought to see that philanthropy is utilitarianism and utilitarianism philanthropy. And that can never be except by carrying theory farther, by looking deeper into causes and farther into consequences than

---

[1] The latest contribution of importance to the literature of this subject is Mr Wharton's *Philosophy of Criminal Law.*

either philanthropist or utilitarian can see from his own exclusive point of view.

Now it is wholly needless to conceal from ourselves that what occurs exceptionally in the other departments of jurisprudence is still the rule, as regards the law of nations. There is scarcely one of its doctrines with reference to which a scientific determination has been arrived at, or even a ripe public opinion has been formed, nay, with reference to which two hostile parties at least do not find themselves face to face, the moment it is mentioned.

Let us, without descending to specialties, take the three leading doctrines of Recognition, Neutrality, and Intervention, as set forth by text-writers, and partially recognised by treaties, and see whether what I have said be exaggerated.

That a doctrine of recognition of some sort must form the basis of the positive law of nations, is a subject on which there is, I believe, no difference of opinion. The *de facto* existence of the nation being given, that its *de jure* recognition by other nations becomes a right inherent in it, and a duty incumbent on them, is an application of the *de facto* principle, the universal admission of which in practice, if not in theory, is one of the strongest historical arguments for the soundness of the *de facto* principle itself. So far the rights of the nation are on a level with the rights of the person, and international law is on a level with municipal law.

But when we come to inquire into the characteristics of the nation, and the consequent point at which it enters or quits existence, we find them by no means so clear as in the case of the person. The phenomena of gestation are so accurately known that even incipient personal rights are ascertainable. The period of birth, when the rights of the living person emerge, and of majority when they culminate, can always be ascertained ; and nature marks the point of personal dissolution even more unmistakably. But when national life commences, what are the stages of its progress, when it is completed, and when it ceases, are all of them questions of far greater difficulty. The law of nations, at the very outset, thus gets mixed up with some of the subtlest and least settled questions of another department of jurisprudence—viz., the public law of individual nations. The doctrine of recognition constitutes, in truth, the border-land between these two departments, and before we can cross the frontier line, and enter on the special study of international relations, we find ourselves in an intermediate zone of moral and political jungle, where we are confronted with questions to which science as yet has made no definite response.

Yet the determination of these questions lies at the very root of the definition of the doctrine of international recognition. However desirous we may be of eschewing all contact with national politics, and leaving to the individual State the widest freedom of choice as concerns forms of government, we cannot, as international jurists, avoid asking what a nation is ? We must know at least its *necessary* characteristics; for if these be absent there is nothing to recognise, and we obtain no starting-point.

But even when the international existence of the State is granted in the fullest manner,—when it is placed in a position of what is called "equality" with other States, it is only in the most general way that the doctrine of recognition, as applied to it, can be said to be determined. That it has rights is then conceded; but what are these rights, and what are the corresponding duties which they involve? The relations of citizen to citizen within the State involve the duty of mutual protection to life and property. Is it so with the relations of State to State? Is the recognised State entitled to claim from the recognising State, or from the community of States into which it has been admitted, aid and protection, should aid and protection come to be a condition of its continued existence as a state? To what extent does recognition render the recognised State responsible for the actions of its citizens, or guarantee to them their cosmopolitan freedom as persons? These are questions to which the common law of nations, and the treaties into which separate States have entered on various occasions return conflicting answers, and yet it is from these answers that our doctrines of intervention and neutrality with all the subsidiary doctrines of the positive law of nations must obviously be deduced.

If such, then, be the character of the doctrines which form the backbone of the *corpus juris inter gentes,* there can, I think, be little question of the justice of the opinion which regards the law of nations rather as a branch of scientific inquiry than as a discovered system, or of the prudence of the academical arrangement which maintains its connection with natural law.

CHAPTER II.

OF INTERNATIONAL CUSTOMS AS UNCONSCIOUS INTERPRETERS OF THE LAW OF NATURE IN INTERNATIONAL RELATIONS.

Having considered the manner in which the general ends or objects of international law are determined, or, in other words, the primary source of this branch of jurisprudence, we now proceed to its secondary sources, or the means by which these ends are to be defined in the concrete relations presented by international life.

In every department of jurisprudence, custom, or usage, is the earliest form in which positive law declares itself; and it is in observing and recording this spontaneous manifestation of it that the historical method of its discovery consists. He who would make a better road to kirk or market must first observe the road that has been beaten by the feet of previous travellers. That road may admit of being levelled or straightened; but, if the general direction of it be departed from, we may rest assured that the new road will be abandoned, and the old road will reassert itself, in spite of all the fences and barriers we can erect. The process is precisely analogous to that which takes place in the formation of all real positive law, whether national or international; and if treaties embodied, and text-writers recorded nothing that had not the sanction of custom, they would be trustworthy guides so far as they went, both to science and to practice. Even an antiquated or obsolete custom has always something to teach. It always had a meaning; and customs become misleading only when they are studied without reference to the circumstances in which they prevailed, and attempts are made to revert to them in their old forms.

Though customs appear to arise spontaneously, and are rarely traceable to premeditation, they must always have rested on a previous conception of an object to be attained, and of the means of attaining it. Even a common footpath must have existed in thought before it existed in fact. But the distinctive characteristic of custom consists in this, that its existence proves that its object was possible, and that the means which it employed for its attainment were not wholly inadequate. No custom is ever a pure mistake, as is the case with many theories, and with the doctrines which rest on them. There never was a custom, for example, either of the balance of power or of the *status quo*, though they are perhaps the two most famous doctrines of the written law of nations; and the equality of States and their absolute independence have been steadily repudiated by custom, notwithstanding the unanimity with which the former has been accepted, and the zeal with which the latter has been contended for. It is out of the consuetudinary rejection, indeed, of the very doctrine of international independence, on which private international law was supposed[1] to be founded, that it has really grown up. In this, as in so many other directions, men have drifted into truths which they have failed to explain to themselves, and have gone right when they intended to go wrong.

Of the efficacy of custom in revealing what for generations

[1] *Infra*, Book III. cap. ix.

has proved to be law, I shall give two examples, neither of them belonging precisely to the law of nations, but both kindred to it. The law-merchant, which, as a branch of municipal law, may be regarded as common to all civilised States, and which, as such, has obtained international significance, is almost entirely an embodiment of mercantile custom. The famous sea-laws of the middle ages, the *consolato del mare*, the *rolles of Oleron*, and the rest, though, like the *coutumes* and *usages* of the ancient provinces and cities of France, they ultimately assumed the form of written codes, had no legislative authority, and proceeded from no known lawgiver; and there is every probability that the same was the case with the mercantile jurisprudence of the Phœnicians, of which these sea-laws were partial reproductions. Our admiralty law is, no doubt, partly statutory, and now we have the merchant shipping and other kindred Acts; but these are almost entirely declaratory of usages already well defined and generally observed. In the forms in which it is presented to us in the maritime codes, this consuetudinary legislation corresponds very closely to what the Romans understood by *responsa prudentium*, or what we call judge-made law. It consisted of the awards of arbitrators and of the judgments of consuls, elected by the merchants themselves to preside in the maritime courts, who defined and applied to special cases what was floating about as mere seamen's lore.

I can give you a curious instance of a mercantile arrangement of some nicety and complexity, which, after passing through this process of development, resumed its purely consuetudinary character, and has continued amongst semi-barbarous races to hold its own for ages, as a mere popular tradition. The *lex Rhodia de jactu*, which the Romans borrowed from the Phœnicians, is now in green observance amongst the tribes of the Sahara as the customary mode of distributing the losses incurred by caravans crossing the desert between the company owning the camels, or what in railway language would be called the plant, and the passengers or owners of goods. The Khodja or scribe acts as a supercargo, and is said to be quite conversant with the distinction between general and special average.[1] Whether the indigenous races of North Africa derived this custom from the Carthaginians and other Phœnician colonists directly, or whether it came to them indirectly through the Romans, is a point which it would probably be impossible to determine, and on which they themselves certainly could throw no light. But of the pedigree of the custom there can, I imagine, be little doubt.[2]

My second example comes from a very different region. It is what may be called the consuetudinary code of honour on which so much of the machinery of the British Constitution, and of all the constitutions which are modelled after it, is governed.[3] "We now have a whole system of political morality," says Mr Freeman, "a whole code of precepts for the guidance of public men, which will not be found in any page of either the Statute or the Common Law, but which are in practice held hardly less sacred than any principle embodied

[1] *Alger. Congrès*, 1881, p. 8.

[2] An interesting account of the Caravan trade in antiquity will be found in Lindsay's *Merchant Shipping*, vol. i. p. 86 *et seq.*

[3] *Growth of the English Constitution*, p. 109.

in the Great Charter, or in the Petition of Right. In short, by the side of our written Law, there has grown up an unwritten or conventional constitution. When an Englishman speaks of the conduct of a public man being constitutional or unconstitutional, he means something wholly different from what he means by conduct being legal or illegal.[1] . . . If any officer of the Crown should levy a tax without the authority of Parliament, if he should enforce martial law without the authority of Parliament, he would be guilty of a legal crime. But, if he merely continues to hold an office conferred by the Crown, and from which the Crown has not removed him, though he hold it in the teeth of any number of votes of censure passed by both Houses of Parliament, he is in no way a breaker of the written law. But the man who should so act would be usually held to have trampled under foot one of the most undoubted principles of the unwritten but universally accepted constitution."[2]

The reason of the acceptance of consuetude in this latter instance is, that it was positive law which was so unquestioned that it did not require to become enacted law.[3] Whether this reason may continue to be a sufficient support for the parliamentary code of honour in our own day, seems more than doubtful.

Of bad customs.—No custom, as we have seen, can be wholly

[1] *Growth of the English Constitution*, p. 111.
[2] *Ibid.*, p. 112.
[3] Mr Wallace gives an analogous example in the case of the Russian Village Commune. "The Commune," he says, "is a living institution, whose spontaneous vitality enables it to dispense with the assistance and guidance of the written law."—*Russia*, vol. i. p. 193. The same characteristics belong to the Indian village communities, and, indeed, to all primitive institutions.

dissevered from nature; but there are customs which sprang from it in its partial, abnormal, and ephemeral manifestations. There are consequently customs which are not sources of law, but continuous violations of law.

Bad customs are of three kinds :—

(a) Those which are bad essentially, on the ground that they violate permanent natural laws—*e.g.*, the slaughter or enslavement of prisoners of war; and slavery itself, indeed, in all its forms, except perhaps when it is employed, under very stringent regulations, as an educational institution for the benefit of the inferior races of mankind: the organisation of society into exclusive castes, and in so far as realisable the opposite of this—viz., the establishment of artificial equality, and the obliteration of natural social distinctions. Then there are many forms of crime and folly which differ from ordinary crimes and follies only in that, being committed by large numbers of persons simultaneously, they partake of the character of customs. Customs of this class, though as reactions against each other they occasionally yield a resultant which becomes a source of law, have in themselves no claim to that character. Agrarian or communistic outrages are not sources of law, even in cases in which they lead to more accurate definitions of the natural rights of persons, or of the limits of private property.

(b) Those customs which, continuing after the circumstances in which they arose have changed, no longer generate law. To this class belong feudal and patriarchal customs in modern times, in so far as they do not represent permanent human relations: the maintenance against their will of the dependence of communities that are capable of self-government and self-protection: the retention of civil or religious observances resting on dogmas that have been abandoned, and, in short, all customs which lag behind the spirit of the age. For a reason which I shall point out presently, however, customs have far less tendency to outlive their day than the international treaties or even legislative enactments in which they are embodied.

(c) Customs which have sprung out of reactionary tendencies, and which, consequently, lose their basis of fact when the causes which led to the reaction have been removed, and the pendulum of opinion, or of fashion, or immediate interest swings in the opposite direction. Whilst the vast majority of each generation are ready to accept its proclivities as indications of permanent laws of national and international life, there are always exceptional persons who, detecting their one-sided character, are tempted to dismiss them as mere traditionary hallucinations. It is hard to say in which direction the risk of error is greater, but the only safeguard against it obviously consists in the possession of some test of truth which shall be independent of the influences either of individual temperament, or of local and temporal hopes and fears. The true relation between neutrals and belligerents, for example, can be determined neither by the recent tendency to exaggerate the obligations of neutrals, nor by the previous tendency to exaggerate the rights of belligerents against which it was a reaction.

Custom is, as it were, an intermediate stage through which opinions or conceptions ought almost always to pass, before assuming the form of enacted law. We can seldom mount by a single leap from a recognised conclusion to a legislative act. It is by contributing to the formation of customs more and more in accordance with natural laws, that morality, religion, and science must, for the most part, be contented to contribute to the development of positive law. So dependent is international law, in particular, on this intermediate factor, that to many it has seemed impossible that it should ever advance beyond it. This was the view which Count von Moltke took of it in his celebrated letter to Professor Bluntschli on the Manual of the Laws of War, prepared by the International Institute at its meeting at Oxford in September 1880.[1]

It is no doubt true, as Count von Moltke says, that the weak point of international law is the want of any central authority to enforce its rules, and that this deficiency, to a certain extent, is supplied by custom. Custom is itself a sanction; and what is "sanctioned by custom," as we say proverbially, is enforced by a compulsitor which acts scarcely less forcibly on nations than on individuals. Shame and vanity minister to its support. Like fashion, too, custom is infectious. It consequently penetrates regions that are impervious to argument, and that can neither be reached by remonstrances nor threats. Brutality and even stupidity give way before it, and, though a silent, it thus often becomes a more powerful international factor than either selfishness or terror.

There is no direction in which it is more necessary that we should keep the subjective channel to natural law distinctly

[1] *Times*, February 1, 1881. *Revue de Droit International*, 1881, tome xiii., No. 1, p. 79.

before us than when we are called upon to distinguish between good and bad customs, because customs themselves claim to be objective witnesses to the very law by which their qualities must be tested. To a very considerable extent, indeed, the art of legislation consists in thus applying to customs a test which they partially supply, and its importance becomes apparent when we reflect that the effect of a legislative enactment is to stereotype the customs which it embodies.

Even after a custom is sufficiently recognised to secure its own enforcement, so long as it continues to be a custom merely, it retains a self-adapting and self-modifying character, and may die away into entire desuetude. A right of way which cannot be stopped will be abandoned if the object which it served has ceased. Laws, on the other hand, which have been formally enacted must be formally repealed. Treaties which have been formally negotiated ought to be binding till they are formally renounced. It is in this consideration that the great objection to codification consists, whether as applied to national or international law. The elasticity of custom maintains for it an unbroken connection with the sources of law, which, in the case of enacted law, can be maintained only by the continual action of the legislative factor, which, in international law, is almost wholly wanting. Even where the legislative factor is in full operation, obsolete positive law has a tendency to get encrusted in a mass of intricate technicality, from which it is exceedingly difficult for common-sense and common honesty to dislodge it. From this trivial cause it may become a serious impediment to social progress, where the private interests of a particular class of practitioners are involved in its preservation. Of this we have a famous instance in the laws of feudal conveyancing, which needlessly impede the transference and diminish the value of landed property in this country. So effectually has professional ingenuity contrived to shelter this cherished branch of our legal system, that every fresh legislative assault directed against it by popular indignation has only added to its complications. In quite recent times we have had nine conveyancing statutes in Scotland, and nineteen in England; and the feudal system which, for a century and a half has been dead to consuetude, still lives in the courts of law. The case is emphatically one in which the lawyers have "taken away the key of knowledge." They have not entered in themselves, and them that were entering they have hindered.

In making these remarks, it is not my intention to depreciate the conscious as contrasted with the unconscious elements in jurisprudence. As regards international law, in particular, I am fully alive to the benefit resulting from labours which make us more accurately acquainted with customary rules, and indicate the extent to which they conform to, or have drifted away from natural laws. It is in this direction that the combined action of the jurists now forming the Institute of International Law is likely to prove most valuable. What I wish to point out is merely that in the absence of an international legislature for their perpetual revision, very serious entanglements may arise from the stereotyping of customary rules in international treaties. Special treaties, as I shall have frequent occasion to point out, are often serious impediments to progress; and the same character, it is much to be feared, might attach to any general treaty for the adoption of an international code, however well it was adapted to the existing circumstances, or reflected the prevailing tendencies of a particular epoch.

CHAPTER III.

OF TREATIES.

We have seen that no single treaty can have the value of a well-established custom as a guide to our knowledge of the law of nations, either in itself, or as interpreted by the international consciousness of a particular epoch. A treaty indicates only what the parties to it have consented to hold as the relation subsisting between themselves at the period of contracting it; and, inasmuch as this consent may have been brought about, not by coincidence of reason and ultimate will, but by violence or selfishness on the one side, and fear or stupidity on the other, it is quite possible that a treaty may not have the value even of an isolated and temporary instance of international understanding. It may never have been carried out at all, either on the ground that one of the parties to it promised what was impossible, or what he had no intention of performing, except under the continuance of the compulsitor with which he had agreed to dispense. Such, I think, has been the character of all the treaties concluded between the European powers and the Ottoman Empire during more than a century. The Porte could not have fulfilled them if it would, and would not have fulfilled them if it could. Even between the European powers themselves, the character of a mere makeshift has belonged to so many of these arrangements, that they can be regarded in no other light than as marking the various stages in the progress of a war which one of the belligerents was unable or unwilling to prosecute for the time being, but which he retained both the will and the power to resume. The whole mass of treaties concluded by the Allies, first with the French Republic, and then with the French Empire, from the Treaty of Basle in 1795 down to the Treaty of Vienna in 1815, can claim no higher character than this. Those which belong to the first twelve years of the present century serve no other purpose than that of enabling us to trace the victorious progress of a tyrant who was guilty of almost every crime of which humanity is capable, murder included, and whose ambition never rose above personal aggrandisement and the gratification of personal and national vanity. For the next three years,—from 1812 to 1815,—they indicate the footprints of the Nemesis that chased him to his doom. If you will turn over the pages of Martens, in which they are recorded, or glance at the analysis of them which President Woolsey has given in the Appendix to his book,[1] you will find that they tell a story which reads like the plot of a Greek tragedy, every actor in which was soiled by the vices and degraded by the weaknesses of the hero of the piece. It was with this mournful page of history specially in view that Wordsworth exclaimed—

[1] *Introduction to the Study of International Law*, App. ii. pp. 3, 4, 5 et seq.

is thus by no means measured by their success or permanence as international transactions. Of treaties which are directly instructive, the most memorable is the great Treaty of Westphalia. In many directions it brought law into harmony with fact, and in these directions it regulated the destinies of a large portion of mankind for well on to a couple of centuries, and still contributes, in an important manner, to the international conceptions even of those who were not parties to it. The recognition *de jure* of the political consequences of the Reformation in Germany, and of the independence of the Netherlands and of Switzerland, were emphatic and very authoritative assertions of the principle that rights and facts are in their nature inseparable, and that the law of nations must accept them as it finds them. With all its faults, the Treaty of Westphalia was a successful treaty, and it is not wonderful, therefore, that we should derive positive instruction from it. But let us look at the negative instruction which may be derived from unsuccessful, or partially successful, treaties. The "solemn declaration," which was a sort of doctrinal annex to the Treaty of Paris of 1856, in affirming the principle "free ship, free goods," and in defining blockade and abolishing privateering, made permanent contributions to the law of nations. With these exceptions, it must, I think, be regarded as a failure. But does not the speedy abandonment of the limitations which the Treaty of Paris attempted to impose on the supremacy of Russia in the Black Sea, confirm and enforce the lesson which the constant violations of the Treaty of Vienna might well have taught, as to the futility of spasmodic efforts to maintain an artificial *status quo*, in viola-

> * * * "Earth is sick,
> And Heaven is weary of the hollow words
> Which states and kingdoms utter when they talk
> Of truth and justice."[1]

That many heroic qualities were displayed in the wars of which these treaties are the memorials, is unquestionable; but all that remained as the results of this display was material impoverishment and moral degradation. Not a single permanent law of international life was disclosed or vindicated. The famous Treaty of Vienna left the natural relations of the races by whom Europe is peopled as obscure as they had been before the conflagration burst forth; and, before the signatures to the final act were dry, the act itself was in process of becoming waste-paper.

On the other hand, however, treaties have always a basis of reality, for the simple reason that they testify to actual occurrences, and rest on accomplished though ephemeral facts. The greater treaties are justly regarded as summing up the international experience of the epochs of history to which they belong; and when we consider the frightful cost at which they were purchased, it would be sad indeed if they taught us nothing. To regard them simply as monuments of objectless effort and fruitless suffering would be to disbelieve in the wisdom not of man but of God. They are themselves instructive events. There is no treaty which, if studied in relation to its causes and its effects, is not calculated, often at the distance of a very few years, to shed precious light on the inalienable and imperishable rights and duties of nations. The instruction which treaties are fitted to convey indirectly

[1] *The Excursion*, Book V.

tion of the necessarily changing character which belongs to all true positive law? It tells us that, though the function of law be to declare facts, we must be very sure of the facts which we declare. A treaty is a synthetic process, the value of which will depend on the completeness of the analysis on which it rests; and yet, in an epoch which justly prides itself on the success with which analytic processes have been applied to physical investigations, it is curious to remark that the failure of modern treaties may in general be traced to the shrinking which their negotiators have exhibited from an honest and searching analysis of the relations which they pretended to define, or sought to adjust. More than even in former times, diplomatists have confined their investigations to the existing conflict of passions, prejudices, and supposed interests, and given little heed to the normal elements of international life.

But whatever the absolute value of treaties may be, they are, between the parties to them, whilst they subsist, authoritative declarations of positive law. If the good faith of nations is to have any meaning, the words of a treaty must be as sacred to the ministers of the contracting states as their own statute law is to their judges. Nor can the effects of treaties be honestly limited by their words. Any proposition which logically, and as such, inevitably results from their terms, must possess, for the contracting parties, the character of *res judicata*. However strongly we may condemn them as private persons, or as scientific jurists, as citizens we are bound by their principles not less than by their words. Should the principles which two nations have embodied in a treaty be at variance with the common law and common usage of nations, the former and not the latter must, for the time being, be accepted by both as positive law. It is this consideration which renders the contracting of treaties, and even the enacting of municipal laws which have reference to international relations, so very anxious a proceeding. Concessions made or obligations undertaken from motives of present convenience may be found to involve consequences which were not contemplated by one, or perhaps by either party; and by a series of such treaties and enactments, even the consuetudinary law of nations may undergo alterations at variance with the natural law of the relations which it had correctly defined. Examples of both phenomena are presented, if I mistake not, by the Foreign Enlistment Acts and by the Treaty of Washington. When we come to study the subject of neutrality, we shall find that the principles of these enactments imperil the freedom both of speech and writing in neutral countries; and that, if logically carried out, they would involve the entire renunciation of trade,—consequences certainly not contemplated by the contracting parties, but which are now being claimed by others whose immediate objects they seem to advance. But the leading objection to treaties as a source of the law of nations, as well as the chief cause of their untrustworthiness as separate transactions, consists in the necessity which exists, or is supposed to exist, for their being negotiated and even ratified by the executive independently of the legislative factor in national affairs, and the consequent risk of their failing to represent the national will. To what extent this objection may be inevitable, is a question which belongs to constitutional rather than to international law; and I shall reserve what I have to say regarding it till, in discussing the doctrine of recognition, we come to consider the State in its international aspect. For the present I shall only say, in passing, that the international effect of this supposed necessity is to reduce treaties negotiated by constitutional States very nearly to the level of those negotiated by despotic States.

As sources of international law, treaties may be divided into three classes, though all of them are frequently comprised in a single international transaction, which is still popularly regarded as a single treaty.

First, Those which determine an isolated fact in dispute between two nations, in accordance with a recognised principle—*e.g.*, which define the limits of international rights or responsibilities on predetermined international principles, or fix international boundaries in accordance with geographical or ethnographical principles already agreed on. Such treaties correspond to isolated decisions in municipal jurisprudence, and are of value to the scientific jurist only in so far as they illustrate the meanings attached to the principles.

Second, Those which define or determine a principle in dispute, by which it is intended that, as between the parties, a certain course of action shall in future be regulated—*e.g.*, which determine whether and to what extent neutral States shall be responsible for the actions of their citizens; whether, in defining boundaries, the parties will be guided by geographical or ethnographical considerations alone, or will take the immediate will or wishes of the populations into account. Treaties of this very important class, which include treaties of commerce, extradition, copyright, and a host of others, correspond in many respects to legislative enactments. Their value for the jurist will depend on the honesty and intelligence of the parties by whom they are negotiated, and of the States by which they are entered into, the frequency with which they are contracted, and the consistency with which they are observed.

Third, Those which profess to declare the absolute law of nations, and to which the parties not only bind themselves, but which they urge on the acceptance of other nations. To this class belong the treaties which abolish and condemn the slave-trade; which define the rights and duties of belligerents *inter se*, and of belligerents and neutrals; which recognise free trade, the equal rights of foreigners and natives before the municipal law, &c.

Treaties of this class profess to be direct contributions to the science of jurisprudence, and their value will depend in no small measure on the eminence of their negotiators, and their freedom from misleading influences at the period at which their work was performed. Mere frequency of repetition will count for very little in favour of doctrines even thus enunciated, and, if not followed by acceptance, may even tell against them. No principles have been repeated more frequently or authoritatively than the equality of States and their absolute independence, except perhaps their counterparts, the balance of powers, and the *status quo*; and all of them may now, I think, be safely said to have been repudiated by history, as they always were by reason.

The value of treaties, as a source of the positive law of nations, is supposed to have been greatly enhanced by the annex to Protocol No. I. of the conferences held in London in 1871, respecting the clauses of the Treaty of Paris of 1856 which have reference to the neutralisation of the Black Sea. The protocol is in the following words: "The plenipotentiaries recognise that it is an essential principle of the law of nations that no Power can liberate itself from the engagements of a treaty, nor modify the stipulations thereof, unless with the consent of the contracting Powers by means of an amicable arrangement."

But the circumstances in which the plenipotentiaries had met, on that very occasion, were sufficient to show how little reality there was in the "amicable arrangement" by which they arrived at the "unanimity" to which they no doubt formally attained. Nothing but a threat of war by Russia, supported as she was known to be by Germany, could have induced either France or England to accept her propositions.

In the previous correspondence Lord Granville had observed, very truly, that "the assumption contained in the Russian circular of the right of one Power to deal singly with a European treaty was one which was fatal to the validity of all international engagements." That Lord Granville's own faith in the validity of such engagements, however, was not very great, may be gathered from the suggestion which immediately follows: "If, instead of denouncing the special convention annexed to and embodied in the treaty of 1856, the Russian Government had asked her Majesty's Government, as well as the other Governments parties to that treaty, to consider whether there were not reasons which would justify some modifications being made therein, her Majesty's Government would, in conjunction with the other co-signatories, have taken into consideration the merits of such a request; and, by such a course on the part of the Russian Government, whatever might have been the result, they would have avoided the risk of future complications, and of making a precedent dangerous to all international engagements."[1]

To this Prince Gortschakoff replied : " We regret to see that Lord Granville lays stress principally on the form of our communications. It was not chosen by us. Certainly we should have asked for nothing better than to obtain our purpose by an understanding with the signatories of the treaty of 1856. But the principal Secretary of State of her Britannic Majesty well knows that all attempts made, at different times, to assemble the Powers in common deliberations, with a view to remove the causes of complication which disturb the general peace, have repeatedly failed. The prolongation of the actual crisis, and the absence of a regular Power in France,[2] removes still further the possibility of such concert."[3]

So far from being, as the protocol assumes, an element of strength, it is the unanimity supposed to be necessary both for the conclusion of treaties and for their modification or repeal which is the main element of their weakness, and it is this which constitutes the great inferiority of treaty law to statute law. There are very few statutes that are either enacted or modified unanimously. It is true that this requirement in international transactions logically results from the doctrine of

---

[1] *Correspondence*, p. 12.
[2] The siege of Paris was then in progress.
[3] *Correspondence*, p. 25.

the absolute independence of separate States. Citizens do not claim to be absolutely independent of each other; and this doctrine, when applied to States, as we shall see hereafter, amounts to a total repudiation of international responsibility: it is a denial of the existence both of international rights and international duties, and, as a necessary consequence, of the possibility of international law, either public or private. So long as this lawless doctrine is maintained and acted on, no international organisation for jural purposes is conceivable, and international legislation, whether proceeding from Congresses of Sovereigns or from Conferences of Diplomatists, can have no binding force. Whether the unanimity demanded be real or pretended, the result is the same. The moment that one of the parties changes his mind the unanimity ceases, and the basis on which the treaty rested is cut away. Each single State, in the exercise of its absolute independence, may free, not itself alone, but all the other signatories, from a treaty by its single intimation; whereas a statute, enacted by a majority, requires a majority for its repeal. It was through the loophole thus supplied by the protocol itself that Russia logically escaped from the treaty to which the majority of the contracting Powers were still anxious to adhere. Unanimity was possible only by the majority giving way to the minority.

It may be that, in virtue of the very limited renunciation of absolute independence implied in the indefinite league into which the great Powers entered at the Congress of Aix-la-Chapelle, Russia, as one of them, was precluded from intimating her change of resolution simply in a despatch. But there can, I imagine, be no doubt that she was entitled to invite her co-signatories to meet with her for the consideration of such changes as she might suggest on the treaty of 1856, or even its repeal; and that in the conference when met, or apart from the conference if it refused to meet, she might have renounced the treaty either in whole or in part. Nor would any new *casus belli* have resulted to the other Powers from such an act in itself, to whatever extent the act might have revived the causes which led to the war of which the treaty was the result. If Russia committed an error then, it was the formal error which Lord Granville alleges against her, and his allegation rests, as we have seen, on a statement of fact as to the willingness of the Powers to reconsider the treaty, which Prince Gortschakoff denies. These observations hold true, I think, even where the unanimity from which a treaty resulted was real, because all consent is necessarily conditional, and a change of circumstances swept away the conditions on which it rested. If the unanimity was pretended, as was the case with the Congress of Paris in 1856, and must always be the case with a congress held at the termination of a war, to which the vanquished belligerent is a party, the treaty which may be agreed upon scarcely rises above the rank of a truce. The only compulsitor by which it can be enforced being a renewal by the victorious party of the war by which it was made, the moment that a renewal of that war is no longer to be apprehended, it rests on no material basis at all.

Is there, then, a moral obligation to observe it on the side of the party on whom it was involuntarily imposed? It is generally assumed in this country that, in availing herself of the opportunity which the Franco-German war afforded her of withdrawing from the Black Sea clauses of the Treaty of Paris, Russia sinned, if not against positive, at all events against natural law, or, in other words, that she was guilty, if not of an illegal, at all events, of an immoral act. By breaking down the unanimity requisite for its support, she repudiated an obligation in virtue of which she had obtained a treaty of peace. But the assumption, apart from the consideration that it separates law from morality, is an extremely doubtful one, and would be so even if her assent to the treaty of 1856, in place of being involuntary and extorted, had been voluntary and spontaneous. The treaty, in her opinion, rested on a "situation" which had ceased to exist, and its only effect now was to produce discord and trouble. There is thus much force in Baron Brunnow's assertion, that the permanent character claimed for the interdiction of Russia from the Black Sea "exceeds the bounds of possibility." The words are: "The waters and ports of the Black Sea are in perpetuity interdicted to the flag of war of the Powers possessing its coasts." And Baron Brunnow remarks: "In the order of human affairs, it is in the power of no one to proscribe or to deny the action of time."[1]

How, then, was a treaty, the observance of which in the eyes of Russia, who was as well entitled to judge of it as any or all of the co-signatories, had become unjust and impossible, to be got rid of? The contingency which had arisen was one by which all treaties are necessarily limited: the unanimity to which it owed its formal validity was gone, and yet, short of a transference of that unanimity to the side by which it

[1] *Correspondence*, p. 13.

was assailed, international law furnished no machinery for its repeal, or even for its revision. Russia could scarcely be blamed for not anticipating so extraordinary a change of opinion, and but for its occurrence, a *casus belli* would certainly have been presented to her. In the absence of any other means of solution she would have been entitled to cut with the sword the bonds which the sword had imposed.

Nor can it be doubted that, had they retained what we must assume to have been their original opinion, a similar *casus belli* had arisen to the other signatories. All treaties, as an inevitable result of changes of circumstances for which they make no provision, thus become occasions of future wars, and must continue to do so till some better arrangement than "unanimity" is devised for their revision and their repeal, as well as for their enforcement. If statute law stood on no firmer basis, every obsolete statute would hold *in gremio* the seeds of a civil war. It is to continuous legislative activity alone that it owes its continuous binding force. But it is needless to conceal from ourselves that any such arrangement must imply a sacrifice of the absolute independence of the States that enter into it. It was the failure of the plenipotentiaries at the Congress of Aix-la-Chapelle to face this fact, which has given to the public law of Europe, which they are supposed to have established by the Protocol of 15th November 1818, the feeble character which it so constantly exhibits.[1]

---

[1] The following is the Protocol, signed at Aix-la-Chapelle, on the 15th November 1818, by the Plenipotentiaries of the Courts of Austria, France, Great Britain, Prussia, and Russia:—

"1. That they (the Plenipotentiaries) are firmly resolved never to depart, neither in their mutual relations, nor in those which bind them to other States,

CHAPTER IV.

OF PRECEDENTS.

As there are no international judges, there can, of course, be no international judgments, and, as a precedent is the result of a series of consistent judgments, there can be no international precedents, in the sense in which there are national precedents. But as treaties supply, in an imperfect manner, the place of

from the principle of intimate union which has hitherto presided over all their common relations and interests—a union rendered more strong and indissoluble by the bonds of Christian fraternity which the sovereigns have formed among themselves.

"2. That this union, which is the more real and durable, inasmuch as it depends on no separate interest or temporary combination, can only have for its object the maintenance of general peace, founded on a religious respect for the engagements contained in the treaties, and for the whole of the rights resulting therefrom.

"3. That France, associated with other Powers by the restoration of the legitimate monarchical and constitutional power, engages henceforth to concur in the maintenance and consolidation of a system which has given peace to Europe, and which can alone secure its duration.

"4. That if, for the better attaining the above declared objects, the Powers which have concurred in the present act should judge it necessary to establish particular meetings, either of the sovereigns themselves, or of their respective ministers and plenipotentiaries, there to treat in common of their own interests, in so far as they have reference to the object of their present deliberations, the time and place of these meetings shall, on each occasion, be previously fixed by means of diplomatic communications; and that in the case of these meetings having for their object affairs specially connected with the interests of the other States of Europe, they shall only take place in pursuance of a formal invitation on the part of such of those States as the said affairs may concern, and under the express reservation of their right of direct participation therein, either directly or by their plenipotentiaries."—*Annual Register for* 1819, pp. 131, 132.

legislative enactments, the awards of arbiters and the judgments of mixed courts of prize appointed under treaties, to a corresponding extent take the place of judicial decrees; and a series of such awards or judgments, if tolerably consistent, would loosely correspond to precedents. It is in this direction, almost exclusively, that many persons look for the development of the positive law of nations; and, though the hopes excited by the transactions which took place in the Alabama case were extravagant, there is no reason to doubt that arbitration under special treaties, and even a species of judicial action under general and permanent treaties, will henceforth form an important factor in the progress of international law.

The inherent weakness of arbitration, when regarded from this point of view, lies in the fact that the treaty, or other arrangement which it seeks to apply, is, for the most part, the result of a compromise already accepted between interests which conflict, or are supposed to conflict, rather than an agreement as to the principles or ultimate law which governs the relation in which the parties stand to each other. When we come to the subject of neutrality we shall see but too much reason to believe that even the Treaty of Washington of 1871, though professing to determine the relation between belligerents and neutrals permanently, was in reality a compromise by which neutral rights were sacrificed to the extent which, on that particular occasion, was requisite to avoid a fratricidal war. Before the award of the arbiters who met at Geneva could be applied as a precedent, a new treaty embodying the famous "Three Rules" would require to be negotiated; and it is extremely unlikely that either England or any other neutral Power would again agree, beforehand, to pay damages for the fulfilment of the impossible engagements which these rules impose. The judicial soundness of such an award is thus no guarantee for its value as a precedent.

Assuming the logic which governed the deduction of the arbitrators to be irrefragable at every point, it will do nothing to strengthen a premise which rests on no authoritative legislative basis sufficient to prevent its truth from being called in question. Other cases may, no doubt, occur, in which the end, being peace, will more than justify the concession to belligerent susceptibilities which may be the only means of securing it. But no series of such concessions will advance the definition of the true relation between belligerents and neutrals; and the only hope of rendering concessions unnecessary lies in the definition of that relation by some form of international agreement, in circumstances from which belligerent susceptibilities are absent. At the termination of a war their presence is inevitable; and to make a rule of conceding to them to the extent of forbidding trade between belligerents and neutrals, which, we shall see, would be the logical result of the three rules, would be to put a premium on war. In the absence of an international legislature it is by the formation, first of sound opinions and then of sound customs, alone, that we can arrive at rules sufficiently definite to supply the place of precedents. In such minor matters as the rules which regulate the transaction of diplomatic business, and even the international recognition of private national law, custom already performs the part of precedent fairly enough. For a similar advance in such graver matters as recognition, neutrality, and intervention, it is to the progress of scientific jurisprudence, rather than to the negotiation even in times of peace of treaties of arbitration, that we must still mainly trust. The minds of men must be clearer as to the rules which they ought to adopt, before they can formulate them in treaties which shall have any chance of permanent or even of general acceptance.

CHAPTER V.

OF SCIENTIFIC OR CONSCIOUS INTERPRETATION OF THE NATURAL LAWS OF INTERNATIONAL RELATIONS.

Though customs are the most trustworthy, and treaties the most direct, and, as regards the parties to them during their subsistence, the most authoritative form in which the law of nations declares itself, neither one nor the other has that object directly or consciously in view. It is only inferentially that a knowledge of that law transcending the special circumstances in which they have declared it, can be derived from them. Intellectual processes of analysis, comparison, and generalisation become necessary before they can yield general results, and the ultimate value of these results must be further tested by bringing them in contact with the permanent laws of human nature revealed to us by the history of events, and by the moral and physical sciences. A custom, or a treaty, which is at variance with these laws, offers no contribution to the positive law of nations in the absolute or scientific sense. However great may be its influence on the relations of particular parties for the time being, it is an abnormal manifestation of human volition—an exceptional historical occurrence—a mistake, in short, the consequences of which, in order to avoid a still more flagrant violation of natural law, those who have made it may be bound to accept, but which to mankind in general is a warning—not a guide. Its teaching is thus purely negative; and in order to obtain from it even this negative teaching, scientific action is indispensable.

There are three agencies by which the intellectual processes to which we must look for our systematic knowledge of the law of nations may be performed.

I. *Sovereigns and their ministers, and in constitutional countries the legislative assemblies which act as the advisers of the executive.*

Sovereigns, legislative bodies, ministers of state, and diplomatists, in such circumstances, assume the function of scientific jurists; and when we consider the advantages for procuring information and skilled labour which they derive from their position, there seems, at first sight, no reason why they should not perform it to a much greater extent than they have hitherto done. The great obstacles to their success are the special interests, or supposed interests, which pervert their views, and the more pressing, though not more important, daily and hourly occupations which absorb their time and their energies. These obstacles, except in very rare cases, are probably insuperable.

Perhaps the most remarkable enterprise of this description is the so-called *Grand Dessein* of Henry IV. of France, of which he and our Queen Elizabeth are said to have been the joint-authors, and of which Sully has given so interesting an account in the 30th book of his celebrated *Memoirs*.[1] Bluntschli, in his papers in the *Gegenwart*, of which I shall speak hereafter, attaches great, and I think exaggerated, importance to it.

A vague design of making something like a permanent contribution to the law of nations seems also to have floated before the minds of the three great sovereigns who entered, in 1816, into the convention commonly known as the Holy Alliance.[2]

The famous doctrine of the balance of power, and more especially the Treaty of Utrecht in 1713, the object of which is said expressly to have been *ad conservandum in Europa equilibrium*, was also no doubt intended to stretch beyond the exigencies of the occasion. The same may be said of the "Solemn Declaration" regarding neutral property at sea and blockade, embodied in the Treaty of Paris of 1856, and of the Treaty of Washington of 8th May 1871, as further determining the responsibilities of neutrals in maritime warfare. The Protocol No. I. of the Conferences at London in 1871, with reference to the conditions on which treaties may be modified or repealed, of which I spoke in the last chapter, is another instance directly in point.

---

[1] Vol. iii. p. 355. As to the authenticity of the project, otherwise than as the work of Sully himself, see Sir G. C. Lewis's *Methods of Observation*, &c., vol. ii. p. 285.

[2] *Annual Register*, 1816, p. 381, and *ante*, p. 50.

Most important of all, for practical purposes, is the attempt which is now being made to establish a sort of permanent international executive, by means of the concert of the six great European Powers. The weak part of this arrangement, which it shares with the balance of power, is the necessity for perpetual readjustment which it presents, and its consequent inability to give any permanent direction to its own activity. It does not contain the element of self-control, on which even its external action is dependent; it never can be either wiser or stronger than the particular treaty which it professes to execute.

II. *Scientific jurists acting in conjunction, whether in their private capacity, or together with the constituted authorities of one or more States.*

This agency, which has frequently proved so powerful in the development of municipal jurisprudence, has scarcely, as yet, been brought to bear on the definition of international relations, and the Institute of International Law is probably the first organisation by which it has been attempted to call it into permanent activity.[1] When the period of codification of international law arrives, its action will, no doubt, be very important, and its influence on consuetude may, in the meantime, be of great value. As a means of developing doctrine, and determining the objects of international law, however, it must trust, in the main, to the efforts of its separate members, and can scarcely aid them otherwise than by criticising their labours, and affording them opportunities of interchanging their views.

[1] *Revue de Droit International*, 1873, vol. v. pp. 667-712.

III. *Scientific jurists acting in isolation.*

It is on this agency, hitherto, that the law of nations has been mainly dependent for its scientific development, and on it, for an indefinite future, it must to all appearance, continue to depend. What I have said of the necessity of a clearer definition of the objects of international law before defining its rules, indicates plainly enough, that it is of intellectual labour that we are still in want, and all such labour must be labour of the closet. It is a mistake to suppose that the concurrence of many minds strengthens a conclusion as it strengthens a resolution. In the former case quality is everything, in the latter quantity counts for much. Those who would come nearer even to relative truth, must be contented to approach it, as we must each of us come into the presence of absolute truth at last—alone.

The different relations of States of the most dissimilar character to each other and to their respective citizens, must be analysed with all the light which history and experience afford, and which the sciences kindred to jurisprudence can be made to contribute. In each case the jural ideal must be discovered to which the real is to approximate, otherwise there will be nothing to realise.

As the subject of political ideals, of which I have frequent occasion to speak, is one on which much misapprehension prevails, and regarding which much that is foolish and ignorant is constantly talked and written, in this country more especially, it may be well to quote what was said of it by an Englishman who was alike eminent as a theoretical and a practical politician. "Everything," says Sir G. Cornewall Lewis,[1] "in the nature of an *improvement* in human affairs, implies a preconception of a state of things different from their actual state. Before an improvement can be executed, it must be devised by somebody. Everything real, which is not a mere reproduction and mechanical imitation of something already existing, must have previously been ideal. Every human contrivance, of which *better* can be predicated,—which, in comparison with other things of the same sort, has attained a higher degree of excellence,—must have existed as a mental conception before it was reduced to practice. If we consider all the great items of political progress—such as the introduction of monogamy, of government by a political body, of representative institutions, of the abolition of slavery, of the liberty of the press, of religious toleration, of permanent embassies, of a standing army, of a government post, of a civil police, &c., we shall find that every one must, when it was newly introduced, have been conceived by its author as an ideal scheme. It is true that important political institutions of this kind are rarely or never produced at a single cast; they are the result of a series of accumulations, and they are formed by a gradual process of accretion. Still, each new institution may be analysed into a series of successive steps, and each of these must have been made by persons who conceived it as an untried novelty, so that the aggregate may be described as partaking of this character."

It is a mistake, I believe, to suppose that for the conception of such ideals in general—in our own case for the discovery

[1] *Methods of Observation and Reasoning in Politics*, vol. ii. p. 288.

of the ideal jural relations which we must seek gradually to realise—any peculiar class of faculties is requisite, differing in kind from those which belong to the higher class of practical minds. But these faculties must be differently used, and perhaps differently trained. The work demands far more consecutive thought, and must consequently be performed with far greater deliberation, than the mere application of ready-made rules to special instances. It requires more knowledge of the country, and more measurement and calculation, to make a shorter road between any two points, even supposing the points to be determined, than to plod along the old road, or even to repair it. But it does not follow that the workmen need be dissimilar to anything like the extent that is generally imagined, or that, in favourable circumstances, they may not even be the same. What has retarded the progress of international law has been the smallness of the number of really efficient workmen of any kind who have devoted their energies continuously to this kind of work. There has been less consecutive thought and labour devoted to it than to any other branch of jurisprudence. Had the hundredth part of the skill and industry been brought to bear on it, that has been expended on the development, or even on the criticism of the municipal law of Rome, or on the administration, during half a century, of the municipal law of any single European country, the law of nations could not possibly have been in the condition in which we find it. But, in place of being, like the municipal systems, the result of the calm and persistent efforts of the best legislative and judicial minds of successive generations, the law of nations is left to be determined on the special occasions on which it is about to be administered, always more or less afresh, by party leaders and diplomatists who are endeavouring to overreach each other, or by legal practitioners, to whom for the most part the whole subject is new. The consequence is, that the objects which they hastily assign to it are dictated, not by them, but to them, by the circumstances in which the contending parties are mutually entangled, into which they have permitted themselves to drift, or into which the one has dragged the other. The involuntary or onesided decisions thus arrived at, are then embodied in treaties, recorded by the text-writers, and generalised into the so-called "principles of international law."

Nor has the case been much better, when the subject has been discussed apart from special occurrences, by those whose lives were devoted to speculative inquiries. With them, too, it has been for the most part a πάρεργον, taken up from motives of philanthropy, and thrown aside when its magnitude and difficulty were realised. Even the great work of Grotius occupied but a very small portion of his long and active life; and though he lived for twenty years after it was written, doing practical work of doubtful value at the time and long since forgotten, it does not seem that he ever even seriously revised it. The important contributions which Leibnitz made to the science can be regarded only as happy accidents in his philosophical career. The same may be said of Wolff; whilst Kant, and Trendelenburg, and Whewell became interested in it only towards the close of their long and laborious lives. There is, so far as I know, no single instance of a man of first-rate speculative ability who ever made the law of nations, as a science, the study of his life; and yet it has been by the occasional efforts of such men that it has been mainly advanced. The hopelessness of direct or immediate practical results from their labours, which soon became apparent to themselves, has, no doubt, been the chief cause of the discouragement of so many who entered the international field with the loftiest aspirations. But they erred, as it seems to me, in failing to recognise the necessity of the intermediate stages of gradual and partial consuetudinary recognition which, in all such matters, lie between theory and practice, and which no logical consistency of argument can surmount. Their error has been the error of all doctrinaires, an error from which I am far from imagining that I am myself exempt. But in proof of the assertion that it is to thinkers rather than to compilers or even to actors that we owe such progress as has been made in defining international relations, let us carry back our historical retrospect to an earlier time.

Of the connection between international law in the modern world, and the recognition of the necessary relation between rights and duties in antiquity, I have elsewhere spoken.[1] It was the Stoics who traced out the ethical doctrines of the Socratic school in this special direction, and to them the paternity of international law, as a science, has been justly ascribed. But the Greek Stoics did little to develop the system of universal jurisprudence which their ethical doctrines had rendered possible, and the Romans were shut out from it by the exclusiveness of their national system. Still, the

[1] *Institutes of Law*, pp. 117, 155.

advantages of the natural and philosophical conceptions of the sources of jurisprudence which the Romans derived from their acquaintance with Hellenic ethics acted upon it indirectly. The idea of the *persona* contained the germs of that cosmopolitan system, the realisation of which the ancient world was not privileged to behold, and which we ourselves, even now, have seen but in part.

The sentiment of a brotherhood of mankind, it is true, is one of those innate conceptions which belong to humanity as such. Were its absence conceivable from any sane mind, we should be compelled to relinquish our doctrine of the necessary recognition of the rights of the *non ego*; and when we find the "golden rule" pervading the religious literature of India and China, it is only what we should have anticipated *à priori*. But it was in the hands of the Stoics, as I have said, that this conception assumed the more definite form which gave it practical value as a source of international law. "The Cynics alone," says Zeller, "appear as the precursors of the Stoa, attaching slight value to the citizenship of any particular State, and great importance to citizenship of the world. Still, with the Cynics this idea had not attained to the historical importance which afterwards belonged to it; nor was it used so much with a positive meaning to express the essential oneness of all mankind, as, in a negative sense, to imply the philosopher's independence of country and home. From the Stoic philosophy it first received a definite meaning, and became an idea of general utility. The causes of this change may be sought, not only in the historical surroundings amongst which Stoicism grew up, but also in the person of its founder. Far easier was it for philosophy to overcome national dislikes, when the genial Macedonian conqueror had united the various nationalities comprised within his monarchy, not only under the forms of a central government, but also under those of a common culture." [1]

But even after the cosmopolitan conception had been attained, though jurisprudence in other directions was cultivated as a science of nature, it was long before any serious attempt was made to trace its laws in the relations of State to State. When we come to the subject of private international law, we shall see that it is historically traceable to the Roman conception of the *jus gentium*, and, more particularly, to the doctrines of *origo* and *domicilium*. But, as regards the *jus inter gentes*, the utterances of Cicero, who, when dealing with other departments of jurisprudence, speaks as a professional person, were scarcely more definite than the ethical commonplaces of Seneca and Epictetus; whilst the practical lawyers, whose *dicta* compose the *corpus juris*, by whom the doctrine of the *persona* was only partially understood, are altogether silent on the subject. Even after the Roman Empire was broken up into separate kingdoms, the same continued to be the case. There was no study of public international law at Bologna, or at any of the older universities. That the labours of the civilians, in all the departments of national law, contributed enormously towards consolidating the new societies, is admitted on all hands. Even in the face of the feudal institutions, they succeeded in vindicating the private rights of the subject Roman populations, and thus laid the foundation of the doc-

[1] *Stoics and Epicureans*, Richel's translation, pp. 308, 309.

trines of international jurisdiction which we call private international law. Both Bartolus and Baldus belong to the fourteenth century, so that in a chronological sense, at least, private may be looked upon as the mother of public international law. But the civilians were Imperialists, and down to the period of the revival of letters, and the renewal of the study of Greek philosophy, which was the happy compensation for the loss which Christendom and humanity sustained by the taking of Constantinople by the Turks, the *jus gentium* never transcended the limits which they assigned to it. It was either the vague cosmopolitanism of the Stoics, or else it was the recognition of what Savigny calls "particular rights," existing in persons of different races within the same State. The only traces of a wider conception of it, as determining the relations between separate States, are to be found in the ecclesiastical writers. Of this, M. Nys, in his able and learned work on *The Laws of War and the Precursors of Grotius*, has pointed out an earlier instance than is generally supposed to have existed in so definite a form:—

"Isidore de Séville, qui écrivait au commencement du VIIe siècle, divise le droit en *jus naturale, jus civile et jus gentium*. Le *jus naturale* est pour lui : '*Jus commune omnium nationum, et quod ubique instinctu naturæ, non constitutione aliqua habeatur.*' Il range sous cette rubrique le mariage, la procréation et l'éducation des enfants ; dans son langage, le *jus naturale* remplace ainsi le *jus gentium* des Romains. Le *jus gentium* d'Isidore correspond au contraire, presqu'entièrement à notre droit international : '*Jus gentium est sedium occupatio, ædificatio, munitio, bella, captivitates, servitutes, postliminia, fœdera, paces, induciæ, legatorum non violandorum religio, connubia inter alienigenas prohibita.*' En dehors de cette classification, Isidore de Séville admet le jus militare: '*Jus militare est belli inferendi solemnitas, fœderis faciendi nexus, signo dato egressio in hostem, vel pugnæ commissio. Item signo dato receptio; item flagitii militaris disciplina, si locus deseratur; item stipendiorum modus; dignitatum gradus; præmiorum honor, veluti cum corona vel torques donantur. Item prædæ decisio et pro personarum qualitatibus et laboribus justa divisio; item principis portio.*'"[1]

Between the death of Boethius and the birth of Isidore there was an interval of only about half a century, so that Stoical as well as Christian influences may have told on him directly.

But M. Nys mentions another curious fact connected with this matter. These definitions were admitted into the collection of Gratian, towards the middle of the twelfth century, and thus became part of the *Corpus juris canonici*:

"Les définitions d'Isidore de Séville reçurent la plus haute consécration qu'il leur fût possible d'obtenir; elles prirent rang dans le décret de Gratien et traversèrent ainsi la seconde moitié du moyen âge, faisant l'objet de perpétuels commentaires, sans que, même à la veille de l'époque moderne, les auteurs aient su tirer profit de la terminologie si rationnelle qu'elles offraient."[2]

It is strange that this remark should hold true even of so acute a writer and of one so well acquainted with the work of Isidore and so much occupied with kindred subjects, as Thomas

---

[1] *Le Droit de la Guerre et les Précurseurs de Grotius*, pp. 12, 13.
[2] *Ib.*, p. 13.

Aquinas. The chief of the schoolmen made valuable contributions to the science of natural law, regarding it not only as a branch of ethics, but as the basis of jurisprudence. But it was not in the direction of the *jus inter-gentes* that he sought the application of the principles which he evolved; and Dante's theory of the divine character of a universal empire would have swept away international relations from the civil, just as the theory of Gregory VII. of a universal Church would have swept them away from the ecclesiastical side. Between these two latter theories, however, there was this difference in favour of the former: Dante did not condemn the Church as the device of Satan, as Gregory did the empire. Like the secularists of our own day, Dante was an advocate for the total separation of Church and State, whereas Gregory's scheme, like that of Mahomet, was that the Church should swallow up the State. It is on this ground that Gregory is justly stigmatised as the founder of the non-reciprocating principle which, even in secular affairs, clings to Roman Catholicism in our own day.

Neither Francis à Vittoria, in his *Relectiones Theologicæ* (1559), nor his pupil and successor at Salamanca, Dominic Soto, in his *De Justitia et de Jure* (1568), made any advance in developing the conception of international relations, though the former deserves much credit for the application which he made of it in pleading the cause of the American Indians; and though Conrad Bruno,[1] Balthazar Ayala,[2] and Alberico Gentili[3] dealt with branches of the subject, none of them entertained

---

[1] *De Legationibus*, 1548. [2] *De jure et officiis bellicis*, 1581.
[3] *De jure belli*, 1589.

any adequate conception of its scope as a separate branch of the science of jurisprudence.

The value of what was indirectly effected by Thomas Aquinas, who, in jurisprudence, as in ethics and theology, stands out in solitary majesty, and by Soto, whom we may regard as the immediate founder of the dynasty of jurists which culminated in Grotius, when contrasted with the labours of the civilians—from Bartolus and Baldus down even to Bynkershoek—consisted in this: that, whilst the civilians contented themselves with applying municipal rules to international relations, the scholastic jurists remounted to nature, and sought to discover laws of which the validity was universal. Their endeavour, which in the instances we have mentioned was anything but unsuccessful, was to lay deeper foundations for jurisprudence as a whole, by tracing the *jus gentium* back to its ethical basis; and their reward consisted in the discovery that this basis was adequate to support the new superstructure of positive law, of which the Europe of their day had come to be so sorely in need.

But neither Thomas Aquinas nor Soto was altogether aware of the value of the work which they performed for this purpose; and it was to the eyes of Francesco Suarez of Grenada, so far as I know, that the vision of this fresh sprout from the tree which Isidore had planted so long ago first presented itself in something like a definite shape. Suarez is perfectly fair to his predecessor: " *Quantum ex Isidoro, et aliis juribus et auctoribus colligo,*" he says, referring probably to the *Decretus Gratiani* and its commentators. But Suarez was himself a great man. Hallam has said of him that "he was beyond question the greatest man in the department of moral philosophy whom the order of Loyola produced in this age, or perhaps in any other;" and Grotius was of opinion that he had hardly an equal in point of acuteness amongst philosophers and theologians. The passages of his work[1] in which he treats of international law, though not of the same absolute value as the portions devoted to general jurisprudence, are full of interest when we regard them from a historical point of view. At first it seems as if he had scarcely got hold of the distinction between laws which, independently of local peculiarities, almost all States find it necessary to enact, and which they may, consequently, without fear of injustice, administer to foreigners, and laws by which separate political entities define their mutual relations. The idea of the Roman *jus gentium* was still uppermost in his mind. But as we proceed, he glides, as it were, insensibly into the trains of thought to which the abstract principles which he himself and his predecessors had enunciated could not fail ultimately to lead, and which the necessities of the time were originating. At last we have the *jus inter-gentes*,—as Zouch, the successor of Gentili at Oxford, not long after happily called it,—very clearly indicated, its true character and general objects pointed out, and the fact that it is a branch of *positive* law, and as such distinguishable from, though dependent on, the law of nature—a fact which the successors of Grotius have often been reproached with having forgotten, and to which Grotius himself did not always give adequate expression—strongly insisted on. His words are: " Ratio autem hujus partis, &

[1] *Tractatus de Legibus et Deo Legislatore*, 1611.

juris est, quia humanum genus quantumvis in varios populos, & regna divisum, semper habet aliquam unitatem non solùm specificam, sed etiam quasi politicam, & moralem, quam indicat naturale præceptum mutui amoris, & misericordiæ, quod ad omnes extenditur, etiam extraneos, & cujuscumque nationis. Quapropter licèt unaquæque civitas perfecta, respublica, aut regnum, sit in se communitas perfecta, & suis membris constans, nihilominus quælibet illarum est etiam membrum aliquo modo hujus universi, prout ad genus humanum spectat: nunquam enim illæ communitates adeò sunt sibi sufficientes sigillatim, quin indigeant aliquo mutuo juvamine, & societate, ac communicatione, interdum ad melius esse, majoremque utilitatem: interdum verò etiam ob moralem necessitatem, & indigentiam, ut ex ipso usu constat. Hac ergo ratione indigent aliquo jure, quo dirigantur, & rectè ordinentur in hoc genere communicationis, & societatis." Then, as to its positive character, he adds: "Et quamvis magna ex parte hoc fiat per rationem naturalem: non tamen sufficienter, & immediatè quoad omnia: ideoque aliqua specialia jura potuerunt usu earumdum gentium introduci. Nam sicut in una civitate, vel provincia consuetudo introducit jus, ita in universo humano genere, potuerunt jura gentium moribus introduci."

The subject is worked out in the same strain, at considerable length, in the chapter from which I have transcribed these sentences,[1] the distinction between the *jus gentium* of the Romans and this other kind of *jus gentium*—as he calls the *jus intergentes*—when once seized, being clearly maintained. There is no attempt at a detailed system; but the remarks which are

[1] Lib. II. cap. xix. sect. 9, p. 109, ed. 1679. Read from p. 103 to p. 111.

interspersed on the special subjects pertaining to this branch of jurisprudence—such as the privileges of embassy, the laws of war, of treaties of peace, suspensions of arms, and the like — show, I think, that it was probably more the accident of his profession, and of the party to which he adhered, than his personal characteristics, that prevented Suarez from anticipating Grotius, and becoming the author of a practical treatise on international law.

From these few observations you will have no difficulty perceiving the extreme injustice of the manner in which, down to our own time, it has been customary to speak of the scholastic jurists.[1] Learned as Barbeyrac was, the few perfunctory sentences which he devotes to them in his celebrated preface to Puffendorf,[2]—which he adopts in his preface to Grotius[3] as serving for both works,—are no exception. The fact is, that ever since the Reformation the prejudices of Protestants against Roman Catholics have been so vehement as to deprive them of the power of forming a dispassionate opinion of their works, even if they had been acquainted with them, which they rarely were. Recently these prejudices have been

---

[1] I believe that no more valuable contribution could be made to the literature of jurisprudence at the present time, than a collection and translation of the portions of these works which have reference to general jurisprudence and international law. M. Nys has remarked that there is not one of the precursors of Grotius who has written pages on the subject of war so cruel and pitiless as those which Bynkershoek wrote after him; and I venture to affirm that the scholastic jurists kept the ethical basis of jurisprudence before their eyes far more steadily than either Bentham or his successors. The consequence is that the science of jurisprudence, which was then before the age, is now behind it; and that popular opinion for the present has become the ultimate as well as the proximate source of legislation.

[2] P. cxv.   [3] P. 11.

extended to Churchmen of all denominations who, as such, are supposed to be incapable of recognising any other source of knowledge than direct revelation. Should the movement for the separation of Church from State be successful, this prejudice, which, as regards the Established clergy, both in England and Scotland, is beginning to give way, will very soon become as inveterate in this country as it has already become almost everywhere on the Continent. " Presbyter " will then be indeed but " Priest writ large," and the same exceptional character will be ascribed to him.

Grotius, elsewhere I believe, speaks of Suarez as a moralist with admiration, but he does not mention him amongst the jurists whom he had consulted when composing his great work;[1] and there is no reason to suppose that he had any adequate acquaintance even with the portions of the *De Legibus* which treat of his own immediate subject. That Grotius was not a very careful reader, even of those of his predecessors whom he mentions by name, may be gathered from the fact that he accuses them generally,[2] and Balthazar Ayala in particular, of not having treated of the justifying causes of war —" *Causas, unde bellum justum aut unjustum dicitur, Ayala non attigit,*"—whereas the subject was a favourite one with them, and the second chapter of Ayala's first book is entirely devoted to it. Probably the fact mentioned by Barbeyrac,[3] that Grotius had no library at his command when his book was written, may, to some extent, account for this seeming injustice, as well as for the extent to which he quoted from memory. Yet not I think wholly. Barbeyrac himself was no better than Grotius

[1] *Proleg.*, sect. xxxviii.   [2] *Ib.*   [3] See on this subject, Nys, p. 72.

in his treatment of the ecclesiastical jurists, though he was a more careful worker in general, and had adequate resources at his command. In speaking of Grotius, of whom he was not an extravagant admirer, he says, that "but for him there might still have been no passable system of the science of natural law,"[1] an assertion which he certainly could not have made if he had compared the famous *Prolegomena* and the other portions of Grotius's work which treat of the subject, with the works of Suarez, of Soto, or of their far greater predecessor, Thomas Aquinas. Grotius's own shortcomings as the founder of a new branch of jurisprudence, in consequence of the frequency with which he lost hold of the guiding principles of natural law, are pointed out by Barbeyrac with much truth and impartiality.[2] "The general principles of Grotius relating to natural law," he says, "are very solid; but Grotius does not develop them sufficiently, and it requires a great deal of meditation to follow them out. He does not sufficiently show the chain of consequences which result from them when they are applied to particular subjects. This has occasioned certain authors, not very penetrating or very just, to say of him, that after having laid down his principles, he leaves them there without making any use of them, and founds his decisions on different things altogether. Grotius might have prevented these rash judgments by amplifying a little, and making more obvious on each occasion, the connection between the proofs which he adduces, and the principles which he deduces from them."

---

[1] *Preface to Puffendorf*, p. cxxii.
[2] *Preface to Grotius*, p. xxx.

The fault which Barbeyrac here indicates, that—viz., of failing consistently to maintain, or at any rate to exhibit, the logical connection between the ethical and jural principles which he discovered in the nature of international relations, and the rules for the realisation of these principles in the conditions in which the relations were manifested in the world which surrounded him, was unquestionably the leading fault of Grotius, as it has been of so many other representatives of the school which he founded.

The name which is inseparably associated with that of Hugo Grotius is that of Samuel Puffendorf. Feeling the imperfection, whilst recognising the soundness of the basis in nature which his predecessor had endeavoured to lay for his system, Puffendorf resolved to remedy the defect by demonstrating in every department the inseparable connection between natural and positive law. His conception was a magnificent one, and in the effort which he made to realise it, he has left behind him a work which, notwithstanding the unpardonable amount of commonplace which it contains, and its consequent dulness, is entitled to the respect of all future jurists. It was nothing less than an attempt to evolve, from the study of human nature, a system of jurisprudence which should be of universal and permanent applicability. I have explained in another connection [1] the grounds on which, and the extent to which the conception that gave rise to it, and to the class of works of which it is the most prominent example, must be regarded, if not as scientifically unsound, at least as practically unrealisable.

[1] *Institutes of Law*, p. 524 et seq.

Unlike the work of Grotius, Puffendorf's book was not written with special reference to the relations of State to State; and though entitled *The Law of Nature and Nations*, only a very small portion of it—the last seven chapters of the eighth book—is devoted to international law. But here, if anywhere, his method was in place; for the relation of international law to natural law, though not exceptional in kind, is, as we have seen, exceptional in degree. Puffendorf accordingly makes little advance on Grotius in defining international relations himself, and he falls behind him in exhibiting the manner in which they were defined by custom. It is doubtful, indeed, whether, in consequence of the misapprehension of Grotius's system to which it gave currency, Puffendorf's work did not retard rather than promote the study of international law. And yet the fault did not lie wholly with Puffendorf. Grotius, as I have elsewhere pointed out,[1] had unfortunately spoken occasionally of the positive law of nations, when opposing it to natural law, as "voluntary law" (*jus voluntarium*). To any one who read Grotius's book as a whole it ought to have been apparent that, where this phrase went beyond the assertion that the laws which govern human relations, though immutable, are not inviolable, or that the conditions on which the relations depend are, to some extent, subject to human volition, it was mere looseness of expression. No one was ever less disposed than Grotius to separate any branch of jurisprudence from its moorings in nature, the laws of which are independent of human will at any rate. The conception of a law which had no deeper roots than

[1] *Institutes of Law*, pp. 257, 258.

human "sovereignty"[1] was left for the palmy days of our own Georges. To suppose that even Hobbes was contented to stop short at the fiat of his own *Leviathan* would be to do him exceeding injustice. Still there can be no doubt that Puffendorf ascribed this error to Grotius, that his learned and judicious translator and commentator Barbeyrac endorsed the opinion, and that both of them bounded over to the opposite and not less erroneous opinion, that as there could be no voluntary law, there could be no variable law. Seeing clearly, as they did, that there could be no positive law which was not natural law realised in time and place, they unhappily jumped to the conclusion that there was no natural law which was not positive law, apart altogether from such realisation. It did not occur to them that the recognition of natural law by human intelligence, and its realisation by human will and human power, were not necessary consequences of the necessity of its existence, and that their definitions of it, however accurate, could have no permanent or universal application to practical affairs. The following passage from Barbeyrac, which I quote as being far clearer and more concise than any of Puffendorf's numerous statements to the same effect, places this assertion beyond dispute: " M. Puffendorf," he says, " often refutes Grotius, with reason, as one may see at once by glancing at my Index of Authors; and in order to be convinced that Grotius had ideas on several subjects which were false, or at least confused, it will suffice to consider one of his opinions, which is spread over his whole system,—I mean the distinction which he supposes

[1] *Vide* Austin and his followers, *passim*.

to exist between the law of nature and a certain law of nations, which he conceives to rest on the tacit consent of peoples."[1]

It sounds strange to hear the discovery of the positive law of nations thus made a reproach against Grotius. Mainly, of course, it was a dispute about a word, for the word "voluntary" was not intended by Grotius to convey the meaning which Barbeyrac assigns to it. But it was not without practical consequences, of which the most unfortunate was that of gradually alienating men from the study, not of the positive law of nations, as founded on consent, but of the natural law of nations of which this consent was, *or ought to have been*, the expression. The positive law of nations was thus deprived of the scientific basis on which the other departments of jurisprudence rested, and on which Zeno and the Stoics had placed it at the first, which was certainly very far from the intention of Grotius. Feeling that the dictates of natural law in the abstract were incapable of application, and that in the concrete they varied with the circumstances by which they were brought into play, practical men abandoned their investigation altogether, and sought in the circumstances which were to determine the form of its realisation the law which was to be realised. The ideal of which positive law is the temporal and local expression was thus lost sight of; jurisprudence drifted away from ethics; and positive law, and the law of nations more especially, came to be regarded as *jus voluntarium* in the literal sense. If not dictated by absolute caprice, it was supposed to owe its origin to nothing more binding than convenience, comity, utility, and the like,—to

[1] *Pref. to Puffendorf*, p. 122; see also liv. ii. chap. iii. sect. 23.

be, in short, what was called an "imperfect obligation," which each nation might observe or not observe as it felt disposed. It is true that this result did not follow immediately. The hitherto unpublished fragments on natural law which Leibnitz left behind him, recently given to the world by Professor Trendelenburg,[1] show, even more strongly perhaps than his writings previously known to us, how greatly he was averse to this tendency. It was Leibnitz's impatience of Puffendorf's dulness which prevented him from discovering the extent to which they certainly agreed, and he himself continued occasionally to make use of the unfortunate expression, *jus voluntarium*, which had scared Puffendorf and his followers into error.

Nor did Wolff or Vattel succeed in saving the science from the rising tide of empiricism, and from the consequences of the separation of law from ethics, which resulted from the distinction between perfect and imperfect obligations, advocated by Thomasius, and adopted by Kant under modifications which I have elsewhere explained.[2] Yet how just and clear their own views were will be apparent from the following passage from Vattel, whom we may accept as Wolff's exponent: "We must apply the rules of natural law to nations," Vattel says, "in order to discover what their obligations are, and what are their rights; and, consequently, the law of nations is, in general,[3] nothing else but the law of nature

---

[1] *Bruchstücke in Leibnitzen's Nachlass zum Naturrecht gehörig. Historische Beiträge zur Philosophie.* Von Adolph Trendelenburg. Vol. ii. p. 257.

[2] *Institutes of Law*, p. 295.

[3] *Ordinairement.* This unfortunate word shows that Vattel himself did not always avoid the very error which he was reproving.

applied to nations. But as the application of a rule cannot be just and reasonable unless it is made in a manner appropriate to the subject, we must not suppose that the law of nations is precisely and in all respects the same, so that we have nothing more to do but to substitute as its subjects nations for individuals. A civil society, a State, is a very different thing from a human individual, and hence result, in virtue of the law of nations itself, obligations and rights, in many cases extremely different. The same general rule applied to two subjects does not yield the same decisions, because a special rule that is entirely just in the one case may be quite inapplicable in the other. There are, consequently, many cases in which the law of nature will not yield the same decision between State and State which it yielded between individual and individual. We must know how to apply it in a manner appropriate to each subject; and it is the art of applying it with justice founded on reason which makes of the law of nations a special science. What we speak of as the necessary law of nations thus consists of the application of the law of nature to nations. It is necessary because nations are absolutely bound to observe it. This law contains the obligations which the law of nature imposes upon States, and on them this law is not less obligatory than on individuals, because States are composed of men; their deliberations are the deliberations of men, and the law of nature is obligatory on all men, whatever may be the relations in which they act."[1]

Vattel thus, as you observe, vindicates for the positive law

[1] *Droit des Gens*, vol. i. p. 39, edition 1820.

of nations its scientific character by tracing it back to nature; whilst, by repudiating the *jus voluntarium*, he brings it within the scope of the *jus strictum*, and places it on a level with national law. It is true that neither Leibnitz nor Wolff nor Vattel himself wholly discontinued the use of the term "voluntary law," though thus protesting against the literal sense in which their adversaries accepted it; and this was at least a grave literary mistake on their part. But surely nothing can justify men, with such passages as that which I have quoted before them, for writing such nonsense about the opinions of Vattel and his predecessors as is still contained in almost every English, and in many foreign books.[1]

The real fault of the elder jurists was, that they were not careful enough in their study of the circumstances of the State life in which they sought to realise the necessary law, and that they argued too much from false or partial analogies between the life of the State and the life of the individual,—a fault which, scientifically at least, is less heinous than that of not knowing that there is a necessary law at all, either for States or for men, or any analogy between its manifestations in the various branches of jurisprudence. It is this study of circumstances, without any definite object, which has been the fault of the vast majority of their successors, and which is the fault of what is now called the Historico-practical, but ought rather to be called the Historico-empirical school.

The distinction between the two classes of writers and the

---

[1] Take, *e.g.*, as a good popular source, Chambers's *Encyclopædia*, *voce* "Vattel," where we are told that his conception of natural law was that of an "imaginary system"!

two methods, may be thus summed up. Down to the time of Vattel,[1] and including it, the effort had been to discover the ideal law of the relation, Kant's "shortest line;" and that, or the nearest approach that could be made to it with the knowledge of the circumstances possessed by the writer, was held to be the necessary, and as such, the common law of nations. Occasional or even consuetudinary aberrations from it, or what were sometimes too hastily held to be such, were dismissed as exceptions having no claim to general recognition. Such was the theory, however imperfect the practice may have been.

From Vattel's time, again, till our own, partially including the latter, the effort has been to determine the consuetude, which is accepted as the common law, without reference to any absolute or necessary standard, and positive law is criticised or amended only in accordance with prevailing sentiments, or with such experience of its results as recent historical events are supposed to afford. Even where these experiences amounted to a custom, which we have seen to be one of the most important sources of the law of nations, Savigny's[2] profound remark that "custom is the mark by which we recognise positive law, not the

[1] As Vattel (1714-67) was the last of the philosophical, Moser (1701-86) appears to have been the first of the empirical jurists. President Woolsey says, p. 421, "From this time the positive and practical tendency has prevailed—in some writers to the neglect of the principles of general justice." It is curious to observe that the tendency to determine the relation between neutrals and belligerents by considerations of immediate convenience, as opposed to ultimate principle, which still prevails, first manifested itself about the same period.— Hall's *International Law*, p. 511.

[2] *Die Gewohnheit is das Kennzeichen des positiven Rechts, nicht dessen Entstehungsgrund.*—*System*, vol. i. p. 35.

ground from which it springs," was entirely overlooked. It is not on the ground that they are recorders of experience, that I object to the writers who followed Vattel. I have elsewhere[1] explained that the utilitarian or empirical method, when employed for the purpose of investigating nature, with a view to the discovery of natural, and as such necessary laws, whether in the abstract or in the concrete, is a perfectly legitimate branch of the inductive or observational method. When confined to the observation of external phenomena, and conducted exclusively by means of the external senses, it is indeed one-sided, and can yield no trustworthy results. We cannot legislate till we know the beings for whom we are legislating, and the relations in which, as such, they stand to each other; and the science of jurisprudence cannot be successfully prosecuted, in any department, if the ethical phenomena of consciousness be left out of account. But the phenomena of consciousness can in no way be better ascertained than by studying the history of human opinion, provided that the sphere of observation be sufficiently wide. Each generation, moreover, has its special function, and if the function of the generation which followed the French Revolution was to supply external factors for the solution of international problems, those who feel the necessity of internal factors also have no right to undervalue the gifts which they have received. If we do not know much more either of ourselves or of others than our fathers did, our means of knowing both have been vastly widened; and it is only when we forget the object for which we acquired our knowledge that we lose the good of it.

[1] *Institutes of Law*, p. 50.

It is only when the necessary law is lost sight of in its concrete manifestations, that empiricism, utilitarianism, and the like, degenerate into mere objectless groping amongst lifeless facts and life-destroying fictions.

The more or less clear and definite perception of the object of their search, then, rather than the means which they adopt for its discovery, is the test which we must apply if we would distinguish between the writers on the law of nations since Vattel's time who are jurists, on the one hand, and those who are chroniclers and party politicians, on the other. I have said that there has been all along a sad lack of consistent application to this subject by men of first-rate ability; and I doubt whether we can point to a single recent writer to whom the scientific character can be ascribed without qualifications. If this be so, an enumeration of names and characteristics would be an ungracious and unprofitable task, and special references must be reserved. On the other hand, however, it would be very unjust to the schools of jurisprudence which have recently sprung up in Germany, Belgium, and Italy, and which are now making their way into America, and even into England, if we were to represent their members as insensible to the claims of science, or incapable of occupying an absolute point of view. That a very important revival has taken place quite recently, will be obvious to any one who will take the trouble to contrast the writings of Bluntschli, or Mancini, or Rolin Jaequemyns, with those of Wheaton, or Story, or Heffter. Let us take Wheaton and Bluntschli as typical instances. The friend of Senior and Austin, and through them an inheritor of Benthamite traditions, Wheaton, who was bred as an American case-lawyer, never had a clear conception of the necessary character of positive law at all; he never saw the distinction between it and what, whether rightly or wrongly, had been held to realise it. To him, whatever is recognised by custom or established by treaty, is, *eo ipso*, positive law; and this equally, whether it conforms to or violates the necessary law of the relation—whether, absolutely, it be right or wrong. Whatever is necessarily variable, or, as he would say, " dependent on circumstances," he regards as dependent on human will, as *jus voluntarium* in the sense in which men like Grotius and Leibnitz certainly did *not* mean it. Positive law, as he views it, thus varies not only with circumstances, but—in so far as human will is free—in the same circumstances; so that there may be half-a-dozen answers, all equally true, to the same question,—half-a-dozen centres to the same circle. It is in consequence of this want of any definite object of search that Mr Wheaton constantly abandons the position of a jurist employing the historical method, for that of a chronicler of events, or an advocate of American interests and prejudices, and records conflicting lines of policy without the slightest attempt to reconcile them, to try them by an absolute standard, or even the slightest conception that there is any absolute standard, any necessary law governing the special relation, by which they may be tried. As a record of what was believed or held to be the law of nations in his time, his books are valuable beyond perhaps any other books; and if he is not always dispassionate, he certainly always means to be so. As the work of an honest and experienced diplomatist, they possess an authority for practical purposes which can never attach to the writings of those who have not had the same experience of affairs; and in Mr Lawrence they have found an editor and continuator not inferior to their author. But they help us over no theoretical difficulties, and can scarcely be regarded as a contribution to scientific jurisprudence, otherwise than by chance.

Bluntschli, on the other hand, who, like Grotius, was a philosopher and a theologian, has a clear conception of the necessary character of the law to be recognised; and he describes the efforts of Congresses, when issuing such documents as the Solemn Declaration of Paris in 1856, to have been to declare it rather than to enact it. "They had no intention," he says, "of creating a conventional law, because they could bind only the contracting parties, or the signatories to the protocols. But they wished to determine [*poser*] general principles for the European world, and which all the States of Europe would respect. They did not desire to create an arbitrary law, which could last no longer than the force which supported it. They wished to recognise a necessary law and necessary principles [*un droit et des principes nécessaires*], based on the nature of the relations between peoples, and the duties of civilised nations to humanity as a whole."[1] And again: "In the treaties concluded between different States are to be found dispositions which possess the essential character of laws [*sont lois par essence*], and are not simple articles of a treaty,—dispositions which formulate principles and a necessary law, and are not the result of the good pleasure of the contracting parties."[2] It is somewhat doubtful whether the insight which Bluntschli here ascribes to the

[1] *Droit International Codifié*, p. 4.   [2] *Ib.*, p. 5.

negotiators of whom he speaks, really belonged to them; but it is plain enough that it is between these essential laws and those which result from the good pleasure of the contracting parties, that the writers, of whom Mr Wheaton is the most eminent representative, fail to distinguish. If the good pleasure of the parties be in conformity with the essential laws, the provisions of the treaty are then no doubt positive laws in the fullest sense which the science of jurisprudence attaches to that epithet. However imperfect the machinery for their enforcement may be, they possess, in virtue of the treaty, a weight which science alone can never confer. But it is a weight which science may go far to take away; for if they can be shown to be destitute of this character, they are only new blunders, destined sooner or later to follow the old blunders which they superseded into that limbo, first of condemnation, and ultimately of forgetfulness, which has swallowed up so many of the treaties which encumber Mr Wheaton's pages, and which still form the almost exclusive subject of study by international lawyers.

CHAPTER VI.

OF CONTEMPORARY PUBLIC OPINION.

From the narrow scope of our vision and the shifting character of the scene presented to it by human affairs, the conclusions of reason with reference to the means by which ends or objects, even when determined, may be realised in special circumstances, seldom rises above probability. To these probable conclusions we give the name of opinions or convictions, as opposed to traditions, which we accept on the authority of others, or prejudices, which are imposed on us by our own imperfections. When a decided preponderance of evidence is recognised as existing in favour of a particular conclusion, we arrive at what is called a ripe opinion, and in a ripe opinion we behold the proximate source of positive law. Nay, when opinion is so strong and fixed as to declare itself in the form of custom, we have seen that it becomes the immediate spring of action, and by asserting for itself the character of positive law, obviates the necessity for legislation. Nor is there any department of jurisprudence in which this phenomenon is more frequently exhibited than in the formation, development, and enforcement of the law of nations. The better part of that law is, and probably always will continue to be consuetudinary; and as the function of the scientific jurist is to influence consuetude by moulding opinion, his labours are of peculiar value in this department.

But it is mere delusion on the part of the scientific jurist to imagine that, however unassailable his arguments may be, he can, single-handed, procure for his conclusions such acceptance as shall render them self-legislative. He may originate and shape opinion, but he cannot disseminate it; and the populariser, if not the legislator, must thus stand between him and immediate action. The motive power which he seeks to turn in a particular direction is that of many wills; and in order that these wills may be brought into harmony they must be approached by a thousand by-ways of sentiment, prejudice, interest, and the like. These secondary motives point only indirectly to the goal which reason indicates, and the utmost that reasoning can achieve is to control those who are to control them. The scientific jurist must farther be contented to see his arguments presented in a one-sided form, and his conclusions only partially apprehended by those who accept them, and who will often profess and believe that they have worked them out for themselves. Still, as a counterpoise to the impediments created by the imperfections of popular exposition, it must never be forgotten that in the greater strength and activity of this intermediate factor between theory and practice lies the special element of hope which modern, as opposed to mediæval life, holds out to the international jurist. Public opinion on international subjects is the offspring of those appliances for stimulating and disseminating thought which follow in the wake of national freedom. Where the moral tone of society is high, it may even anticipate the conclusions of science, and it may act beyond the boundaries of the States in which it originates, either directly by influencing international action, or indirectly by developing international organisation. Of its fallibility, on the other hand, and its tendency to be misled, the popularity which in their commencement has almost always attended the most disastrous wars is a melancholy proof.[1] Popular opinion, like scientific opinion, further runs the risk of being misunderstood by its professed interpreters. We have not to go far back into the history of this country for an instance in which it was found to be at variance with that of its official expositors, and of a large portion of the metropolitan press. But on this very occasion its power was very strikingly manifested. In the case of Lord Beaconsfield's foreign policy, the interesting phenomenon was exhibited of public opinion holding both a ministry and a parliamentary majority of extraordinary docility in check, till a constitutional opportunity of repudiating them arrived. The uncertainty which clings to the science of political meteorology is made ludicrously apparent by the docility with which the 'Times' constantly braves public ridicule by changing sides.

The power which public opinion already possesses with us it is gradually asserting even in those countries in which it acts on internal government less immediately; and it is not too much to say, that the influence of international law, as a factor in the life of humanity, now depends almost exclusively on the extent to which public opinion can be brought into harmony with reason. Much in this direction has still to be done. If such elementary truths as the *necessary* interdependence of States, and the *inevitable* solidarity of their interests had reached the stage of ripe European opinions, it is inconceivable that

[1] Mr Gladstone's speech on Mr Richard's motion, April 29, 1881.

Germany should still think it, or find it, necessary to have an army of 1,800,000 ready to march in ten days.[1] Either Germany is wasting her resources in objectless precautions, or else there is a vast amount of unreason somewhere, against which she has to use such formidable safeguards.

[1] *Statesman's Manual*, 1881, p. 10.

BOOK II.

OF THE RECOGNITION OF STATE-EXISTENCE AS
THE FUNDAMENTAL DOCTRINE OF
THE LAW OF NATIONS

CHAPTER I.

OF THE DISTINCTION BETWEEN INTERNATIONAL RECOGNITION
AND INTERETHNICAL RECOGNITION.

NO modern contribution to science seems destined to influence international politics and jurisprudence to so great an extent as that which is known as ethnology, or the science of races. Ethnology is still in its earlier stages; but when we consider that it is not yet a hundred years since Peter Camper died, since Blumenbach commenced his famous *Collectio craniorum diversarum gentium*, or since Pritchard was born, we must regard as very wonderful the results which it has yielded. These results have often been in directions altogether outside and beyond the contemplation of its founders. By them it was regarded chiefly, if not entirely, as a contribution to comparative physiology; but in other hands comparative physiology has led to comparative philology, which, in its turn, has quite recently become the parent of comparative theology. In the political direction the influence of these studies has hitherto been almost unobserved, but they have insensibly modified the old historical and geographical conceptions of nationality; and there seems no reason why they should not ultimately yield us sciences of comparative ethics, politics, and jurisprudence, which will become important factors in the development of the positive law of nations.[1]

Even at the stage of knowledge which we have reached, our data seem sufficient to suggest the inquiry whether, as there are groups of human beings wider than those which we call nations, there are not also corresponding jural relations of a more general kind, which claim our attention before we venture to define the relations of the separate nations of which these groups are composed. Is it not possible that separate ethnical groups may, by their very nature, be directed towards political and social ideals so dissimilar as to prevent them from ever following the same lines of progress? May it not be that under these diverse ethnical impulses diverse types of nationality must necessarily grow up, and that these, though permanently dissimilar, may be of equal ethical value with that which our ethnical genius has imposed upon us, and equally entitled to international recognition by us and by the other nations of Western Europe? Are we right in measuring the progress of a nation which belongs to a different ethnical group from our own by the approach which it makes to our conception of an organised community? Ought we not to distinguish between differences of kind and differences of degree, and, *within the lines of natural law,* to measure nations rather by the approach which they make to their own ideals than to ours? If we attempt to construe Turanian or Mongolian politics or positive law from an Aryan point of view,

---

[1] To this enumeration I might add "comparative religion;" because, though it is the ethical side of religion alone that bears on politics and jurisprudence, ethical study may derive important aid from comparing the forms in which common ethical ideals are exhibited in various religious systems.

is it not very much like attempting to construe Chinese or Turkish by the grammatical laws which are more or less common to the Romanic and Teutonic languages?

Even within the wider groups into which ethnologists have divided the human family, may not the ethnical subdivisions which so often penetrate and transcend the limits of nationality, generate social and political conceptions permanently irreconcilable and yet mutually entitled to recognition? It is said that the population of Europe includes eighty millions of Slavs; and though the Slavs are a branch of the Aryan race, there is reason to believe that the Slavonic ideal of social and political organisation, as regards the life of the family, the tenure and transmission of land, and the administration of justice, differs from the Teutonic and Romanic ideals in many essential particulars. What in Western Europe we understand by political organisation rests on individualism and aims at self-government, which always tends to assume the form of constitutionalism. Now constitutional government acts by means of the representation as opposed to the delegation of national power; and this conception of national life is apparently at variance, not only with the history and traditions, but with the present sympathies and aspirations of the whole Slavonic race. Starting with the Mir and ending with the Czar, Slavonic organisation, in so far as it has grown from Slavonic roots in Russia, has hitherto been communal and autocratic; and to these conditions of existence, amidst all their contradictions and inconsistencies, the whole national party, from the most moderate Slavophile to the wildest Nihilist, still clings.

In his careful and thoughtful book on Russia, Mr Mackenzie Wallace has indicated as the cause of the failure of the Germanising party in that country their inability to "see things from the inside;" and that when seen from the inside they mean a preference for communalism over individualism, and for the delegation of power over the direct political activity of the citizens in their own behalf, are points on which Mr Wallace and all the other writers of authority seem to agree.[1] It is from an irrational and aimless hatred to government in every form, and not with a view to the limitation of his power, that the attacks of the Nihilists are directed against the Czar; whilst it is to the communal element, which pervades the whole social structure, that the national party, we are told, look for protection against the proletariat, which they believe to have arisen from exaggerated notions of individual freedom, and regard, not without reason, as the greatest danger threatening Western civilisation. It is not probable that this view, either as to the origin or the means of checking the growth and accumulation of the pestilent residuum of our city populations, will commend itself to statesmen and economists in Western Europe; and we may possibly regard, with some complacency even, the difficulties which it occasions us when contrasted with the hidden workings of those elements of social disintegration of which communalism, at any rate, has not hindered the activity. But the question is not whether the Teutonic and Romanic races are to adopt Slavonic conceptions, but whether the Slavonic race is to be permitted to retain them in the hope that it may raise upon

---

[1] See in particular *Russia before and after the War*.

them a political superstructure more in accordance with its genius than it can derive from the imitation of foreign institutions. Whatever may be the influence of biological laws in future ages, there are no historical examples of political assimilation between alien races being effected otherwise than either by absorption or amalgamation. Mere conquest has always been wholly ineffectual. Where there has been no admixture of blood, the absence of the *idem sentire* has continued to prevent the *idem velle atque nolle*. Now as no such intermixture, on a great scale, between Slavonic and Teutonic or Romanic populations seems possible, and the extermination of either by the other is inconceivable, the conclusion seems to be forced upon us that ethnical will continue to produce political differences which international law must accept as permanent factors.

It is conceivable that a corresponding ethnical divergence may count for more than we are willing to admit amongst the causes which have hitherto rendered our own Celtic problem insoluble; and that the study of Celtic history, and of the Celtic language and literature, in themselves of no great value, may be important for political as well as for philological and archæological purposes. Germs of incipient State-existence may possibly come to light when the old Brehon laws and the clan-system have been carefully and dispassionately looked into. In another direction, it may modify our condemnation of the system of communal ownership in other races, when we reflect that the relation of landlord and tenant amongst ourselves seems no longer able to bear the strain of advancing democracy, and when the adoption of some modified form of permanent tenure by the occupier and cultivator of the soil, even in cases in which he is incapable of direct ownership, seems to have become inevitable. But these are considerations which belong to national rather than to international organisation. The international question is, whether, in the presence of ethnical differences which for jural purposes we must regard as indelible, we are entitled to confine recognition to those branches of alien races which consent to separate themselves from the rest, and, ostensibly or professedly, to accept our political conceptions. If Slavophile aspirations, in their constructive aspect, aim at the attainment of order and liberty, is it wise to impede their realisation by appointing German princes to rule over Slavonic populations, and by urging those populations to accept what we understand by constitutional government?

Now these are questions for the answers to which we must look to the future progress of ethical and jural ethnology. All that the scientific jurist can do, for the present, is to point out the importance which must continue to belong to the absolute and unchangeable ethical element which underlies all the relative forms of its manifestation. His function is to emphasise the distinction between the universal ethical, and the local, even if permanent, ethnical elements which enter into every political and international problem. No mere accumulation of ethnical facts will help us to an opinion with reference to the claims of a race or a nation to recognition, unless we have an absolute standard by which to measure the ethical results of its political activity; and for this absolute standard we must go back to those laws of our common nature which govern all races and nations alike. Ethnology will probably teach us that the ethical ideal may be realised in accordance with ethnical ideals more diverse than we at present imagine; but, unless we keep this common goal in sight, we shall be in continual danger of mistaking licence for liberty, and apologising for crime. We may hesitate to condemn a positive policy the professed objects of which are not anti-jural, on the ground that the means which it proposes to employ for their attainment seem to us inadequate or mistaken; but no toleration must be shown to a policy of mere negation, which aims at nothing but disorganisation, and which trusts to means which the common conscience of humanity repudiates. Such a policy as that of Nihilism or Fenianism or Communism must be dealt with as a manifestation of that element of jural contradiction which it is the object of jurisprudence to remove. It has thus no claim even to the ephemeral or tentative recognition, which, under certain conditions, may be jurally extended to the abnormal relations of States,[1] and the terrors of lawlessness must be responded to, if need be, by the terrors of the law.

Apart altogether from any influence which it might exert on our ultimate policy in Ireland, there is no nation for which the subject of race has such momentous importance as for our own, because it is on the views· which we form of it that must depend not only our future attitude to such countries as Russia, China, and Japan, but the ultimate destiny which we attempt to shape for our great Indian empire. That the

[1] *Infra*, Book III.

natives of India are being rapidly instructed, the activity and ability of the native press abundantly testify. But are they being Anglicised, or Teutonised, or Europeanised in their sentiments or their aspirations, so as to lead to the hope that they will ultimately develop either into a semi-autonomous English colony, or into a separate State on the European model? Of neither result does there seem to be any substantial promise. The native populations of India differ far more from Englishmen than Slavonians differ from Germans; and if the Germanising of Russia, or the Russianising of the German provinces on the Baltic which politically belong to her, has proved impossible, what shall we say of the Anglicising of India? The alternative thus seems to lie between the entire subjugation of these races — which, even if it were desirable, we shall scarcely be able to maintain — and the gradual development of some oriental form of political organisation hitherto unknown to the history of politics. There is no reason to suppose that the latter solution is permanently shut out by the superstitious observances with which Brahmanism and Buddhism have obscured the ethical traditions of the Aryan race. But the problem is complicated by the presence of the Mahometan element in the population, with reference to which, for reasons which I shall state hereafter, the same hopeful view cannot be entertained. The greater or less tenacity with which this latter creed is held may, however, be largely a question of race.

But however great may be the influence of the ties of race on the development of cosmopolitan or political relations, it is obvious that they do not bind communities together to the extent of enabling them to assert jural rights or to discharge jural obligations. We cannot recognise Slavs or Celts or Teutons simply as such. The analogy between the person and the State may not be very close, but when we come to deal with ethnical groups, we drift away from it altogether; and it is only when, by the action of historical and geographical factors, these have crystallised into political bodies,[1] that they come within the scope of a treatise on the law of nations.

CHAPTER II.

OF INTERNATIONAL RECOGNITION IN GENERAL.

As a political phenomenon, humanity, in its present condition, divides itself into three concentric zones or spheres—that of civilised humanity, that of barbarous humanity, and that of savage humanity. To these, whether arising from peculiarities of race or from various stages of development in the same race, belong, *of right*, at the hands of civilised nations, three stages of recognition—plenary political recognition, partial political recognition, and natural or mere human recognition. Intensively, the first of these forms of recognition embraces the two latter; extensively, the third embraces the two former.

The sphere of plenary political recognition extends to all the existing States of Europe, with their colonial dependencies, in so far as these are peopled by persons of European

[1] *Infra*, p. 128.

birth or descent; and to the States of North and South America which have vindicated their independence of the European States of which they were colonies.

The sphere of partial political recognition extends to Turkey in Europe and in Asia, and to the old historical States of Asia which have not become European dependencies—viz., to Persia and the other separate States of Central Asia, to China, Siam, and Japan.

The sphere of natural, or mere human recognition, extends to the residue of mankind; though here we ought, perhaps, to distinguish between the progressive and non-progressive races.

It is with the first of these spheres alone that the international jurist has directly to deal; but inasmuch as jural progress consists not merely in perfecting the relations which arise within the sphere of political recognition, but in its gradual expansion, he is brought into continual contact with the external spheres, and must take cognisance of the relations in which civilised communities are placed to the partially civilised communities which surround them. He is not bound to apply the positive law of nations to savages, or even to barbarians, as such; but he is bound to ascertain the points at which, and the directions in which, barbarians or savages come within the scope of partial recognition. In the case of the Turks we have had bitter experience of the consequences of extending the rights of civilisation to barbarians who have proved to be incapable of performing its duties, and who possibly do not even belong to the progressive races of mankind.[1] Should the Japanese, on the other hand, continue

[1] Persons who have had the best means of judging, Englishmen more especially,

their present rate of progress for another twenty years, the question whether they are not entitled to plenary political recognition may have to be determined.

Lastly, any doctrine of recognition which professes to correspond to fact must take account, within the sphere which it covers, of the distinction between absolute and relative equality, as elsewhere explained.[1] Even within the sphere of plenary political recognition, States are no more equal to each other, in the absolute sense, than their citizens are equal. They differ in powers, and consequently in rights; and the recognition which they are entitled to claim from each other is proportioned to their powers and rights.

We have thus forced upon us by science the difficult, and, at the existing stage of international organisation, I fear, the practically insoluble problem of relative recognition.

Recognition, in its various phases, constitutes the major premise of the positive law of nations, when stated as a logical system. To the communities which it subsumes, international rights and duties result from it logically, and consequently jurally; and this, however imperfectly they may be realised, or realisable, under the existing conditions of the body cosmopolitan.

bear almost unanimous testimony to the good qualities of the Turkish peasantry, even as contrasted with the Christian races amongst whom they live. Against the upper classes, on the other hand, testimony, even when reluctant, is scarcely less unanimous; and there is probably no other instance of a people that has been so long in contact with civilisation without producing one single individual who has been distinguished in any intellectual pursuit. The art of war is the only art that they seem capable of acquiring, and even in it their success is the result of courage rather than of skill. The subordinate position into which they are rapidly sinking, seems to be that for which nature has designed them.

[1] *Institutes of Law*, p. 375 et seq.

CHAPTER III.

OF PLENARY POLITICAL RECOGNITION.

Plenary political recognition may be defined as a formal declaration of the result of an inductive process, by which one separate political entity has satisfied itself that another entity, phenomenally presented to it, possesses a separate political existence; or, in other words, is capable of performing the duties, and, consequently, is entitled to the rights which centre in international existence.

That the life of the State, like life in general, is the source of rights, and that these rights imply corresponding duties, is a proposition which amounts to nothing more than an assertion, in the concrete relations of State to State, of the abstract principle which governs all jural relations whatever. It is the *de facto* principle, which we studied in the *Institutes of Law*, in one of its innumerable applications. If international law be a doctrine of rights and duties at all, it can rest on no other foundation than that which lies at the root of jurisprudence as a whole. And any doctrine of recognition which stops short of asserting recognition as a right on the one hand, and accepting it as a duty on the other,—which professes to regard it as an act of courtesy, comity, or the like, the exercise of which may be jurally withheld,—deprives international law of a permanent basis in nature, and fails to bring it within the sphere of jurisprudence.[1] In separating it from natural, it separates it from positive law, and hands it over to the dominion of mere human caprice. When such doctrines appear in the text-books, then, whether on public or private international law, they are to be regarded, not as intended to cover their logical consequences, but as proofs of deficiency in scientific insight, or of precision in thought or language, on the part of the writers. The case is one of the many in which practice has been more philosophical than theory; for there is probably no historical instance of recognition being refused to a State on any ground which did not, substantially, amount to a denial of the existence, as a State, of the community which claimed it. In granting recognition, practice has not always been equally loyal to the *de facto* system.

CHAPTER IV.

OF THE RIGHT TO DETERMINE THE FACT OF JURAL STATE-EXISTENCE.

The right to determine the fact of the jural existence or non-existence of a claimant for recognition rests with the State, or States, from which recognition is claimed.

As the present stage of international organisation presents

[1] This, though not very consistently, is now recognised by the better class of international jurists, as it was, with reference to jurisprudence generally, by Savigny, long ago.—*System* I. b. ii. sect. 15.

no central authority superior to the individual State, recognition is necessarily, in all cases, a transaction between separate States. It is an act of mutual municipal legislation.

Though recognition is often spoken of as admission into the family of nations, it leaves the State which has claimed and obtained it from one State only, in the same position in which it formerly stood to every other State.

A valuable though irregular expedient has often been adopted, by means of which something approaching to a general character is communicated to the act of recognition. This expedient consists in the joint action of several recognising powers. Generally it takes the form of a clause in a treaty, and is carried out by the simultaneous presentation to the court of the claimant of identic notes of recognition, along with their credentials of appointment as ministers, by the representatives of the parties to the treaty already resident as consuls. On the same occasion, or shortly thereafter, treaties of commerce are usually negotiated between the recognising powers and the recognised power. Of this proceeding the recognition of Roumania, in 1880, is a recent example.

Where the great Powers unite, as in this instance, to take the new-comer by the hand, the smaller States, in general, are only too thankful to welcome it; because, from the conditions of the case, it must almost always be an addition to their own number.

This concert between States is the progressive element in international organisation on which the development of the law of nations almost wholly depends. It is an agency, however, which must be called into action afresh on each separate occasion, and which demands such delicate adjustment of opinions which really and of interests which apparently conflict, that its regular action is impossible. The decision of each individual State, on the vital point of recognition, is thus not only technically and formally, but, in the majority of cases, really final. It cannot be called in question even diplomatically, as may be done with the judgment of a prize court; because, previous to recognition, there are no diplomatic relations between political communities. The judgment of the individual State can thus be disputed only *vi et armis;* and this judgment, be it remarked, extends not only to the facts, but to the law by which these facts are to be measured. Each State is to say, not only whether or not a given community fulfils the requirements of international existence, but is, moreover, left to determine what these requirements are. It can thus twist both facts and law to the gratification of its passions or its prejudices. So long as the definition of State existence is thus exposed to the influences which so often distort the judgments of individual States on the occasions on which treaties are negotiated, it is obvious that international law can possess but very partially the character of a positive system.

Even in cases in which the facts are no longer disputed, it leaves continually open a side-door of opinion with reference to principle, through which the State appealed to can escape from the consequences of its international obligations without calling in question their *de facto* origin. Without the aid of an international legislature, it is impossible that this door should ever be effectually closed; but it may be possible to narrow it by the help of science, and, at all events, it is our duty to try.

CHAPTER V.

OF THE FUNCTION OF SCIENCE IN DETERMINING THE FACT OF JURAL STATE EXISTENCE.

The conditions which, if satisfied, imply a right to plenary political recognition, may be determined scientifically, and enunciated as permanent maxims of international law.

So long as the independence of individual States is asserted, even to the extent of leaving them to be the absolute judges of the facts alleged by the States claiming recognition, any doctrine of recognition must be merely formal or hypothetical. If such and such conditions admittedly exist, a State exists. Farther than this the scientific jurist cannot go. But it may comfort us to reflect that it is the judicial and executive functions, only which science, of necessity, thus abandons to the individual State. When science says that if such and such facts are found to exist in the claimant by the State from which recognition is claimed, then, whatever the other facts of the case may be, we are dealing with a political entity from which recognition can no longer be withheld without a repudiation of the principles of jurisprudence altogether, it has said all which a national legislature, apart from the executive, says to the judge, or which a judge says to a jury. By defining the necessary characteristics of the State, science is thus in a condition to supply the legislative factor of positive law. Substantially it is this which has been attempted by international jurists. The results at which they have arrived are vague and often contradictory, but in so far as they are real results, I think they may be summed up under the following heads :—

In order to be entitled to recognition, a State must presumably possess ;

(a) The will to reciprocate the recognition which it demands.

(b) The power to reciprocate the recognition which it demands.

CHAPTER VI.

OF THE PRESUMPTION OF RECIPROCATING WILL.

Jurisprudence is essentially the science of relations ; and the jural unity of humanity, when exhibited as a consequence of the common source of rights and duties, and of the indissoluble link by which rights and duties are bound together, is its last and highest lesson. From an economic point of view, again, this unity admits of being exhibited as resulting from the coincidence of human interests ; and, in this doctrine, we have the final lesson of political economy. Both of these doctrines have now been established with a precision which falls little short of mathematical demonstration. But the capacity to apprehend either doctrine, intellectually, still more to reason it out into its concrete results, so that jural or economical solidarity shall be accepted as a practical necessity, is a requirement which obviously can never be imposed on a political community in its corporate capacity. The very fact of its separate existence brings up an opposite class of considerations. Patriotism seems to conflict with cosmopolitanism, and the reconciliation of duties and interests in entities which are not only separate, but which, *ex hypothesi*, must continue to be so, appears to involve the difficulties which in ethics and theology surround the reconciliation of personality and pantheism, and of liberty and necessity. Even when the matter is looked at from the international side, the independence of the State which, in a certain sense, is rightly insisted on as one of the conditions of recognition, seems to shut recognition out as a jural doctrine. A jural starting-point is no sooner asserted than it is abandoned; and international jurisprudence, at its very outset, is made to rest on a contradiction.

Must recognition, then, in each separate instance, wait on the removal of this intellectual stumbling-block? Can no State be recognised till it has reached the point of intellectual development at which interdependence is perceived to be a cosmical necessity, involved in the vindication of its own existence as a separate political entity? Will no reciprocating will suffice which does not possess the character of a result logically deduced from the postulate of coexistence?

Happily, in the pursuit of truth, the heart of man often outruns his head, and in this case, when its action is unfettered, it leaps forward spontaneously to the solution at which science arrives only slowly and painfully. The golden rule, as we have seen,[1] is common to humanity, and the golden rule involves the doctrine of reciprocal recognition. All that science adds to it is the demonstration of its ultimate necessity and universal beneficence, and of the coincidence of liberty with order, and of self-interest with duty. "Do unto others *for. thine own sake*, what thou wouldst that others should do unto thee; and, in doing so, *accept a law from which thou canst not escape.*"

Experience, too, often carries a practical belief in the inevitable character of results into minds to which their causes continue to be unknown. Of this our ready acceptance of physical laws which we do not attempt to explain is a familiar instance. In an analogous manner, the dependence of each upon all and of all upon each becomes a practical rule of life to many whose thoughts never extend beyond the rights of nationality and the duties of patriotism.

Of the higher guarantee which intellectual insight affords for the presence of reciprocating will there can be no question; and, when we come to speak of the relative value of States, we shall dwell on the international importance of culture. But what we are here concerned with is the presence or absence of reciprocating will; and what I assert is, that, being a characteristic of normal humanity, its presence in the aggregate as in the individual, if not disproved must be presumed.

But if the State be entitled to the same ethical presumption which we extend to the citizen, why is it that even civilised States should still belie it so frequently, and that all States should have belied it till quite recently? What is it that

[1] *Institutes of Law*, pp. 44, 122.

has given rise to the opinion, not yet quite abandoned, that the natural relation of separate States to each other is one of perpetual hostility? and that the only rule by which they can consult their separate interests is that of "beggar my neighbour"? Why is it that international law is the greenest branch of the science of jurisprudence?

The reason is that, from the absence of any central organisation, the moral requirements which international law makes on each State are very much higher than the moral requirements which the State makes on each citizen. Between citizen and citizen the link of reciprocity, or fraternity, is strengthened, and, if need be, supplied, by the link of subjection, or paternity, which subordinates the will of each to a common will, and by a happy arrangement, has been made to assume a separate objective character. Between State and State, on the other hand, the reciprocating will stands alone; and each State must exhibit it, not as a general sentiment, but on the special occasions when its passions and prejudices run highest. International law in all cases is wholly dependent on the presence of this ethical factor in *each* of the separate subjects with which it must deal; and international jurisprudence, though willing to assume it in the absence of any contrary indication, must of necessity be inquisitorial up to this point. The citizen may profess a religious or political creed which is at variance with the recognition of reciprocal rights and duties, but so long as he does not act upon it, his creed is assumed to be that of the law which he obeys; and when he does act upon it, the State subordinates his will to its own. It is on this ground that citizenship, in this country, is extended, without question to Jews, and Mahometans, and Atheists, and Communists, and Nihilists. But no such possibility exists in the case of the non-reciprocating State. If a State *professes* a non-reciprocating creed, the doctrine of recognition must take it at its word.

CHAPTER VII.

OF RELIGIOUS CREEDS WHICH EXCLUDE THE PRESUMPTION OF RECIPROCATING WILL.

Plenary political recognition has hitherto obtained only between Christian nations. The very important question consequently arises—is this limitation imposed by Christianity, or does it arise from other causes? Does our belief in Christianity, as the only true revealed religion, bind us to exact the same belief from all other nations, as a condition, *sine qua non*, of their admission to the international rights which spring from political existence? Or:—is it not rather in flagrant opposition to the teaching of Christ that His disciples should exhibit, in this matter, an exclusiveness which He universally condemned?

But if the latter alternative be accepted, where are we to stop? If Christianity be not the test of the presence of reciprocating will in religious creeds, what test have we? If Christianity be *alone* true, all other religions must be false;

and what guarantee can a false religion afford even for its secular influences?

Now the distinguishing element between those non-Christian religions which do and those which do not, in this respect, conflict with Christianity, however much they may fall short of it, will become apparent, I think, if we take note of the element in which Christianity differs from all other religions which claim to rest on direct revelation. It is Christianity alone which, in opening to humanity a new avenue to the knowledge of God's will, and of those ultimate and absolute laws which lie behind and beyond all religions, does not close the avenue to this knowledge which nature has opened to mankind. In claiming to be a direct revelation to humanity, it does not repudiate the indirect revelation through humanity. On the contrary, it is on its coincidence with the latter, so far as the latter goes, that Christianity mainly bases its claim to our further acceptance. Its divinity is guaranteed to our nature by the divinity which addresses us through our nature. It was as the Son of Man that the Son of God spoke to us; and our consciousness tells us that, in carrying us beyond our nature, the religion which He taught is still carrying us along the lines which our nature indicates. Christianity explains us to ourselves; and the law which it teaches us, in being divine, is not on that account the less, but the more, human law. Now, between Christianity in this absolute, necessary, and universal sense — the sense in which Saint Augustine says that it existed before Christ came in the flesh — and the nature-religions of the Aryan races, in so far as these religions are the genuine outcome of human consciousness and human

INTOLERANT RELIGIOUS CREEDS. 115

reason, there is no conflict, any more than there is a conflict between God and nature. Ethical monotheism is the subject-matter and as such the fundamental creed of both. It is a creed which may be so faintly accepted, so feebly held, or so overlaid by idolatrous ritual and irrational superstition as to be inoperative, even as a basis of jurisprudence. Such, for the present, I fear, is the case with all the Aryan religions of Asia.

But it must not be forgotten that similar causes have frequently deprived the Roman Catholic Church, more particularly as represented by the Jesuits, of an ethical character. It was on this ground that, even during the existence of the temporal power of the Pope, international recognition was withheld from the Papacy by Protestant States;[1] and one of the strongest of the many insuperable objections to granting a separate international position to Ireland is, that her ecclesiastical ties to Rome would render it unsafe for England to recognise her as a reciprocating political community. The nationalisation of Churches was the most precious fruit of the Reformation when seen from an ethical or political point of view, but it was a fruit which unhappy Ireland failed to reap.

Nor can even Protestant Churches always lay claim to an ethical character on any other ground than the flagrant inconsistency of their doctrines. Every Church, indeed, which in virtue of its dogmatic teaching separates itself from the secular

---

[1] See *The Papacy and International Law*, by M. Ernest Nys, and my attempt to answer his contention that diplomatic relations ought still to be maintained with the Vatican, published in the *Journal of Jurisprudence* for October 1879, and translated by my dear and lamented friend Dr Pauli in the *Zeitschrift für Kirchenrecht*, B. xv.

life of the community, and seeks to constitute an *imperium in imperio*, weakens the presumption in favour of reciprocating will in the community in which it exists. In this consideration we perceive a powerful international argument against the Disestablishment of National Churches; for there can, as it seems to me, be no question that the tendency of separation between Church and State is to weaken the ethical as contrasted with the dogmatic element in the national theology. It is a reopening of the door to priestcraft, and a partial undoing of the work of the Reformation; and it is surprising that it should be advocated by Liberal statesmen.

But these are aberrations which weaken, not fundamental errors which take away, the right to recognition. No Christian or Aryan creed, as such, fails to affirm the ethical postulates on which jurisprudence rests, or contains any element which need prevent the States which adhere to it from reciprocating international obligations with States which are willing to enter into them. Nor need this statement be confined to the religions of the Aryan races. As regards the ancient creed of China, my learned colleague Professor Flint has said: "There is probably not a single moral precept in the Christian Scriptures which is not substantially also in the Chinese classics. There is certainly not an important principle in Bishop Butler's ethical teachings which had not been explicitly set forth by Mencius in the fourth century B.C. The Chinese thinker of that date had anticipated the entire moral theory of man's constitution expounded so long afterwards by the most famous of English moral philosophers." [1] However much, then, their

---

[1] *St Giles' Lectures: The Faiths of the World*, p. 419.

theological dogma may, for a time, impede the development or recognition of an ethical system of universal validity, it does not exclude it, and the right to recognition on the part of the States or races which hold these creeds thus becomes a question of fact :—Do they or do they not, at the stage of progress or retrogression which they have reached, possess an operative ethical system ; and does this system, for the time being, produce political and jural results which bring them within the category of States ?

As regards the Roman Catholic States of modern Europe, we may answer this question in the affirmative without hesitation, for in them the danger to which Christianity is now exposed is that the ethical should absorb the dogmatic, not the dogmatic the ethical element. Roman Catholicism is moribund, not only as a form of Church government, but as a system of historical dogma. It is physical science and not theology, which in our day has entered into conflict with philosophy, and which, consequently, threatens to generate superstition. Whether materialism may not be found to sap the foundations of ethics more effectively than even fanaticism, is one of the gravest and deepest problems of the time. Hitherto, however, it has not assumed the same attitude of active intolerance ; and though its relations with anti-jural political theories have often been suspiciously intimate, no proposal has been made since the early days of the French.Revolution to propagate it by the sword.

What we have said of Christianity is altogether reversed when we turn to the religions which claim to rest *exclusively* on direct revelation. Even if such a revelation, in other respects, were coincident with Christianity, it would conflict with it in this very element of exclusiveness. The postulate of each such religion is that it is the only channel through which God has communicated His law. It repudiates anthropology as a source of knowledge altogether. The God within man is silenced by the God without him. Man becomes a mere listener to external commands which all must obey, but which are addressed only to the faithful; and, even to them, not directly, but only through a prophet, of whose mission others, at all events, have no evidence beyond his own assertion. The system of ethics, and consequently of jurisprudence, which results from such a religion is bounded by the theocracy which it establishes. Unless this theocracy becomes universal, God's law can neither be known nor vindicated; and, if it becomes universal, the recognition by it of any other is, *eo ipso*, shut out.

Now this is the position, so far as I know, which all the Semitic religions arrogate to themselves. Each of them repudiates every revelation, whether direct or indirect, except that which it claims to transmit. This was the position of Judaism in so far as Judaism was merely the national religion of the Jews. None who were not of the seed of Abraham were under the Jewish law; and, as there was no other law of God, all others were outlaws. "The one religious portal, through which all must pass to be saved, was Judaism."[1] It is true that this conclusion is much modified by the fact that the law which Jehovah revealed to the Jews—the *Torah*—

---

[1] *Judaism.* By Professor Taylor. *St Giles' Lectures: The Faiths of the World,* p. 357.

was originally coincident with the absolute law which God has imposed on humanity, and which He reveals through consciousness,[1] and that this was not the case with the other Semitic revelations, or pretended revelations. But this coincidence, which ought to have liberalised the national mind, was not perceived by the people, or even by the priests, as the culminating event of their religious history terribly demonstrated; and, much as the Jews have suffered from the unchristian persecution of Christians, there is no reason to suppose that, had the circumstances been reversed, they themselves would have been more tolerant, or that they would be so now. " But for the impossibility, Judaism would undoubtedly have propagated itself like Mahometanism by the sword."[2] Even in the beautiful story of Esther the conduct of Mordecai bears a sadly close resemblance to that of Haman, when his turn to play the persecutor came; and it would fare very badly with the Russian peasants at the present day, I fear, if the Czar were to send forth a writing similar to that which was sealed with the ring of King Ahasuerus. That much of the teaching of the Hebrew prophets was inspired by a far higher and wider spirit is unquestionable; but it was not till the coming of Christ that the ethical element became prominent, and that the doctrine that the Gentiles " having not the law, are a law unto themselves,"[3] was consistently proclaimed in Jewish ears. The failure of modern Jews to

---

[1] See an interesting discussion of the "Leading Principles of the Divine Law, as manifested in the Pentateuch," by Bishop Cotterill, in *The Pulpit Commentary*, vol i.

[2] *The Faiths of the World*, p. 355.

[3] *Romans*, ii. 14.

accept this doctrine, is no doubt the cause of the alien character which everywhere belongs to them.[1]

It is true that ethical sentiments lay all along hidden in the recesses of every Jewish, as of every other human heart; and when we remember that by the renewed influences of divine grace Christianity ultimately came out of Judaism, we must not despair of the future even of the other Semitic religions. It is possible that Mahometans may accept the ethical, even though they should continue to reject the dogmatic teaching of Christianity, or that another and greater prophet than Mahomet may reveal an ethical system which shall bridge the gulf by which the Mahometan world, for the present, is divided from the rest of mankind. Failing both occurrences it is probable,—nay, on the assumption of the existence and continuous action of a divine element in the development of humanity, it is certain, — that ultimately anthropotheistic influences will make themselves felt. But apart from exceptional individuals, like a certain Sheikh el Bakay, mentioned by Barth in his travels to Timbuctoo, or Spinosa and Neander amongst modern Jews, the action of these influences may be manifested in the Semitic races only in those indefinite reaches of time which Mr Darwin has taught us to regard as the atmosphere through which we must contemplate all important changes, whether material or moral. The unspeculative character of the Semitic race, which is traceable, I am told, even in their forms of speech, warns us that ethical development from the human side, in their case, can come but

---

[1] The restoration of the Jews to Palestine would be the most curious and interesting political experiment that ever was made.

very slowly. The highest forms of Semitic culture have exhibited no traces of that introspective tendency which brought the philosophy of the Greeks, on its ethical side, to the very borders of Christianity. As a necessary consequence of this peculiarity, their law of status, as I have elsewhere remarked,[1] has always been rudimentary and barbarous as compared with their law of contract. No political organism of any importance has ever been produced by them; and it is a fact, not without significance in the same direction, that the only great religious movement which has agitated the Mahometan world since the prophet's death—that of the Wahabis—has had for its object to reiterate and emphasise the intolerance which he taught. Even where European culture has been superinduced on Oriental traditions and conversion to Christianity has taken place, the case, as regards individuals, generally remains unaltered. The sympathies of modern Jews do not extend beyond the nationality to which they have become attached by birth or residence; and their loyalty even to it is subordinate to the wider allegiance of race. The late Lord Beaconsfield's imperialistic foreign policy was directly at variance with the idea of reciprocity. In so far as was consistent with Semitic sympathies, there is no reason to doubt the sincerity of his English sympathies. Nay, as contrasted with other Gentile nationalities, he clung to that which he had embraced with exclusive and exceptional loyalty. But when he said that "God never spoke except to an Arab,"[2] he probably was as much in earnest as was consistent with his character. So far as the "Asiatic mystery," which formed the

[1] *Institutes of Law*, p. 77.   [2] *Tancred*, p. 269. See also p. 261 *et seq*.

creed of this strange and gifted man, and influenced for a time the foreign policy of England, can be gathered from his writings and his speeches, it appears to have been this. He believed in a direct revelation, not to the Hebrews exclusively, but to the Semitic race. The divine law, of which this revelation was the sole channel, it was the mission of the Semitic race to impose on mankind, and for the accomplishment of this mission England was the favoured instrument. Of an ethical law revealed to humanity as a whole, not from without but from within, Lord Beaconsfield had not the slightest conception. He did not know what it meant; and it probably was this unspeculative character, relieved from the vulgarity of materialism by the halo of mystery which he shed around them, that commended his views to the practical English mind. He was an oracle whose responses saved his followers from the necessity of thinking out any rule of life for themselves, without degrading them in their own eyes.

It is a curious indication of this Semitic peculiarity, too, that Lord Beaconsfield and his disciples always spoke of rhetoric, in circumstances in which Europeans are accustomed to speak of logic. Whether this latter peculiarity may not have been intentionally adopted from the feeling that the logical results of the Semitic faith were not of a kind which could be safely presented to unbelievers, is another question; for there can be no doubt that its last word is, "Allah or the sword!"[1]

[1] In granting even belligerent recognition to Mahometans, Christian nations ought to bear in mind the risk which they run of becoming sharers in the bloodguiltiness which their creed imposes, without being able to share the apology which it offers to them. In 1877 I took occasion, in my introductory lecture, to

Lastly, it is to be noted that, as culture in other than ethical directions leaves the intolerant character of the individual unchanged, so, in like manner, no improvement in the internal government of any community is of substantial value for international purposes so long as it adheres to a non-reciprocating ideal. Nations like men are happily illogical in the right just as often as in the wrong direction, but to their ideal they will always revert, even in cases in which from passion or apparent self-interest they may be untrue to it for a time. The Turks, as a race, are probably incapable of the political development which would render their adoption of constitutional government possible. But were this otherwise, and had the purpose with which Turkish constitutions were promulgated in 1856 and in 1876 been as honest as they were the reverse—nay, had they even come into actual operation, the international character of Turkey would not have been improved. The Korân would still have stood between it and the world without, and contradicted its constitutional professions of reciprocating will. We say this altogether apart from the merits or demerits of the Korân, in other respects. Whatever may be the absolute truth or falsehood of an exclusive religion, it is always false when seen from an international point of view; and a false theory, like a wrong road, only carries us the farther from our destination the longer we follow it. To.talk of the recognition of Mahometan States as a question of time, is to talk nonsense.

point out the shameful position in which this country was then placed by the Turkish practice of slaughtering prisoners of war.—*Journal of Jurisprudence*, November 1877.

Unless we are all to become Mahometans, that is a time which Mahometanism itself tells us can never come. We are thus driven to assume towards it the same uncompromising attitude which it presents to us. So long as Islam endures, the reconciliation of its adherents, even with Jews and Christians, and still more with the rest of mankind, must continue to be an insoluble problem; and it is a problem, unhappily, which presents itself not only to the whole of Europe in the Eastern question, but to the Russians and to us in Asia, and to the French in North Africa, in each case on a prodigious scale. To us it is aggravated by our national traditions and feelings, which forbid us to refuse to any portion of mankind the ultimate prospect of self-government. But prejudice, when based on false dogma, is the toughest of all forms of error, and these religions will die hard. For an indefinite future, however reluctantly, we must confine our political recognition to the professors of those religions which, by conscious or unconscious processes, have been reasoned out from the facts of nature, and which preach the doctrine of "live and let live." As regards the others, we must strive to commend to them the religion in which we believe, by convincing them of its accordance with the promptings of that human nature which is common to them and to us. They may repudiate our dogma as we repudiate theirs; but if we can bring them up to the stage of intellectual development which will enable them to understand the questions at issue, they cannot refuse to fight us on the field of nature. It is on that field that our missionaries must be prepared to encounter them. They must seek to lead them "through Nature, up to Nature's God:"

and not be too much discouraged if, in the earlier stages of their progress, they are able to trace His laws chiefly as they are manifested in the physical universe. The creed of all barbarians may be described as materialism sublimated by superstition, and the intellectual efforts by which the superstition is overcome are rarely strong enough to combat the materialism, in the same generation. In Roman Catholic countries the men become materialists, whilst the women continue to be idolaters. Even amongst ourselves, we must remember that for one individual whose ethical conceptions rise above instinct, or whose religious or political opinions are more than prejudices, there are fifty who have fairly rational notions about physical phenomena. What we find it fifty times easier to learn ourselves, we need not be surprised if others learn fifty years sooner. The Japanese, like the French, we are told, are all becoming materialists; in both cases from the same cause, no doubt, that makes the backward boys at our public schools run to the "modern side," and the shallow students at our universities "hate metaphysics." It is a pity that ethical and jural relations cannot be exhibited to the eye like chemical affinities and organic structures, or that reciprocating will cannot be "stored" and exported to non-reciprocating nations.

CHAPTER VIII.

OF SECULAR CREEDS WHICH EXCLUDE THE PRESUMPTION OF RECIPROCATING WILL.

We have seen that intolerant religions give rise to political, or what are commonly called theocratic systems, which, partaking of their intolerance, are necessarily unrecognisable. We are now to consider whether there be secular creeds generating political systems which are open to the same objection.

In the eyes of their adherents theocracies are infallible, and the first duty of the faithful, to God and to man, is to impose upon all, the infallible laws which they embody. Are there, then, secular systems which inspire the same absolute faith, and impose on their adherents the duty of exacting the same universal obedience? Do any special interpretations of the revelation through nature claim the same universal acceptance which is claimed by each special interpretation of the revelation to nature? We have seen that the reality of the revelation through nature is a fact which claims the character of a necessary truth. It belongs to the "things which cannot be shaken."[1] We may not consciously accept it, but we cannot consciously reject it. To do so would be inconsistent with mental sanity. But if the fact of the revelation be thus incontrovertible, why should we distrust the form in

[1] *Institutes of Law*, pp. 55-59.

which it presents itself? Is there not contradiction in declining to listen to a voice which, without the interposition of any prophet, tells us directly what, *to us*, is necessarily true, whatever may be its ontological truth or falsehood? We may reject a theocracy which claims our acceptance on the ground that the revelation on which it professes to rest has not come to us. But how can we reject a monarchy, or an aristocracy, or a democracy which professes to rest on an indirect revelation which, by our own admission, must have come to us? We cannot decline the consequences of our own creed.

It is on some such train of reasoning as this, more or less conscious, that the political intolerance which has been the cause of so many wars in times past, and is the source of so much disorder and distrust still, no doubt rests. Its fallacy, of course, consists in the claim which it makes to the infallibility not only of the law which is declared, but of the organ which declares it, and its failure to recognise the relative character which the conditions of the realisation of political truths in the concrete necessarily impose on local and temporal legislation. The infallible and unchangeable character which belongs to the divine idea of a human relation can never be realised, still less can it be realised permanently, in a human conception of that relation; and any secular form of government which claims universal acceptance thus deprives the State which adopts it of its right to recognition. Are there, then, such forms of government?

1. *Of Intolerant Monarchies.*

The very name of monarchy savours of exclusiveness; and

us we have seen that political exclusiveness cannot, in the nature of things, find its realisation in the form of absolute independence, it is driven to seek it in the form of intolerance. There are, consequently, few instances in which the monarchical idea, if not tempered by other conceptions, has not sought to assert itself beyond the limits of the State. A very large portion of the political history of mankind is made up of the history of aggressive monarchies. The old Roman Empire set universal dominion before it as its object. This object it transmitted to its feebler successors, both in the East and in the West; and it may be doubted whether, under the guise of a Hegemony, it has even yet ceased to be cherished. During the first six years of the present century, the precedence, if not the supremacy, of the Holy Roman Empire formed an element in the scheme of European organisation. No sooner were imperialist traditions extinguished in Germany than they were revived in France, and brought nearer to realisation by the first Napoleon than by any preceding monarch since the time of Charlemagne. The "*idée napoléonienne*" never assumed the same formidable aspect in the person of the third Napoleon, but it was still the old idea of universal supremacy, and, as such, it was not till the battle of Sedan that it ceased, from time to time, to haunt the dreams of sovereigns and diplomatists. It is in the same threatening aspect, in so far as it assumes a definite form of any kind, that the Slavonic idea presents itself to the imaginations of Russophobists in this country and in Germany.

Now that monarchies or empires of this class are anti-jural phenomena, and, as such, fall beyond the sphere of international recognition, is obvious ; and there is no more hopeful indication of the progress which the principle of reciprocity has made in recent times, than the fact that no secular monarchy at the present moment does professedly or avowedly belong to this class.

But what shall we say of those vast ethnico-political agglomerations, to the formation of which the ethnological conceptions, of which we have already spoken, have given so powerful an impulse within the last half-century ? Of these the German and Russian empires are the great European examples, whilst the British empire is the great cosmopolitan example. In these combinations the sentiments of affinity of race and community of interest find expression, and it is through them that the natural and necessary interdependence, which is the main factor in the development of international law, mainly acts. They are the counteracting elements to the tendency to isolation which springs from the spirit of nationality. Though fraught with many of the evils of centralisation, the advantages which attend them within their own sphere are undeniable. Whether, when their internal development is more advanced, the prodigious forces which they wield are destined to be hurled against each other, and order to be shipwrecked in the struggle for supremacy; or whether the sentiment of interdependence, which is now consolidating them internally, will ultimately bind them to each other, so as to subsume the whole under one all-embracing autonomous organism,—is a problem which future ages alone can solve. As an optimist I cling to the latter belief, and I am fain to imagine that it obtains some support from considerations special to ourselves.

If cosmopolitan development adheres to the direction which it has followed so consistently during the present century, and if Great Britain and the United States of America, as seems probable, become reunited in sentiment, by far the greatest of all ethnico-political groups must be that of the English-speaking race. M. Prévost-Paradol said that, with the exception of Europe, England and the United States divide this planet between them, and that in two centuries at the most, the world will be Anglo-Saxon.[1] But, though bound together by ties of blood and speech and historical associations which are strong enough to prove of the utmost importance for international purposes, the English race has already divided itself up into separate political communities which, from the value they attach to political autonomy, from their wide dispersion, and the heterogeneous elements which they have absorbed from other races, it seems impossible should ever amalgamate into a single nation. They can never form a political organism sufficiently consistent to impose one single municipal system either on other ethnico-political organisms, or on the Romanic States of continental Europe, which latter seem scarcely likely to form an ethnical bond. Each group of our colonies promises to crystallise round a separate centre, and thus to form itself into a composite State, just as the United States of America did in the end of last century. At no distant period each of these composite States will probably send representatives to an imperial council, in place of the imperial government, as at present, sending representatives to them. From the loyalty which they exhibit, not only to their respective central gov-

[1] *La France Nouvelle*, pp. 397-403.

ernments, but to the imperial government itself, there seems no prospect of their claiming independence, either of each other or of the mother country. Whilst forming separate States, politically autonomous, they will continue to combine for cosmopolitan purposes; and it is surely not impossible that this idea of combination, with a view to the realisation of freedom, not from each other or from the whole, but through each other and through the whole, when exhibited on so great a scale, may extend itself to other ethnico-political groups. Without infringing on the freedom either of separate States or of ethnico-political combinations of States, an autonomous cosmopolitan organism thus becomes conceivable. When elevated to the clearer atmosphere of cosmopolitan conceptions, jurisprudence may come to see, that as national order is the condition of personal freedom, and international order is the condition of national freedom, so it is in cosmopolitan order that international freedom of action must be sought; and it is strange and interesting to reflect that the Old World may thus learn from the New a lesson which her own experience has failed to teach her.

2. *Of Intolerant Republics.*

Intolerance is a vice which clings to the bones of humanity, and no delusion can be greater than to imagine that we shall get rid of it by abolishing monarchy, either despotic or constitutional. Of republican intolerance the example still most memorable to us is the proclamation of the French Convention in 1793, by which the duty of propagating the principles of the Revolution by the sword was imposed on all the generals of the Republic. It was an attempt to realise the dogma of the infallibility of the sovereign people, by substituting the despotism of all over each for the despotism of one over all, and then imposing it on mankind as of absolute and universal validity. Except in its object "this doctrine of Rousseau and his terrible school," as M. Prévost-Paradol[1] has said, differed in nothing from that of the Inquisition, or, I will add, of the Korân. Almost all the States of Europe, in full accordance with the fundamental principles of the law of nations, accepted this proclamation as a declaration of war. They withdrew their ambassadors from Paris,—which is the diplomatic method of announcing that recognition has ceased,—and a war commenced against the intolerant Republic, and continued against the intolerant Empire which succeeded it, till both were overthrown. It was not till the restoration of a limited monarchy that the presumption of reciprocating will, on the part of France, was regarded as sufficient to re-establish her right to readmission into the family of nations.

3. *Of Intolerant Anarchies.*

When a State, by losing control over its citizens, falls into anarchy it ceases to be a State, and the presence or absence of reciprocating will is a question which does not admit of solution. Of this a curious instance occurred during the siege of Paris, when Prince Bismarck refused to negotiate a peace, on the ground that France, for the time being, had ceased to exist as a political entity. The refusal was temporary; but had the Commune triumphed, its principles would have justified, and would no doubt have led to its continuance, and to a renewal of the war. On similar grounds, were the Nihilists to triumph

[1] *Essais de Politique*, vol. iii. p. 6.

over the present, or any other Government of Russia, the international recognition of Russia would immediately cease.

The overthrow of the rational will of any single State thus becomes the warrant for the assertion of the rational will of the other States with which it formerly maintained, or with which it ought to maintain, international relations. The question whether or not the assertion of this rational will necessitates the application of force, is a question of circumstances, which the surrounding States possessing the requisite force are entitled to determine. If they honestly arrive at an affirmative conclusion, war on their part is a duty as well as a right. The error of the peace party, as it appears to me, consists in their failure to recognise the possibility of this occurrence. Would they, as Christian philanthropists and law-abiding citizens, have been satisfied to stand aside and contemplate the final triumph of the first Napoleon, of the French Commune, of Russian Nihilism, or of the Korân?

CHAPTER IX.

OF THE PRESUMPTION OF RECIPROCATING POWER.

The State which claims recognition must present to the State or States from which it claims recognition a reasonable presumption that it is able, as well as willing, to perform the duties incident to international existence. As in the case of the will the presumption of power will suffice, but the presumption imposes at least the negative test of exhibiting no characteristics which are incompatible with the exercise of its reciprocating will. Ostensibly, at least, the State must be able, as well as willing, to reciprocate, or, in other words, it must possess the conditions of jural capacity.

In a very general way we shall be enabled to define this necessary characteristic of the State, if we direct our attention to the analogy which subsists between the law of nations and the other departments of positive law in which natural law has been more fully realised. It was thus, as I have already said,[1] that Grotius and the elder publicists, who were civilians or canonists by profession, proceeded; and though they hampered the progress of international science by the extent to which they bound it in the technicalities of the Roman civil law, it has made so little real progress since their day as to suggest the notion that their method may have been the true one, whatever may be said of the narrow manner in which they applied it.

As the source of rights and duties the State corresponds, in international law, to the citizen in public national law, and to the person in private national law. When the State is recognised, it is placed, as regards other States, in a position corresponding to that in which the citizen who has obtained the suffrage is placed to other citizens, or a person who is *sui juris* is placed to other jural persons, whether natural or artificial. By recognition the State obtains legal capacity; or, more correctly speaking, the jural capacity which it already possessed by natural law it now possesses by the positive law of

[1] *Ante*, p. 80.

nations. It has rights and obligations which an international executive would enforce,—if there were an international executive,—and which the States recognising each other must seek to enforce as best they may.

Now what is the essence of jural capacity as recognised in other branches of positive law? Is it not the presence in the subject, be he person or citizen, of will which, in virtue of its conformity with that all-controlling will which alone is absolutely free, partakes of such a measure of relative freedom as will enable it to exhibit itself within the sphere which the existence of the subject assigns to it as real and ultimate power?[1] And precisely this, as it seems to me, is the essence of jural capacity in the State for international purposes. A State that possesses will which, up to the limits imposed upon it by the other conditions of its own existence, it can freely realise in action, which can consent, which can contract, possesses reciprocating power, and, on this ground, is entitled to jural recognition by other States, just as a citizen in a corresponding position is entitled to the suffrage, or a person is entitled to buy, and to sell, and to marry.

[1] *Institutes of Law*, p. 415 and pp. 426, 427.

CHAPTER X.

OF THE SIZE OF THE STATE.

It is impossible to assign any absolute limits to the local sphere demanded for the display of separate international will and power by the exercise of international rights and the discharge of international duties. The element of quality, both of soil and population, counts for so much as almost to deprive the element of quantity of any claim to separate consideration; and it will, consequently, be convenient to reserve what I have to say regarding it for the subject of relative recognition. All that need here be said is, that the State must neither be so small as to render it incapable of separate international action, nor so great as to impede the action of the international body as a whole. The State can claim recognition only on the ground that its size is such as to warrant the presumption that it will neither prove so weak as to be unable to make its influence felt in the decision of questions of international interest, nor so strong as to decide those questions in accordance with what it may imagine to be its own separate interest. If the principle of relativity, of which we shall speak hereafter, were adopted, nothing but benefit to freedom could result from the recognition of any community which satisfied these requirements, and desired to realise a separate ideal by following out a line of separate development. But so long as such a State as Montenegro, for example, if recognised at all, must be recognised as the international equal of Austria or Russia, its recognition degenerates into a pointless farce, in which one Montenegran is represented as able to hold his own with the hundred and fifty Austrians or three hundred and fifty Russians. Nothing but the widest disparity of race and culture could ever bring such a fiction into accordance with fact.

On the other hand, it is to be remarked that the political inequality between great and small States, whether we regard them from a national or an international point of view, is not anything like so great as their disparities of area and population would lead us to imagine. This circumstance arises from the superior intellectual activity, relatively to their numbers, of the inhabitants of small States. France, for example, has more than seven times the population of Belgium, and more than eight times the population of Holland, and yet, if we measure her by her intellectual productivity, either past or present, in the direction of scientific jurisprudence and international law more especially, it will be impossible to give her an equivalent precedence over either of these countries; whilst as a stable political organism she is inferior to them both. The very fact of living in a small community forces men to occupy themselves with foreign interests,[1] and has thus a directly stimulating effect on their mental development; whereas the momentum of a great State carries the thoughts of its inhabitants lazily and carelessly along the lines of mere

[1] In a thoughtful and original lecture on the *Rôle et Mission des Nations Neutres ou Secondaires dans le développement du droit international*, delivered to the Royal Academy of Belgium, 12th May 1875, M. Rolin Jaequemyns has pointed out the fact that we owe the science of international law almost exclusively to the smaller States.

national tradition. As one obvious effect of the narrowing influences of great nationalities may be mentioned the small number of persons in the greater States of Europe, as compared with the smaller States, who speak or read more than one language.

Of the depressing effect which centralisation exercises on vast masses of men, we have a remarkable and daily increasing example within our own island. London is the greatest city that there is, or ever was,[1] in the world. It already contains 3,814,571 inhabitants, or 80,000 inhabitants more than the whole of Scotland. Now, if we allow this 80,000 to represent the floating population of politicians, men of letters and science, artists, and the like, who are attracted to the metropolis by their occupations, but who do not belong to it by birth, education, sympathy, or even continuous residence, will the most ardent advocate for centralisation maintain that the remaining population of London, though equal in quantity, is equal in quality to that of the whole of Scotland? Does it exhibit the same variety or originality, or evolve the same amount of intellectual or moral power? Or, to avoid the imputation of national partiality, let us contrast London with Switzerland. Switzerland contains only 2,846,102 inhabitants, or 968,469 fewer than London. Is it possible to claim for the remaining 2,846,102 Londoners an equality with the whole Swiss nation?

These considerations seem to indicate the conclusion that

---

[1] The inhabitants of Pekin are roughly estimated at 2,000,000; and Gibbon's calculation was that, at its greatest period, A.D. 408, the population of ancient Rome may have amounted to 1,200,000 souls (chap. xxxi.).

breathing-space is requisite for intellectual and moral, and, consequently, for political as well as for physical development; and that, if great States are ever to enjoy the full benefit of their greatness, it must be by multiplying their centres of national life so as to give the freest possible play to such elements of separate activity as they may chance to contain. There can be no more mistaken aspiration than that after national uniformity. "L'union c'est la force" is true of living organisms only when they are permitted to act in separate spheres. So long as Paris is France and her intellectual life is dominated by a central University, France can never be again what France was once; and if London is to continue to draw away the national life of England from the provinces, the Anglo-Saxon race will soon be dependent for its progressive development on those distant and widely separated centres of life which are springing up in our vast colonial empire.

CHAPTER XI.

OF THE EXTERNAL FREEDOM, OR, AS IT IS COMMONLY CALLED, THE "INDEPENDENCE" OF THE STATE.

We know that no jural entity can be absolutely independent of any other. The conception of independence in this sense is at variance with the conditions of creaturely existence and of cosmical law.[1] To speak of the "independence of the

[1] *Ante*, p. 97.

State," is consequently to use a phrase which is theoretically inaccurate; and which, more than almost any other, perhaps, has been a source of practical error. On the other hand, however, every jural entity must be separate from every other, otherwise neither rights nor duties could centre in it. Its sphere of moral and physical activity must be peculiarly its own. The international State, whether great or small, must thus be a separate State. As the claim to recognition is a logical abandonment of independence, it is a logical profession of separate political life.

This consideration at once cuts off all provinces, colonies, subject States, and States which are placed under the suzerainty of other States, however important may be the contributions which they make to the rational will and consequent power of the States of which they are members, from all claim to recognition; and it relegates the members of political confederations, even when the tie which binds them is of the loosest kind, to the position of imperfect subjects of international law.

The members of those wider ethnico-political groups, of which I formerly spoke,[1] on the other hand, not being bound together by national ties of any kind, preserve their international freedom of action, and consequent reciprocating power unimpaired. Even in the case of so close a connection as that which exists between this country and the United States, it is only in the last instance that ethnical considerations could influence international action; and as all countries must belong to some ethnical group, the limitations thus

[1] *Ante*, pp. 100, 128.

imposed on their reciprocating power may be put aside as possessing no appreciable significance.

The existence of the State as a separate political entity may be the result either of a process of gradual development, or of an act of separation from a State already developed. In the former case, the question of freedom scarcely arises. The other elements of *de facto* existence being present, the presence of freedom is presumed. But in the latter case, as we all know, the question of the presence or absence of freedom is the most delicate question which presents itself in the doctrine of recognition, and causes practical difficulties of the most formidable kind. Apart from the special difficulties of contingent fact which must cling to each special case, there is a general difficulty, common to them all, arising from the fact that the process of separation is a gradual process, and that partial rights arise which claim recognition of an inferior kind to that which will fall to be conceded should the claimant ultimately succeed in asserting its separate political existence. To meet this difficulty, it is held that there are various stages through which the process of the vindication of separate existence and of recognition, in so far as dependent upon it, may pass, each of which has special rights and duties attached to it.

1st, There is the recognition of the inchoate State as a jural claimant for separate recognition—that is to say, the acknowledgment of its right to contend for its recognition, or, to borrow a phrase from municipal law, of its "title to sue." The form which recognition usually assumes, at this stage, is that of a concession of belligerent rights; and this concession may proceed either from the opposite party in the war, or from neutral States alone, or from both.

By recognising belligerent rights neutral powers pronounce no judgment whatever, either on the merits of the claim or the probability of its ultimate vindication. Belligerent recognition is a mere declaration of impartiality. To withhold from the claimant for recognition the rights of belligerency, whilst we extend them to the parent State, would plainly be to take part against it in the war—to violate its blockade whilst we respect that of the parent State, would be a non-neutral act.

It cannot be doubted, however, that, in many points of view, even the presumptive recognition of State-existence, which an open proclamation of neutrality infers, is of the last importance to a new and struggling community. Who can doubt, for example, that the Queen's proclamation of 13th May 1861, and the corresponding documents issued by the French and other European Governments, by placing the Southern States of America, as regarded the war, on a footing of equality with the Northern States, vastly increased their chances of success? A similar proclamation during any of the numerous Polish insurrections would have been hailed by the Poles as a priceless boon; and the same would have been the feeling of the Roumanians in the earlier stages of their struggles for freedom from the Ottoman yoke. In the temper in which as a belligerent she necessarily was, it is not surprising, therefore, that the proclamation of neutrality caused irritation in America. How keen and lasting this irritation was, is apparent from Mr Seward's despatches,[1] not only at the begin-

[1] *North America*, 1863, p. 69.

ning, but during the whole course of the war;[1] whilst the proceedings at Geneva in the Alabama case abundantly testified that this feeling by no means passed away with its successful conclusion. But, though natural, and, in the circumstances, perhaps inevitable, this feeling was unreasonable; for belligerent existence was a fact in the case of the South, just as much as separate existence was a fact in the case of the North—nay, it was a fact of such magnitude that the North itself had been compelled to recognise it. By ignoring it, neutral States would have abandoned the basis of fact on which all jurisprudence rests.

Let us see, then, in what this primary stage of the recognition of State-existence consists. Guided by the teaching of events, the positive law of nations has defined it with somewhat greater accuracy than the final stage. The peaceful privileges which belong to the perfect State it does not confer. Belligerents, as such, cannot send or receive ambassadors, and any communications which foreign States carry on with them are of an informal kind. In the first interview which Earl Russell had with the Commissioners of the Confederate Government, he told them expressly that it was not as a Minister of State that he met them. He " could hold no official communication with the delegates of the Southern States."[2]

This was on the 4th of May 1861, and at that date his words were technically accurate. He stood to the Commissioners in no other relation than if he had been the leader of the Opposition. Nine days later he could not have expressed

[1] *North America*, 1865, No. 9, p. 3.
[2] *Despatch to Lord Lyons*, 1862; *American Papers*, No. 1, p. 36.

himself in the same terms; for, after the proclamation was issued on the 13th, they would no longer have corresponded to the facts of the situation.

From that time forth till the treaty of peace was concluded, the Southern States possessed an international existence which was entitled to representation equally with, though not equal to, that which the Union as a whole, or any other recognised State, enjoyed. Whether the *Disunited* States during the continuance of the war were strictly entitled to be represented in the character which had previously, and which has subsequently, belonged to the *United* States, is a question which was never raised, but which, if raised, must logically have been decided in the negative. If two recognised States go to war, their relation to neutrals remains unchanged. But if one recognised State be broken up into two belligerent States, it seems difficult to contend that, during the recognition of belligerency, either can retain the character to which both lay claim. However unequal the parts may be, no part can be equal to the whole.

Belligerent recognition, then, confers all the rights of public war, and it binds the States which confer it to all the duties of neutrals. A proclamation of blockade by the Southern States would have been treated by the European Powers with the same respect as was shown to that by the North, from which our own trade suffered so grievously. Had New York been physically blockaded it would have been jurally blockaded, just as Charleston was.

It is an established rule, moreover, that all acts by which the parent State endeavours to deal with a revolted province to which this privilege has been granted, as if it were still subject to the provisions of its municipal law, shall be disregarded by the States by which belligerent privileges have been conferred. As an example I may mention the protest of both France and England against the proposal of the President (Lincoln) to close the ports of the Southern States of America by a proclamation following on an Act of Congress,[1] and not by a *de facto* blockade and as a regular act of war. Such a municipal act would, as M. Touvenel remarked, have been practically equivalent to a mere *blocus sur le papier*,[2] whereas (as we shall see hereafter) it is a *blocus effectif* which the law of nations alone recognises; and Earl Russell added this additional objection as to its effects on neutrals—viz., that "it would have given power to the President to confiscate a foreign vessel with its cargo for attempting to enter a port which had not been blockaded, and was not in the possession of the executive, and as to the closing of which none of the parties interested had received any previous notice."[3] A British ship, the Circassian, indeed, was actually seized and confiscated by the American Prize Courts for attempting to run the blockade of New Orleans *after* New Orleans had been retaken and was in possession of the North; and she was restored only under the Mixed Commission appointed by the Treaty of Washington at the close of the war. The Commission held that, as the blockade had terminated by the recapture, the right of a belligerent to exercise the privileges which it conferred against a neutral vessel were at an end.

[1] *North America*, No. 1, p. 60.
[2] *Ib.*   [3] *Ib.*, No. 1, p. 61.

But all that foreign States can do in such a case is to remonstrate against the issuing of a municipal proclamation, and to set it at defiance themselves after it has been issued, leaving the State which has issued it to enforce it against those whom it claims to retain as its subjects, if it be able. Neutral nations, I think, would scarcely be entitled to treat such a proclamation as a direct *casus belli*—though in the case of its being attempted to be enforced against them, more particularly if this were done by such barbarous means as the sinking of ships laden with stones, as was done in Charleston harbour, the case might be doubtful. If the right to issue the proclamation existed in the parent legislature, or executive, previous to the war, it must be held to exist in it, or at all events may be consistently and logically claimed by it as existing, so long as it—the parent State—declines to acknowledge the belligerent rights of its revolted citizens. The chief ground on which the President's proposal was objected to, consequently, was that it was inconsistent with his other acts; that these amounted to a virtual recognition of belligerent rights; and that he could not at one and the same time impose a blockade in accordance with international law, and issue a proclamation closing his ports against neutral nations and imposing on them the penalties of municipal law. He could not go to war and continue to be at peace. It is true that no express recognition of belligerent rights ever proceeded from the American Government, either at the commencement or during the prosecution of the war. But neutral States must judge for themselves of the significance of the facts which come to their knowledge; and they are entitled to have ambassadors resident for the purpose of ascertaining them. On this occasion the preparations were on a scale inconsistent with any other hypothesis than that of actual war. On the 15th April 1861, the President issued a proclamation calling out 75,000 men to suppress what he called "insurrectionary combinations;" on the 19th of the same month he proclaimed a blockade of the ports within seven States of the Union; on the 27th he blockaded two additional States; and on the 3d May he issued a proclamation increasing the army by 22,714 men, and the navy by 18,000 seamen. In addition to these acts, in his Message to Congress, he called for 400,000 men and 400,000,000 dollars.[1] "After a recital of these immense efforts," adds Earl Russell in the despatch from which I have copied these numbers, "it seems quite inappropriate to speak of 'unlawful combinations.' Indeed it cannot be denied," he continues, "that the state of things which exists is a state of civil war; and there is, as regards neutral nations, no difference between civil war and foreign war."

During the Greek Revolution, when the Porte remonstrated with this country against allowing belligerent rights to the Greeks, on the ground that to subjects in rebellion no national character could belong, Mr Canning, then Foreign Secretary, replied, through our minister at Constantinople, that "the character of belligerency was not so much a principle as a fact; that a certain degree of force and consistency acquired by a mass of population engaged in war, entitled that population to be treated as a belligerent, and even if their title was questionable, rendered it the interest, well understood, of civil-

[1] *North America*, No. 1, p. 61.

ised nations so to treat them. Their cruisers must either be acknowledged as belligerents or dealt with as pirates."

Such a reply in the case of the insurrection of the Southern States of America would, I believe, in the eyes of all but Northerners, have fully satisfied the requirements of international law, and justified the recognition of belligerency by the States of Europe. But the case of France and England was, as I have said, vastly strengthened by that other fact of the proclamation of blockade by the North having preceded the European proclamations which acknowledged the rights of neutrality; for the second fact was not only an acknowledgment, but an interpretation of the first fact, by the Northern States themselves. It is on this ground that the recognition of Southern belligerency, which would have been perfectly justifiable on our part, even if the Northern States had consistently refused it, is always alleged by Earl Russell to have proceeded from the States themselves. In the House of Lords, in reply to Mr Bright and the other sympathisers with the North in the Commons, he said: "One of the complaints was that the country, without proper consideration, had granted a belligerent character to the Confederates States; but it was the United States which conceded the character of belligerents to the Southern States by blockading the Southern ports. Any one acquainted with the law of nations knew perfectly well that although a country might put down an insurrection against its authority, it had no power or right to interfere with neutral commerce without giving to the insurgents a belligerent character. When the United States declared the ports of the Southern States to be in a state of

To the same effect Mr Adams, the American minister in London, wrote some years before (on 14th June 1861): "At any rate there was one compensation; the act had released the Government of the United States from responsibility for any misdeeds of the rebels towards Great Britain. If any of their people should capture or maltreat a British vessel on the ocean, the reclamation must be made only on those who had authorised the wrong. The United States would not be liable."[1]

To the credit of the Northern States, it must be remembered that it was in no small measure motives of humanity which, in the first instance, dictated to them a course of conduct which rendered their objection to the recognition of belligerency untenable. Till some sort of belligerency was recognised, prisoners taken on land were traitors, and prisoners taken at sea were pirates; and the ordinary criminal courts of the country had no option in dealing with them as such and condemning them to death. But it was felt very early in the struggle that such a result of the position which the Confederates had assumed was altogether monstrous, whilst its effect in producing retaliation rendered its folly equal to its wickedness. Judge Daly, one of the most respected American jurists, reminded his countrymen of the great historical example of its consequences. The Duke of Alva, during the revolt of the seven provinces of the Netherlands, put 18,000 prisoners of war to death on the scaffold, and "the result was a more desperate resistance, the sympathy of surrounding nations, and the ultimate independence of the Dutch.[2]

[1] Wheaton, p. 44, ed. 1863.   [2] *Correspondence*, No. 1, p. 101.

blockade, Sir A. Milne, commanding our squadron in the American seas, wrote for instructions, and a proclamation was issued declaring her Majesty's neutrality between the belligerents. From that moment her Majesty's subjects were bound to take no part in the conflict, and they disobeyed her Majesty's commands if they gave aid either to one party or the other."

To this allegation the American Government neither did nor could make any other answer than that contained in Mr Seward's despatch, No. 9, 23d March 1865, and so often repeated, to the effect that they regarded the mutual agreement of Great Britain and France to recognise belligerency as "an unfriendly proceeding;" to use the words of the ambassador for the North German Confederation during the Franco-Prussian war, Count Bernstoff, it was not "benevolent neutrality." From Mr Lawrence's edition of Mr Wheaton's principles, published during the very heat of the war, it is plain enough that the better class of American jurists were quite aware that the position which their Government had assumed was entirely untenable; and it is amusing to find the editor endeavouring to reconcile his countrymen to what he well knew to be the law of nations, by reminding them "that it is not always to the advantage of the old Government that belligerent rights should be withheld from the revolutionary Government by foreign Powers; for as long as the proceedings are deemed an insurrection in the body of the State, it might remain liable for the acts of the revolutionists to third parties, as well as be deprived, as respects them, of the belligerent rights of blockade."

2d, The next stage in the process of recognition is recognition for neutral purposes not directly connected with the war. "If the contest be protracted,"[1] says Sir Robert Phillimore, "and there be any appearance of equality between the contending forces, the subsequent conduct of third Powers intending to remain neutral cannot be blamed if they proceed to virtual recognition of the revolted State—*i.e.*, if they recognise its commercial flag, and if they sanction the appointment of consuls to the ports of the new State. So far, there is a recognition of its *de facto* existence fully justified, perhaps indeed imperatively enjoined, by the duties of the third Power towards its own subjects, and in no way inconsistent, according to the practice of nations, with the continued observance of neutrality between the contending parties." It might be contended, I think, that recognition to this extent is consistent with neutrality, on the simple ground that trade between neutrals is not interrupted by war, and that whatever is necessary for neutral trade neutrals may do, so long as they respect the blockade and other strictly warlike arrangements of the belligerents. Even whilst recognition extends no further than to belligerent rights, the necessities of their own subjects may force neutral States to open communications and negotiations with those who, for the time being, possess authority in the State which is fighting for recognition. France and England opened communications with the Southern States, by means of their consuls, in order to induce them to act on the second and third articles of the Treaty of Paris; and when Mr Bunch's *exequatur* was with-

[1] *Correspondence*, No. 2, p. 17.

drawn, the ground which the Northern States took up was not that such negotiations were illegal, but that Mr Bunch had gone beyond them, and, being a consul, had acted in the capacity of an ambassador whose appointment would have amounted not to belligerent, but to full jural recognition.

3d, Formal and public recognition, by which all the rights and privileges of an adult political community are acknowledged to reside in the new-born State. This final stage is marked either by the sending of ambassadors, or by the elevation of the consuls already resident to the rank of ambassadors, as was done in the case of Roumania already mentioned,[1] and by entering into treaties with the new State. In the case of communities that have seceded from a recognised State, this formal recognition must be delayed till the contest by which the secession was effected is finally decided, but, for obvious reasons, it must frequently take place on the part of neutral States long before it is conceded by the parent State. Thus the Treaty of Munster, by which Spain recognised the Republic of the Netherlands, was not signed till 1648, nearly seventy years after the declaration of independence, and after every other State in Europe with the exception of Austria had recognised it. The independence of Switzerland, which was formally recognised on the same occasion, was of still older standing. In like manner the revolt of Portugal from Spain took place in 1640, but it was not till 1688 that Portugal was recognised by Spain in the Treaty of Lisbon; whereas England concluded a treaty of peace and alliance with it

[1] *Ante*, p. 106.

in 1641, the very year after the revolt. Even the fullest recognition by a neutral State, if taking place thus in the fulness of time, does not imply a breach of neutrality by the law of nations. This principle was fully recognised by Mr Seward, the American minister, in his instructions to Mr Adams, the American minister in London, whilst protesting vehemently against the belligerent recognition of the Confederacy. "We freely admit," he says, "that a nation may and even ought to recognise a new State which has absolutely and beyond question effected its independence and permanently established its sovereignty, and that a recognition in such a case affords no just cause of offence to the government of the country from which the new State has detached itself." Though such, unquestionably, is the sound doctrine of international law, I suspect there are very few instances in which a neutral State has recognised the independent existence of a revolted province, previous to recognition by the parent State, without causing the latter serious offence. When France recognised the United States by concluding a treaty with them in 1778, Great Britain immediately declared war against France. Had the issue of the war been in favour of the South, I strongly suspect that the opinion of the North as to whether our final recognition was or was not a non-neutral act would have been governed by the consideration whether America was or was not in a condition to go to war with England.

These three—or, inasmuch as the distinction between the first and the second (between belligerent and mercantile recognition) is not so distinctly marked—let us say these two stages in the process of recognition, produce very different effects not on the relation of the States alone, but on the relation of the individual citizens of the States. Recognition of full jural independence places the citizens of the new State in all respects in the same position as the citizens of other separate nations. The rules of private international law must mean the same thing to them as to the citizens of the oldest communities, otherwise the same grounds of offence will emerge to them. Just as they can send and receive ambassadors in their corporate capacity, so in their individual capacity they can sue and be sued. But as the full rights of independent State-existence do not follow belligerent recognition in the case of the community, neither do full citizen rights belong to its inhabitants. To define these rights, both public and private, is a task which often involves questions of great difficulty. The general answer, in both directions, no doubt is that the rights of belligerents are measured by the requirements of belligerency. Belligerents have an international existence for one purpose only—viz., for the purpose of fighting, and thus ascertaining, by the verdict of battle, their farther right to full jural recognition. What the right of fighting involves, is a question which I shall consider when we come to speak of the laws of war, and the relations between belligerents and neutrals.

CHAPTER XII.

OF THE INTERNAL FREEDOM OF THE STATE.

Freedom from external control on the part of the claimant for recognition will not satisfy the requirements of international law. The international State must be free from itself; it must possess subjective as well as objective freedom; it must be autonomous or self-ruling, as well as autarchous or self-directing. Whether or not an individual State does so govern itself in point of fact, is a question for the practical politician, not for the scientific jurist. But even in order that it may enjoy the presumption which will entitle it to have what we have called the relevancy of its claim sustained, and be permitted, by the recognition of belligerency or otherwise, to go to proof, it must present itself clothed with conditions which render the exercise of reciprocating freedom *possible*. These conditions it is the function of the scientific jurist to define. Two separate inquiries here present themselves.

1st, Whether, assuming the claimant to possess reciprocating will, and this will to be free from external constraint, it is sufficiently in accordance with omnipotent will, or, in other words, with absolute reason, to admit of its vindicating itself as relative freedom?

2d, Whether the form of government under which the claimant professes to live be such as to give expression to his relative freedom, to the extent of enabling him to discharge international obligations?

If either of these inquiries should yield a *negative* result, the claim even to belligerent recognition falls to the ground.

CHAPTER XIII.

OF COMMUNITIES THAT ARE DEPRIVED OF INTERNAL FREEDOM, ON THE GROUND THAT THEY ARE INCAPABLE OF EXPRESSING OR REALISING THEIR RECIPROCATING WILL UNDER ANY FORM OF INTERNAL GOVERNMENT.

We know that it is rational will alone that is free and capable, as such, of exhibiting itself as power. In this indispensable element of reason we have consequently the test of the presence or absence of the internal freedom of the State. Our problem thus comes to be, how are we to determine the presence or the absence of reason in a claimant for recognition?

Now, does the analogy of national or municipal law, as the more developed branch of jurisprudence, still help us here? In national or municipal law, both public and private, a general right to what may be called municipal recognition is admitted on the general ground that human existence raises a presumption in favour of the presence of rational, and, as such, of free consenting will. A man who is not *sui juris* in a jural community, whether in his public or his private capacity, is in an exceptional position. But there are such positions. There are special grounds on which the presumption in favour of the presence of rational will is reversed, and municipal recognition is withheld or suspended. Let us inquire into these grounds and see whether or not they may exist in communities and apply to international recognition.

The internal or subjective grounds which, during their continuance, are held to forfeit or suspend the right of the person to jural recognition by national law are the following:—

1. Nonage.
2. Imbecility, congenital or superinduced.
3. Criminality.

1st, *Nonage*.—The mere lapse of time can supply, in international law, no presumption in favour of the presence of rational will corresponding to that which is derived from it in municipal law. The most barbarous communities are probably as old as the most civilised. Still there is such a thing as political nonage; for, though barbarians may be old children, those of them who belong to capable races are simply the children of the great human family. Their childishness cuts them off from international rights only for a time; but whilst it subsists it cuts them off as effectually as the childishness of a promising child cuts it off from municipal or political rights.

The right of undeveloped races, like the right of undeveloped individuals, is a right not to recognition as what they are not, but to guardianship—that is, to guidance—in becoming that of which they are capable, in realising their special ideals.

2d, *Imbecility*. (*a*) *Congenital Imbecility*.—Whether congenital imbecility exists in the case of races is a physiological problem which it does not belong to our province to discuss. It is sufficient for us to know that if, or to the extent to which, it exists, it will form a permanent bar to recognition in international just as in national law. The relation which it establishes between inferior races and superior races, if such there be, is that of perpetual pupilarity and guardianship. Nor must this attitude of guardianship be abandoned in point of law, in the mere hope that its basis in point of fact may be thereby removed. In this, as in all other cases, law must wait upon fact. The recognition of the equality of the negro with the white races in America is a case in which law has outrun fact, and for the present, at least, it furnishes no precedent of which international law can take cognisance. On the ground that international law, like other branches of positive law, must be satisfied with approximations, the municipal recognition of an inferior race, so long as the preponderance of proximate power remains with the superior race, will count only as an element in determining the relative claim of the superior race to recognition. But the absolute claim of the superior race itself will be cut off, should the preponderance of proximate power pass into the hands of the inferior race.

(*b*) *Superinduced Imbecility.* — The two causes which national law recognises as superinducing imbecility are disease and decay. Insanity and dotage impede the action of the rational will, and even where they do not annihilate it they deprive those who suffer from them of the right to municipal and political recognition. That the same causes, when existing in communities, will produce corresponding international consequences, is obvious. Nor is their occurrence doubtful or unfamiliar. The history of our own time and the aspect of surrounding nations, even at the present hour, present, alas! but too many examples of both. But the difficulty in international as in national law in dealing with imbecility, when superinduced, is very much greater than in dealing with it when it arises from nonage or is congenital. Ostensibly the status of the subject is sufficient, and those who question it are driven to guess out its defects from his actions. If a man who is not supposed to labour under any legal incapacity makes an insane will, the will is as invalid as if it were made by an idiot. The inference derived from the special fact receives, moreover, a general application, and municipal law accepts it as an indication of the position to be assigned to the actor. Even if an insane action should be held to indicate only monomania, it will, in general, invalidate both civil capacity and criminal responsibility. Now precisely the same principles govern international law, and the same function of inferring general conclusions from special actions belongs to it. If recognition is claimed by a community professing to have established or adopted social or political institutions, the realisation of which assumes the existence of impossible facts, the claim will have no international validity, and the fact of its being tendered will deprive the community of the right to claim recognition on any other ground. Communism and Nihilism are thus forbidden by the law of nations. But the process of applying the law is attended with so much difficulty, that few, if any, instances can be given of political insanity being dealt with otherwise than as a *casus belli*. It is in the direction of its adoption, however, as a formal ground for the refusal or withdrawal of recognition, as much as in any other, that a farther development of international law is requisite, and that international may be made to react beneficially on the development of public municipal law. There is a clear distinction between interfering with the internal action of a despotic or democratic government, and refusing to accept them as adequate guarantees for the international trustworthiness of States which profess to live under them. Whilst we continue to recognise Russia, we are forbidden by the law of nations to intervene in behalf of her Jewish subjects, who are now (1882) being persecuted, on the ground that they were not adequately protected by the Government, otherwise than by friendly remonstrances; but we are perfectly entitled to withdraw our ambassador from St Petersburg, and send his passports to the Russian ambassador in London, and by doing so we should afford no jural *casus belli*. We should then stand to Russia in the same position in which we have stood to Mexico since the murder of the Emperor Maximilian. But this brings us to the subject of crime.

3d, *Criminality.*—Crime is a violation of natural law, and, as such, at variance with reason. Though all errors are not crimes, all crimes are errors. The presence of a criminal intention, to the extent to which it exists, is thus a proof of the absence of rational will. In municipal law it is consequently held to involve the forfeiture of the right to jural recognition. The same principle has always been recognised in international law. Grotius lays it down that a band of robbers is not a State. On this ground the Barbary States were never recognised by European nations; and the conquest of Algeria by France was not regarded as a violation of international law. It was an act of discipline which the bystander was entitled to exercise in the absence of the police; and the justification for the present interference of France in Tunis and our own in Egypt, must be sought in the extremely rudimentary character which still belongs to what is beginning to be called the European Concert. In the absence of concerted action, France and England are now doing in Africa what Russia did in the Balkan peninsula when the European Powers declined to enforce their own resolutions on Turkey after the Conference of Constantinople. We must bear in mind, however, that criminality which warrants either the refusal or the withdrawal of recognition, or which, in the case of an unrecognised State, acts as a *casus belli*, must be determined by the object, not by the origin of the community. International law affixes no bastard-badge even to States which have come into existence by means which it repudiates. Had Algeria come to respect the rights of life and property, its history would not have permanently deprived it of the right to recognition. Law follows fact very closely, and a very short prescription will give an international title. Whether or not it be the true view that all criminal law resolves itself into guardianship,[1] there can, I apprehend, be no doubt of the truth of the proposition that such is the character which alone can justify its enforcement by one community on another. The personality of a community is never so complete as to

[1] *Institutes of Law*, p. 306.

enable other communities to impose criminal responsibility on it as a whole, and to make it a suitable object of punishment. Any attempt to punish a community always takes the inhuman character which belongs to reprisals—of making the innocent responsible for the guilty, and can be justified, if at all, only by the necessity which justifies war. The real difficulty which meets the international jurist is to determine in what cases communities which cannot be regarded as barbarous, and which professedly exist for purposes which municipal law does not expressly condemn, are unworthy of recognition on the ground that they do not, and on the face of them cannot, supply that measure of rational consent, on the part of the community in its totality, on which the claim to recognition is founded. This brings us to the inevitable question of the forms of government, or of alleged government, which are compatible with the discharge of international duties.

CHAPTER XIV.

OF COMMUNITIES THAT ARE CUT OFF FROM RECOGNITION, ON THE GROUND THAT THE FORMS OF INTERNAL GOVERNMENT UNDER WHICH THEY PROFESS TO LIVE INCAPACITATE THEM FOR EITHER EXPRESSING OR REALISING RECIPROCATING WILL.

Under the head of relative recognition, we shall consider the value of the various forms of government which, more or less perfectly, satisfy the requirements of absolute recognition. Here we have to do only with those which are repudiated by the law of nations altogether, on the ground that they fail to satisfy these requirements.

To this class belong:—

1st, *Personal governments, whether hereditary or elective, and whether professing to be founded on divine or on human will.*

L'état, c'est moi, is not only an unrealisable fiction, but it is a fiction which, if realised, would cut away the ground on which alone international recognition becomes a right—viz., the contracting will of the community as an organic whole. Just in so far as the community abjures its own will in favour of the will of an individual, it forfeits its own right to recognition. On the other hand, it confers no corresponding right on the individual whom it professes to place in its stead, because an individual is not a nation in point of fact, and never can become one. It is true that something like a representative character is always claimed by the veriest despot. But even supposing this allegation to be true in its extremest form—viz., that the choice of the individual shall have been the act, not only of the universal will but of the rational will of the whole community—he could represent its contracting will only on a single occasion, or for a very brief period. Questions cannot be answered till they are put. Consent cannot be bottled up and handed over for general or for future use. In order to possess validity, consent must have reference to a special matter; and it must be *de præsenti* and not *de futuro*. When a treaty is negotiated, for example, the community must consent to it at the time, and not merely consent that another shall consent to something or other, of which, at the period of its supposed consent, the community knew nothing. The community itself is the only possible witness to its own will; and if a new question regarding its will is to be put to it, it must be recalled and re-examined. The repudiation by the French nation, or by those who were afterwards supposed to represent the French nation, of the Free Trade Treaty of Commerce which Napoleon III. negotiated with this country in 1859-60, is a striking and memorable illustration of this fact. The Emperor had been repeatedly and quite recently chosen by the universal suffrage of the French people as the representative of France: his will in this matter was far more rational than the wills of those who chose him; and yet the will of the Emperor was not the will of France. The recognition of his government, consequently, was the recognition not of France but of him. During his whole reign, other nations had no continuous guarantee offered to them by France beyond that of his personal character and intelligence. That guarantee they were under no international obligation to accept, and in point of fact they did not accept it for a single hour after his personal disappearance from the political scene. According to the strict principles of international law, France would have had no *casus belli* against any State which declined to receive the Emperor's ambassador, if the declinature had been put expressly on the ground that he was not the ambassador of France. The assertion of these principles, however, in this direction, would involve the few States that were entitled to assert them on the ground that they themselves complied with them, in a crusade against all autocratic and despotic States. The nearest approach to a historical example of the refusal of an ambassador on the ground here stated, is Cardinal Mazarin's refusal on the part of France to receive Grotius, on the allegation that he was accredited by Oxenstern and not by the Swedish Government.

In cases, then, in which personal governments are recognised, it is necessary to bear in mind that their claim to recognition rests not on their perfection but on their imperfection, as such. A perfectly personal government would be perfectly unrecognisable; and we shall see, by-and-by, that the international value of governments sinks or rises in proportion to the extent to which other States are entitled to accept them as continuous representatives of the national will. It is on this ground, that in my attempt to solve the ultimate problem of international law, by the formation of an international organism embracing the three factors of legislation, jurisdiction, and execution, I have insisted on the necessity of recognising the action of national legislatures in international legislation; and I am happy to find that, on this point, I have the high sanction of Professor Bluntschli's concurrence.

2d, *Class governments, or governments which rest on the assumption either of the absolute equality or permanent inequality of individuals or of classes—in other words, absolute democracies and exclusive aristocrasies.*

The professed abdication of its inalienable sovereignty by the community as an organic whole in favour of a class, whether democratic or aristocratic, stands, in principle, on precisely the same footing as a similar abdication in favour of an individual. Class governments, like absolute monarchies, are unrealisable fictions; and happily so, because their realisation would be the negation of State-existence, and, consequently, the surrender of the right to recognition by the communities which realised them.

A class is not a nation, and nothing but a nation can be a subject of international law. And this applies to classes which constitute the majority, just as much, and in some cases even more, than to those which constitute the minority of the nation. The extremest instance of this occurs in the case of a community in which a slave population has been recently emancipated and endowed with the suffrage. Even if the freedmen do not themselves constitute the majority they are sure to be got hold of by the most worthless portion of the freemen, and made to turn the elections in their favour. But class government, in the sense we here understand it, may impede the action of the rational will even where a homogeneous community is represented as a whole, if its component parts be represented otherwise than in proportion to the contributions which, as individuals or as classes, they severally make to its contracting will. Universal suffrage, even when coupled with the representation of minorities, does not exclude class government so long as it contains no provision for the graduation of voting power. The existence of absolute equality in the contracting wills of individuals or of classes never is, or can be, a fact, and to recognise it as a fact is to recognise a falsehood. On the other hand, inequality of contracting will may very readily be represented beyond the extent to which it exists; and in this case likewise the organisation of the State rests upon a fiction, which in so far invalidates its right to recognition. In principle, then, both personal government and class government lie under the permanent ban of international law. If either of them could be completely realised, it would have no right to recognition at all, so long as human nature remains as it is. It would not be the government of a human community. It would be a wholly artificial entity, not a natural, and consequently not a jural entity. But inasmuch as God has mercifully set limits to human folly and wickedness, as well as to human wisdom and goodness, by the limitation of human power, nature's laws can be violated by man only partially. No personal or class government ever was, or will be, perfectly realised in fact; and this necessary imperfection may even go the length of saving such governments, practically, from the condemnation to which they are theoretically exposed. The phenomena which they present are often utterly at variance with the principles on which they profess to be founded. The science of public municipal law is still in so early a stage of its development, and the practical influence even of the truths which it recognises is so insignificant, that the best governments we know, either historically or experimentally, are mere masses of inconsistency. Made up of false elements and true elements, they seek objects that are possible and impossible, by means which conduce to them, and by means which defeat them. Practical statesmen and diplomatists must take them as they find them, and often be thankful that they are not more logical than they are. For practical purposes, however, it is very important to bear in mind, that a government which either rests on the assumption of unrealities, or which professedly seeks to realise impossibilities, though its practice may be so at variance with its principles as to render it for the time being not unworthy of recognition, is in process of becoming unrecognisable; whereas a government that takes for granted nothing which does not partially exist, and seeks to realise nothing which is not approximately possible, however imperfect may be its present action, will be continually strengthening its claim to confidence as it advances along its own lines and perfects its internal *modus operandi*. The determination of the point in the upward or downward progress of a nation at which the scale shall turn, and recognition be given or withdrawn, involves concrete considerations which do not admit of any general or formal determination. We cannot determine the watershed by merely looking at the mountain; and as the instruments of our science will not help us here, we must be contented to wait till we see which way the water runs.

CHAPTER XV.

OF THE NECESSITY OF ASCERTAINING THE RELATIVE VALUE OF STATES.

Though the classification of forms of government, too often irrespective of circumstances, has been a favourite subject with publicists, both national and international, from the days of Aristotle downwards, the classification of States, taking their simple or composite character, their forms of government and their adaptation to circumstances into account as elements in the calculation, is a branch of the study of the law of nations which, as yet, can scarcely be said to have been entered upon.[1] In any other sense than as a rule for the admission into, or exclusion from, the family of nations, no doctrine of recognition has been considered possible; and with the exception of some formalities of diplomatic etiquette, now almost obsolete, old States and new States, great States and small States, States that have rational forms of government, and States that have irrational forms of government, have been left to scramble for ascendancy as best they might. It has been a case of—

> " Black spirits and white,
> Red spirits and grey ;
> Mingle, mingle, mingle,
> You that mingle may."

There has been, it is true, no want of theories by which this inevitable question has been sought to be evaded. We have had theories of universal monarchy, resting sometimes on divine right directly, and sometimes on human election, which by reducing the world to one state, proposed to cut off the question altogether. We have had oligarchical theories, by which five or more "great powers," asserting an equality more or less real amongst themselves, excluded all other powers from computation, or admitted some of them perhaps to a

[1] Yet Aristotle pointed it out, not only in the general doctrine of proportion, in the *Ethics*, but specially in the *Politics*: τίς ἑκάστῃ πολιτεία καὶ ποία: κ.τ.λ. —Lib. I. c. ii., and IV. c. iv.

merely "consultative" position, and thus left the question confessedly unsolved. Last, and most baseless of all, we have the prevalent theory of the equality of all powers, a theory which seeks to get rid of the question by denying its existence. Of these three theories it is the last alone which has never been found capable of any practical realisation at all; and yet it is the theory which at the present day you will find set forth in all the books[1] as that which alone is in accordance with nature, and to which practice must, of course, strive to accommodate itself. Now the equality of all States, the moment they are acknowledged to be States at all, is, if possible, a more transparent fiction than the equality of all individuals who are admitted to be jural persons or jural citizens; because in the case of individuals or citizens there are limits to possible size and power, and consequently to inequality, which do not exist in the case of States. A State may be almost of any size or power, both absolutely and relatively; and unless we are to adopt the theory of absolute centralisation and recognise annihilation of nationality as the Nirvâna of international existence, it is of the last importance that the rights of the smaller and weaker States, such as they are, should be carefully preserved.[2] But this will never be effected by placing them in a false position and inducing them to advance claims which they cannot maintain. To assert that, without any superiority in other respects, a State with ten thousand inhabitants is equal to a State with

[1] *Vattel*, p. 47; *Klüber*, p. 116; *Heffter*, p. 48; *Wheaton*, Dana's edition, p. 234; *Martens*, vol. i. p. 322. Even *Bluntschli, Droit International Codifié*, sect. 81, p. 88; German edition, p. 98; *Field's International Code*, p. 10.

[2] *Ante*, pp. 135-138.

ten million inhabitants, or that a State half the size of an English County is equal to a State that covers half a Continent, is just as false as to assert that a thousand is equal to a million, or that the Canton of Geneva is equal to the Continent of Europe.

All this is so obvious, that at first one is tempted to imagine that some equivocal meaning, in this connection at all events, *must* hang around the word "equality," and that, if this were cleared away, the statement would be true, at least approximately true. If all that was meant were that all States are equally entitled to assert such rights as they have, and that they have thus an equal interest in the vindication of law, the assertion would be true of States, as of citizens and individuals. Small States might be more dependent on positive law than great States, but the same may be said of small men as compared with great men. This, however, is not the meaning of the doctrine at all. If we look into the authorities we shall find that what is meant, though of course by no means consistently maintained, is really what is said—viz., that the *rights* of States are equal in themselves, and not merely the *right of asserting* their rights. Let us take Heffter, who, as a German, might be expected to be free from the confusion of mind on the subject of equality generally found in French writers since the Revolution. Heffter then speaks of "Le principe fondamental de l'égalité de toutes les nations souveraines, sauf les modifications qu'il a reçues dans le droit positif."[1] Now this must mean equality in the rights to be recognised, not in their recognition, for the latter (equality

[1] P. 48.

before the law) has suffered, it is to be hoped, no modification from positive law. Again he says,[1] "Les souverains sont égaux entre eux,"—a statement which he supports by the fact that there is a species of social equality, to the extent of intermarrying, recognised between the members of royal families, provided their dominions are hereditary. But the *jus matrimonii* everywhere in Europe extends to all classes under royalty, and in England has been permitted to penetrate its ranks.

Klüber,[2] also a German, is even more explicit: "Tous les États jouissant d'une personnalité morale et libre, *chacun* d'entre eux peut pretendre à *tous*[3] les droits qui dérivènt de cette personnalité; *leurs droits sont par conséquent égaux.* D'ailleurs, les rapports *naturels* entre les États étant partout les mêmes et par consequent *essentiels,* cette égalité ne peut-être altérée par des qualités ou attributions accidentelles d'un État, telles que son ancienneté, sa population, l'étendue de son territoire, sa puissance militaire, la forme de sa constitution, le titre de son souverain, l'état de la civilisation sous toutes ses formes, la considération dont il jouit, les honneurs qu'il reçoit de la part d'autres États, &c. Cette égalité de droit est particulièrement incompatible avec les prétentions à la précédence, à la supériorité, à la jurisdiction, au pouvoir criminel, vis-à-vis d'autres États." There can be no mistake about the doctrine here. Martens and Bluntschli are much more guarded in their expressions of adhesion, and pretty well explain the doctrine away. Still they hand it down as a doctrine fundamentally irrefragable; whilst Field, as a republican, asserts,

---

[1] P. 105.   [2] *Klüber,* sect. 89.
[3] The italics are in the original.

without hesitation, that "all nations are equal in rights."[1] Strangely enough the only approach to a solution of the question of the arrangement of States in accordance with their real value, and a consequent advance in international law, with which I am acquainted, was made by a Pope. In 1504, Pope Julius II. issued an order fixing the rank of the ambassadors according to the importance of the States which they represented, and thus, by implication, the rank of the States themselves. But on what principle his calculation proceeded we can only conjecture. That it was not a principle that found much acceptance, even at the time, is apparent from the fact that his arrangement was soon observed only at the Papal Court, and there only with respect to the first four sovereigns on the list, of whom the second—taking precedence of the kings of France and Spain, of everybody but the Emperor—was the King of the Romans.[2]

On the 10th December 1814, the plenipotentiaries of the eight Powers who had signed the Peace of Paris, named a commission to determine "the principles for regulating the rank to be assigned to the different crowns, and the consequences of such regulation,—"des principes à établir pour régler le rang entre les couronnes, et tout ce qui en est une conséquence." In the meeting of 9th February 1815, a discussion took place on the project of the Commission, which had established three classes of powers relatively to the rank of ministers. One would have expected that the rank of the ministers should be relative to the rank of the powers. But doubts

[1] § 16, p. 10.
[2] *Embassies and Foreign Courts*, by the Roving Englishman, p. 274.

being raised as to this classification, and particularly as to the class to be assigned to the great republics, the question was abandoned, and the plenipotentiaries confined themselves to determining the rank of the diplomatic agents of crowned heads."[1]

The importance of such an arrangement, if really resting on fact—not for purposes of etiquette merely (though even these still mean something)—but for the most serious diplomatic purposes, we shall have occasion to see more fully when we come to study the subject of peaceful intervention. But even here it is well that we should remark the inconveniences to which the want of any recognised order of precedence have led, and must continue to lead; and how public business on the greatest scale has come to be conducted without the precautions which are adopted in the management of the most ordinary affairs. The rudeness of the machinery employed for international purposes, when we examine it closely, is appalling; and it is little wonder if the work which it turns out should be clumsily adjusted and insecurely put together. When the Treaty of Münster was negotiated, all the States of Europe, except England, Poland, Muscovy, and the Ottoman Porte, were present by representatives, and questions of etiquette were discussed with so much keenness as greatly to impede the despatch of business. Six whole years before the plenipotentiaries met were spent in frivolous controversies on points of form, yet no attempt whatever was made to determine the measure of real influence which should be conceded to the various States when they came together. During the five years that the Congress lasted, Münster and Osnabruck

[1] *Klüber*, p. 122.

were scenes of intrigue, misrepresentation, mutual distrust, bullying, and bribery such as the world has rarely witnessed, and which contrast painfully with the serious purpose which, on the whole, was prevalent, and the important and lasting results which were unquestionably obtained. But no arrangement for ascertaining the real opinion—of getting at the rational will of the Congress—was adopted or even attempted. No vote was taken from first to last; and it was only by siding with one or other of the great Powers, or by threatening, in the event of war being renewed, to go over from one of them to another, that the small States succeeded in making their presence felt. The unanimity which in the end was supposed to have been arrived at was the shallowest fiction—like the peace itself, it was a mere expression of exhaustion on the part of the combatants,—and the result practically was that the terms of the treaty were dictated to Germany by France and Sweden.

On a more limited scale, and in a lesser degree, every one of these objections might be made with reference to the Treaty of Utrecht.

At the Congress of Vienna every State in Europe was represented except Turkey; and if its general voice could really have been heard, the Congress of Vienna might have exercised that influence to which, as an Œcumenical Council, it really was entitled. The elements of a representative, and as such of a legislative, assembly were present, if they could have been called into action; and they could have been called into action if their relative value had been known and acknowledged. But it, too, was totally destitute of organisation,—a mere chaos of conflicting interests, passions, and suspicions, out of which such kosmos as was possible was brought by the plenipotentiaries of the great Powers resolving themselves into a sort of board, aided by committees and sub-committees. The representatives of the smaller Powers, who had to trust to persuasion, might, for the most part, just as well have stayed at home; and twenty years had not elapsed before the rupture between the alien populations of Belgium and Holland convinced the greater Powers of the recklessness with which their interests had been disposed of.

The subsequent Congresses of Aix-la-Chapelle, Troppau and Laybach, and Verona, comparatively speaking, were private transactions—consultations with a view to the adoption of a policy in the interest of sovereigns, not as the representatives of States, but as the representatives of dynasties. Whatever may be their historical interest or importance, they scarcely belong to the subject of international law.

The Congress of Paris in 1856 is the nearest approach to an international legislative assembly in our day; and its affairs were conducted on the same principle, or want of principle, as those of Münster and Vienna. The conclusions arrived at were supposed to be the result of general agreement, and were accepted as permanent,[1] in the only sense in which that word can be used in positive law. Yet we all know for how short a time the leading provision for the neutralisation of the Black Sea continued to form part of the public law of Europe, and

---

[1] "Il faut bien le dire," said Baron de Brunnow, sarcastically, "le mot 'à perpétuité' n'a pas été heureusement choisi. Dans l'ordre des choses humaines, il n'est au pouvoir de personne de proscrire et de renier l'action du temps."
—*Protocol of Conferences respecting Treaty of* 1856, *held in London in* 1871.

how practically useless was an "agreement" in which the will of so important a power as Russia, and as it turned out when the Conference was held in London in 1871, that of Germany also, had been counted for nothing. So far from a transaction binding on Europe, and which Europe was prepared to fulfil, it was a mere expression of the wishes of France, England, and Turkey, to which Europe was willing to accede till a convenient occasion should arrive for setting it aside.

Nor is there a single vice of these earlier gatherings which the Conference at Constantinople in 1877, and the Congress at Berlin in 1878, did not exhibit. The first of these occurrences stands conspicuous as the only diplomatic transaction on a great scale which yielded no results whatever, either real or imaginary, even at the time. If it had any indirect effects even, they were in the opposite direction to the resolutions at which it was supposed to arrive ; and the only light in which it is instructive to the international jurist is as a *reductio ad absurdum* of the recognised modes of diplomatic action. Of the Congress of Berlin, except in so far as it recognised the results of the Russo-Turkish war, it would be premature as yet to speak. But we need not hesitate to say that its coming together was a monument of the folly of the recognition of Turkey as a European State, which was the chief object attained by the Congress of Paris of 1856.

It may be that the ultimate course of the world's history is less affected than one would imagine, by thus leaving international arrangements to the rude guidance of the forces which, first in the field and then at the Council Board, chance to be uppermost for the time being. If the world be governed by God, the power which tells in the long-run will be God's power. If right originated in His might, might will end in His right; for in Him the two are identical. But though God has retained the ultimate government of the world to Himself, He has committed the proximate government of it to man; and unless man brings the proximate into conformity with the ultimate by the exercise of reason, God will do it for him at his cost. Power was not of man's giving, and ultimately it is not at man's taking; and the human problem is not to supplant power by reason but to discover it by reason; to distinguish between the powers that be and the powers that only seem to be; and to do this, if possible, without waiting for the terrible *a posteriori* teaching of war. But this, obviously, can never be effected by Congresses called together after wars are concluded, and so constituted as to render it impossible that they should do anything else than register their immediate results. After the Russians are in Constantinople and the French in Egypt, it will be too late to solve the Eastern question, but not too late perhaps for God to punish those who ought to have solved it in the nineteenth century, as He punished those who ought to have solved it in the fifteenth century, and has continued to punish all Christian Europe ever since.

Now, if from these great international transactions in which the reason of men seems to be paralysed by the very magnitude of the interests at stake, we turn to everyday life, and observe the manner in which prudent men manage their ordinary affairs, what do we behold? Is not their first endeavour to calculate forces and tendencies in order that they may estimate probable results ? That various forces will all be realised, or that conflicting forces will all be brought to pull in the same direction, is what they never imagine. Their object is to ascertain the resultant of their action—or, in other words, which of them as real and permanent must ultimately prevail—and then to avoid conflicts by making way for this resultant at once. If external means afford a measure of the forces available for action, as in the case of the shareholders of a company, their computation is an easy matter. The problem of ascertaining the results which must be accepted as ultimate speedily resolves itself into a question of the direction in which the forces will act, of the manner in which they will be applied. It is here that the moral and intellectual elements of power come into play. Men make speeches — each endeavouring to commend his opinion to the unanimous acceptance of his fellows. But they do not deceive themselves as to the improbability of this result, or fail to make provision for an opposite result. In the end they test the effects of all this diplomacy, and ascertain what they must accept as the real state of the case, by voting *in proportion to the money they have invested*, and the shares of which they are at liberty to dispose. They do not pretend to agree whilst they really differ; but they agree to differ *at once* in such a manner as to exhibit the result to which their differences would ultimately lead, and they thus procure the verdict of battle without going to war.

Where the task of ascertaining the value of forces which cannot be measured by external means, and which do not exhibit themselves in diplomacy, has to be encountered, the whole problem of anticipating results becomes vastly more difficult. The value of character, for example, as an element in computing credit, is far less easily determined than the sum which an individual or a mercantile house has invested in a particular concern. Still it is an element which no prudent man will put out of account—nay, which will often be altogether decisive with him as to whether or not he shall enter into a transaction that is proposed to him. He endeavours to compute it, accordingly, as best he may, often, of course, accepting past success as the only available measure of future honesty, straightforwardness, and energy.

Now I cannot see the least reason to doubt that these principles are true of international affairs, and admit of being recognised in international transactions just as much as in national or personal transactions. Their application may be more difficult, but it is the problem *sine qua non* of international law; for to say with Mr Montague Bernard, that "no independent State ever did, and it is unlikely that any such State ever will, submit its rights and interests to the vote of an assemblage of its fellows,"[1] is simply to give up international law as impossible. It is a specimen of the haste and superficiality into which even sensible men are led by the acceptance of such absurd doctrines as absolute equality and absolute independence. It is quite true that no State is ever likely to accept any other dictation than that of *necessity*, which in the last analysis always means *force*. But neither, in general, will a man, or a body of men; and to imagine

[1] *Lectures on Diplomacy*, p. 30.

that *if* the presence of this force can be ascertained by a vote, no State will submit to it till it assumes the form of violence, is just about as reasonable as to suppose that no unsuccessful litigant will pay a debt till his goods are taken from him and sold by the magistrate; or that no defeated ministry will go out of office till it comes into bodily contact with Cromwell's Ironsides or Napoleon's Grenadiers. The question of questions then is, Can international forces be measured, the direction of their probable action determined, and their "resultant" be ascertained otherwise than by conflict? If the question, as hitherto, must be answered in the negative, international law, as hitherto, will be a name and not a thing, and the internationalist, of all jurists, "most miserable."

Of the two branches into which we have seen that the problem of anticipating results divides itself, that of ascertaining the direction in which forces will act belongs to diplomacy, and falls under the doctrine of intervention. Under the doctrine of relative recognition, it is with the forces themselves that we have to do; and the value of the State, as we here understand it, is measured by the influence which it is in a condition to exert in determining the direction of international action.

CHAPTER XVI.

OF THE MEANS OF ASCERTAINING THE RELATIVE VALUE OF STATES.

In estimating the international value of States which have established their right to recognition, there are, I think, four factors which fall to be taken into account:—

1*st*, The extent or size of the State, or the quantity of materials of which it is composed.

2*d*, The content or quality of the State, or of its materials.

3*d*, The form of the State, or the manner in which its materials are combined.

4*th*, The government of the State, or the manner in which its forces are brought into action.

1*st*, *Of the size of the State as an element in determining its relative* [1] *claim to recognition.*

In repudiating the doctrine of the absolute equality of States, we have not only seen the necessity of estimating their value, but we have further recognised the fact that magnitude is an element of value.

It is vain to conceal from ourselves, however, the very great difficulty which attends the estimation of the magnitude of the State. I do not mean the definition of its boundaries. That, at times, it is true, is by no means easy. The difficulties attending it were severely felt both when the independence of

---

[1] As to its effect in determining its absolute claim, v. *ante*, p. 134.

the Spanish colonies was recognised by Mr Canning, and when the Southern States claimed a similar recognition during the great American Civil War. But, in the case of a stationary people, a proximate solution is always possible in the end; and it is very unlikely that any nomadic people will ever become strong enough to satisfy the other requirements for admission into the family of nations. The far more serious difficulty to which I refer arises from the fact that the material with which we have here to deal as a source of power, is always intellectual and moral as well as physical; that the element of quality is *inseparable* from the element of quantity. The right to recognition, as we have seen, rests on consenting will; and it is with consenting will that we have still to do when our object is to measure this right. Population, extent of territory, free revenue, and the like, thus become only secondary elements in the computation. A little cream will not produce so much butter as a great deal of cream, but it will produce more butter than a great deal of milk. A small fertile highly cultivated State, with a small homogeneous population of progressive race and with definite boundaries, may generate more consenting will—more power—than a large State without these other advantages. We have already seen that for this purpose it even derives benefit from its smallness.[1] It may thus exceed it in international value. But it exceeds it in spite of its material insignificance; and only in consequence of its excess in quality or content overbalancing its defect in quantity or extent. Inferiority in size may thus be neutralised by moral and intellectual

---

[1] *Ante*, p. 134 *et seq.*

superiority, by more perfect organisation, or even by advantages of local position, climate, and the like; but *till* it is so neutralised, it is an element of the first importance, of which the doctrine of recognition is bound to take cognisance. Size, or mere physical extent, may thus be distinguished from magnitude, the former as excluding and the latter as including the element of quality or content.

Under the head of size, as thus distinguished from magnitude, fall the two elements of area and population. The rank of the principal States of the world, in so far as it depends on these elements separately, has often been calculated, and is annually published in the *Statesman's Year-Book*.[1]

But it is in combination only that the elements of area and population offer any index to the real value of the State for international purposes; for a population without territory can scarcely be, and a territory without population cannot at all be, a subject of international law. Even when taken together, the slightness of the indication which they afford becomes obvious when we consider that on this footing China would surpass every State in the world! Yet that they are not without weight is apparent from this very instance, for it is on them almost exclusively that the importance of China depends. If China were not bigger than Belgium, or more populous than Norway, we should scarcely hear of it at all; and pretty nearly the same might have been said of Russia, till a very recent period at least.

2*d*, *The content of the State or the quality of the materials of which it is composed.*

---

[1] *Year-Book* for 1881, p. xxxiii.

MEANS OF ASCERTAINING RELATIVE VALUE. 185

(a) *Material Wealth.*—Like its area and population, the material wealth of the State admits of pretty accurate computation. We can calculate, for example, its net revenue, after deducting the interest of its national debt. We can calculate its exports and imports. In these we have measures of the fertility as well as the extent of its soil,[1] of the character of its climate, the advantages or disadvantages of its local position, and the like. Nor is this all. Wealth is the result of the moral and intellectual qualities of the population as much as, if not more, than of the physical means at their disposal; and it measures the former as it measures the latter. Of this Holland and Belgium are conspicuous instances.

(b) *Moral and Intellectual.*—If we bear in mind what we have previously said[2] of reciprocating will and reciprocating power, as conditions of absolute recognition, and if to the elements of material wealth which we have just enumerated we add the military resources of the State, we shall find that the wealth of the State furnishes the best and perhaps the only means available for international purposes, of estimating the moral and intellectual qualities of its citizens.

"Taäke my word for it, Sammy, the poor in a loomp is bad,"[3]

is an assertion, harsh though it seems, which the internationalist, at any rate, I fear, must accept. The wealth of a people in this wide sense unquestionably measures their industry,

---

[1] The average annual production of wheat in the principal wheat-producing countries of the world is exhibited in an ingenious diagram in the *Year-Book* for 1881, p. xxxii.
[2] *Ante*, pp. 113 and 132.
[3] Tennyson's *Northern Farmer*.

frugality, energy, ingenuity, and martial spirit, whether these qualities be the result of race, stage of development, climate, or any other cause or causes. And the measure becomes more accurate if, along with the mere extent of wealth at a given time, we take into account the fact of its being progressive, stationary, or retrogressive. Inherited wealth is not the same guarantee for the qualities we have mentioned as acquired wealth, either in a State or a man. A man who has made £100,000 at the Bar has given very different proof of character from a man who has inherited the same sum from his father; and a man who has doubled his inheritance, from a man who has lost the half of it, though their wealth for the time being may be equal. On the other hand, inherited wealth is more highly prized; for of States as of families it is true that, if they are old because they are frugal, they are frugal because they are old. Of this the contrast between Holland and America is a very striking instance. During the middle ages the Eastern Empire was the richest, and up to the twelfth century, perhaps, it was also the most powerful State in Europe. But its wealth, almost wholly in consequence of its moral degradation, went on diminishing from this period downwards, and it ceased to be the most powerful whilst it was still the wealthiest of States.

Of the more strictly intellectual element of international value, it is conceivable that a more direct test than we have hitherto possessed might be furnished by educational statistics. The proportion of a population that can read and write, or that has received the higher instruction, might be ascertained and taken into account in determining the relative value of the State to which it belonged. How important an element education is, even when power asserts itself in the form of violence, was brought strikingly before the world in the late Franco-German war, as it has been for centuries whenever our Scotch regiments go into action. That, numbers, strength, and even courage being equal, educated men will overcome uneducated men in any department of effort, from a campaign to a ploughing-match, is matter of certainty; and education, consequently, is an element of international value of which account ought unquestionably to be taken. But the accumulation of wealth is a direction in which education tells, not always in the individual case certainly, but in the "loomp," as much as in any other; and wealth is so much more easily measured in other directions than in that of knowledge, that in the case of a whole people the safest course probably would be to accept the former as our test of the presence or absence of the latter. History seems to indicate that the moral takes precedence of the intellectual, and the intellectual of the material progress of a people, whether upwards or downwards. All progressive States become first moral, then intelligent, and then rich; and all retrogressive States become first immoral, then stupid, and then poor. In individual progress and retrogression the same order may generally be observed. In external as in internal politics the recognition of the principle of graduation, even on the basis of material wealth, would be a vast stride in advance when compared with its absolute repudiation by the doctrine of equality. If, in the progress of political science, the application of more accurate means of measuring the value either of States or of citizens should become practicable, then by all means let them be adopted. But do not let us shut our eyes to the value of that which we already possess.

3d, *The form of the State.*—The relative value of different forms of the State is a subject of inquiry apart from, though of course intimately connected with, the inquiry into the relative value of different forms of government. The most general classification of States, in form, is into those which are simple and those which are composite. Whether simple or composite, a State may be governed either monarchically, aristocratically, or popularly; or its government, like that of England, may partake of all these three elements at once. We have historical examples, indeed, of almost every possible combination of forms of States with forms of governments.

Nor does experience, so far as I know, indicate any natural or necessary alliance between special forms of government and special forms of the State. It is true that confederations have been more frequently governed as republican than as monarchical States, and on this ground it would seem, at first sight, as if republican and federal governments were only internal and external manifestations of the same principle. On the other hand, it must be remembered that the tendency of advancing republicanism, or at any rate of democracy, both in America and in Switzerland, has been to sacrifice the local to the central power. The American Civil War was a war in which the North fought and conquered in behalf of centralisation, far more than against slavery. And republicans would do well to remember that centralisation is the highroad to Cæsarism. To what extent this may have proceeded in America from special causes, or may be simply ascribed to the tendency of democracy to pull down whatever exists either in form of government or form of State, it would be difficult to say. In Spain it seems to run in the opposite direction, perhaps for no other reason than that Spain for many centuries has been a single State. In France the republic has as yet exhibited none of the decentralising influences which many of her best politicians expected from it.

Taking forms of the State, then, for the present apart from forms of government, and endeavouring to estimate them, for international purposes, on their own merits, the only general proposition which it seems safe to lay down is the following:—

The value of forms of the State will be greater or less in proportion to the completeness with which, by concentrating the expression of its rational will, and guaranteeing its reality, they enable it to contract as a single person.

We shall find the justification of this proposition if, adhering to the method we have hitherto adopted, we turn from international to national law as the more developed system. The legal or corporate person with whom men can most safely contract, and whose credit, consequently, stands highest, is that which approaches most nearly to the natural person. Unless a corporate name be a reality, the credit of the corporation still rests on the credit of its partners, as individuals. The corporation itself counts for nothing—nay, its existence tends to diminish the faith which we should otherwise repose in its individual members, if personally bound, and hence we seek to bind them *singuli in solidum*. But when that is done, the value of the corporation, *qua* corporation, sinks to its lowest point. The burden which it ought to have borne, has fallen back on the shoulders of its individual members; and of the strength or weakness of these shoulders it offers no indication. On the other hand, even though the responsibility of the partners should be limited, the credit of the corporate body will be good if it can prove to the world that it has at its disposal an amount of paid-up capital equal to the enterprise which it has undertaken, and that the partners have renounced all interest in the capital otherwise than as partners. Up to the amount of this corporate capital it is a legal person, and can contract just as much as if it were a man. But this contracting power rests wholly on these facts: 1st, That the existence of the capital is beyond question; and, 2d, That the capital has been placed beyond the reach of the shareholders, or the directors or managers whom they employ, as individuals.

With the first of these facts we are concerned only in so far as its verification depends on the form of the company. Let the slightest suspicion arise, either that the nominal capital, or other resources of the company, cannot be made forthcoming, or that the directors, according to the constitution of the company, are not wholly precluded from employing it for other purposes than those of the company, and the credit of the company is gone. The capital is no longer its capital *exclusively*, and will be available to it, only to the extent to which the partners are known to have merged their individual fortunes in its corporate fortunes. A limited liability company's credit extends only to the limits of the ascertainable liability of its members, not to the extent of their fortunes; but up to that point, it offers a better security to shareholders than an unlimited liability company, because the extent of its means is more readily ascertainable.

Now, in precisely the same manner, the international credit, and consequent value of a political person or body politic, will be proportioned to the completeness with which it can prove to the world,—1st, That the power which it professes to wield is a reality; and, 2d, That that power is wholly at its disposal for international purposes. If the extent of its resources be unknown or uncertain, though a halo of mysterious grandeur may hang over it, its contracting power and real international weight will be limited to the portion of those resources which is really ascertainable. If the action of the central power be dependent on the more or less independent action of its constituent parts, it will be limited by the extent to which it is so. That it will act as a whole cannot be safely taken for granted so long as, in accordance with its constitution, it *may* act otherwise.

If we classify States, then, in accordance with : the assurance which they afford —1st, Of the reality of the power which they profess to wield; and, 2d, Of their own hold on that power; we shall have—

(*a*) *Simple States.*—All States may be regarded as simple, the internal and external affairs of which are controlled by the same organisation. The means which the State possesses of satisfying the first of the two elements of credit we have mentioned, by affording assurance of its real power, depends on the form of its government, more perhaps than on its form as a State. Publicity is of the very essence of constitutional government, whether monarchical or republican. Despotic and even oligarchic governments may tell a false story to the world; but a constitutional government thinks aloud, and invites the world to listen. Hence the exceptional international confidence which constitutional States always inspire. International society is not more charitable than national society, and concealment always gives rise to suspicion. But if the whole story be published to the world, an open and outspoken State enjoys the same confidence that is conceded to an open and outspoken man. Still the form of the State is not unimportant for this purpose; and the best form is the simplest. Such a State is the nearest approach to a single man; and, other things being equal, it is easier to ascertain both the mind and the means of one man than of two, and, of two, the less their affairs are separated. In like manner, supposing two States both to possess the same internal form of government—both to be constitutional States, we shall say, but the one simple and the other composite—it is easier to ascertain the policy and the resources, and consequent trustworthiness, of the simple than of a composite State. In the latter case, even where professedly there is a central organisation for international purposes, so long as there are separate internal governments, there continues to be a question of the solvency, so to speak, and of the loyalty of each of the partners of which the central organisation is composed. It is only partially that the central government relieves the external world from the necessity of computing for itself the value of the powers which revolve around local centres, and this computation the external world is necessarily very little in a condition to make for itself.

But the advantages of the simple State are still greater when it comes to supply the second of the elements of credit to which we have referred—the assurance of its hold on and control over the power which it really possesses. It can speak as a whole, and speak without the fear of self-contradiction. The most perfect example of the simple State would be a State which not only constituted a single organism for the time being, but which was composed of the same race, dwelling upon a united territory, and which had never been broken up into separate nationalities. Of such a State, however, the history of Europe presents no perfect example. All exhibit a mixture of races, and even populations of the same race have generally lived under different local governments. The nearest approach to simple sovereignty is thus where there has been a complete renunciation of political independence by the parts, even for national purposes—or what is called "integral union." Even integral union, however, is not always a guarantee for complete unity of feeling; and it cannot be denied that, though professing to be thus united, this country presents many of the characteristics of a confederation. The political union which was forced on the Irish people did not remove that diversity of race and religion which renders Ireland a source of weakness rather than of strength, and would almost warrant its deduction from the elements of international value. Then the colonies, which have become locally self-governing, can no longer be regarded as integral parts of the mother-country, though community of race and closeness of sympathy, arising from the very recent character of a large part of the emigration to which they owe their existence, render them still willing to accept the external policy of England as their own. The tendency of some of them to repudiate the doctrine of free trade, however, is an instance of a difference of internal policy which gravely affects other nations, and consequently the relations in which we of the mother-country stand to them. Then India is still, and probably always will continue to be, merely a subject-State, the international value of which can be reckoned at little more than the contribution which it makes to our material wealth. To count the vast area and population of India as part of the British Empire, and thus to raise England above Russia in population, and above Germany in *both* area and population, as is done in the *Statesman's Year-Book*, is a very hasty, and, if adopted as a basis of international organisation, would be a most misleading computation. Nor ought Russia, probably, burdened as she too is with new and doubtful conquests, to receive credit for one half of her nominal extent in either direction; or Austro-Hungary to be regarded as a simple State, on the ground of the union of the two States under one sovereign, or of the central controlling power as regards external policy being intrusted to the Delegations.

(*b*) *Composite States.*—All States are composite of which the internal affairs are governed by separate political organisations, whatever may be the arrangement with reference to their external affairs.

The line between simple and composite States is one which, as we have seen, cannot, in practice at least, be very sharply traced. All simple States, in point of fact, are more or less composite, and as international law knows nothing of the parts of which the State is composed, otherwise than as an element in estimating its value, its international existence and consequent recognition is limited to the extent to which it is represented as a single body by a single diplomatic corps. The international rights possessed by the separate States of the former Germanic Confederation were limitations of, and deductions which fell to be made from, the international rights of the Confederation itself; and the right of the Kaiser to represent the Empire internationally (*das Reich Völkerrechtlich zu Verträten*) is still limited by the existence of the *Bundesrath*, without the consent of which he cannot declare war that is not defensive. It is further limited by the fact that *chargés d'affaires* still reside at several of the minor courts; and that there is not·one even of the smallest of the twenty-five States of which the Empire is composed that does not possess a measure of local autonomy greater than now belongs to any one of the "three Kingdoms." Austro-Hungary, though a bipartite State, and even Switzerland and the United States of America, though confederations, inasmuch as the separate parts possess no power of separate external action, thus approach more nearly to the character of simple States, formally considered, than the Germanic empire even now. But ethnologically considered, the Germanic empire is far more homogeneous; and it is race even more than history that binds communities together. To what extent its defect in form is supplied, or overbalanced by the fact that the central government of Germany is monarchical, whereas the governments of Switzerland and the United States are republican, is a question which will fall to be considered under the head of the relative value of forms of government. It is a question of great importance in this point of view; but it is not one which affects the relative value of the form of the State. Seen in this light, both the German empire, on the ground that its internal affairs are managed by various governments, several of them, such as those of Bavaria, Saxony, and Wurtemberg, being nearly independent; and the Austro-Hungarian empire, on the ground that it consists of two parts which are only loosely held together by the Crown and by the Delegations, must, for the present at least, be classed with composite States.

It is wonderful to how great an extent municipal relations affect international relations, particularly in free States. So long as the component parts retain a separate internal life, anything approaching to a political nationality, they will always, from time to time, exhibit a tendency to vindicate for themselves some approach to international recognition. The occasions on which this tendency from a dormant becomes an active power, will be those in which the several members have become dissatisfied with the treatment which they receive at the hands of the central body. If satisfaction be refused them by the confederation, their next thought will be to seek it by forming alliances beyond its boundaries; and finally, by renouncing its allegiance, and throwing off its yoke. The so-called American rebellion from 1861 to 1865 was, to some extent at least, only a more formidable result of causes similar to those which led to our own rebellions in Scotland and Ireland.

Notwithstanding these very obvious considerations, there have not been wanting, either in ancient or modern times, those who have extolled the composite, or federal, State as the last and highest effort of political science. Let me quote to you the words in which Mr Freeman, in his *History of Federal Governments*, explains and commends what he correctly characterises as the federal ideal.

"There is," he says, "what may be called a certain federal ideal, which has sometimes been realised in its full, or nearly its full, perfection; while other cases have shown only a more or less remote approximation to it. . . . That ideal, in its highest and most elaborate development, is the most finished and the most artificial production of political ingenuity. It is hardly possible that federal government can attain its perfect form except in a highly refined age, and among a people whose political education has already stretched over many generations. Two requisites seem necessary to constitute a federal government in this its most perfect form. On the one hand, each of the members of the union must be wholly independent in those matters which concern each member only. On the other hand, all must be subject to a common power in those matters which concern the whole body of members collectively. Thus each member will fix for itself the laws of its criminal jurisprudence, and even the details of its political constitution. And it will do this, not as a matter of privilege or concession from any higher power, but as a matter of absolute right, by virtue of its inherent powers, as an independent commonwealth. But in all matters which concern the general body, the sovereignty of the several members will cease. Each member is perfectly independent within its own sphere; but there is another sphere in which its independence, or rather its separate existence, vanishes. It is invested with every right of sovereignty in one class of subjects; but there is another class of subjects on which it is as incapable of separate political action as any province or city of a monarchy, or of an indivisible republic. The making of peace and war, the sending and receiving of ambassadors, generally all that comes within the department of international law, will be reserved wholly to the central power. Indeed the very existence of the several members of the union will be diplomatically unknown to foreign nations, which will never be called upon to deal with any power except the central government. A federal union, in short, will form one State in relation to other powers, but many States as regards its internal administration. This complete division of sovereignty we may look upon as essential to the absolute perfection of the federal ideal. But that ideal is one so very refined and artificial, that it seems not to have been attained more than four or five times in the history of the world."[1]

Now the only remark which I wish to make on these passages is, that the federal ideal is one, the historical realisation of which I deny in point of fact, and the future realisation of which, under any conceivable conditions of human life, appears to me to be impossible. And when I say that it is impossible, I do not use that word simply in the sense in which we may say that the perfect realisation of any ideal is impossible to imperfect human beings. I say it is impossible, because I believe it to embrace conceptions which

[1] Pp. 2, 3, 4.

are contradictory,—that the realisation of either of the two elements which it embraces necessarily excludes the realisation of the other, and that the more perfect a federal government becomes in the one direction the less perfect it will always be in the other direction.

The reason of this is, that internal and external interests cannot, from their nature, be so separated as to render it possible for the central power to legislate with reference to the one and the local power to legislate with reference to the other, irrespective of each other's legislation. It is the case of Church and State over again. They are members of one organism, discharging different functions on which they are mutually dependent, and if you separate them, you lose both. If, in any particular instance, it were wholly unlawful for the central power to interfere with internal legislation, there are many circumstances in which it would be impossible for it to bind the confederation to the discharge of international duties. Just take the case of criminal jurisprudence, which Mr Freeman instances, and suppose that any one of the States composing the confederation were to become a nest of pirates. Is it possible to imagine that the external relations of the federal government should not be thereby affected? No one of them, of course, could either negotiate an extradition treaty on its own account, or prevent the confederation from doing so for it; and what becomes in either case of its freedom of action with reference to criminal law? Then, on the other hand, if the local members are to be independent, and may appeal to foreign powers when they conceive their internal freedom to be sacrificed, what becomes of the freedom of the central power? From whichever side we regard it, you will thus see that separate action of the parts and of the whole within the limits of the same confederation is excluded.

Let me further illustrate this statement by two examples which, I daresay, have already occurred to you. A question arises between the central Power and a foreign State with reference to slavery, or free trade. Are the interests which the former institution, or the latter line of policy involves, exclusively those of the general body, or are they both general and local? You will not, I imagine, have much hesitation in answering that they are *both;* or in seeing that, if they are dealt with either by the central or the local government to the exclusion of the other, one or other of the conditions of perfect federal life will remain unsatisfied.

The consequence, then, of a federal government being, as Mr Freeman has said, " in its essence a compromise between two opposite political systems," seems to be that it tends necessarily to its own dissolution. Progress with it, in any other sense than that of more perfect adjustment of its elements at the existing stage of their development, means progress towards dissolution. You cannot develop the two principles which it contains *together*, because if neither is to give way they will hold each other back; and the moment you develop either the one or the other *separately*, you destroy the relation which subsisted between them. Your government or State will tend to become something else than a confederation. If you develop the central element, it will tend to become one homogeneous State,—if you develop the local element, it will tend to become several separate States.

The only condition on which the federal ideal becomes realisable is that of a stationary condition in which the two forces shall hold each other permanently in check; and that is not a condition in which humanity can continue to exist, or at any rate, can fulfil the objects of its existence.

I do not say, on this account, that there are not circumstances in which confederations may be eminently useful. Manifestly they combine many of the advantages both of great and small States. They may, and often have enabled political neighbours, not sufficiently united to form a single State, to defend themselves against a common enemy; and many are of opinion that, in place of permitting our colonies to leave the parental roof, we ought, with that object, to bind them to the mother-country and to each other, by a confederate tie. On the merits of this proposal I offer, for the present, no opinion beyond the prediction that such an arrangement would be a mere stepping-stone to their establishment as separate States, which, in all probability, is their ultimate destiny. But what I allege is, that in the abstract the "federal ideal," in place of being the most finished production of political ingenuity, is a temporary makeshift—an expedient for the attainment of proximate objects by means of a form of government which will always be found, ultimately, to be, both nationally and internationally, imperfect. In the relations of States, as in the relations of persons, the only ties that will bear the strain of progressive development are the ties of blood and race; and nothing tends to strengthen these ties so much as the removal of political entanglements. Of this the increasing cordiality between the American Union and the mother-country since their separation, furnishes a remarkable and happy example.

That even a cosmopolitan confederation for exclusively international purposes—for realising, within the sphere of international jurisprudence, the action of the three indispensable jural factors of legislation, jurisdiction, and execution—that even such a confederation would have in it an element of weakness, arising from the causes here indicated, is quite undeniable. It, too, could be but a makeshift; and it is only as a makeshift, imposed upon us by motives more urgent than those which lead to the formation of confederate States, that it admits of a higher defence.

On taking thought, however, we shall find that the combination of separate political entities, in every form of its conceivable realisation, is a makeshift. It is harmonious action alone that is consistent with freedom. In every other direction we arrive at finality only when we arrive at unity; and unity is to be found, if at all, only in infinity,—in the infinitely great or the infinitely small. Our ultimate choice, as idealists, would thus lie between the universal monarchy of Dante, and the absolute autonomy of the human person, of M. Emile Acollas. The first alternative annihilates international law, and the second sweeps away law altogether. But when we take the concrete conditions of coexistence into account, we perceive that it is by the counteracting forces of centralisation and decentralisation that political organisation exists, just as it is by the counteraction of centripetal and centrifugal forces that physical organisation exists. All States in this sense are and must be composite States, and they must be contented to accept, as the condition of that partial harmony which is the source of life and development, a conflict of forces which shall result in their final dissolution. Its action in the body politic may be likened to pulsation in the animal frame, which is, at once, the condition of life and growth, and the cause of decay and death. In this consideration we behold the limitation which nature has imposed upon political as upon every other form of organic life. Even if we had perpetual motive power, we could not have perpetual motion, in consequence of the presence of friction and the perishable nature of the material of which our mechanism must be composed. And even if we had perpetual motion we could not have perpetual growth, for growth is the result of an effort which goes beyond the mere perpetuation of life, and which exhausts the very organs which it develops.

4th, *The form of government, or the manner in which the materials of the State are brought into action.*

In estimating the relative value of possible forms of government, as formerly in distinguishing between those forms of government which, on the ground of their conformity or nonconformity with necessary conditions, are possible and impossible,[1] we come upon a branch of the doctrine of recognition in which external come in contact with internal relations, and international comes in contact with national law. It is in vain to argue that this contact is undesirable, and to shut our eyes to its necessity on the ground of its delicacy. That all forms of government which may be possible in given circumstances, or, in other words, which would fulfil the conditions

[1] *Ante*, p. 161.

of State-existence to the extent of supporting a claim for recognition, are not equally adapted to those circumstances, and consequently will not contribute equally to the value of the State, is a fact which reason indicates, which experience demonstrates, and which we must consequently accept and make provision for as best we may.

It is quite true that nothing has done more to bring ridicule on the study of political science, whether national or international, than the futile attempts which have been made to discover the best abstract forms of government, and then to urge their universal adoption, irrespective of all conditions of time, place, race, and the like, as if they could be realised *in vacuo*. A like ridicule would justly attach to any attempt abstractly to classify the forms with which we are historically conversant, and then without further inquiry to accept the category to which they belonged as the measure of their value in the concrete instance. The value of a form of government, as an element in the value of a particular State, can be estimated only when its relation to the condition of that State and of other existing States is kept fully in view. The immediate aim of government, like that of law, as opposed to ethics generally,[1] is perfection in the relation, not in the objects related; and the most perfect government for a particular State will be that which places it, *as it is*, in the most perfect relation with the States by which it is recognised, *as they are*. It is this form of government which will secure for it the fullest measure of freedom. But perfection in relation is an element in the perfection of the

[1] *Institutes of Law*, p. 356.

objects related. It does not simply become so after their character is fixed; for they would not have had the same character if their relations had been different.[1] Jurisprudence is thus one of the many rills which contribute to the river of the State life from without as well as from within.

At first sight, then, it seems as if the whole question of forms of government were relative, and as if absolutely they were indifferent, their whole value depending on the pre-existing circumstances by which they were called into existence. For each particular moment, indeed, this necessarily is so. As there can be but one straight line between two points, so there can be but one right government in a given State for the time being, and that government will be indicated by the circumstances, if we can understand them, just as the line will be traced to us if we can but see the points. But this is only the first aspect of the matter. When we look at it more closely we shall see that this government reacts on the circumstances as the circumstances act on the government—nay, that it is itself part of the circumstances with which it must deal. Moreover, we perceive that it is just the part of the circumstances which is, in general, most under the control of the human will. It is the only element of State value which can be contributed almost wholly by conscious internal effort, and which even conscious external effort may do something to call forth. Now it is, I believe, the more or less definite recognition of these facts which has so often led to the forgetfulness of the narrow limits within which they are practically operative internationally. Recog-

[1] *Institutes of Law*, p. 357.

nising the fact that constitutional government, for example, is realisable in favourable circumstances by human means, and that, if realised, it becomes in itself an element, and a very important one, in the value of the State, there has been a tendency to establish nominal constitutional governments *ab extra*, in circumstances in which they were not realisable, and then to count them as elements of value, just as if they had been realised. Abandoning the fatalistic belief in "circumstances," the theory of the absolute independence of States, and the consequent position that international law could do nothing to modify national law, men have rushed to the opposite extreme of assuming that it could entirely change it; and constitutional monarchies and constitutional republics have been recognised which never existed anywhere except in the imaginations of those who recognised them.

Nominal forms of government are worthless, whatever be their form, and we cannot tell whether they are nominal or real otherwise than by entering into the circumstances of each particular case. But these facts do nothing to invalidate the allegation that, when realised, governments of certain forms contribute more extensively to the value of the State than governments of certain other forms. Nor does the question, whether or to what extent particular forms may be realisable by international means, belong to the present discussion. It is a question which internationalists are bound to discuss, and an approximation to the solution of which I by no means regard as hopeless. But it is a question which falls clearly under the doctrine of intervention; and the doctrine of recognition, as such, has nothing to do with it.

In inquiring into the value of forms of government as elements in the value of States, we must assume that their realisation, which we have ascertained to be humanly possible, has become actual.

It is true that realisation, in human affairs, is a relative term; and it is also true, that in practice more or less perfect realisations may balance, or overbalance, more or less value in the forms realised. Security is the first requisite of all government; and even a firm despotism, if there be such a thing, would be preferable to a constitutional monarchy or republic which gave signs of instability. But here, again, we are back into a question of circumstances which is irrelevant to our present subject. In order to compare governments, we must assume that, though not perfectly, they are equally realised. If we would measure their height we must not only make them stand upright, but we must give them the same footing, and make them stand on the same level.

In estimating forms of government from this point of view, very much as in estimating forms of the State, the tests which we must apply to them, as it appears to me, are the following :—

(*a*) *To what extent do they enable the State claiming recognition, by concentrating its whole rational will, to contract as a single individual ?*

(*b*) *To what extent do they enable the State claiming recognition to satisfy the States from which recognition is claimed, that its apparent is coincident with its real rational will ?*

Tried by these tests, the forms of government with which

history is conversant would rank, I believe, in the following order:—

1st, Constitutional monarchies, in which the constitution embraces the whole population, individuals being classified, and counted not as equally but as relatively or proportionally endowed with rational will.

Universality of relative political enfranchisement being equally attainable in monarchies and republics, the ground on which international precedence is claimed for monarchies is, that in them the whole rational will finds utterance through a single permanent organ. But there are many indirect advantages attaching to monarchies which are by no means destitute of international value. Society is more stable under a form of government which recognises classes without stereotyping them as castes, and thus gives free play to individual tendencies, whether acting in an upward or a downward direction. The safety-valve thus afforded to individual ambition no doubt might be, though it scarcely ever has, been attained to the same extent under a republican form of government. It is by preventing the isolation of States that monarchical government contributes to international progress and to the consequent value of the States by which it is adopted in a manner altogether peculiar.

I do not think that we, in general, recognise at all to its full extent the international importance of the cosmopolitan character which belongs to the royal families of Europe, and specially to our own. It is no small matter that at the top of the social pyramid in each country there should be placed a family whose ties of blood with all the other families similarly situated constitute, as it were, a private link of sympathy between nations. Channels both of information and influence are opened by the domestic intercourse of near and often, no doubt, dear relatives, which are closed equally against the wiliest diplomatist and the most audacious "correspondent." For the preservation of this characteristic of royalty it appears to me that, where it does not involve individual hardship of a very special kind, the rule prohibiting the intermarriage of the members of these families with subjects ought to be strictly adhered to. The limitation in point of numbers which this rule imposes on the family group is one of its greatest advantages for international purposes. The effects of these alliances are no doubt less direct and ostensible than in former times, but it does not follow that they are the less real. It is their power for mischief, mainly, that they have lost, in consequence of the limitations imposed on monarchy by the increased strength of the popular will. But their power for good remains unimpaired, and depends, in no small measure, on the preservation of their exclusive character. Had the Duke of Edinburgh, for example, married the daughter of an English duke in place of the daughter of the Czar, who can doubt that the danger of this country and Russia drifting into war in 1876-77 would have been increased? One cannot but hope that the more constant intercourse to which the facilities for locomotion have given rise may lead to more frequent intermarriages between all classes of Europeans; and when these take place between the territorial magnates of various countries, advantages may be anticipated similar, if not equal, to those which result from royal marriages. Each nation, like each individual, must no doubt retain, and if need be defend, its own separate sphere of activity. On this ground it is very undesirable that national sentiments should be weakened by international sympathies; but it is surely equally undesirable that they should be strengthened, as they have been hitherto, by international antipathies. One of the most precious results of the progress of physical science is, that we now have our planet more in hand, so to say, than at any previous period in the history of mankind. Even Alexander the Great had mere parochial conceptions of its character and of the races which inhabit it, when compared with those which are now the common property of all. Gradually our moral horizon will no doubt widen with our physical conceptions, and we shall cease to regard with terror and aversion any portion of a world round which an English commoner and his wife and children can sail in their own yacht on a tour of friendly visits.[1]

2*d*, *Constitutional republics, where the constitution rests on the rational will of the community.*

A republic which elects a single president will, in general, be superior to a republic which elects two or more; and the longer the period during which he holds his office, the greater will be the security which it offers to the external world. If it were not for the dangers attendant on his election, a single president for life would, in some respects, no doubt, be a better head to the State than even a hereditary monarch. The guarantees for his ability would be higher, but not those for his impartiality, and he would want much of the social *prestige* which, in the hands of a king or a queen, when worthily

---

[1] See *A Voyage in the Sunbeam*, by Lady Brassey.

employed, tells as so important a factor even beyond the limits of the individual State. Publicity will be equally attained by republican and monarchical constitutional governments, and external States will have equal means of judging of the sincerity of the professions which they make.

3*d, Constitutional States, where the constitution embraces the rational will only to a partial extent.*

The rational will of the whole *may* find expression through that of the part, and thus the realisation of the true government of the whole is not here impossible as in the case in which the individual members are represented as equal. Such a State may consequently tell the truth, and its real may coincide with its apparent will. But we have no guarantee for such coincidence, and the probability is that such a State will appear more rational than it is. This probability will increase as the representation narrows itself to an oligarchy, particularly if it be an oligarchy of intellect. Plato's State, governed by philosophers, would have been very far from a trustworthy member of the community of nations. And as the first great educationalist, Plato himself strove to remedy this defect by providing that, in so far as seemed to him possible, the governed should be imbued with the sentiments of the governing class.

4*th, Non-constitutional States, where the general will finds expression only through the organic structure of society.*

States of this class may ostensibly assume any form of government. Their value is to be judged of by their historical antecedents, and the real guarantee for State qualities which they offer may rise far higher than the formal guarantee. Such States, however, are in general in a transition state, for public opinion, when once recognised as a power, very soon becomes directly legislative.

5th, Pseudo-despotic and pseudo-democratic States.

Despotic and democratic States, as such, being unrealisable, belong to the category of impossible States. Failing to fulfil the conditions of absolute recognition, any claim to an international position which they can jurally put forth, must rest on the ground that the names by which they are called do not correspond to the things which they profess to signify. States that are spoken of as despotic are very often indirectly governed by public opinion, and States which are spoken of as democratic often indirectly concede to property and education an amount of influence which they profess to deny them. Being founded on false principles, however, they have a downward tendency, and the more nearly they are realised the worse they become—*i.e.*, the more nearly they approach to anarchy, which is the negation of State life, national and international. In estimating their value we must consequently be guided by the paradoxical principle that they get better as they get worse, and worse as they get better.

6th, Of the power by which the relative value of the State is to be determined and its international position assigned to it.

Supposing the relative value of States to be ascertainable with more or less accuracy by the means we have indicated, or by any other means, the final question which presents itself is, how are these means to be made available for the object in view? Very great difficulty must attend the operation of assigning to separate, and, above all, to old and powerful States, a relative rank which they will voluntarily accept, and I am far from ignoring the still greater difficulty of imposing it upon them. But the question is one not of the difficulty but the possibility of an operation on which the progress of international organisation, and the freedom of the smaller States, unquestionably depend. As regards the "great Powers," the principle of absolute equality for an indefinite period must, no doubt, be retained; and in their case, fortunately, it conflicts less flagrantly with fact than when applied to the relations between them and the lesser States. To the latter, and to new States more especially, an international position, corresponding in some measure to their real importance, might, without any great apparent difficulty, be assigned, just as their national position is assigned to new constituencies when any redistribution of electoral power is made within a constitutional State. But by what international body is this function to be performed? In the doctrine of relative as in that of absolute recognition, the really weak point of international law as a positive system consists in the absence of an international legislature, with its attendant judicature and executive. Till this defect is supplied, its doctrines, in a practical sense, will never rise greatly above the character of appeals to the rational will of individual States; and how little such appeals are to be relied on is manifested by the whole course of history. But the discussion of the means by which this defect is to be supplied belongs to the branch of our subject which deals with intervention rather than recognition. All that need be said here is that, failing such international organisation, the ultimate decision of the rank to be assigned to the State claiming recognition, like the fact of the existence of the right to recognition itself, must be with the State or States from which recognition is claimed. The claim originally propounded by the individual State would no doubt in general be extravagant; and that it should be dealt with impartially, so long as it was dealt with by individual States, is not to be expected. But it would probably be dealt with just as impartially as the primary claim for recognition itself; and, as in that case, almost any definite solution of it would be better than none. Even if proceeding from an international legislature, such decisions, of course, could be merely temporary, and some arrangement for their periodical revision would form one of the most indispensable characteristics of such an institution. The progress of States ought not to be, and the retrogression of States cannot be, prevented by other States; and even in the event of an individual State standing still for a time, the progress or retrogression of its neighbours would inevitably change its relative position towards them.

A change for the worse in the internal position of a State would, of course, be the first step towards the withdrawal of recognition; and as resistance to this step would form a legitimate *casus belli* on the part of the recognising States, an occurrence so unfortunate would serve as a significant hint to the degraded State of the international extinction which awaited it, if it persevered in the downward course on which it had entered. That it would inevitably resist, where resistance was deemed possible, shows the necessity of the presence of a powerful international executive at the back of any international legislature or judicature which was to be of practical

CHAPTER XVII.

OF PARTIAL RECOGNITION.

Partial recognition is the recognition which States that accept each other as equals in quality, however much they may differ in quantity, extend to States which they regard as their inferiors in quality. Even between States on the same level of civilisation, international recognition does not imply entire or unqualified acceptance by the recognising State of the definitions of legal relations which may obtain in the recognised State. When we arrive at the subject of the recognition of public and private municipal law, we shall see that such recognition does not extend to cases in which the notions of morality, or public policy, on the part of the recognising State, are at variance with those on the part of the recognised State. An American in England is not entitled to all the privileges of a "free and enlightened citizen;" and a divorce pronounced in Germany will not liberate the spouses from a marriage contracted in France. No free State puts either its conscience or its judgment wholly into the keeping of any other, and there is thus no such thing as plenary recognition in the absolute sense. The right to interpret its own consciousness is of the essence of rational existence in the State as in the person, and no entire agreement amongst States in their conceptions of their rights or their duties has yet been attained. But between

value; and it is on this ground that I have always insisted on keeping the question of international organisation apart from the dreams of the extreme peace party. It may be vain to talk of a cosmopolitan legislature or a cosmopolitan tribunal altogether, but it is vainer still to talk of their vindicating their decrees or their judgments without the possibility of that ultimate appeal to force which is indispensable to a school board, or the court of a justice of the peace. As the loss of position, if at all extensive, would in general be coincident with a period of great national weakness, there seems reason to believe that it would, in most cases, be peaceably accepted at the hands even of individual States. When it was the act of a powerful State, it would be irresistible, and the smaller States would be tolerably safe in following the lead of the great Powers. Without an international organisation, however, all consistency of action would be hopeless; and the same State might have different positions assigned to it by each of its neighbours. In the recognition of the necessity of so undesirable an event, we see how entirely a doctrine of relative recognition hangs on the possibility of a developed doctrine of intervention, embracing the establishment of a self-vindicating international legislature. That involves, obviously, the substitution for international purposes of international for national armament; or, in other words, the placing of the executive, in so far as it had reference to external action, under central control. Is the amount of centralisation which such a necessity would involve possible or desirable? We here touch the most perplexing of the many questions which attend on the great question of international organisation.

civilised States, progress towards such agreement has reached the point at which acceptance becomes the rule, and repudiation the exception. Whatever may be their relative importance, each of them intrusts its citizens to the other, and, as a rule, each accepts the other's municipal law and the decisions of its courts, both civil and criminal. But in the relations between civilised and semi-barbarous States, the case is different. Even when diplomatic relations have been established between them, the recognition of a semi-barbarous State by a civilised State does not extend to its municipal law, either public or private, except as regards its own citizens within its own frontiers. The recognising States consequently maintain separate courts, exercising separate jurisdiction within the borders of the partially recognised State; and to these courts is intrusted the decision of all questions between the citizens of the recognising States, *inter se*, and, in many cases, between them and the citizens of the partially recognised State. The practice of our own country in this respect is still mainly regulated by the important statute known as the "Foreign Jurisdiction Act" (6 & 7 Vict. c. 94),[1] passed in 1843. This statute, with the corresponding memorandum issued by the Foreign Office for the guidance of consuls in the following year (July 2, 1844), has reference chiefly to the Ottoman empire; but the recognition of China and Japan, by this and the other European States, is similarly limited. At the stage of progress which they have reached, these States stand to the Western Powers in a relation midway between that of recognised and pro-

[1] Phillimore, vol. ii. p. 272.

tected States; and it is very desirable that some qualifying adjective should be conjoined with the term recognition in all cases in which it is applied to them. The difficulty of doing so consists in the fact that, as interference with their internal government as regards their own citizens is so often called for on grounds of humanity, they are constantly relapsing into the position of protected States; and this evil is aggravated when, as in the case of Turkey, their nominal citizens consist of various races who are continually claiming the protection of the civilised world against the tyranny of the ruling race.

A step in advance in the direction of the recognition of semi-barbarous States has been attempted to be made in Egypt by the establishment of mixed courts, but it can scarcely be said to have passed the stage of an experiment. Such courts may be presided over by a judge, appointed either by the partially recognised State or by the States which profess to accept his judgments; and the other arrangements may give a greater or less preponderance to the native or foreign element, as circumstances demand.

Such partial recognition of municipal law is the only form in which the principle of relativity has as yet been accepted in international organisation. With the single exception of Turkey, which, in consequence of its technical recognition, occupies a wholly anomalous position, no partially recognised State has as yet been permitted to take part in the counsels of civilised nations, though their right to relative recognition, in this as in other respects, in virtue of their trade alone, seems incontestable. On what ground of absolute justice can China, for example, be precluded from bringing her standing grievance against us with reference to the opium trade to the notice of other nations? As every State in Europe now receives her ambassadors, why should a seat and a vote, if proportional voting were admitted, be denied to them in diplomatic gatherings? As the greatest of all the Asiatic powers, China could not have been indifferent to much that took place at the Berlin Congress of 1878 ; and it is impossible that she should have regarded our Afghan war in 1879, otherwise than as an interested neutral.

BOOK III.

OF THE NORMAL RELATIONS OF STATES

CHAPTER I.

OF THE DISTINCTION BETWEEN NORMAL AND ABNORMAL RELATIONS; AND BETWEEN ABNORMAL RELATIONS WHICH ARE JURAL AND THOSE WHICH ARE ANTI-JURAL.

HAVING completed our survey of the necessary and contingent characteristics of States, and traced the doctrines of absolute and relative, and of plenary and partial recognition, our next task must be to determine the rights and duties of States, or, in other words, the relations to each other in which, as separate though not isolated communities, they must seek the realisation of that freedom which is the object of their jural existence.

These relations, as already indicated,[1] may be broadly distinguished into:

(*A*) Normal relations, or relations in accordance with the general scheme of the universe; and

(*B*) Abnormal relations, or relations at variance with the general scheme of the universe.

(A) Normal relations may again be divided into:

1*st*, Normal relations by the law of nature, between communities within and without[2] the pale of recognition.

[1] *Introduction,* chap. ii. p. 5 *et seq.*
[2] Communities without the pale of recognition, not being States or nations,

(a) Relations of mutual forbearance.

(b) Relations of pupilarity and guardianship.

When it becomes necessary for the realisation of these latter relations, that they should be enforced by the guardian community, they pass into the abnormal jural relations of coercion and obedience; and when unnecessarily enforced, or enforced beyond the point of necessity, they pass into the anti-jural relations of subjugation and slavery.

When resisted by the community in pupilarity to the point necessary for the preservation of its separate existence, they pass into the abnormal jural relation of war; when resistance is carried beyond this point, they pass into the abnormal anti-jural relation of insubordination.

2*d*, Normal relations by the law of nations between communities within the pale of recognition.

(a) Relations of mutual confidence.

1*st*, Political or diplomatic intercourse.

2*d*, Commercial or consular intercourse.

3*d*, Recognition of each other's public municipal law.

4*th*, Recognition of each other's private municipal law.

(b) Relations of mutual aid.

1*st*, Pacific co-operation in behalf of freedom,—*c.g.*, the European Concert.

2*d*, Warlike[1] co-operation in behalf of freedom,—*e.g.*, the Grand Alliance.

(B) *Abnormal jural relations.*

the jural and anti-jural relations which subsist between them by the law of nature, do not fall within the scope of the law of nations.

[1] Though war is always an abnormal relation between the parties at war—when jural, it becomes a normal relation between allies.

We have already seen[1] that all abnormal relations, on the ground that they are at variance with the general scheme of the universe, absolutely or ontologically regarded, are anti-jural. Ethically regarded, however, those of them are jural which, in the case of the parties related, are inevitable and involuntary. But being justified by necessity alone, they are jural only so long, and in so far, as that necessity subsists. Its disappearance marks the point at which they become anti-jural.

1*st*, Abnormal jural relations by the law of nature between communities within and without the pale of recognition.

(*a*) War for the establishment or maintenance of guardianship.

(*b*) Involuntary abstention from such war.[2]

2*d*, Abnormal jural relations by the law of nations between communities within the pale of recognition.

(*a*) *Active.*—1*st*, War in behalf of subjective freedom.

2*d*, War in behalf of objective freedom.

(*b*) *Passive.*—1*st*, Involuntary submission to overwhelming objective power.

2*d*, Neutrality, or involuntary abstention from war in behalf of objective freedom.

(C) *Abnormal anti-jural relations.*

These relations, being voluntarily at variance with the scheme of the universe, are anti-jural both relatively and absolutely.

1*st*, Abnormal anti-jural relations by the law of nature

---

[1] *Ante*, p. 7.
[2] See note on normal relations by the law of nature, *ante*, p. 224.

between communities within and without the pale of recognition.[1]

2*d*, Abnormal anti-jural relations by the law of nations between communities within the pale of recognition.

(*a*) Violation of objective freedom.

(*b*) Voluntary failure to maintain subjective freedom.

(*c*) Voluntary failure to defend subjective freedom.

(*d*) Voluntary neutrality, or failure to intervene in behalf of objective freedom.[2]

CHAPTER II.

OF THE NORMAL RELATIONS BY THE LAW OF NATURE BETWEEN COMMUNITIES WITHIN AND WITHOUT THE PALE OF RECOGNITION.

Though international recognition defines, it does not create the jural relations which subsist between separate communities. It is in the fact of conscious[3] coexistence that these rights and duties, like all other rights and duties, originate; and power is the measure of their extent and the warrant for their enforcement. It is thus that communities at stages of advancement so different as to forbid the acceptance of

---

[1] See note to normal relations, *ante*, p. 224.

[2] As the separate treatment of each of these subjects with any degree of exhaustiveness would involve much repetition, I shall modify this scheme in the sequel as may seem convenient.

[3] Mere coexistence establishes relations; but it is conscious coexistence which generates rights and duties.

each other's jural definitions, are nevertheless bound together by mutual obligations. The relations in which communities thus situated stand to each other may be either negative or positive.

1*st, Negative.*—If two communities are so widely separated, geographically or otherwise, as to be incapable of ministering to each other's advancement, their reciprocal rights and duties are limited to what I have characterised as mutual forbearance. All that they are called upon to do is, to let each other alone. This rule, self-evident though it be, is not always observed in the dealings of civilised races with savages. Seeing the miserable and degraded condition in which savages live, civilised men are tempted to interfere with them when they can do them no good, and when their interference involves an expenditure of their own resources which is wholly objectless. The simple fact that savages behave themselves as such—that they enslave, and murder, and eat each other —creates neither rights nor duties towards them on the part of civilised men. It is in the power to help them that the duty and even the right to interfere with them originates; and the right and the duty are measured by the power.

2*d, Positive.*—The moment that the power to help a retrograde race forward towards the goal of human life consciously exists in a civilised nation, that civilised nation is bound to exert its power; and in the exercise of its power, it is entitled to assume an attitude of guardianship, and to put wholly aside the proximate will of the retrograde race. Its own civilisation having resulted from the exercise of a will which it regards as rational, real, and ultimate, at least when contrasted with the irrational, phenomenal, and proximate will of the inferior race, in vindicating its own proximate will, it is entitled to assume that it vindicates the ultimate [1] will of the inferior race—the will, that is to say, at which the inferior race must arrive when it reaches the stage of civilisation to which the higher race has attained. But the obligation and the right of a civilised nation to interfere with a retrograde race, even where such interference might be for the benefit of the latter, is limited by the proviso, that, in so doing, it does not so burden its own resources as to cause a greater loss of the means of progress to itself and others than it confers on the retrograde race. This latter proviso seems more generally to be forgotten in our own day than the duty which it defines. The expenses of the Zulu war of 1879 for a single month were estimated at a million and a half, and probably greatly exceeded that amount — a sum which would have endowed the whole of the learned institutions of Scotland up to the point that is requisite to place Scotland on a footing of equality with the most learned nations of continental Europe. It seems scarcely doubtful that the gain to civilisation on the whole, and ultimately even to the civilisation of the Zulus, would have been greater had the home duty been attended to in the first instance, and—provision being made for the defence of our colony—the Zulus left to enjoy their proximate will for another generation. Time is an element in the action of civilising influences, the importance of which is not always

---

[1] As to the distinction between ultimate and proximate will, see *Institutes of Law*, p. 432.

sufficiently kept in view. Neither warlike nor peaceful contact acts immediately—nay, the first generation subjected to the influences of either is frequently inferior to that which preceded it. The pagan temple is in ruins, and the Christian Church has not been built. The old rude rule of life has been abrogated, and no better rule has yet taken its place. In many cases it becomes a question of the utmost delicacy, whether appeals to the reason, the conscience, and the self-interest, even of savages, through missionaries, traders, and neighbouring settlers, be not more potent than the closer contact and more direct guidance which results from political subjection if unaccompanied by actual colonisation. It is too true that colonisation often acts as an improving influence only by improving those subjected to it off the face of the earth; but its action admits of being so regulated by the mother country as that it shall ultimately assign to her retrograde children the position for which they are suited by the characteristics of the race to which they belong, and the stage of progress which they have reached, or, in the case of old communities, at which they stand for the time being. The great difficulty always consists in understanding those whose circumstances differ from our own often more widely than their characters; but this difficulty is one which Scotchmen have a peculiar gift for overcoming. Englishmen are quite as successful in their dealings with savages and barbarians, but they seem to have less capacity for entering into the thoughts and feelings of races that lie nearer to themselves. Had the preliminary negotiations with the Boers been conducted by Scotchmen, it is conceivable that we might have been spared the misunderstandings which ended in the Transvaal war; and it is not unworthy of remark that the only portions of Ireland in which any real progress has been made are those that have been colonised by Scotchmen.

CHAPTER III.

NORMAL RELATIONS BY THE LAW OF NATIONS BETWEEN COMMUNITIES WITHIN THE PALE OF RECOGNITION.

(*A*) *Of the relations of mutual confidence in general.*

That the normal relations of States are relations neither of hostility nor indifference—as is alleged, not very justly perhaps, to have been the ancient opinion—nor of mutual jealousy and distrust, which is still too much the modern opinion, but of amity and reciprocal confidence, is the logical inference from the doctrines of natural law which we have elsewhere established. It is on this inference that all the doctrines of the law of nations rest, and its conquest, as a conscious starting-point, is justly regarded as the greatest achievement of science in this department of inquiry. The much profaned principle of *fraternité*, when thus understood, brings the whole moral hemisphere within the range of scientific vision, and holds out to us a prospect of its practical exploration. Expanding from the person to the family, from the family to the State, and from the State to the community of States, the doctrine that " love, which worketh no ill to its neighbour," is " the fulfilling of the law," by bringing the law of nations within the range of ethics, is preparing it gradually to assume the character of a positive jural system.

But mutual goodwill by no means implies mutual interference, or even co-operation, in ordinary circumstances. On the contrary, the capacity for self-support and self-government being, as we have seen, conditions of recognition, non-interference may be enunciated as the primary duty which separate communities, simply as such, owe to each other. That in the normal relations of jural entities, the negative takes precedence of the positive principle,[1] is a maxim of universal application in jurisprudence which follows as a corollary from the subjective[2] origin which we have assigned both to rights and duties. As the first subjective right of every separate rational entity is the right to the unfettered exercise of the powers which God has conferred on him, and his first subjective duty is to exercise these powers in his own behalf, so, in like manner, the first objective right which this entity must acknowledge is the right of others to be relieved by his personal efforts of the burden of his support, and the first objective duty towards him is the duty of permitting him to energise for this purpose. Now separate States are such rational and responsible entities. It is on this ground, as we have seen,[3] that their right to recognition rests—and in their case, consequently, just as in the case of individuals that are *sui juris*, the rule must be in favour of non-interference.

---

[1] The grounds on which this maxim is reversed in the abnormal relations, has already been indicated, pp. 7 and 225, and will be fully explained in Book IV.
[2] *Institutes of Law*, pp. 212, 235.   [3] *Ib.*, p. 101 *et seq.*

As time rolls on, and the experience of ages accumulates, the importance of this rule, not only for the sake of those in behalf of whose liberties it is invoked, but of those on whose ambition, or philanthropy, or restlessness, its restrictions are imposed, comes to be more and more clearly admitted. The interest of each is felt to be the interest of all; and the interest of each, with few and often doubtful exceptions, will be better promoted by leaving him to follow the bent of his own genius, than by any rules that we can impose upon him, or even by any aid that we can afford him. Within the State—freedom of speech, freedom of the press, freedom of religious opinion and worship, free contracting power, free access to offices and honours, and self-government—that is to say, government in accordance with conditions that are imposed by subjective reason: and without the State, freedom of trade, freedom of intercourse and interchange of thoughts and opinions, freedom to adopt and renounce nationality, and, above all, freedom from interference with the internal activity and the spontaneous development of the national resources,—these are the modern instruments of progress. Though they have not always been wisely or happily applied, the results which have attended their gradual and steady introduction into the system of European life, during the last two centuries, have, on the whole, been such as fully to warrant our belief in their efficacy. To the abstract question, then, whether or not we ought to interfere with the free exercise either of individual or of national power, even with the benevolent object of delivering it from the self-imposed restraints of ignorance, superstition, or passion, the answer is—don't. However unsuccessful or even irrational that exercise may seem to us to be, so long as it does not encroach on objective rights, the rule both of municipal legislation and of international law is to give it free scope, leaving the individual or the nation to learn wisdom by the consequences of its misapplication. This rule is so peculiarly in accordance with the genius of English life, that the duty of teaching it to the rest of mankind might, not inappropriately, be stated as the political mission of the Anglo-Saxon race, and it is a mission to which, on the whole, we have not been unfaithful.

Few internationalists, however, appear to have remarked, and still fewer of them to have reconciled themselves to the fact, that the advance of the ethical tide, which we have here signalised as the progressive element of the law of nations, is sweeping away some of its most cherished traditions.

The doctrine that non-interference is the jural attitude of States, so long as the relations in which they stand to each other continue normal, negatives the two famous doctrines of the balance of powers and of the *status quô*. The practice of the law of nations is often more logical than the theories of its professed exponents, or the rules of which it is supposed to consist. Of this a conspicuous instance is furnished by the tenacity with which these two doctrines[1] are clung to by text-writers and political orators, after they have become practically obsolete, and the confidence with which they continue to state them alongside of ·principles which yield the very opposite results.

But, further: the doctrine of non-interference forbids the exhibition either of exclusive favour or of special disfavour to individual States. As this rule of conduct is generally

[1] As to the doctrine of equality see *ante*, p. 171 *et seq.*·

regarded in its bearing on relations of neutrality, it may be asked whether, in accordance with the doctrine which we have here enunciated, no greater favour must be shown to one nation than to another, even in time of peace. Is a "favoured nation's clause" in a treaty, for example, by which the goods of the favoured nation are admitted on easier terms than those of other nations, an injury to non-favoured nations and a breach of international friendship? If we enter into a treaty of extradition with one nation, must we do the like with every other recognised nation that offers to contract with us? Must there, even in time of peace, be no such thing as the benevolent neutrality which Count Bernstorff expected England to exercise towards Germany during the Franco-German war? As a general rule the answer to this question must be in the affirmative. Non-interference means absolute impartiality. Free trade to all, but favoured trade to none. Not the acceptance only, but the offer of reciprocity. The ties of kindred and neighbourhood, of course, must affect the relations of States as they affect the relations of individuals. A man is not bound to behave to his next-door neighbour as he does to his life-long friend, or to the members of his own family. He is not entitled to do so; he cannot do so; he would not be a good friend or neighbour if he did. From the centre of the family to the circumference of humanity his relations go on diminishing in depth or content as they increase in width or extent; and in the case of States in like manner, by favouring those which lie nearest to us, locally or otherwise, in proportion to their nearness, we do the best that we can for those which, though further off, still participate indirectly in favours which they cannot directly enjoy. With reference to them we are still conforming to Kant's "Law Universal," and our right to do so is recognised by the positive law of nations.[1] But if, by treaty or otherwise, we favour those who are near to us beyond the relation of their nearness, geographical, ethnological, historical, or otherwise, or if we show preference for one of two that stand equidistant from us, then we violate this rule, and are guilty of a wrong which circumstances may magnify into a *casus belli*. The care with which all such occurrences should be watched in time of peace is manifest from the fact that the jealousies of national friends frequently exceed those even of personal friends. The difficulties of maintaining an impartial attitude between friendly powers is by no means confined to the occasions on which one of them goes to war. Nor does it seem true, as is often assumed, that this difficulty is diminished by the increase of communication between nations incident to the progress of material civilisation. Many an indiscreet speech which, in former times, would never have gone beyond the ears to which it was addressed, by the aid of reporting and newspaper and platform commenting, now brings us to the very brink of war. Lord Beaconsfield's speech at the Lord Mayor's banquet in 1876 is an instance in point. But however great may be the discretion of those in authority on their own part, it is impossible in free countries wholly to avert this danger. Governments cannot and must not attempt to gag the press or to silence the Opposition, but they have the remedy of full and explicit explanation in their hands, and the application of that remedy is one of the most important objects of modern discussion and of modern diplomacy.

[1] Heffter, sec. 27, p. 49.

CHAPTER IV.

OF POLITICAL INTERCOURSE—OF LEGATION.

1*st*, *Legation results from recognition.*
We have seen that States are *necessarily* interdependent.[1] They consequently recognise each other as such; and the rights and duties of intercourse resulting from interdependence thus flow from the rights and duties of recognition.

These obvious considerations, as it seems to me, supersede the needless, and, I think, mistaken discussions, into which Grotius and the elder jurists have entered, as to whether the right of legation rests on the law of nature, or on the law of nations. It rests, and must rest, on both. In so far as it is a right resulting from the fact of State existence, it rests on the law of nature; in so far as it is a right resulting from the recognition of this fact, under certain conditions of time, place, and other circumstances, it rests on the interpretation which the positive law of nations puts on the law of nature. I believe that Grotius, and many other jurists along with him, sin against the spirit of their own system when they treat this and other legal relations as arising from a *jus gentium* or a *jus inter gentes*, which they call voluntary. There are no voluntary jural relations; and the rights and duties of legation rest, in my opinion, most clearly on the inalienable

[1] *Ante*, p. 139.

right and inevitable duty which clings to every moral entity, to assert its own existence and to recognise every other moral entity, as it is.

2d, *Legation is measured by recognition.*

The second question commonly discussed by writers on this subject—viz., Who may send or receive ambassadors, and other ministers? has also received, by anticipation, the only general answer of which it admits. Recognition, we have seen, implies separate existence, not potential only but actual. Only a community which already possesses a separate will can be recognised as entitled to express that will through separate diplomatic agents. This limitation cuts off the right of legation not only from all colonies, however important or distant from the parent State, but from all protected States and members of confederations, except to the extent to which they are internationally recognised as retaining it. An international treaty may, for example, reserve to a State which has been annexed by another State the right of sending consuls to protect its trading interests, of carrying a mercantile flag, or the like, as was done in the case of the Ionian Islands when attached to Great Britain; or it may reserve to a State which has become a member of a confederation the right of sending diplomatic agents to watch over such separate political rights as it still possesses, as is at present the case with Bavaria.

But the agents can represent no interests beyond those which the principal possesses; and these interests, in the case of States, are determined, not by the doctrine of legation, but by that of relative recognition.

Again, a community, however numerous or important, which

has not yet separated itself from another community, having in no circumstances a right to recognition as a State, has no claim to legation in its completed form. If we revert to the analogy between the State and the person, we may regard such a State in the light of a child that is still in its mother's womb. It can neither speak nor be spoken to. It can neither send ambassadors nor receive them. On the other hand, from the moment that it gives unequivocal signs of separate life, the State, like the child, can no longer be regarded as wholly denuded of separate rights; for rights originate in life. Here the difficulties of the subject of legation begin; but they are difficulties of fact, not of principle,—and of facts, moreover, which belong to the subject, not of legation, but of recognition. All that need be said in the present connection is, that every right which calls for recognition involves a corresponding right to legation; and that the one right, like the other, is measured by the duty which the entity claiming it is in a condition to perform. Belligerent recognition thus involves belligerent legation—*i.e.*, intercourse with the recognising States, by accredited agents, with reference to all subjects bearing on the conduct of the war. Under the head of recognition, I have already observed [1] that the commissioners of the Southern States of America, subsequently to the recognition of belligerency by the Queen's proclamation, on 13th May 1861, were strictly entitled to be received officially, by the Minister of Foreign Affairs in this country, though they were not, of course, entitled to be received as the ministers of a recognised State. And such is the practice as well as the theory of legation.

[1] *Ante*, p. 144.

Messrs Mason and Slidell were received in Europe as officials under the protection of international law; and it was on this ground that the attempt to treat them as contraband of war was mainly resisted, when they were seized in the Trent. " For the purpose of avoiding the difficulties which might arise from a formal and positive decision of these questions (questions relating to the recognition of new States), diplomatic agents are frequently substituted (for ambassadors), who are clothed with the powers and enjoy the immunities of ministers, though they are not invested with the representative character nor entitled to diplomatic honours."[1]

Another limitation to the rights and duties of legation may arise from the partial character, not of the separate will of the State, but of its rational will. When the autonomous power of a State is limited from this cause, we have seen that its recognition suffers corresponding limitations. Semi-barbarous States like Turkey, China, and Japan, whose municipal law and the judgments of whose courts are not recognised by civilised nations, are in this position. They belong partly to the category of recognised and partly to the category of protected States, and the ambassadors sent to them possess greater rights and responsibilities, whilst the ambassadors whom they send possess smaller rights and responsibilities than the ambassadors whom States in the same stage of civilisation interchange. The English or Russian ambassadors at Constantinople, and the Turkish ambassadors in London

[1] Wheaton, p. 379, Laurence's edition, quoted by Lord J. Russell, *Parliamentary Papers*, 1862; *North America*, No. V. p. 34.

and St Petersburg, are cases in point. And yet, so imperfect is the law of diplomacy as a positive system, that Lord Stratford de Redcliffe and Musurus Pasha were placed by the Treaty of Paris of 1856, technically and formally, on a footing of equality. It is scarcely possible to imagine a more absurd or even ludicrous result of the failure of positive international law to recognise the relative side of the doctrine of recognition.

3*d*, *A public minister represents the sovereignty of the State which sends him, as a whole, and not any separate branch or function of that sovereignty.*

The question whether the power of legation resides in the Crown or in Parliament, and, consequently, whether legation be an executive function or a legislative function of government, is wholly a municipal question. Whatever be the department of government by which his commission is issued, and whatever be the rank which it confers on him, so long as the minister's action is within the limits of his commission, or even within the limits of his office, as these are understood by the common law of nations, he binds his State to the bargain which he makes. It is for their own sakes, therefore, in the first instance, that all civilised countries ought to be, and that most of them are, so careful in training and selecting those who are to represent them abroad.

But the rule that a public minister represents his State as a whole has important international as well as municipal consequences. It is for the common interest that common affairs should be in the hands of men who are not only technically but really representative of the States which employ them; and this can be the case only when the various departments of government in the sending State act in unison. If the executive department be in conflict with the legislative, or feebly or doubtfully supported by it, a minister who possesses the fullest confidence of the former, and obeys it with the greatest fidelity, may be pursuing a line of policy which will be repudiated by the occurrence of a domestic revolution, or even a change of ministry. In States which are ruled despotically, it is always difficult to ascertain whether the executive will and the general will of the community be or be not coincident; and hence the low value which must always belong to them in an international point of view. Where democracy and despotism come together, in the form of government known as Cæsarism, even a plebiscite will not determine the fact, as was proved in the case of France shortly before the fall of the Napoleonic dynasty. But constitutional governments exist for the purpose of securing this coincidence, and its presence at a given time, or in the case of a particular ministry, may always be ascertained more or less perfectly, in proportion to the greater or less perfection of the constitution, by a fresh appeal to the constituencies. Whether such a step might not be internationally insisted upon without violating the rights resulting from recognition, before entering into grave transactions with an executive which is suspected of holding views at variance with those of the community, is a question on which I shall not venture to offer an opinion.

4th, Of the ranking of international agents.

If it be true that the right of legation is measured by the

right of recognition, it necessarily follows that the value assigned to the State determines the rank of its international agents. The principle of relativity, which this proposition embodies, though eagerly repudiated by almost every writer on the subject since the French Revolution, has not failed to vindicate for itself a partial and irregular practical acceptance. So long as no attempt is made to realise the doctrine of the equality of States by means of positive institutions, its claim to adorn the pages of text-writers of democratic proclivities need scarcely be disputed by practical jurists.[1] Whilst vanity and jealousy continue to be human characteristics, it will not want advocates; and comfortable fictions will be invented to hide uncomfortable facts.

But when facts and fictions actually come in contact, the fictions have a bad time of it; and there is no branch of international law in which this occurrence is more inevitable. The very object of legation is to bring separate sovereignties in contact; and it is only at a distance that a giant seems no bigger than a dwarf, even to the dwarf. It is not surprising, then, that the principle of relativity should have forced itself into recognition in the doctrine of legation; and that such rude attempts at the ranking of international agents, as have been made from the days of Pope Julius II. in 1504, down to the Congress of Vienna in 1815, should have been founded upon it.

Only the great Powers possess the highest class of agents, technically called ambassadors, at all; and they only send them to each other. The other classes are employed by

[1] *Ante*, p. 169 *et seq.*

and sent to the smaller States, each State, as a rule, reciprocating in kind. So far the relative principle has asserted itself mainly, no doubt, in consequence of the inability of the minor States to support the costly establishments of the great Powers. This inevitable recognition of inequality, however, is attempted to be neutralised by treating it as merely ceremonial; and when affairs of general importance, in which several Powers, great and small, are interested, come to be decided by their representatives, their mutual jealousies have hitherto necessitated the nominal recognition of a mock equality, which, by preventing the adoption of any system of voting, has given to European congresses, conferences, and other diplomatic gatherings, the character of mere intrigues amongst the greater Powers.[1]

The smaller States, unless their representatives chance to be individuals of unusual ability and force of character, scarcely obtain even a hearing; and no combination for the purpose of delivering them severally from the dictation of the greater States, in whose neighbourhood they are situated, is possible amongst them. The question as to the possibility of substituting any self-adjusting organisation for this rude and often fallacious mode of asserting the supremacy of physical force will be considered hereafter.

The following is the existing diplomatic hierarchy, as fixed by the annex to the Treaty of Vienna, of 9th June 1815, and by the Protocol, No. XIV., of the Conferences of the five Powers at Aix-la-Chapelle, of November 21, 1818.

[1] *Ante*, p. 174 *et seq.*

"REGULATIONS ANNEXED TO THE VIENNA CONGRESS TREATY OF JUNE 9, 1815.

"In order to prevent the inconveniences which have frequently occurred, and which might again arise, from claims of precedence among different diplomatic agents, the Plenipotentiaries of the Powers who signed the Treaty of Paris have agreed on the following Articles, and they think it their duty to invite the Plenipotentiaries of other crowned heads to adopt the same regulation:—

"Article I. Diplomatic Agents are divided into three classes: that of Ambassadors, Legates, or Nuncios; that of Envoys, Ministers, or other persons accredited to Sovereigns; that of Chargés d'Affaires accredited to Ministers for Foreign Affairs.

"II. Ambassadors, Legates, or Nuncios, only, have the representative character.

"III. Diplomatic Agents on an extraordinary mission have not, on that account, any superiority of rank.

"IV. Diplomatic Agents shall take precedence in their respective classes, according to the date of the official notification of their arrival. The present regulation shall not cause any innovation with regard to the representatives of the Pope.

"V. A uniform mode shall be determined in each State for the reception of Diplomatic Agents of each class.

"VI. Relations of consanguinity, or of family alliance between Courts, confer no precedence on their Diplomatic Agents. The same rule also applies to political alliances.

"VII. In Acts or Treaties between several Powers which grant alternate precedence, the order which is to be observed in the signatures shall be decided by lot between the Ministers."

"PROTOCOL OF CONFERENCE OF THE FIVE POWERS, AIX-LA-CHAPELLE, NOVEMBER 21, 1818 (*Ministers Resident*).

"In order to avoid inconvenient discussions which might in future arise upon a point of diplomatic etiquette, which appears not to have been anticipated in the Annex to the Treaty of Vienna, whereby questions of precedence were regulated, it is agreed between the five Courts, that Ministers Resident accredited to them shall form, with respect to their precedence, an intermediate class between Ministers of the Second Class and Chargés d'Affaires."

5th, The right of legation involves the conditions of its exercise.
The general principle that every right carries with it the conditions of its exercise, each of which conditions thus becomes a separate right in itself, finds many illustrations in the case of legation.

Every right and privilege, inseparable from the complete discharge of his duties, thus centres in every political agent, and evokes its corresponding *debitum justitiæ* on the part of the State to which he is sent.

These rights and privileges, being limited to the requirements of the office, vary with the circumstances in which they are claimed. They are dependent both on time and place, and an exhaustive enumeration or definition of them would consequently carry us into historical and local details inconsistent with the objects of this work. Speaking generally, and with reference to the present conditions of European society, they may be thus stated.

(a) *The right of passage through intermediate States.*

The right of legation, being coextensive with the right of recognition, is valid, not only between the State which sends and the State which receives an international agent, but between these States and all other States by which they are recognised. The point is one which has given rise to much discussion;[1] but if we dismiss the false distinction between perfect and imperfect obligations, I do not see that it need cause us any difficulty. In order to vindicate for himself the peculiar rights of exterritoriality, inviolability, and the like, which belong, as we shall presently see, to the international agent, his public character must, of course, be made known to the State through which he claims to pass. If that State be at war with his own State, their mutual recognition being, *eo ipso*, suspended, his right of passage, in so far as it flows from the postive law of nations, is, for the time being, at an end. If he is to pass at all, it must be in virtue of a safe-conduct which derives its validity, not from the doctrine of recognition, but from the limitations which the law of nations, following natural law, imposes on the rights of war. If, on the other hand, the State to which he is destined, be at war with that through which he claims to pass, that State cannot in accordance with the law of nations, withhold its permission, for between it and the neutral State to which he belongs,

[1] Wheaton, p. 418.

recognition is unimpaired. In every case, the State through which he passes is entitled to protect itself against any dangers which he or his suite might occasion it; and this right, of course, will warrant a stricter watch being set over his actions when the place of his destination is a hostile State.

(b) *The right of holding personal intercourse with the representative of sovereignty in the State to which he is sent.*

The State to which the agent is sent determines the arrangements by which it may be most convenient for it to conduct its own business for the time being. Even in monarchies, as a general rule, the minister for foreign affairs acts as the deputy of the sovereign, in his business transactions, with the agents of foreign States. No agent, of whatever rank, is entitled to object to an arrangement of such manifest necessity that even sovereigns, when they meet in person, usually adopt it. On the other hand, the State which sends a message is entitled to some guarantee for the fact that it has really reached the centre of affairs ; and, even in limited monarchies, the only possible guarantee consists in the recognition of the right of the messenger to approach the person of the constitutional sovereign. Every agent, then, whatever his nominal rank may be, who is the sole representative of a recognised State, may claim access to the sovereign to whom he is sent. The distinction in this respect between agents who do, or who do not possess the representative character, who are, or are not entitled to royal honours, and even between those accredited from sovereign to sovereign, and those accredited from minister to minister, are rather distinctions of etiquette than distinctions which seriously affect the conduct of affairs.

Like the ceremonial arrangements for the reception of ambassadors and other international agents, which occupied so much of the attention of the earlier writers, they belong to what would now be regarded as *les enfantillages de légation;* and one cannot but wonder and regret that they should have absorbed so much of the time and energy of such a man as Grotius in his later years. In so far as they are still observed, they are stated in all the ordinary text-books. Their only real significance consists in the partial expression which they give to the principle of relativity.

(c) *The rights of exterritoriality and inviolability.*

Amongst the conditions which experience has indicated as inseparable from the right of legation in the existing conditions of society, and which thus become subsidiary rights in themselves, the most peculiar is the right of the international agent to exemption from the municipal jurisdiction of the State in which he resides, or through which he passes. A sharp distinction is here rightly drawn between his character as an international agent and as an individual foreigner. In the former character, and in it alone, he is held to carry the municipal laws of his own State along with him. An English ambassador, with his family and his suite, whilst abroad in the public service, is domiciled in England, and his house is English ground. Beyond the necessities of self-protection, the State in which he resides can deal with him only diplomatically, even in the event of his transgressing its laws—*i.e.*, it must call on his own State to deal with him, through its agent there resident; and debts incurred, in his public capacity, must be sued for in England.

In his character of a private individual, on the other hand, if that character be deliberately assumed by him, for example, by entering into private speculations, or by purchasing property in the country of his residence, that country deals with him as a private foreigner—the exterritorial gives way to the territorial jurisdiction. It was towards tracing this line that the work of Bynkershoek, *De Foro Legatorum*, offered such important contributions. But even in Bynkershoek's hands it was found scarcely to admit of definition; and its necessity has been evaded by the prohibition which most States impose on their diplomatic and even their higher consular agents to enter into private transactions in the States in which they reside.[1]

The right of inviolability, though often treated of separately, is merely another aspect of the right of exterritoriality, which extends, as we have said, not only to the person of the international agent, but to his house and his suite. It cannot be entered, and they cannot be arrested. Here, as usual, jurists get into confusion about perfect and imperfect obligations. Is inviolability, it is asked, a privilege which the receiving State is entitled to withdraw? The answer, of course, is, that if it is necessary it is covered by the right of recognition; and that if it be necessary is a fact which the positive law of nations for the time being must determine. By withholding or withdrawing the rights of legation, as so defined, the State would unquestionably renounce its own

---

[1] In this respect a distinction is commonly made between those consuls who are sent out by the State (*consules missi*) and residents in the place who are appointed to do consular duties.

claim to recognition by the State claiming them, indeed by the whole family of nations. The State immediately offended would withdraw its agents, or treat their forcible detention as a *casus belli*. The Abyssinian war in 1867-68 would have been equally justifiable had Abyssinia been a recognised European State. Even inability to protect diplomatic agents would have the like effect. There can be no doubt that the murder of the persons attached to the embassies at Athens in 1870 deprived Greece, for the time, of her international title to the character of a State; and this, even on the assumption that the brigands were protected, or even instigated by the Turkish authorities in Albania. Recognition, in the case of Greece, being rather nominal than real, her true position being that of a protected State under the guardianship of the great Powers, all that they thought it necessary to do was to increase their vigilance, by sending additional ships to her waters.

The privileges accorded to ambassadors led to many scandalous abuses in former times, none of them greater than those which arose out of the inviolability of their residences, or what was technically known as the *franchise de l'hôtel*. Whole quarters of populous cities—Rome, Venice, Madrid, and Frankfort, during the assembly for the election of the emperor—were taken possession of by foreign ministers under this guise. By the simple expedient of placing the arms of their sovereigns over the doors of as many houses as they thought proper to hire, and letting them out as asylums for offenders against the laws of the countries in which they dwelt, enormous profits were realised. Even Callières, who was not scrupulous, was shocked at the practice. "It is impossible," he says, " sufficiently to blame foreign ministers who abuse the right of asylum by sheltering criminals and bandits condemned to death for atrocious crimes, and make a shameful traffic of the protection they afford them." [1]

Grotius declares that the "*droit d'asile*" has no warrant in international law, and Bynkershoek limits it to the person, the family, and the suite of the minister. Such, in recent times, has come to be the universal rule, with this additional proviso, that the ambassador is required to furnish to the minister for foreign affairs a list of the names of the persons in favour of whom he claims the privilege. Even as regards his own domestics, it is scarcely consistent with modern usage for the minister to exercise magisterial functions; and in criminal cases, he either sends the delinquents for trial to their own country, or delivers them to the local tribunals. One of the privileges of the *hôtel*, however, is still maintained, —that, viz., of holding religious worship within its precincts, in accordance with the national faith of the ambassador; and this not only for the benefit of his household, but for that of his other countrymen resident in the place. The use of external rites—such as processions, bells, and the like—for obvious reasons, is generally interdicted. Marriages which take place in the chapels of our embassies, are held, in English law, to have taken place in England, and to be valid, independently of the local law; but the point of their international validity is one on which grave doubts exist, both in this country and in America, and which has been decided in the negative in France.[2]

[1] P. 161.   [2] Fraser, *Husband and Wife*, vol. ii. pp. 1312 and 1520.

(d) *Exterritoriality of ships.*

Difficulties analogous to those which arose in former times out of the privileges conceded to the residences of international agents arise in our own day out of the privileges conceded to ships. The question is one of special interest to this country, in consequence of the exceptional extent to which our intercourse with the rest of the world is necessarily carried on by sea, and it may therefore be not inappropriate that I should here interpolate a section on the subject.

A State, even physically considered, does not consist exclusively of earth and stone. A ship is a portion of it, whilst within its waters, just as much as a house, and just as obviously as a floating jetty, or a bridge of boats. If the decks of our whole shipping were measured, it would be found that many acres of England are continually afloat; and of the whole area of England, including the towns, these acres are unquestionably the most valuable, and probably the most populous. The mere fact of their being afloat, so long as they float either on English waters or on the high seas, which are the common property of all nations, can obviously have no effect on their jural character. An English ship and its crew, in such circumstances, is as much under the local jurisdiction of England as if it were lying in a London dock. If there are foreigners on board of it, they are foreigners in England. They and their goods are subject to English law, or to the law of nations, as the law of England accepts and interprets it. So far there is no difficulty; and the principle on which the immunity of the neutral flag rests is as unassailable as that which guarantees the immunity of England.

EXTERRITORIALITY OF SHIPS. 253

But what is the jural position of the ship, when she gets into foreign waters, or enters a foreign port? Here the theory of the law of nations still seems clear,[1] though the close contact into which two systems of municipal law, possibly inconsistent, are brought, introduces difficulties as to its realisation. The rights and duties arising out of the necessary interdependence of States carry with them the conditions of their exercise, and these conditions have been found by experience to involve the recognition of the exterritoriality of ships, and their consequent exemption from foreign jurisdiction. Within her own territory—*i.e.*, on board—the ship and her crew are still under the municipal law of England; and in their relations to each other with reference to wages and the like, that law will be administered to them by the English consul at the port, in the first instance, or, failing him, by the local judge, in the exercise of what is called "concurrent jurisdiction."

But these relations are the accidents, not the objects of the voyage. The intercourse for which the ship has come carries her crew on shore; and the moment that a sailor goes on land himself, or rolls a cask on land, the distinction between him

[1] Mr Field says that "ships are no longer regarded as part of the territory of a nation" (*Code*, p. 160, n. 4), but on what ground he accepts the change of opinion or expression is not obvious, seeing that he holds the jurisdiction of the nation over them to be "exclusive, except in the case of a private ship within the limits of another nation, in which case it is concurrent with that of the other nation" (p. 159, § 309), "the territorial jurisdiction taking precedence only in the case of conflict" (§ 311, p. 161); and as regards criminal jurisdiction, under the condition that "no punishment shall be inflicted on board of the private ships of one nation, within the territorial jurisdiction of another, greater than is allowed by the law of the latter, for the like offence committed on board of domestic ships" (§ 648, pp. 435, 436).

and any other foreigner of his nation is at an end. If his ship is a public one, the case is different; and so long as he acts in his public capacity, or does only what his presence in that capacity necessitates, or reasonably implies, the inviolability which covers international agents will cover him; but, apart from exemptions resulting from special treaties, the converse is the case as regards persons attached to foreign private ships. Having landed for their own purposes, they are under the territorial law.

But if the Englishmen on board becomes a foreigner by stepping on shore, does the foreigner on shore become an Englishman by stepping on board? Does the obligation to accept or the right to claim foreign law on shore involve the right to claim or the obligation to accept English law on board? Here are two separate municipal jurisdictions actually touching each other, or connected by a plank. Are these jurisdictions mutually exclusive? Does the one end where the other begins, or do they overlap and mutually limit each other, thus creating as it were a neutral territory governed by a law which may differ from both? It is this question, as is well known, which has given rise to so much difficulty with reference to the treatment of slaves; and as it is an open question, it is well that we should consider it on principle.

We have seen that the independence of the State is not absolute, but that, on the contrary, it is limited in its own nature by the reciprocal obligations which are inseparable from its exercise. Amongst these obligations, that of recognising and enforcing the private rights of foreigners holds a prominent place. The State, as a condition of its claim to be recognised as such, undertakes, when necessary for the ends of justice, the duty of ascertaining and enforcing the rights of the citizens of other States, whose separate existence it recognises. But the independent existence of a part of a State cannot exceed the independent existence of the State as a whole. If the ship, then, be a part of the State, its right to the recognition of its existence, as separate from other States, must be conditioned by its acceptance of this duty. It must recognise and vindicate the rights of foreigners within the limits of its jurisdiction. A foreign contract, if valid in England, is consequently valid in a British ship, whether on the high seas or within foreign waters; and failure to enforce it, or to permit its enforcement, if necessary, by the local authorities, is a violation of the law of nations. In like manner, a crime committed on a foreigner on board of it must be punished, or jurisdiction of the local authority must be invoked.

But the validity of the contract in itself, and the criminal character of the act, are here assumed; and the rule that contracts valid in one country are valid in another, or that crimes in one State are crimes in another, is not, as we have seen, without exceptions. The recognising State does not wholly forego its right of judgment, even on the production of the decree of a foreign court of justice, the general validity of whose decrees it recognises. If the contract or the crime thus authenticated be at variance with the conceptions of morality, or of natural law entertained by the recognising

State, or if it be inconsistent with its public policy as a nation, the decree will not be enforced. Gaming debts, polygamous marriages, and the like, though voluntarily entered into by both parties, and valid in a foreign State, are invalid in England. And what is true of immoral engagements, voluntarily entered into, must be still more true of those which are involuntary on one side. The law of England, in refusing to enforce the relation of slavery, in accordance with her conceptions of natural law, thus acts in accordance with the law of nations, which is natural law in given relations, as she conceives it. But if a British ship be only a part of England elsewhere, what is true of the whole must, in this case, be true of the part; and there is no principle of the law of nations which overrides English conceptions of morality on board of her ships more than anywhere else in England.

So much for the civil aspect of the question. Nor is the case less clear if, in place of regarding escape from slavery as a violation of contract, it be viewed as the commission of a crime. The duty of surrendering acknowledged criminals, we shall see hereafter, is binding by the common law of nations apart from the existence of treaty obligations altogether. But escape from slavery is not a crime, as we understand criminal law, any more than it is a breach of contract, as we understand civil law; and it is our understanding of the one law, as of the other, and not the understanding of our neighbours, that determines its international character *for us*. Here the case of the slave is on all-fours with that of the political offender. Both alike are entitled to the benefit of our indulgent, happily now not exceptionally indulgent, law.

So long as the exterritoriality of British ships is maintained, therefore, no claim logically resulting from the law of nations can, as I conceive, be urged for the surrender of fugitive slaves. By receiving them and protecting them in our ships, we are entering on no new crusade against slavery; we are simply acting, within our own borders, on the view of it which we have long proclaimed to the world. We are acting at sea as we have long acted on land. But if, on the other hand, the exterritoriality of our ships, whether public or private, be abandoned — as Mr Wheaton was originally inclined to do, and as Mr Field seems still inclined to do, in the case of private[1] ships—then the practice becomes utterly indefensible. In that case, a ship is under foreign jurisdiction; and the retention of the slave is a plain violation of the municipal law of a foreign State — a breach of recognition, and, apart from treaty, a legitimate *casus belli*.

In saying this, I express no opinion on slavery. I by no means assert, either that our view of its character is correct, or that this is the best means of vindicating it. Slavery, for the inferior races of mankind, may be one of the processes of gradual development which nature demands; and we may be hindering their progress in place of advancing it, and defeating our own ultimate object, by abandoning slavery, and urging others to abandon it. Or, being right in our conception of the character of slavery, we may be mistaken in the means

[1] P. 191.

by which we seek its abolition. It might possibly be wiser, and it certainly would be more dignified, openly to proclaim war against it, than thus to oppose it by half-acknowledged means, which give to slave-holding Powers a grievance of which they may justly complain. Finally, on the principle that subjective are as valid as objective rights, no right which can exist in the slave to the protection of English law can bind Englishmen to forego the rights of self-preservation. The first duty of the captain of a ship, whether public or private, is to see to its safety, its efficient working, and the health of its crew. If any of these objects would be endangered by permitting his ship to become a refuge for fugitive slaves, filthy, idle, immoral, and diseased as the poor wretches must necessarily be, his duty is simply to clear his decks of them, without reference to where they are to go. In such circumstances, talk about "sending them back to slavery" degenerates into claptrap, unworthy of jurists, and very unlikely to influence the conduct of sailors. It was not the captains of our ships who instituted slavery, and they must not seek to abolish it by carrying "deck cargoes," which will endanger the lives of their crews.

My slave circular would, consequently, be a very brief one. I would tell the captains, both of H.M.'s ships and of trading vessels, that they were not bound to surrender slaves on the requisition of the slave-holding State: that if they could employ them in the ship, or even accommodate them, they might do so; and if the danger of their being treated with inhumanity at home was great, they ought to do so; but that they were under no obligation, and had no right, to retain them or even to receive them, to the prejudice of the interests of the ship, its crew, or its owners.

The ultimate question thus resolves itself, as usual, into a question of fact, and of that question the captain of the vessel must, as it seems to me, be the sole and practically the irresponsible judge. And this is precisely the position in which, after so much irrelevant talking and writing, the celebrated Slave Circular of 1876 has left him.

"Instructions respecting reception of fugitive slaves on board her Majesty's ships:—

"To all commanders-in-chief, captains, commanders, and commanding officers of her Majesty's ships and vessels, the following instructions are to be considered as superseding all previous instructions as to the receipt of fugitive slaves:—

"1. In any case in which you have received a fugitive slave into your ship, and taken him under the protection of the British flag, whether within or beyond the territorial waters of any State, you will not admit or entertain any demand made upon you for the surrender on the ground of slavery.

"2. It is not intended, nor is it possible, to lay down any precise or general rule as to the cases in which you ought to receive a fugitive slave on board your ship. You are to be guided as to this by questions of humanity, and these considerations must have full effect given to them whether your ship is on the high seas or within the territorial waters of a State in which slavery exists; but in the latter case you ought at the same time to avoid conduct which may appear to be in breach of international comity and good faith.

"3. If any person within territorial waters claims your protection on the ground that he is kept in slavery contrary to treaties with Great Britain, you should receive him until the truth of his statement is examined into. This examination should be made, if possible, after communication with the nearest British consular authority, and you should be guided in your subsequent proceedings by the result.

"4. A special report is to be made of every case of a fugitive slave received on board your ship."

With the exception of the unmeaning flourish about what "may appear [to whom?] to be in breach of international comity and good faith," these instructions seem to me to be not only reasonable but inevitable.

(*e*) *Exterritoriality of foreign armies.*

On grounds analogous to those on which it is conceded to the crews of public ships on shore, exterritoriality is granted to a foreign army passing through, or stationed within the territory of a friendly State, or sailing over its waters.[1] And this rule would seem to apply to fugitives interned in a neutral State, who, as prisoners of war, are present in their public, not their private capacity.

CHAPTER V.

OF POLITICAL INTERCOURSE—*continued.*

Of the negotiation and ratification of treaties.[2]

A treaty is the definition, by two or more separate States, of a specific jural relation actually subsisting between or

---

[1] Wheaton, p. 191.

[2] Of treaties as sources of international law we have already spoken, p. 49 *et seq.*

among them, which definition they engage to accept and enforce as positive law.

I have no hesitation in preferring some such definition of treaties as this to those in which they are spoken of as founding purely conventional laws (*Eigentliches vertragsrecht* [1]), and creating and terminating rights. There is no such thing as a purely conventional law; [2] and a treaty can no more create a right than it can create a man. Rights, moreover, can be terminated in law only when they are terminated in fact; and a treaty for their termination becomes possible, only when the relation of which they were the expression has, by human activity or otherwise, been changed for a new relation, which the treaty defines. Whether as a means of making a right or of unmaking it, the treaty in itself is mere *brutum fulmen*. Nor does this inaccuracy of language, and the confusion of thought which it reveals, affect the science of international law alone. It has largely influenced diplomatic action, and, as we have seen, when examining treaties as sources of international law, its practical effects have been of the most disastrous kind.

As treaties profess to be contracts, the rules for their negotiation, seen from a merely jural point of view, do not differ from those for the constitution of valid contracts in any other department of jurisprudence. As the law of contract forms a very important branch of study in all municipal systems, the fragmentary manner in which it is presented in many treatises on international law seems scarcely warranted by the occasion. Its importance for the diplomatist indicates very clearly, how-

---

[1] Bluntschli, § 402.   [2] *Code*, p. 79.

ever, the wisdom of the arrangement by which a complete course of legal study is imposed on those who enter the diplomatic service of all civilised countries, except England.

But, without entering into the general law of contract, it is necessary that we should indicate certain conditions which affect the constitution of contracts between separate political communities in an exceptional manner.

We have seen that recognition implies the possession by the recognised State not only of rational will, but of the means of expressing such will. Every State, whatever be the form of its internal organisation, must thus present to the external world an exponent of its will whose exposition may be safely accepted by other States. But rational will, as we have likewise seen, converts itself into power; and as it is in this aspect that it becomes apparent for the most part to the external world, it is through the executive factor of government, not the legislative, that external relations are formally defined and adjusted, and that treaties are concluded. But the executive, even when it centres in a single individual, can seldom speak directly. In general it must speak by deputy; and the link which binds the deputy to the deputing power thus becomes a matter of great practical importance. It is not surprising, therefore, that considerable difference of opinion should exist amongst writers on international law as to the extent to which a treaty, negotiated by a plenipotentiary duly accredited, binds the sovereign for whom he acts, without subsequent ratification. Without troubling you with the controversy, I shall endeavour to place its results before you.[1]

[1] Wheaton, p. 443.

The acts of public ministers, even when armed with "full powers," have, from very early times, been considered still to be subject to ratification. Barbeyrac gives an example of a treaty between Justinian and Corroes, King of Persia, which was formally ratified by the two sovereigns, and there are many other early instances; whilst the modern understanding is thus stated by Sir Robert Adair: "A plenipotentiary, to obtain credit with a State on an equality with his master, must be invested with powers to do, and agree to, all that could be done and agreed to by his master himself, even to alienating the best part of his territories. But the exercise of these vast powers, *always under the understood control of non-ratification*, is regulated by his instructions."[1] In order that there may be no mistake on this point, it is stated by Vattel that, even in his day, it was customary for princes expressly to reserve to themselves the power of ratification, or rather of *non*-ratification, in the treaty itself. Still, even where this is done in the most formal manner, it is plain that the doctrine of ratification must be very strictly guarded, otherwise "full powers" would become a meaningless expression, and negotiation would be impossible. Vattel, consequently, asserts that before a sovereign can refuse to ratify "he must have strong and solid reasons, and in particular, he *must show that his minister has deviated from his instructions.*" To this latter statement, if intended to imply that deviation from instructions was a necessary ingredient in "the strong and solid reasons," and that such deviation alone would justify non-ratification, Mr Wheaton very justly demurs; and he has

[1] *Ib.*, p. 447.

embodied the reasons which appear to him valid in the following propositions.

" 1. Treaties may be avoided, even subsequent to ratification, upon the ground of the impossibility, physical or moral, of fulfilling their stipulations. Physical impossibility is where the party making the stipulation is disabled from fulfilling it for want of the necessary physical means depending on himself. Moral impossibility is where the execution of the engagement would injuriously affect the rights of third parties."

As this proposition, both in its physical and moral aspects, raises questions of fact on which the two contracting parties are very unlikely to agree, it opens doors of escape from the treaty to both parties, which both or either may construe into a *casus belli.*

" 2. Upon the ground of mutual error in the parties respecting a matter of fact, which, had it been known in its true circumstances, would have prevented the conclusion of the treaty."

Mutual admission of mutual error, where the error must tell in favour of one party only, will always, I fear, be a rare occurrence. The St Juan affair of 1872-73 may be instructively studied as bearing on this subject.

" 3. In the case of a change of circumstances on which the validity of the treaty is made to depend, either by express stipulation, or by the nature of the treaty itself."

As circumstances *always* change, there is no treaty which, after the lapse of a few years, is not voidable on this ground, whether ratified or not.

Mr Wheaton himself, indeed, has remarked that every one of these occurrences would void a treaty even after ratification; and the same, I think, may be said of every other conceivable fact which would really justify non-ratification. It is for this reason, as we have seen already,[1] that in the absence of an international legislature, by which these provisions can be brought into harmony with existing conditions, treaties fall short of the character of legislative enactments, or even of successful contracts. Practically, then, the reservation of the right of subsequent ratification is of less importance than it at first appears; and in present circumstances the formal conclusion of a treaty may be safely left in the hands of the plenipotentiary.

But whilst the value of his action, in giving formal validity to a treaty, by appending his signature to it, has increased, the influence of the plenipotentiary in determining its character has greatly diminished since Mr Wheaton wrote. The increased rapidity of communication in our day, and above all, the invention of the telegraph, by enabling the home government to superintend the proceedings of foreign ministers with a minuteness which was impossible in former times, has shifted both the powers and responsibilities of diplomacy, in no small measure, from the shoulders of the ambassador to the shoulders of the minister for foreign affairs. But, though the changes thus effected in diplomatic intercourse must more and more deprive States of the apology which they once possessed for not ratifying their treaties, examples of ratification being withheld on the ground of

[1] *Ante*, p. 49 *et seq.*

res noviter veniens, are not awanting in recent times. Sir Travers Twiss has given three, of which the earliest is in 1841.[1]

The great difficulty with reference to the negotiation of treaties in our own day arises from the risk of conflict, not between the diplomatic and the executive factor of government, the former, where they are not identical,—as in the case of treaties negotiated by sovereigns or their prime ministers in person,—being now the mere mouthpiece of the latter, but between the executive and legislative factors. That the ambassador expresses the will of the executive which he represents, is no longer questionable; but whether or not the executive at a given time represents the national will, may be questioned, and is questioned, indeed, more and more.

In 1873 (March 3), in consequence of the universal dissatisfaction felt with the Treaty of Washington, and the results of the Geneva Arbitration, Lord Stratheden, very inconsistently with the attitude which he assumed in the discussions relating to the Eastern question, moved, in the House of Lords, that "an humble address be presented to her Majesty, praying that all treaties or conventions by which disputed questions between Great Britain and a foreign Power are referred to arbitration, may be laid upon the table of both Houses of Parliament six weeks before they are definitely ratified." This was resisted by the Government (Earl Granville Foreign Secretary, and Lord Selborne (Roundell Palmer) Chancellor, on the ground that it would hamper the executive to so great an extent as to

[1] Vol. i. p. 276.

render the negotiation of treaties almost impossible. Lord Granville said : " There could be no doubt that the discussions which had taken place while the fate of the Treaty of Washington was as yet uncertain had a most unfortunate effect. They probably suggested not only the ' Indirect Claims,' but many arguments which were used against us at Geneva with great effect, and especially a far more elastic construction of the 'three rules,' than that of which they were naturally susceptible." The Lord Chancellor, speaking from his own experience, as the counsel who conducted the English case at Geneva, confirmed the remark. " The inconvenience of such discussions as had taken place in Parliament," he said, " was very sensibly felt at Geneva ; " and he then proceeded to explain the proper form of parliamentary action. " It had been said that the honour of the Crown was so far pledged to the Treaty of Washington in the course of its negotiations that it was impossible to refuse to ratify it. That, however, he denied; although, no doubt, the honour of the Administration was so far committed that they must have retired from office if an address praying her Majesty to refuse ratification had been carried." From a constitutional point of view, the answer was, no doubt, sufficient. But if Parliament were to proceed on the assumption that the honour of the nation, when repudiating the action of the executive, was saved by simply turning an Administration out of office, I suspect the international effect would be pretty much the same as if Parliament were to limit the powers of the executive constitutionally, as Lord Stratheden suggested. Indeed, as a less honest proceeding, it would, I fear, even more decidedly, sacrifice the confidence of foreign States. The executive may be controlled, but it must not be repudiated. Such was the outcome of the debate, and of a similar discussion which took place on the 13th of June 1878, when Mr Ryland called attention to the treaties of 1856 and 1871. Many incidental remarks of importance on the relation between Parliament and the agents of the executive will also be found in the discussion on Mr Richard's motion, on 29th April 1881, though the motion itself had reference rather to the position of the governors of colonies, and other officers exercising executive functions abroad, than to our diplomatic representatives. Mr Gladstone's chief defence of the existing arrangement rested on the allegation that public, and even parliamentary, sentiment in this country, is more impulsive than that of the executive, or even of its responsible agents; and that the rashest acts, however strongly they may have been reprobated afterwards, were generally popular at the time. It is in counteracting this tendency to the indulgence of national pride and passion, rather than in controlling the executive on particular occasions, that the chief value, not only of Parliament, but of the Peace Society, the Anti-aggression League, and similar philanthropic associations, consists. "What you really want," said Mr Gladstone, on this latter occasion, "is not merely the improvement of the machinery by which the central authority controls its extraneous agents, it is the improvement of the central authority itself,—the formation of just habits of thought; it is that we should be more modest and less arrogant; it is that we should uniformly regard every other State, and every other people, as standing on the same level of right as ourselves. It is that, in the prosecution of our interest, we shall not be so carried away by zeal as to allow it to make us forgetful of the equal claims and the equal rights of others. That is a very grave question indeed, and one upon which I am bound to say I believe the central authority is quite as much in need of self discipline and self-restraint as its extraneous agents."

CHAPTER VI.

OF POLITICAL INTERCOURSE—*continued*.

The literature of legation.

The considerations on which I have dwelt in the preceding chapters indicate very plainly the character of the changes which more advanced conceptions of international relations must effect, and, to some extent, have already effected both in the functions of diplomatic agents, and in the qualifications requisite for their discharge. When mutual confidence is substituted for mutual suspicion, speech, in the mouth of a foreign minister, loses its value as an instrument for the concealment of thought. The ambassador's duty is no longer "to lie for his country," but to tell the truth for her better than she can tell it for herself, and to remove any misapprehensions which may have arisen with reference to her opinions or intentions. If honesty be the best policy, the perfect ambassador must be an ideally honest man. The slightest suspicion of double-dealing which attaches to him will cling to his country, and the path of honest negotiation, for her, will be beset with thorns. One single discovery will breed a thousand suspicions; and as the deepest secret is not unfathomable, the only safety for the diplomatist consists in having no secrets to fathom. International politics is no limbo from which the light of morality is excluded; and the ethical commonplaces which apply to the intercourse of individuals apply to the intercourse of States.

But such was not the conception which, in former times, was attached either to the functions or the qualifications of a political agent, or which was placed before him in the books that were written for his instruction. His calling, on the contrary, was regarded as one which could be exercised only in the twilight of imperfect obligations, and amid the *demi-monde* of intriguers and deceivers. He himself was to be honest only for the sake of appearances, and only up to the point at which dishonesty might better serve the interests of his own country. That these interests were always in ultimate conflict with those of the State in which he resided was the hypothesis which justified his mission, and his duty was to watch for the turn of affairs at which this conflict declared itself in their actual relations. When this occurred, whilst still professing neutrality, he became a secret belligerent. His personal was superseded by his official conscience, and lying and cheating took the rank of stratagems of war. It cannot, I fear, be maintained that the mutual jealousies which gave rise to this conception of the ambassador and his functions, have entirely disappeared from international politics;[1] but the general advance in international morality has been sufficient to deprive the old literature of legation of much of its importance; and in a work which aims at presenting the positive law of nations as it logically results from the relations of separate States as they really exist, rather than as they are supposed to exist, a very slight sketch of it will suffice.

Grotius describes the diplomatic intercourse of the nations of antiquity, from the Jews to the Romans; and Barbeyrac, as usual, has largely supplemented his learning. But the classical nations have left us no express treatise on the subject; nor has even the title of any work come down to us which would lead us to suppose that any such ever was composed. Like the other doctrines of the law of nations, the doctrine of legation rests on the doctrine of recognition; and as the Romans recognised no State but their own, there is no trace of any literature of legation in the Roman jurists. The passages relating to the *legatus* and his functions, which occur in the *Digest* and the *Code*, have reference, as might naturally be supposed, to the duties of delegates sent to represent the interests of a city or province of the empire at Rome, and not of a separate or independent State.[2]

---

[1] See Blue-books with reference to the relations between this country and Russia during the Russo-Turkish and Afghan wars, and Russian correspondence found at Cabul—*Central Asia*, No. 1, 1881.

[2] I do not think the single passage quoted by Mr Wheaton in his history, p. 237, is really an exception to this remark. "Si quis *legatum hostium* pulsasset, contra jus gentium id commissum esse existimatur: quia sancti habentur legati" (*Dig.*, lib. 1. tit. vii., De Legationibus, leg. ult.) The *legatus*, in this case, corresponds, as it seems to me, not to an ambassador, but to an officer bearing a flag of truce. His credentials proceed from the general commanding the army of the

But the increased importance which the subject received, on the breaking up of the Roman Empire, immediately attracted the attention of the scholastic jurisconsults, several of whom treated it incidentally; and when the separate States of Europe were ultimately established, it became a favourite subject of literary treatment by jurists and politicians of every class. Hotman,[1] Besold, and others, furnish lists of these writers; but I shall mention only a few of the most conspicuous.

The first writer who published a separate treatise on the subject seems to have been Conrad Brunus, a German civilian and Roman Catholic, whose work, *De Legationibus*, appeared at Mainz in 1548, exactly one hundred years before the Peace of Westphalia.[2] The work can scarcely have attained much celebrity, for it is nowhere mentioned by Grotius, and neither Barbeyrac nor Hallam seems to have been acquainted with it; but I agree with Mr Wheaton in regarding it as by no means destitute of merit; and the objection which he makes to it—that its doctrines are buried under a load of needless quotations from civilians, canonists, theologians, fathers of the Church, poets, philosophers, and historians—is an objection which he might have made to any other work of the period. Even as

State which he serves, and he represents the State only in its belligerent, not in its general character, which is essential to the conception of an ambassador, or other international minister. The section of the Commonplace-Book of the Emperor Constantine VII. (Porphyrogenitus), which bears the title, Περὶ Πρεσβειῶν (*De Legationibus*), is a mere collection of historical extracts, chiefly from Priscus.

[1] Not Hottoman, the author of the famous *Antitribonianus*,—v. Hallam, vol. ii. p. 74.

[2] *De legationibus libri quinque: cunctis in republica versantibus, aut quolibet magistratu fungentibus* perutiles, *et* lectu jucundi. It is printed along with two other treatises,—the one on the use of ceremonies, the other on that of images in the church.

LITERATURE OF LEGATION. 273

regards the technical part of the subject, Mr Wheaton admits that Brunus distinguished accurately between the full powers, the letters of credence, and the instructions of a public minister; and in other directions he entered, not without intelligence, into the wider questions relating to peace and war, which Grotius and the other publicists afterwards discussed. The arrangement of his subject, too, is very much that which subsequent writers on legation adopted;[1] and my own impression is that, as in the case of Suarez and others, his Protestant successors were more indebted to him than they were willing to acknowledge.

The next work is the far better known treatise, *De Legationibus*, published in 1585, by Alberico Gentile, the Italian Protestant refugee, who for some time occupied the chair of Civil Law at Oxford, and to whom Grotius expresses his obligations. In virtue of his subsequent work, *De Jure Belli*, the first portion of which appeared in 1588, Gentile is entitled, in the opinion of some, to contest with Grotius himself the honour of being regarded as the father of international law; and Barbeyrac considers him as the first writer on the subject of legation whose name deserves to be mentioned. His work, apart from its direct claims to notice, is interesting from two

---

[1] The following are the titles of his books :—

1. *De personis eorum qui mittunt Legatos, deque mandatis et rebus Legationum.*

2. *De personis eorum qui Legati mittuntur : de scientia item et virtutibus Legatorum.*

3. *De officiis Legatorum.*

4. *Privilegiis et immunitatibus Legatorum.*

5. *De personis corum ad quos mittuntur Legati, et de officio corum in suscipiendis dimittendis que Legationibus.*

S

adventitious circumstances: the first, is its dedication to Sir Philip Sidney; the second, that it contains one of the earliest defences of Machiavelli from the charge of being a teacher of tyrants—a defence, the soundness of which is still a subject of controversy.

But it is not to these accidents, or to the party to which he belonged alone, that Gentile's work was entitled for the hold upon public attention which it obtained. There are few branches of the important subject of legation on which he has not shed the light of thought and learning which must have been new to his contemporaries, in this country at all events; and till Bynkershoek appeared, he was unquestionably the leading authority.[1]

With the next set of writers whom Bynkershoek enumerates, I have not made, and I confess do not feel tempted to make, acquaintance. There was Charles Pasqual, whose work,

---

[1] Professor Holland, as the successor of Gentile at Oxford, with filial piety has revived his fame in England, and from similar motives he has been ably seconded by the Italians. Ample amends have thus been made to him for the neglect into which he had fallen. The impression which he leaves upon us is that of a careful and industrious rather than a gifted man. In the interesting inaugural lecture which he devoted to him, Professor Holland tells the following characteristic story. Mathew, the father, with his two sons, Albericus and Scipio, spent some time in Carniola, as a temporary resting-place in their flight from the persecution to which, as Protestants, they had been subjected in their native Perugia. "It may have been at this time that, while the three were sitting one winter evening round the fire, the father said to his two sons, 'Take each of you a piece of coal. I will give you a sentence in prose, and do you turn it into verse, which you can write with the coal on the stove.' While Scipio expressed the idea in three lines, Albericus nearly covered the stove with poetry. The father encouraged Scipio to go on writing verses, but made Albericus promise to give up the practice" (pp. 9, 10). Perhaps this occurrence may have had something to do with the bitter hatred which, in after-life, Albericus felt for the "Humanists."

entitled *Legatus*, appeared at Rouen in 1598, and was afterwards augmented and republished by the author at Paris in 1613; Hermann Kirchner, author of the *Legatus ejusque jura, dignitas et officium*, published in 1603, and which ran through several editions; Fredericus de Marselaer, whose *Legatus* first appeared at Antwerp in 1618,—and others. To the same class of books may be referred Abraham de Wicquefort's *Mémoire touchant les ambassadeurs*, and *L'ambassadeur et ses fonctions*, still well-known works, and which Barbeyrac tells us, in his time, were the best known and the most esteemed and sought after.

Amongst the number, though not of separate, certainly of important works, is the chapter on the subject in Grotius, which, with Barbeyrac's notes, ought to be read in connection with the still more important work of Bynkershoek, who has also had the advantage of having Barbeyrac as his translator and commentator. Bynkershoek's work, though treating ostensibly only of a particular question—viz., the *forum competens legatorum*, or tribunal to which ambassadors are amenable, is the best treatise that I know on the general subject. In the French dress which Barbeyrac bestowed on it, and in which I recommend it, though published separately, it appeared also as a supplement to the longer though by no means equally satisfactory work of Wicquefort. It is written with great clearness by a man of unquestionable ability, and, though it is short in comparison with most works on the subject, it touches on almost everything that one cares to know or to discuss.

We owe Bynkershoek's work to an accident, and it bears

traces of haste; but its value is enhanced by the fact that it proceeds from a man whom nothing but a pressing State occasion could have called from his important judicial duties to the scientific elucidation of a general subject.

Bynkershoek was President of the Court of Holland and Friesland; and he tells us that he writes, *festinante calamo et non aliter quam solent occupatissimi*. The occasion which called Bynkershoek from the bench to wield the pen in illustration of the duties and privileges of ambassadors was curious. The envoy of the Duke of Holstein to the States-General had got into debt, in consequence of his connection with the South Sea Company. His creditors applied to the Court of Holland, which arrested the effects of the minister, in so far as they were not necessary for his personal use, and cited him to appear before them. The envoy complained of this act to the States-General, as an infraction of the law of nations in his person. The Court of Holland justified its proceedings in a letter which it addressed to the States; but the affair made a great noise, and our author was often questioned regarding it in private conversation. As the matter scarcely admitted of being fully explained otherwise, he was led to promise that he would publish his sentiments regarding it—a promise which he fulfilled shortly afterwards.

So much for the earlier and more recondite literature of the subject. To go further in this direction would be simply to furnish a list of modern text-writers on international law, all of whom have treated it with more or less completeness.[1]

---

[1] A good selection of works and documents relating to international law, including collections of treaties, will be found in Appendix I. of the fifth edition

Amongst these Wheaton stands conspicuous, on the ground not only of his great ability, but of his having so long discharged the functions of an ambassador himself.

But there is another class of books which treat of the art of negotiation, and of the qualities requisite for a good negotiator from a personal and social rather than a scientific point of view; and as there are few departments of professional literature in which more amusing reading is to be found, I am unwilling to pass them over in silence. On the grounds which I have already indicated, much that is disparaging might be said of their absolute value, because, almost invariably, they proceed on the assumption that the interests of States necessarily conflict, and that an attitude of constant suspicion alone is fitting for a negotiator. But, apart from these and other objections which might be taken to the spirit in which they are written, they contain many shrewd remarks, which are applicable not only to all classes of public agents, but which may be read with profit by all persons who are intrusted with the management of transactions of which the success depends on a knowledge of human feelings, interests, prejudices, and passions. As it is in the direction of want of sympathy rather than of want of honesty that our countrymen usually fall short of their foreign colleagues, these antiquated dissertations on the *savoir faire* seem peculiarly fitted to convey instruction to English diplomatists.

of Woolsey's *Introduction to the Study of International Law*. For information on the curious art of cryptography, or secret writing, to which the necessity of conveying intelligence by telegraph without its being understood by the officials, gives importance even in our own time, a very careful article in Chambers's *Encyclopædia* may be consulted.

These works may be divided into two classes: those which treat of the art of negotiation and the character of the negotiator expressly; and those, often not less important, which touch on these subjects only incidentally. Under the former class are comprehended *Le parfait Ambassadeur*, which was originally published in Spanish by Don Antonio de Vera, long the Spanish ambassador at Venice, and was subsequently translated into all the languages of Europe; *L'ambassadeur et ses fonctions* of Wicquefort; the *Principes des Négociations* of the Abbé Mably; and the works of Pecquet and Callières. To the latter class belong the Despatches of the Cardinal d'Ossat, the *Political Testament* of Richelieu, many portions of Machiavelli's works, the Letters of Grotius and Mazarin, the Negotiations of the President Jeannin, the Memoirs of Walsingham, Bellièvre, Sillery, and the like. More formal works are those of M. Flassan, *L'histoire de la diplomatie Française*, and the Comte de Ségur's compilation from the papers of Favier, one of the principal secret agents of Louis XV., entitled *Politique de tous les Cabinets de l'Europe, pendant les règnes de Louis XV. et de Louis XVI.;* and one of the very best and most useful for our purpose, notwithstanding its more popular aspect, the *Embassies and Foreign Courts* of the Roving Englishman.

M. de Callières's *Manière de négocier avec les Souverains*, is, on the whole, that which I should be disposed to select as the best example of this class of books. True, it is based on so low an estimate of the morality of those with whom the diplomatist must come in contact, that, *mutatis mutandis*, it might almost serve for a detective's manual.

Still it is a charming book, as racy, and almost as shrewd, as Aristotle's *Ethics* and Bacon's *Essays*. Nothing can be more inimitable than the manner in which Callières contrasts the *habile négociateur*, "*qui ne croit pas légèrement tous les avis qu'il reçoit*," who takes into account the interests and passions of his informants, who considers how they *made* their pretended discoveries, and what relation their intelligence has to what he has received through other channels, *et quantité d'autres signes*, from which an able and penetrating man may draw conclusions, — with him to whom nature has denied the qualities requisite for the occupation, "*qui n'est pas né avec les ouvertures d'esprit nécessaires en pareil cas*," and to whom there is no more use in explaining the rules of good diplomacy than if he were deaf and dumb.

Callières was at first the secret agent, and latterly the acknowledged plenipotentiary, of France at the Treaty of Ryswick; and to all appearance was himself quite an upright and honourable man. He had a lofty notion of the qualities requisite for negotiation—even the moral qualities—as *he* understood morality. It is not sufficient that the good negotiator possess the most brilliant intellectual qualities, "*toutes les lumières, toute la dextérité et les autres belles qualités de l'esprit*," he must have those also which depend on the sentiments of the heart, "*car il n'y a point d'emploi qui demande plus d'élévation et plus de noblesse dans les manières d'agir.*"[1] He even goes the length of saying that a sagacious and able negotiator ought to be a good Christian, though he slily adds that it is *at least* equally necessary that he should

[1] Callières, p. 35.

appear to be so. In the abstract he is very sincerely, I believe, an advocate for honesty—and where a straightforward course seems to him to be possible, he always recommends it; but the small extent to which he evidently thought such a course was possible, and the perfect coolness with which he contemplates the adoption of a very different line of conduct, presents to us anything but a pleasing picture of the diplomatic morality of the earlier part of the eighteenth century.

As regards the people of the country in which the ambassador resides, and the intelligence which may be derived from them, he says:[1] "When a negotiator serves a great prince, the surest and shortest means is to gain over to the interests of his master some member of the Council of the Prince, or of the State, to which he is sent, by means of which a negotiator, who is discreet and able, knows very well how to avail himself when his master has put them at his disposal; but he ought to know how to choose his correspondent, lest he should become his dupe.

"There are in negotiations, as in war, double spies, who get paid by both parties, and there are those who give, in the first instance, really good advice in order that they may be able in the long-run more completely to deceive the negotiator who has consulted them. There are even princes so guileful (*assez fins*) as to detach one of their confidants, who, under the appearance of a secret *liaison* with the foreign minister, gives him false information in order better to conceal the designs of his master; and there have been ambassadors so little sharp-sighted as to allow themselves to be deceived by

[1] Callières, p. 145.

such a scheme." I am sorry to say that the example which Callières gives of this dexterous proceeding is taken from the Court of our own Charles II., the victim being a Dutchman whom our countrymen succeeded in inducing to persuade the States-General that we had no intention of making war upon Holland. Corruption, in Callières's day, seems to have been everywhere a matter of course; and he praises the sage custom of the Spaniards, which placed a regular fund at the disposal of their ambassadors for the purpose. "An ambassador," he says, "is called an honourable spy, because one of his principal occupations is to discover the secrets of the Courts in which he resides, and he acquits himself badly of his duty if he does not know how to make such an expenditure as may be necessary in order to gain those who are able to give him information."[1] He was quite of Lord Palmerston's opinion as to the value of a good dinner. "A good table," he says, "facilitates the means of ascertaining what is going on. . . . It is the property of good cheer to conciliate *les esprits*, to promote familiarity, to open the hearts of the guests; and the warmth of good wine often brings important secrets to light."[2] Nor would that genial statesman have probably dissented from the following observations on the snare which pedantry is likely to prove to a bookish diplomatist. Callières insists on the moderation with which the negotiator must make use of any acquaintance which he may possess with the higher

[1] As to the openness with which bribery was practised at the Congress of Munster, see Bernard's *Lectures on Diplomacy*, p. 25; Puffendorf's phrase, "*Muneribus demulcire*," is quite in Callières's vein.

[2] Callières, p. 156.

departments of thought and knowledge. "It is very useful," he says, "and becoming, that those who are charged with the interests of States, and on whose conduct often whole nations are dependent, should have a general acquaintance with such sciences as tend to enlighten the understanding; but they must possess them without being possessed by them— that is to say, that they are not to esteem them beyond their real value, and that they are to regard them as means of rendering themselves more wise and able, and not as a subject of pride, or as a ground on which they are entitled to despise those who are not possessed of similar acquirements."[1]

In strong contrast to the small value which he attaches to book-learning, is the high estimate which Callières forms of the natural endowments necessary for a diplomatist. His remarks on the subject are full of wit. "A man," he says, "who is eccentric, of an unequal temper, and who is not master of his whims and his passions, ought not to undertake the employment of negotiation. War is much better suited for him; for as war consumes a great number of those who devote themselves to her service, she is not so delicate in the choice of her subjects, but resembles those good stomachs which digest all kinds of food and turn them to profit."[2]

Before taking leave of Callières, I shall quote to you only one other passage, which is too characteristic of him and of the other writers of the class to which he belongs, to be omitted. "If the habits of the country in which the negotiator is resident," he says, "permit of free intercourse with the ladies, he

[1] Callières, p. 228.   [2] Ib., p. 68.

ought not to neglect to get them on his side by contributing to their pleasure, and rendering himself worthy of their esteem. The power of their charms is such as often to contribute to the most important resolutions on which the greatest events depend. But in his efforts to please them by his magnificence, by his politeness, and even by his gallantry, he must take care that he does not lose his heart. He must bear in mind that love is in general accompanied by indiscretion and imprudence, and that the moment that he allows himself to be subject to the wishes of a beautiful woman, however sage he may be, he runs the risk of being no longer master of his own secret. Grave inconveniences have arisen from this sort of weakness. The greatest ministers are not exempt from falling into it, and it is not necessary to go beyond our own times in order to find memorable examples."[1] One thinks of Madame de Longueville at Munster; but Callières's instances were probably more recent.

Cardinal Mazarin is, of course, Callières's model of a negotiator; but in place of translating what he says in his praise, I shall, in justice to an age which was not wholly given over to Mazarin, quote to you the sentences in which the writer on embassies and foreign Courts contrasts his maxims with those of the Cardinal d'Ossat. "Of those French negotiators with whom we are most familiar," he says, "we shall perhaps hardly find two examples more worthy of note than the Cardinals Ossat and Mazarin. The former appears to have invariably adopted the most perfect frankness and truth in all his dealings. His idea of statesmanship was based on the fair

[1] *Ib.*, p. 59.

and open principle of sincerity; and indeed such a policy will be found, in all cases where it has been adopted, to have been eminently successful. In a frank plain statement there is always something attractive even to the most crooked-minded man. The negotiator has also told the worst, and every day softens the first effects of his communication; whereas if he begins by glozing over a disagreeable matter, which must be discussed in its true form at last, his affairs are every day growing worse, and he has nothing to hope from a future, which will certainly plunge him into deeper difficulty. Ossat believed, therefore, that it was in the first place necessary to state his case clearly, and then he trusted always to carry the matter in hand by appealing to the reason of his adversary, and forcibly pointing out the advantages of the measure he advocated. Nothing escaped his fine understanding and penetrating intellect which could in any manner contribute to so legitimate an object. The arguments he adduced, in the first place, were always as well considered, as just and unanswerable as possible. All his skill, we are told, therefore consisted in reiterating them again and again, with unshaken constancy, and in an easy agreeable manner. This made him a most perplexing antagonist, for he always maintained his point with as much courtesy as firmness. Mazarin had not been bred in so noble a school. He owes his reputation altogether to cunning and to intrigue. He was so profound a dissembler, that deception became the habit and custom of his life. It was a rule with him to treat the affairs of which he most desired the accomplishment with apparent indifference. In this he seems to me to have made a capital mistake, for such a proceeding could only cool the zeal of friendship, and give a troublesome confidence to opposition. Mazarin, however, had that trickster mind which has often characterised bad women in places of power, or the slaves and eunuchs of the East. He loved deceit for its own sake. He had more pleasure in deception than success, and he would have considered himself robbed of half his triumph if he had not been able to boast of the unworthy means by which he attained it."[1]

It is gratifying to find, from the expressions of opinion by the most eminent diplomatists of our day, which Mr Montague Bernard has collected in his valuable and interesting little book,[2] that it is Ossat and not Mazarin who represents the prevailing conception of the "perfect ambassador." When Lord Clarendon was asked whether, in his judgment, any special art was required in diplomacy, he answered, "No; I think the special art required is this—to be perfectly honest, truthful, and straightforward."[3] To this characteristically English utterance I would only add, "and to possess sufficient dexterity to prevent your straightforwardness from being mistaken for selfishness, and your shyness for pride."

Whether we regard it from an international or a national point of view, it is scarcely possible to overestimate the importance of the character attached by foreigners to the representatives of this branch of the public service. The extent to which a nation enjoys that undefinable power which is known by the name of *prestige*, and the due employment of which so often supersedes the necessity for an appeal to more formid-

[1] P. 46.   [2] P. 127.   [3] P. 129.

able factors, depends as much on the sympathetic and conciliatory manners of its official representatives as on the reputation of its soldiers for valour or its citizens for wealth. Our transatlantic descendants have always been specially mindful of this fact; and it has often occurred to me that their astuteness in this respect may have something to do with the greater goodwill that is shown to them than to ourselves by Continental nations. When the Alabama arbitration occurred, Continental sympathy was on the American side to a far greater extent than was warranted by the merits of the cause; and no Englishman who ever heard a maritime question discussed by Continental jurists, can have failed to see that their judgments were not altogether unaffected by anti-English sentiments.

That a people, whose substantial good qualities others so freely admit, should be so unpopular as the English unquestionably are, betrays superficial faults of character which we ought to correct. All of us in our travels ought to bear in mind that every Englishman abroad is a representative of his country,—that the honour of England is in his hands,—that by cordial, cheerful, courteous, and intelligent intercourse with foreigners, he contributes to his nation's greatness; whilst by a display of petulance, a senseless attempt to assert a fancied superiority, or to conceal a consciousness of the imperfections of his theoretical culture by professing to be "practical," he detracts from her glory and her power. And if this be true of every one who, by bearing the name, has constituted himself a representative of his country, how much more is it true of those to whom the country herself has formally and officially confided this character?

CHAPTER VII.

OF MERCANTILE INTERCOURSE.

The consular office.

We have now to study the character of an office less dignified and less highly privileged, but scarcely less important, than that of the Ambassador—the office of the Consul.

The object of the institution of consuls is to protect the commerce and the navigation of the country which appoints them : to represent the interests of their fellow-countrymen to the authorities of the country in which they are resident: to exercise, under certain conditions, jurisdiction over them : and to furnish to their own Government information and suggestions which may tend to promote the prosperity of commerce.

A keen controversy was carried on amongst the publicists of the seventeenth and eighteenth centuries as to whether consuls were, or were not, public ministers. Wicquefort refused to consider them in any other light than as commercial agents, and mercantile judges. Vattel, Martens, and Klüber following him, without taking account of the changes which had taken place in the institution, also refused to consuls any place in the diplomatic corps. Such is also the opinion of Wheaton and of Fœlix. It is certain that consuls cannot pretend to the ceremonial honours of public ministers, though many treaties accord to them the right of hoisting the flag of their nation, and placing the arms of the sovereign whom they represent over the doors of their hotels. Several modern writers, on the other hand—for example Steck, in his *Essai sur le Consul;* De Clercq and De Vallat, *Guide pratique des Consulats;* De Cussy in the *Dictionnaire du Diplomate et du Consul, et Phases et Causes Célèbres du droit Maritime des Nations*—ascribe to consuls the character of public ministers. According to these authors, whatever may be the rank assigned to consuls in the diplomatic hierarchy —whatever may be their position of subordination relatively to other political agents, whether they act and speak in their own name, and under their own responsibility, or in virtue of express instructions received from their ambassadors, consuls are not the less clothed with a public character. As officials, sent and accredited, and, as frequently happens, left behind in charge of the archives of the embassy after diplomatic relations have been suspended by their country, they are ministers, and their persons and their residences ought to participate in the respect which is due to their nation. "Without going to the full length of these latter authors," says Vergé,[1] in his recent edition of Martens, "we may, however, affirm in general, that consuls and other agents for commercial relations, and the persons attached to consulships, enjoy, like other public ministers, the right of inviolability as regards their persons, though they are not entitled to the privileges of exterritoriality. They are not entitled to claim the free exercise of their religion in a country in which it is not tolerated. As regards their private affairs, they are subject

[1] *State Papers*, No. 3175, 1863.

to the ordinary tribunals of the place of their residence, and must submit to the same modes of execution as other strangers resident in the State in which they are established. It may, however, happen that a consul receives from his Government a special diplomatic mission. In these circumstances he is regarded as the representative of his sovereign, and enjoys all the immunities which belong to public ministers."[1] These statements embrace very nearly the views now prevalent in this country as to the nature of the consular office,[2] more particularly if along with them we take into account the distinction which Martens afterwards makes between those who are resident in Europe and those in the Levant, along the African shores of the Mediterranean (with the exception of Algeria, which is now a European possession),[3] and in many other places which are either entirely or partially beyond the range of ordinary European diplomatic arrangements. Arrangements of the kind here referred to were made between this country and Morocco by the treaty of peace and commerce signed at Fez on the 28th July 1760, and many later examples might be given.[4] In many places the exercise of their religion has been accorded to consuls; and in the Foreign Office list you will find an enumeration of upwards of forty consulships to which chapels are attached, and partly supported by her Majesty's Government, under the Act 6 Geo. IV. c. 87.

[1] Martens's *Précis*, vol. i. p. 366.
[2] See decisions of municipal tribunals as to consuls, *Phill.*, vol. ii. p. 260, and the case of Viveash *v.* Becker, *Phill.*, vol. ii. p. 199.
[3] *Maule* and *Selwyn*, p. 284.
[4] *Précis*, p. 370.

Like the other institutions of the middle ages which had the protection of commerce for their object, that of the consulate originated with those merchant communities which at an early period sprang up around the shores of the Mediterranean. The best authority on the early history and development of the Consulate is Alexander von Miltitz, whose *Manuel des Consuls* appeared in London and Berlin in 1837; following upon the *Essai sur les Consuls* of Herr von Steck, published in Berlin in 1790. The work of Miltitz is in five thick volumes, executed with all the fidelity and something of the prolixity of German *Gelehrsamkeit*—a statement which will explain to you the impossibility of my even attempting to present you with a *résumé* of it here. I shall endeavour, however, to state, in a few sentences, the view which he takes of the history of the office—a subject on which you will find nothing that is satisfactory in the popular treatises.

And first, of the name. Having been continued as a mere empty title, long after it had lost its ancient significance, by the emperors of the West, and adopted by their rivals and successors at Constantinople, the name to which so many magnificent associations cling was arrogated to themselves for a time by the kings of France and Italy and Germany. Even the Saracen princes in Spain coveted it; and it became a most incongruous addition to their other titles. The consequence of its popularity was that it fell into entire disrepute. "Having lost its *éclat*," says Miltitz, "from the multitude of little princes who adorned themselves with it, the Greek emperors, and in imitation of them the other greater monarchs, abandoned it, towards the commencement of the tenth century.

When thus repudiated by sovereign princes, the title of consul was adopted by the chief magistrates of the free towns of Italy. On the establishment of the *Commune* in France, in the twelfth century, municipal officers were appointed who, in the southern provinces, were called consuls, and who corresponded to the *maires, échevins, jurats,* and *conseillers de l'hôtel de ville,* elsewhere.

In his preface to Haliburton's *Ledger* (p. xlviii) Professor Innes says: "The consuls and *prudhommes* in Southern France, the *maires* and *échevins* in the Langue d'Oil, the *schaut* and *schepens* of the Low Country cities, and many another name of magistrature, hardly differ in essentials from our own aldermen, provost, bailies, and councillors."

Many other examples might be given of the generic sense in which the term was used, corresponding to a certain extent to the loose and general way in which we ourselves often speak of a magistrate. But some of the uses thus made of the term might disturb the complacency of the present dignified holders of a title at which once "the world grew pale." From the learned pages of Miltitz, they might learn that in the fourteenth century the tailors and the broom-makers of Montpelier had each a consul of their own. On board ship, the officer under whose charge the provisions were placed, and who thus corresponded to the modern steward (an epithet, by the way, of great historical dignity amongst ourselves), was known as the consul. The eleventh section of the *Consulato del Mare* provides that if this dignitary should be guilty of cheating the owners (actor or art and part), he should be burned on the forehead with a hot iron. But enough of antiquarianism, by which, as by statistics, it would often seem that anything can be proved.[1]

The next step, by which it was specially appropriated to domestic judges in maritime affairs, was an easy and natural one. The statutes of the city of Pisa of the year 1169 vest, it is said, in the *Consules Marinariorum et Mercatorum*,[2] authority to counsel, to advise, and to judge in all matters relating to the interests of the mercantile community, and impose upon them the duty of advancing, by every means in their power, the maritime and commercial interests of their country. These latter judges were the *consules maris*, out of the recorded decisions of whose courts the maritime codes of the middle ages grew.

The last stage in the transition of the word from its ancient to its modern signification, presents us with the institution of the consulship pretty nearly in its completed form. In foreign ports consuls were appointed whose functions very closely resembled those of the domestic magistrates whom I have just mentioned.

Of these *consuls d'outre mer*, or *consuls à l'étranger*, traces appear at a very early period. Their first establishment was probably a consequence of the wise policy which induced the barbarian conquerors of the Western Empire to recognise the municipal laws of Rome as governing the city communities; and accordingly we find in the *Codex Visigothorum* a distinct recognition of the right of seafaring strangers and foreigners to

---

[1] Those who desire to pursue the subject farther, in addition to Miltitz, are referred to Heeren, *Ideen über die Verkehr der Völker des Alterthums*.

[2] Tuson, *Consul's Manual*.

be judged by magistrates and arbiters of their own nation, and according to their own laws.[1] But though such was probably the origin of the consular office in Europe in medieval times, there can be little doubt that it has existed whenever and wherever a permanent foreign trade has been established. Whether Heeren and Miltitz may or may not have succeeded in finding traces of it in the very remote ages in which they have sought them, I shall not hesitate to believe that there were Phœnician consuls at any rate, of whose courts the Rhodian and other earlier maritime codes were the digested decisions, just as the codes of the middle ages were the decisions of the courts of their successors.[2]

The popular view of the matter assigns to them, however, a far shorter pedigree. The prevailing opinion appears to be that foreign consuls were first appointed during the Crusades, in consequence of permission granted by the Franks to the trading towns of Italy, France, and Spain, to send magistrates into Asia to protect the commercial interests of their own citizens, and to act as judges amongst them.

The advantages resulting from these appointments induced several States of Europe, towards the commencement of the thirteenth century, to obtain from each other the privilege of sending consuls. Martens[3] gives examples, ranging from 1256 to 1291; and Miltitz mentions the existence of a

Reddie, p. 166.

See an interesting paper on "The Influence of the Shemitic Races on the Development of Mercantile Law," written originally as a prize essay in my class, by Mr David J. Mackenzie, advocate, and afterwards published in the *Journal of Jurisprudence*, April 1876.

[3] Heeren's *Versuch einer historischen Entwickelung des wahren Ursprungs des Wechselrechts*, p. 52.

diploma, bearing date 9th May 1190, by which the city of Naples conferred on the merchants of Amalfi the power of naming consuls to judge in such disputes as might arise amongst them. Whether the so-called Table of Amalfi, if it ever existed, was the code by which these judges were guided, is a subject on which Miltitz speculates, but into which we cannot follow him. In Pardessus, and in Reddie, who repeats him, you will find clear indications of the existence of the Consulate at Genoa in 1250, and at Pisa in 1298; and it seems probable that the trading communities of Spain were not slow, in this and in other respects, to follow the example of their Italian rivals, if, indeed, from their more extensive connection with Phœnicians and Carthaginians in early times, they did not precede them.

But, though its origin was thus venerable, it was not till the beginning of the fifteenth century that the practice of sending consuls to foreign ports became general; and in many instances, both as between different European States and between these and the partially recognised States in other portions of the globe, it is much more recent. The first foreign consul appointed by England, according to Tuson, was Leonardo Strozzi, at Pisa in 1485, or as Lindsay, in his *History of Merchant Shipping*,[1] says, in 1490. Two other Italians were appointed in the earlier part of the following century, one at Candia in 1522 and one at Scio in 1531; and Mr John Tipton was "Commissary" at Algiers in 1584.

But it was by the Hanseatic League that the consular system was chiefly developed; and it is said that, at one time, this

[1] Vol. i. p. 460.

great trading body maintained more than a hundred foreign consuls in different parts of the world. Traces of the existence of a *Hanse* have been discovered in Scotland so early as the reign of David I.,[1] a century before the date commonly assigned to the great Baltic Association. David's reign commenced on the 27th April 1124, so that if the consulate formed a part of the early Scottish *Ansum*, as it did of the more famous *Hanse* of the north of Europe, we may claim to have had consuls, as we certainly had resident ambassadors, long before the date assigned as that of their general institution in Europe. The effect of this statement, however, is not to found a claim for priority to the Scottish institution, but to show the fallacy of the date commonly assigned to it elsewhere, because our trading institutions, in all probability, came to us from the Continent. Much interesting information on this subject will be found in Mr Innes's *Scotland in the Middle Ages*, as well as in the work referred to below; and Mr Jeffrey, in his *History of Roxburghshire*,[2] gives some additional details relating to the trading colonies of Flemings, who established themselves in most of the towns of Scotland about the same period. "In every district, from the Tweed and the Solway to the Clyde and the Moray Firth, the Flemings, he says, obtained settlements; and so powerful did they become, that they obtained the right to be governed

---

[1] King William the Lion (who reigned 1165-1214) granted to the northern burghs of Scotland "*ut habcant liberum ansum suum.*" The same king grants privileges to burghs, "*sicut consuetudo et assisa fuit tempore Regis David avi mei,*"—not as David made the law, but as he found it.—Professor Innes's Preface to Haliburton's *Ledger*, p. xlviii, note.

[2] Vol. iii. p. 105.

by their own laws." These laws we may safely assume were administered by their own magistrates; so that the consulate in the twelfth century in all probability extended to all the more important trading communities of Scotland. There is a curious instance of the extension of this privilege, even to a semi-barbarous people, which appears in our statute-book at a later, though still an early period. King James V., by a writ in the Privy Council Register dated 15th February 1541, granted to Johnnie Faa, king of the gypsies, power to administer justice upon his people conform to the laws of Egypt.[1]

A famous Scotch consular establishment, to which very extensive privileges were conceded, was that of the conservatorship of the privileges of the Scotch nation in the Netherlands, over which Andrew Haliburton, to whose *Ledger*, extending from 1492 to 1503, we have already referred, presided. The Scottish *staple*, it is said, was transferred from Bruges to Campvere in 1444, in consequence of the marriage of the lord of Vere with Mary, the sister of James I.; and if a *staple* or factory implied a consulate, or something equivalent, we may assume that there was a Scotch consul at Bruges long before the appointment of Strozzi to be English consul at Pisa in 1485 or 1490.

But we are not left to conjecture on this subject. "In 1456 we read of the appointment, with the express consent of the magistrates of Aberdeen, of a certain prudent man (*providus vir*) Lawrence Pomstrat, burgess of Slusa, who shall be the host and the receiver of all Scotsmen, merchants or others, that may visit the town of Slusa in Flanders. This,

[1] Jeffrey, vol. iii. p. 316.

I take it," continues Mr Innes, "is the first appointment of a Scotch consul on record, and Lawrence Pomstrat was evidently the predecessor of our Haliburton."[1]

Though the connection between England and the Continent, after the loss of the French provinces, was less intimate than that between Scotland and the Continent, the reverse was the case up to that period;[2] and as the trade of England must always have been more extensive, it is not probable that an institution of so much importance as the consulship was known in Scotland before it was known in England. I am consequently disposed to think that the statement that Strozzi was the first English consul is erroneous.

Foreign consuls were originally elected by the merchants of their nation at the port at which their duties were to be performed. Such was the case with those appointed at Naples by the merchants of Amalfi; and such appears to have been the case also with Lawrence Pomstrat, who was a burgess of Slusa, and was appointed by the merchants, with consent of the magistrates of Aberdeen. But it soon became apparent, that in order to strengthen their authority and give efficacy to their decisions, it was necessary to obtain the approbation of the prince to whom they were subject. Subsequently governments began to see that it belonged to their interest and their dignity to choose consuls for themselves; and examples are frequent of their reserving the right of establishing them in treaties. Pinhiero Ferrara blames Martens, and the publicists who have followed him, for not perceiving that it was at this stage that consuls became public ministers. I confess

[1] *Burgh Registers*, p. 20. [2] Haliburton's *Ledger*, p. lxxxi.

I cannot see that the circumstance of their being *chosen* by their fellow-countrymen resident abroad, in place of being selected by the Government at home, provided that their appointment afterwards received the sanction of their native sovereign, made any essential difference in their public character. An ambassador might have been so indicated, and provided his appointment was afterwards ratified by his sovereign, he would have been a public minister, representing the interests of his country not the less in consequence of the mode of his selection. So long as no ratification of their appointment took place, consuls were, of course, merely the private agents of the merchants who selected them, and arbiters in such disputes as they chose to submit to their decision.

The consular service of this country consists of five classes: 1. Agents and consul-generals; 2. Consul-generals; 3. Consuls; 4. Vice-consuls; 5. Consular agents. The general instructions for her Majesty's consuls issued by the Foreign Office[1] thus fixes the rank of these various offices. "Agents and consul-generals rank with, but after, rear-admirals, or major-generals. Consul-generals rank with, but after, brigadiers and commodores. Consuls rank with, but after, colonels and captains R.N. of three years' standing. Vice-consuls rank with, but after, lieutenants R.N., navigating lieutenants of eight years' standing, or majors in the army. Consular agents rank with, but after, captains in the army, other lieutenants and navigating lieutenants in the navy. Consuls take rank amongst their colleagues, at the port of

[1] Paragraph 26.

their residence, in accordance with the rules prescribed by the Congress of Vienna for diplomatic agents—by seniority according to official title, and priority of arrival.

To these various grades—as a connecting link between the consular and diplomatic corps—fall to be added those agents who hold both political and consular appointments. From the Foreign Office list there seem to be only *five* officers of this class,—resident in Egypt, Tunis, Bucharest, Jassy, and the Sandwich Islands. But at other places, as at Tangiers, there are consul-generals who are at the same time ministers-resident; and at others, as Bolivia, Lima, St Jago, &c., there are agents who combine the offices of *chargé d'affaires* with those of consul-general. Many irregularities of this sort are to be found, which seem to prove the futility of attempting to draw an absolute line between the diplomatic and consular corps. The Envoy Extraordinary and Minister Plenipotentiary in China is called the chief superintendent of British trade; whereas his colleague in Japan, performing very similar functions, is a consul-general. But the latter, as well as the former, has a complete ambassadorial staff, with the addition of a considerable body of student interpreters. Student interpreters are likewise attached to the consuls at Canton and Foo-chow-foo, and elsewhere in China; and to the minister plenipotentiary in Japan,—a liberal and wise arrangement, and one of the many indications to be found in the Foreign Office list of the present tendency to take advantage of the machinery of the diplomatic service for the promotion of civilisation in every possible direction.

Another arrangement which binds the two services together

is the habit of transferring individuals from the one to the other. A very considerable number of those who hold the higher consular appointments commenced their career as *attachés* to embassies, and instances are not wanting of ministers and envoys extraordinary who at one stage of their progress were consuls. Prescott observes, in a note in his *Ferdinand and Isabella* (vol. i. p. 90), speaking chiefly of Spain, that in the "middle ages consuls filled in some sort the post of a modern ambassador or resident minister, at a period when this functionary was only employed on extraordinary occasions." As a rule, the same functions seem to be confided to him still, wherever no minister is resident.

The shortest method by which I can convey to you a conception of the very varied and onerous duties which fall to be performed by the consul, will be by quoting to you a few passages from the general instructions for her Majesty's consuls, issued by the Secretary of State for the Foreign Department, which, together with copies of the treaties and other documents having reference to the particular place to which he is sent, are furnished to the consul on his appointment. As the consular service of this country does not differ in essentials from those of the other European States, these instructions, *mutatis mutandis*, are of general validity.

First, with reference to the *exequatur*, or authority from the foreign State to act within its jurisdiction:—

"Upon the arrival of the consul at his post, he will announce himself to the principal public authorities, and will show them her Majesty's commission, or a copy thereof; and he may, if required, give them a copy stamped with the consular seal.

"The original commission should be forwarded to her Majesty's ambassador, or minister, at the Court of the country in which the consul has to reside; with a request that the said ambassador, or minister, will apply to the proper authorities for the usual *exequatur* to enable him to enter officially upon his consular duties.

"Her Majesty's commission and the *exequatur* will secure to the consul the enjoyment of such privileges, immunities, and exemptions, as have been enjoyed generally by his predecessors, and are usually granted to consuls in the country in which he resides; and he will be cautious not to aim at more."

The *exequatur* granted by one Government, unless formally withdrawn, is recognised by any subsequent Government which may spring up in the State to which the consul is sent.

With the sections having reference to the consular fees, and the forms which are prescribed for their correspondence and accounts-current to be rendered by consuls, I need not trouble you; but the commercial instructions which they receive are of general interest.

"It will be the particular study of the consul to become conversant with the laws and general principles which relate to the trade of Great Britain with foreign parts; to make himself acquainted with the language and with the municipal laws of the country wherein he resides, and especially with such laws as have any connection with the trade between the two countries. . . .

"He will bear in mind that it his principal duty to protect and promote the lawful trade and trading interests of Great Britain, by every fair and proper means, taking care to conform to the laws and regulations in question; and whilst he is supporting the lawful trade of Great Britain, he will take special notice of all prohibitions with respect to the export or import of specified articles, as well on the part of the State in which he resides as of the Government of Great Britain; so that he may caution all British subjects against carrying on an illicit commerce, to the detriment of the revenue and in violation of the laws and regulations of either country: and he will not fail to give to this department immediate notice of any attempt to contravene those laws and regulations."

With reference to the advice and assistance to be given to British subjects, the consul is directed "to give his best advice and assistance, when called upon, to her Majesty's trading subjects, quieting their differences, promoting peace, harmony, and goodwill amongst them, and conciliating as much as possible the subjects of the two countries upon all points of difference which may fall under his cognisance.

"In the event of any attempts being made to injure British subjects, either in their persons or property, he will uphold their rightful interests, and the privileges secured to them by treaty, by due representation in the proper official quarter. He will, at the same time, be careful to conduct himself with mildness and moderation in all his transactions with the public authorities; and he will not upon any account urge claims on behalf of her Majesty's subjects to which they are not justly and fairly entitled. If redress cannot be obtained from the local administration, or if the matter of complaint be not within their jurisdiction, the consul will apply to her Majesty's consul-general, or to her Majesty's minister, if there be no consul-general in the country wherein he resides, in order that he may make a representation to the higher authorities, or take such other steps in the case as he may think proper; and the consul will pay strict attention to the instructions which he may receive from the minister or consul-general."

Under the head of correspondence, public and private, the consul is directed to "keep her Majesty's minister regularly and fully informed of all occurrences of national interest within his consulate, respecting either the trade of her Majesty's subjects or that of other nations at peace or at war with Great Britain. He will likewise not fail to transmit to him such correct intelligence as he can procure respecting the arming, the equipment, or the sailing of any public or private armed vessels belonging to the enemies of her Majesty; and whenever it may appear to him essential that her Majesty's Government should be directly informed of the subject of his communications to her Majesty's minister, he will transmit copies of them to this department.

"The consul will not, however, upon any account, correspond with private persons on public affairs; neither will he recommend his private friends abroad or at home for employments of trust or profit under the Government of the country in which he resides; and he will not ask or accept favours of that Government for himself."

That the duties of the consul, though primarily commercial, are not regarded by Government as entirely exclusive of politics, and consequently that, to a certain extent, every consul is a political agent, is apparent from the prohibition contained in the following section against corresponding with Lloyds on politics: "Such of her Majesty's consuls as are agents for Lloyds are specially directed not to correspond with Lloyds on the subject of political occurrences." "The consul," it is farther stated, "will not hold any correspondence on such subjects, excepting that which it is his duty to hold with the Secretary and Under-Secretary of State, and the superintendent of the consular service, or with her Majesty's minister and consul-general in the country where he resides, or with consuls and naval or military officers in her Majesty's service who may be employed in his neighbourhood, and to whom it may be necessary to communicate immediately any event of public interest."

With reference to protection on board of British ships, the consul is informed that "misconception having arisen with respect to the degree of protection which commanders of British ships may afford to any individuals seeking refuge on board of those ships, he shall take notice that the commanders of British ships, lying in the ports of a foreign country, are not authorised to harbour any persons, even if British subjects, who may seek refuge on board of their vessels, in order to evade, or resist, the due execution of the laws to which, by reason of their residence in the country, they have rendered themselves amenable; and the consul will bear in mind, in all applications that may be made to him on behalf of individuals so circumstanced, that such persons are liable to be taken by due process of the laws of the country."[1]

On the very important subject of the commercial report, the following are his instructions: "The consul will forward to the Secretary of State, in duplicate, so soon as the information he can collect will enable him so to do, but at any rate within a period of six months from the date of his arrival at his residence, a general report on the trade of the place and district, specifying the commodities, as well of the export as of the import trade, and the countries which supply the latter, together with the increase or decline in late years, and the probable increase or decline to be expected, and the causes in both cases. He will state the general regulations with respect to trade at the place where he is resident, and their effects. He will give the average market prices within the year of the several articles of export and import. He will particularise what articles, if any, are absolutely prohibited to be imported into the country wherein he resides; what articles are prohibited to be imported from any other place than from the place of their growth or production; whether there be any privileges of importation, and what those privileges are, in favour of ships that are of the build of or belonging to the country wherein he resides; whether there be any difference in the duty on goods when imported into that country in a foreign ship, and if so, whether it be

[1] As to fugitive slaves, see *ante*, p. 256 *et seq.*

general, or applicable only to particular articles; what are the rates of duty payable on goods imported into the said country; whether there be any tonnage duty or other port dues (and what?) payable on shipping entering at or clearing from the ports of that country; whether there be any (and if so, what?) ports in that country wherein goods may be warehoused on importation, and afterwards exported, with or without payment of any duties, and under what regulations."

The consul is farther instructed to make annual returns of trade, quarterly returns of corn and grain; to make public the Act of Parliament and Order in Council relating to quarantine; to report any appearance of yellow fever, plague, or other contagious or infectious disease at the place of his residence; to furnish intelligence to the commanders of her Majesty's ships trading upon the coast, and to obtain for them, when required, supplies of water and provisions; to exert himself to recover all wrecks, cables, anchors, &c., belonging to the Queen's ships, when found at sea by fishermen or other persons, and brought into the port where he resides. He has to grant certificates of facts, to attest documents to *viser* and grant passports, to advance money to distressed British subjects, and to render account of the same in accordance with rather troublesomely minute regulations with which he is furnished.

But these are only his *general* instructions. In almost every case the consul has duties of a special kind, arising out of the local circumstances of his residence; and when the first Merchant Shipping Act was passed in 1854, an additional set of instructions were issued relating to matters affecting the British Mercantile Marine. These instructions contain the substance of those parts of the Act which specially relate to the consul's duties; but he is told—rather unfairly, I think that "he will remember that the instructions do not dispense with the obligation under which he lies of making himself acquainted with the Act itself." What he is to do in the not improbable case of his reading of the Act differing from that embodied in the instructions, whether he is to set Parliament or the Foreign Office at naught, is not mentioned. Surely it would have been better, if an intelligible Act could not be constructed, that Government should have taken upon itself the responsibility of construing it, and of furnishing consuls with instructions by which they should have been bound, without reference to its provisions. To add to his perplexity, the consul is informed that the common law, except where altered by statute, remains still in force; and as the instructions apply not only to consuls-general and consuls, but to vice-consuls and consular agents, many of whom are foreign merchants, and some of whom are little better than barbarians,—a man who is not an Englishman at all, may be called upon to discover, in an island in the middle of the Pacific Ocean, or in a village of native huts or tents on the coast of Africa, what is the common law of England, and whether or not, or to what extent, it has been altered by statute! But in this matter, as in most other English matters, the practice is not so bad as the theory. Though they do not relieve him from the responsibility of exercising his own judgment as to the provisions of the Act, the instructions are framed with so much clearness and precision, as practically, in the majority of cases, to obviate the difficulties we have imagined. The following passages are so instructive that I need make no apology for quoting them.

The first has reference to the interference of foreign courts of justice:—

"In considering how far the interference of foreign courts should be allowed or invoked, the first question to be looked at is, whether there are any treaties on the subject existing between this country and the country in which the consul is acting. To the express stipulations of such treaties all general rules of international law are subject; and the consul will therefore be guided by them in the exercise of his own functions, and will call upon the local authorities to act in accordance therewith.

"Subject to any such treaties as aforesaid, the consul will remember that every country has the right of enforcing its own criminal law and police regulations in its own ports and harbours; and that if any offence against such laws or regulations is committed in such ports or harbours, on board a British ship, the offender is liable to be dealt with accordingly. In such cases the consul's duty will be confined to seeing that the offender is fairly tried, and that justice is properly administered. If the laws or regulations of the place are in fault, it will be a matter for representation to the British minister in the country, or to her Majesty's Secretary of State.

"In cases where the offence is one which is punishable both by the law of the place above mentioned, and also by

British law, and where the local authorities are willing to interfere if required by the consul to do so, but not otherwise, he will consider whether the ends of justice will be best met by calling for such interference, or by sending the offender to trial in some British court of justice. The questions he will have to consider are,—which is the speediest and most certain mode of obtaining justice,—which course is the best for the convenience of the ship and the witnesses,— and, above all, whether the principles and practice of the foreign court can be relied on, and whether its proceedings and modes of punishment are such as would be considered proper and humane in this country.

"In any case in which, from whatever cause, any British seaman is committed to prison, or otherwise punished in any foreign country, the consul will see that the place of confinement and mode of treatment is such as would in this country be considered proper and humane; if not, he will report the case to the British minister in the country, or to her Majesty's Secretary of State.

"Subject to the exceptions mentioned above, the consul will remember that, according to well-established rules of national law, a British ship carries British law with her, and that all offences committed on board such a ship, on the high seas, and all mere breaches of discipline in foreign ports, as well as all matters arising out of the contract with the crew, are to be judged of by British law. In some foreign countries the local courts of justice will take notice of and adjudicate upon such contracts; but in these cases it is usual for such foreign courts to act, in the case of a British ship, not according to their own law, but to British law, so far as the construction of the contract is concerned. Except in cases where the consul cannot settle the matter otherwise, it is extremely undesirable that disputes between the masters and crews of British ships should be taken in foreign courts; but whenever this is done the principles above mentioned should be adhered to. The consul should explain the British law; and if this is not followed he should report the case to the British minister, or her Majesty's Secretary of State.

"In cases where British seamen are employed in foreign ships, the consul will remember that, in accordance with the principles mentioned above, they are, whilst so employed, subject to the law of the country to which the ship belongs, and not to British law. If, therefore, the consul is called upon to interfere in their behalf, he should, either in applying to the local authorities, or in taking any other steps that may be necessary, endeavour to obtain the assistance of the consul of the country to which the ship belongs."

The next section has reference to *Naval Courts*.

"The power of summoning these courts, in the absence of any officer commanding one of her Majesty's ships, is given to consuls; and in cases where such an officer is at hand, the consul should, if he considers there is a case for a naval court, apply to such officer to refer the parties to him. The cases in which a naval court may be summoned are the following:—

"(a) If the master or any of the crew of any British ship

make a complaint to the consul which appears to him to require immediate investigation.

"(b) Whenever he thinks that the interests of the owner of the ship or cargo require it.

"(c) Whenever a British ship is wrecked, lost, or abandoned within or near his consulate; or whenever the crew, or part of the crew, of a ship which has been wrecked, lost, or abandoned abroad, arrives at any place in his consulate.

"The court is to consist of three, four, or five members, and the question of which of these it should consist must depend upon circumstances. Whenever it is possible, one of those must be an officer in the navy, of the rank of a lieutenant, or some higher rank; one a consul; and one a master of a British merchant ship. If the court consists of more than three, the remainder may be either naval officers, masters of merchant ships, or British merchants. If there is either no naval officer, or no consul at the place where the court is held, able to attend, his place may be filled up by a master of a British merchant ship, or a British merchant."

Many very clear and simple directions follow relating to the mode of proceeding, and the powers of the court, but into these my space does not permit me to enter. The only other passage which I shall quote is that which has reference to crimes committed on the high seas and abroad.

"Crimes committed on the high seas, on board any British ship, and offences against property or person committed at any place, in foreign countries, by any person who, at the time of the commission of the offence, belongs to any British ship, or by any British subject who has within the previous three months belonged to any British ship, are subject to the same punishments, and may be tried in the same manner as if they had been committed within the jurisdiction of the admiralty in England—that is to say, according to the common criminal law of England."

In the section which follows, the consul is again reminded that, subject to any special provisions by treaty, offences against the municipal law of a foreign country, committed within its limits, although by British subjects, on board a British ship, are liable to be tried by the courts and according to the law of that country, and that British subjects on board a foreign ship are subject to foreign law. But where the crime has either been committed on the high seas, or where the local tribunals decline to interfere, the consul may, either at his own instance or in consequence of a complaint having been made to him, inquire into the case upon oath, and may summon witnesses before him for that purpose. "And if there is evidence which, in the opinion of the consul, is sufficient to substantiate the charge, he may send the offender to some place in the British dominions at which he can be tried." As sending home prisoners involves very serious expense, and as prosecutions in such cases have often failed for want of the observance of the requisite formality, or of witnesses, very precise rules are laid down for the consul's guidance. He is not to send any offender home at the public expense, unless the crime is "murder, attempt to murder, piracy, slave-trading, manslaughter, aggravated assault, wilful destruction of the ship, deliberate and concerted mutiny, or some other offence of a very serious nature, involving risk to the life or welfare of others."

In minor offences the consul is, in no case, to send the offender home, unless the master or agent of the ship, or some other person against whom the crime has been committed, undertakes to prosecute, and to pay the expenses of sending home the offender and the witnesses.

I formerly mentioned to you that jurisdiction of a very much more ample kind than that which they exercise in Europe belongs to her Majesty's consuls and to those of other civilised Powers in the Levant, and in other places out of Christendom. The nature of this jurisdiction, and the sources from which it arises in Turkey, are very clearly defined in the following sentences from the memorial which was issued by Lord Aberdeen's Government in 1844, along with the Order in Council made in pursuance of the powers vested in her Majesty by 6 & 7 Vict. cap. 94, commonly called the Foreign Jurisdiction Act.

" The right of British consular officers to exercise any jurisdiction in Turkey, in matters which in other countries come exclusively under the control of the local magistracy, depends originally on the extent to which that right has been conceded by the Sultans of Turkey to the British Crown, and therefore the right is strictly limited to the terms in which the concession is made.

" The right depends in the next place on the extent to which the Queen, in the exercise of the powers vested in her Majesty by Act of Parliament, may be pleased to grant to any of her consular servants authority to exercise jurisdiction over British subjects; and therefore the Orders in Council, which may from time to time be issued, are the only warrants for the proceedings of the consuls, and exhibit the rules to which they must scrupulously adhere.

"This state of things in Turkey is an exception to the system universally observed among Christian nations, but the Ottoman emperors having waived in favour of Christian Powers rights inherent in territorial sovereignty, such Christian Powers in taking advantage of this concession are bound to provide as far as possible against any injurious effects resulting from it to the territorial sovereign; and as the maintenance of order and the repression of crime are objects of the greatest importance in every civilised community, it is obligatory upon the Christian Powers, standing as they do in Turkey, in so far as their own subjects are concerned, in the place of the territorial sovereign, to provide as far as possible for these great ends. . . .

"The consuls will observe that three courses of proceeding are prescribed by the Order in Council, namely: a summary decision; a decision with the assistance of assessors, chosen from the British community; and recourse to the criminal tribunal of Malta."[1]

A subsequent Order in Council was issued the 24th April 1847. These orders contain a pretty complete code of law for the administration of justice amongst her Majesty's subjects in the Levant, and are, of course, far too extensive to admit of my presenting you with even a synopsis of their contents. The same reasons deter me from entering on the

[1] Tuson's *Manual*, p. 145.

subject of the jurisdiction exercised in China by the court of the chief superintendent of trade, and by the consuls at the ports at which they have been resident since the treaty concluded in 1842.

Notwithstanding the care with which these various documents for their guidance have manifestly been formed, her Majesty's consuls complain that, in consequence of the want of those consular treaties which Continental States are in the habit of contracting with each other, they are placed at a great disadvantage, as compared with their foreign colleagues, when seeking to determine their duties, powers, and privileges. In some respects, moreover, these treaties, all of which contain the "most favoured nation" clause, secure for the consuls which act under them advantages which our consuls enjoy only to the extent to which they can be claimed by the customary law of nations. Of this, two examples may be mentioned. A British subject dies, and it is only by permission, as it were, of the local authorities that the consul takes charge of his succession; whereas his foreign colleague, in similar circumstances, has his treaty to fall back upon in case of interference. Then, if the evidence of the two is required by a local court, the British consul may be called upon to appear in person; whereas the treaty usually provides that the foreign consul shall be examined at the consulate. Various exemptions—from the payment of local rates and taxes—are also, for the most part, secured for foreigners by these treaties, to which our consuls are subjected. This appears to be a matter which admits of easy remedy, and, by way of facilitating it, I shall print in a note the consular treaty between

France and Italy. This I do the more willingly because it defines very clearly the conceptions entertained of the consular office by Continental nations.[1]

[1] "Du 24 Septembre 1862.

"NAPOLÉON, par la grâce de Dieu et la volonté nationale, Empereur des Français,

"A tous présents et à venir, Salut.

"Sur le rapport de notre Ministre secrétaire d'État au département des Affaires étrangères.

"AVONS DÉCRÉTÉ ET DÉCRÉTONS CE QUI SUIT:

"ART. 1.—Une Convention Consulaire ayant été conclue le 26 juillet 1862, entre la France et le royaume d'Italie, et les ratifications de cet acte ayant été échangées à Paris, le 13 du présent mois, ladite Convention, dont la teneur suit, recevra sa pleine et entière exécution.

"CONVENTION.

"Sa Majesté l'Empereur des Français et sa Majesté le Roi d'Italie, reconnaissant l'utilité de déterminer, avec toute l'extension et la clarté possibles, les droits, priviléges et immunités réciproques des Consuls, Vice-Consuls, et Agents consulaires, Chanceliers ou Secrétaires, ainsi que leurs fonctions et les obligations auxquelles ils seront respectivement soumis dans les deux pays, ont résolu de conclure une convention consulaire, et ont nommé, à cet effet, pour leurs plénipotentiaires, savoir:

"Sa Majesté l'Empereur des Français, M. EDOUARD-ANTOINE THOUVENEL, Sénateur de l'Empire, Grand-Croix de son Ordre Impérial de la Légion d'Honneur, de l'Ordre religieux et militaire des Saints Maurice et Lazare, etc., son Ministre et Secrétaire d'Etat au département des Affaires étrangères:

"Et Sa Majesté le Roi d'Italie, M. le chevalier CONSTANTIN NIGRA, Grand-Officier de son Ordre religieux et militaire des Saints Maurice et Lazare, Commandeur de l'Ordre Impérial de la Légion d'Honneur, etc., son Envoyé extraordinaire et Ministre plénipotentiaire près de Sa Majesté l'Empereur des Français:

"Lesquels, après s'être communiqués leurs pleins pouvoirs, trouvés en bonne et du forme, sont convenus des articles suivants:

"ART. 1.—Chacune des Hautes Parties contractantes aura la faculté d'établir des Consuls généraux, Consuls, Vice-Consuls ou Agents consulaires, dans les ports, villes et localités du territoire de l'autre Partie.

"Lesdits Agents seront réciproquement admis et reconnus en présentant leurs provisions, selon les règles et formalités établies dans les pays respectifs.

"L'exéquatur nécessaire pour le libre exercice de leurs fonctions leur sera délivré sans frais, et sur la production dudit exéquatur, l'Autorité supérieure du

There is one other subject, of which most of the writers on the consular office treat at great length, on which I have not yet touched. I mean the personal qualifications necessary for

lieu de leur résidence prendra immédiatement les mesures pour qu'ils puissent s'acquitter des devoirs de leur charge et qu'ils soient admis à la jouissance des exceptions, prérogatives, immunités, honneurs et priviléges qui y sont attachés.

"ART. 2.—Les Consuls généraux, Consuls et Vice-Consuls ou Agents consulaires, sujets de l'État qui les nomme, jouiront de l'exemption des logements et des contributions militaires, des contributions directes, personnelles, mobiliéres ou somptuaires, imposées par l'État ou par les Communes, à moins qu'ils ne possèdent des biens immeubles, qu'ils ne fassent le commerce, ou qu'ils n'exercent quelque industrie ; dans lesquels cas, ils seront soumis aux mêmes taxes, charges d'imposition que les autres particuliers.

"Ils jouiront, en outre, de l'immunité personnelle, excepté pour les faits et actes que la législation pénale des deux pays qualifie crimes et punit comme tels, et s'ils sont négociants, la contrainte par corps ne pourra leur être appliquée que pour les seuls faits de commerce et non pour des causes civiles.

"Ils pourront placer au-dessus de la porte extérieure du Consulat ou Vice-Consulat, l'écusson des armes de leur nation avec cette inscription : *Consulat* ou *Vice-Consulat de....*

"Ils pourront également arborer le pavillon de leur pays sur la maison consulaire, aux jours de solennités publiques, religieuses ou nationales, ainsi que dans les autres circonstances d'usage, à moins qu'ils ne résident dans une ville où se trouverait l'Ambassade ou la Légation de leur pays. Il est bien entendu que ces marques extérieures ne pourront jamais être interprétées comme constituant un droit d'asile, mais serviront, avant tout, à désigner aux matelots et aux nationaux l'habitation consulaire.

"Les Consuls généraux, Consuls et Vice-Consuls ou Agents consulaires, pourront de même arborer le pavillon national sur le bateau qu'ils monteraient dans le port pour le service de leurs fonctions.

"ART. 3.—Les Consuls généraux, Consuls et leurs chanceliers, ainsi que les Vice-Consuls ou Agents consulaires, ne pourront être sommés de comparaitre comme témoins devant les tribunaux.

"Quand la justice locale aura besoin de recueillir auprès d'eux quelques déclarations juridiques, elle devra se transporter à leur domicile, pour les recevoir de vive voix, ou déléguer, à cet effet, un fonctionnaire compétent, ou la leur demander par écrit.

"ART. 4.—En cas d'empêchement, d'absence ou de décès des Consuls généraux, Consuls et Vice-Consuls ou Agents consulaires, les élèves consuls, les chanceliers et secrétaires qui auront été présentés antérieurement en leurs dites qualités aux autorités respectives, seront de plein droit admis, dans leur ordre hiérarchique,

a consul. Notwithstanding its unquestionable importance, I conceive that the necessity for discussing this subject has been superseded, partly by what I have said on the qualifications

à exercer par intérim les fonctions consulaires, sans que les autorités locales puissent y mettre obstacle. Au contraire, celles-ci devront leur prêter assistance et protection, et leur assurer, pendant leur gestion intérimaire, la jouissance des exemptions, prérogatives, immunités et priviléges réciproquement reconnus par la présente convention aux agents du service consulaire.

"ART. 5.—Les archives consulaires seront inviolables, et les autorités locales ne pourront, sous aucun prétexte, ni dans aucun cas, visiter ni saisir les papiers qui en font partie.

"Ces papiers doivent toujours être complètement séparés des livres ou papiers relatifs au commerce ou à l'industrie que pourraient exercer les Consuls, Vice-Consuls ou Agents consulaires respectifs.

"ART. 6.—Les Consuls généraux et Consuls pourront nommer des Vice-Consuls ou Agents consulaires dans les villes, ports et localités de leurs arrondissements consulaires respectifs, sauf l'approbation du gouvernement territorial.

"Ces Agents pourront être indistinctement choisis parmi les citoyens des deux pays comme parmi les étrangers, et seront munis d'un brevet délivré par le Consul qui les aura nommés, et sous les ordres duquel ils devront être placés. Ils jouiront des mêmes priviléges et immunités stipulés par la présente convention, sauf les exceptions consacrés par l'art. 2.

"ART. 7.—Les Consuls généraux, Consuls et Vice-Consuls ou Agents consulaires des deux pays pourront s'adresser aux autorités de leur arrondissement, pour réclamer contre toute infraction aux traités ou conventions existant entre les deux pays, et contre tout abus dont leurs nationaux auraient à se plaindre. Si leurs réclamations n'étaient pas accueillies par ces autorités, ils pourraient avoir recours à défaut d'un agent diplomatique de leur pays, au gouvernement de l'État dans lequel ils résideraient.

"ART. 8.—Les Consuls généraux, Consuls et Vice-Consuls ou Agents consulaires des deux pays, ou leurs chanceliers, auront droit de recevoir dans leur chancellerie, au domicile des parties et à bord des navires de leur nation, les déclarations, que pourront avoir à faire les capitaines, les gens de l'équipage et les passagers, les négociants et tous autres sujets de leur pays.

"Ils seront également autorisés à recevoir, comme les notaires, les dispositions testamentaires de leurs nationaux et tous autres actes notariés, lors même que lesdits actes auraient pour objet de conférer hypothèques ; dans lequel cas, on leur appliquera les dispositions spéciales en vigueur dans les deux pays.

"Lesdits Agents auront, en outre, le droit de recevoir dans leur chancellerie tous actes conventionnels passés entre un ou plusieurs de leurs nationaux et d'autres personnes du pays dans lequel ils résident, et même tout acte conven-

necessary for the diplomatist, and partly by the statement which I have given of the multifarious duties the consul has to perform. His acquirements and personal character must

tionnel concernant des citoyens de ce dernier pays seulement, pourvu, bien entendu, que ces actes aient rapport à des biens situés ou à des affaires à traiter sur le territoire de la nation à laquelle appartiendra le Consul ou l'Agent devant lequel ils seront passés. Les copies ou extraits de ces actes, dûment légalisés par lesdits Agents et scellés du sceau officiel des Consulats, Vice-Consulats ou Agents consulaires, feront foi, tant en justice que hors de justice, soit en France, soit en Italie, au même titre que les originaux, et auront la même force et valeur que s'ils avaient été passés devant un notaire ou autre officier public de l'un ou de l'autre pays, pourvu que ces actes aient été rédigés dans les formes requises par les lois de l'État auquel appartiennent les Consuls, Vice-Consuls ou Agents consulaires, et qu'ils aient ensuite été soumis au timbre et à l'enregistrement, ainsi qu'à toutes les autres formalités qui régissent la matière dans le pays où l'acte devra recevoir son exécution.

"Dans le cas où un doute s'élèverait sur l'authenticité de l'expédition d'un acte public enregistré à la chancellerie d'un des consulats respectifs, on ne pourra en refuser la confrontation avec l'original à l'intéressé qui en fera la demande, et qui pourra assister à cette collation, s'il le juge convenable.

"Les Consuls généraux, Consuls et Vice-Consuls ou Agents consulaires respectifs pourront traduire et légaliser toute espèce de documents émanés des autorités ou fonctionnaires de leur pays, ces traductions auront, dans le pays de leur résidence, la même force et valeur que si elles eussent été faites par les interprètes-jurés du pays.

"ART. 9.—En cas de décès d'un sujet de l'une des parties contractantes sur le territoire de l'autre, les autorités locales devront en donner avis immédiatement au Consul général, Consul, Vice-Consul ou Agent consulaire dans la circonscription duquel le décès aura eu lieu. Ceux-ci, de leur côté, devront donner le même avis aux autorités locales, lorsqu'ils en seront informés les premiers.

"Quand un Français en Italie, ou un Italien en France, sera mort sans avoir fait de testament ni nommé d'exécuteur testamentaire, ou si les héritiers, soit naturels, soit désignés par le testament, étaient mineurs, incapables, ou absents, ou si les exécuteurs testamentaires nommés ne se trouvaient pas dans le lieu où s'ouvrira la succession, les Consuls généraux, Consuls et Vice-Consuls ou Agents consulaires de la nation du défunt, auront le droit de procéder successivement aux opérations suivantes :

"1º, Apposer les scellés, soit d'office, soit à la demande des parties intéressées, sur tous les effets, meubles et papiers du défunt, en prévenant de cette opération l'autorité locale compétente, qui pourra y assister et apposer également ses scellés.

be such as to enable him to discharge these duties; and the more fully, in addition to the indispensable minimum of linguistic, commercial, and legal knowledge imposed on him

"Ces scellés, non plus que ceux de l'Agent consulaire, ne devront pas être levés sans que l'autorité locale assiste à cette opération.

"Toutefois, si après un avertissement adressé par le Consul ou Vice-Consul à l'autorité locale, pour l'inviter à assister à la levée des doubles scellés, celle-ci ne s'était pas présentée dans un délai de quarante-huit heures, à compter de la réception de l'avis, cet Agent pourra procéder seul à la dite opération.

"2º, Former l'inventaire de tous les biens et effets du défunt, en présence de l'autorité locale, si, par suite de la notification susindiquée, elle avait cru devoir assister à cet acte.

"L'autorité locale apposera sa signature sur les procès-verbaux dressés en sa présence, sans que, pour son intervention d'office dans ses actes, elle puisse exiger des droits d'aucune espèce.

"3º, Ordonner la vente aux enchères publiques de tous les effets mobiliers de la succession qui pourraient se détériorer et de ceux d'une conservation difficile, comme aussi des récoltes et effets, pour la vente desquels il se présentera des circonstances favorables.

"4º, Déposer en lieu sûr les effets et valeurs inventoriés, conserver le montant des créances que l'on réalisera, ainsi que le produit des rentes que l'on percevra, dans la maison consulaire, ou les confier à quelque commerçant présentant toutes garanties. Ces dépôts devront avoir lieu dans l'un ou l'autre cas, d'accord avec l'autorité locale qui aura assisté aux opérations antérieures, si, par suite de la convocation mentionnée au paragraphe suivant, des sujets du pays, ou d'une puissance tierce se présentaient comme intéressés dans la succession *ab intestat* ou testamentaire.

"5º, Annoncer le décès et convoquer, au moyen des journaux de la localité et de ceux du pays du défunt, si cela était nécessaire, les créanciers qui pourraient exister contre la succession *ab intestat* ou testamentaire, afin qu'ils puissent présenter leurs titres respectifs de créance, dûment justifiés, dans le délai fixé par les lois de chacun des deux pays.

"S'ils se présentaient des créanciers contre la succession testamentaire ou *ab intestat*, le paiement de leurs créances devra s'effectuer dans le délai de 15 jours après la clôture de l'inventaire, s'il existait des ressources qui puissent être affectées à cet emploi; et, dans le cas contraire, aussitôt que les fonds nécessaires auraient pû être réalisés par les moyens les plus convenables, ou enfin dans le délai consenti, d'un commun accord, entre les Consuls et la majorité des intéressés.

'Si les Consuls respectifs se refusaient au paiement de tout ou partie des créances, en alléguant l'insuffisance des valeurs de la succession pour les satis-

by examination, he possesses the acquirements of an accomplished gentleman, a scholar and a man of the world, the more nearly will he attain to the ideal of the perfect consul.

faire, les créanciers auront le droit de demander à l'autorité compétente, s'ils le jugeaient utile à leurs intérêts, la faculté de se constituer en état d'union.

" Cette déclaration obtenue par les voies légales établies dans chacun des deux pays, les Consuls ou Vice-Consuls devront faire immédiatement la remise à l'autorité judiciaire ou aux syndics de la faillite, selon qu'il appartiendra, de tous les documents, effets ou valeurs appartenant à la succession testamentaire ou *ab intestat*; lesdits Agents demeurant chargés de représenter les héritiers absents, les mineurs et les incapables.

" En tous cas, les Consuls généraux, Consuls et Vice-Consuls ne pourront faire la délivrance de la succession ou de son produit, aux héritiers légitimes ou à leurs mandataires, qu'après l'expiration d'un délai de six mois à partir du jour où l'avis du décès aura été publié dans les journaux.

" 6°, Administrer et liquider eux-mêmes, ou par une personne qu'ils nommeront sous leur responsabilité, la succession testamentaire ou *ab intestat*, sans que l'autorité locale ait à intervenir dans lesdites opérations, à moins que des sujets du pays ou d'une tierce-puissance n'aient à faire valoir des droits dans la succession ; car, en ce cas, s'il survenait des difficultés, provenant notamment de quelque réclamation, donnant lieu à contestation, les Consuls généraux, Consuls, Vice-Consuls et Agents consulaires n'ayant aucun droit pour terminer ou résoudre ces difficultés, les tribunaux du pays devront en connaître selon qu'il leur appartient d'y pourvoir ou de les juger.

" Lesdits Agents consulaires agiront alors comme représentants de la succession testamentaire ou *ab intestat*, c'est-à-dire que, conservant l'administration et le droit de liquider définitivement ladite succession, comme aussi celui d'effectuer les ventes d'effets dans les formes précédemment indiquées, ils veilleront aux intérêts des héritiers et auront la faculté de désigner des avocats chargés de soutenir leurs droits devant les tribunaux. Il est bien entendu qu'ils remettront à ces tribunaux tous les papiers et documents propres à éclairer la question soumise à leur jugement.

" Le jugement prononcé, les Consuls généraux, Consuls et Vice-Consuls ou Agents consulaires devront l'exécuter, s'ils ne forment pas appel, et ils continueront alors, de plein droit, la liquidation qui aurait été suspendue jusqu'à la conclusion du litige.

" 7°, Organiser, s'il y a lieu, la tutelle ou curatelle, conformément aux lois des pays respectifs.

" ART. 10.—Lorsqu'un Français en Italie ou un Italien en France sera décédé sur un point où il ne se trouverait pas d'Agent consulaire de sa nation, l'autorité territoriale compétente procèdera, conformément à la législation du pays, à l'in-

X

The subjects of examination and other arrangements for admission to the diplomatic and consular services are published annually in this country in the Foreign Office List, and

ventaire des effets et à la liquidation des biens qu'il aura laissés, et sera tenue de rendre compte, dans le plus bref délai possible, du résultat de ses opérations à l'Ambassade ou à la Légation qui doit en connaître, ou au Consulat ou Vice-Consulat le plus voisin du lieu où sera ouverte la succession *ab intestat* ou testamentaire.

"Mais, dès l'instant que l'Agent consulaire le plus rapproché du point où serait ouverte ladite succession *ab intestat* ou testamentaire, se présenterait personnellement ou enverrait un délégué sur les lieux, l'autorité locale qui serait intervenue devra se conformer à ce que prescrit l'article précédent.

"ART. 11.—Les Consuls généraux, Consuls et Vice-Consuls ou Agents consulaires des deux États, connaîtront exclusivement des actes d'inventaire et des autres opérations pratiques pour la conservation des biens et objets de toute nature laissés par les gens de mer et les passagers de leur nation qui décéderaient à terre ou à bord des navires de leur pays, soit pendant la traversée, soit dans le port de leur arrivée.

"ART. 12.—Les Consuls généraux, Consuls et Vice-Consuls ou Agents consulaires pourront aller personnellement ou envoyer des délégués à bord des navires de leur nation, après qu'ils auront été admis en libre pratique: interroger les capitaines et l'équipage ; examiner les papiers de bord ; recevoir les déclarations sur leur voyage, leur destination et les incidents de la traversée ; dresser les manifestes et faciliter l'expédition de leurs navires ; enfin les accompagner devant les tribunaux et dans les bureaux de l'Administration du pays, pour leur servir d'interprètes et d'agents dans les affaires qu'ils auront à suivre ou les demandes qu'ils auraient à former.

"Il est convenu que les fonctionnaires de l'ordre judiciaire et les Officiers et Agents de la Douane ne pourront, en aucun cas, opérer ni visites ni recherches à bord des navires, sans être accompagnés par le Consul ou Vice-Consul de la nation à laquelle ces navires appartiennent. Ils devront également prévenir en temps opportun lesdits Agents consulaires, pour qu'ils assistent aux déclarations que les capitaines et les équipages auront à faire devant les tribunaux et les administrations locales, afin d'éviter ainsi toute erreur ou fausse interprétation qui pourrait nuire à l'exacte administration de la justice.

"La citation qui sera adressée à cet effet aux Consuls et Vice-Consuls indiquera une heure précise ; et, si les Consuls et Vice-Consuls négligeaient de s'y rendre en personne, ou de s'y faire représenter par un délégué, il sera procédé en leur absence.

"ART. 13.—En tout ce qui concerne la police des ports, le chargement et le

THE CONSULSHIP. 323

similar sources must be examined for corresponding information with reference to other countries. Till Faculties of Law, in the wider sense in which they exist abroad, are established

déchargement des navires et la sûreté des marchandises, biens et effets, on observera les lois, ordonnances et réglements du pays.

"Les Consuls généraux, Consuls et Vice-Consuls ou Agents consulaires seront chargés exclusivement du maintien de l'ordre intérieur à bord des navires marchands de leur nation ; ils régleront eux-mêmes les contestations de toute nature qui seraient survenues entre le capitaine, les officiers du navire et les matelots, et, spécialement celles relatives à la solde et à l'accomplissement des engagements réciproquement contractés.

"Les autorités locales ne pourront intervenir que lorsque les désordres survenus à bord des navires seraient de nature à troubler la tranquillité et l'ordre publics, à terre ou dans le port, ou quand une personne du pays ou ne faisant pas partie de l'équipage, s'y trouvera mêlée.

"Dans tous les autres cas, les autorités précitées se borneraient à prêter tout appui aux Consuls et Vice-Consuls ou Agents consulaires, si elles en sont requises par eux, pour faire arrêter et conduire en prison tout individu inscrit sur le rôle de l'équipage, chaque fois que, pour un motif quelconque, lesdits agents le jugeront convenable.

"ART. 14.—Les Consuls généraux, Consuls et Vice-Consuls ou Agents consulaires pourront faire arrêter et renvoyer, soit à bord, soit dans leur pays, les marins ou tout autre personne faisant, à quelque titre que ce soit, partie des équipages des navires de leur nation qui auraient déserté.

"A cet effet, ils devront s'adresser par écrit aux autorités locales compétentes, et justifier, au moyen de la présentation des registres du bâtiment ou du rôle de l'équipage, ou, si le navire était parti, en produisant une copie authentique de ces documents, que les personnes réclamées faisaient réellement partie de l'équipage. Sur cette demande ainsi justifiée, la remise des déserteurs ne pourra être refusée. On donnera, en outre, aux dits Agents consulaires, tout secours et toute assistance pour la recherche et l'arrestation de ces déserteurs qui seront conduits dans les prisons du pays et y seront détenus à la demande et aux frais du Consul et Vice-Consul, jusqu'à ce que celui-ci trouve une occasion de les faire partir.

"Cet emprisonnement ne pourra durer plus de trois mois, après lesquels, et moyennant un avis donné au Consul, trois jours à l'avance, la liberté sera rendue au prisonnier, qui ne pourra être incarcéré de nouveau pour la même cause.

"Toutefois, si le déserteur avait commis quelque délit à terre, l'autorité locale pourrait surseoir à l'extradition, jusqu'à ce que le tribunal eût rendu sa sentence, et que celle-ci eût reçu pleine et entière exécution.

in our universities, the training both of our diplomatists and consuls will continue to be greatly inferior to that of their foreign colleagues. For the present it is utterly unscientific, and scarcely rises above the character of " cram."

"Les Hautes Parties contractantes conviennent que les marins ou autres individus de l'équipage, sujets du pays dans lequel s'effectuera la désertion, sont exceptés des stipulations du présent article.

"Art. 15.—Toutes les fois qu'il n'y aura pas de stipulations contraires entre les armateurs, chargeurs et assureurs, les avaries que les navires des deux pays auront souffertes en mer, soit qu'ils entrent dans les ports respectifs volontairement ou par relâche forcée, seront réglées par les Consuls généraux, Consuls, Vice-Consuls ou Agents consulaires de leur nation, à moins que des sujets du pays dans lequel résideront lesdits Agents, ou ceux d'une tierce-puissance, ne soient intéressés dans ces avaries; dans ce cas, et à défaut de compromis amiable entre toutes les parties intéressées, elles devraient être réglées par l'autorité locale.

"Art. 16.—Lorsqu'un navire appartenant au Gouvernement ou à des sujets de l'une des Hautes Parties contractantes, fera naufrage, ou échouera sur le littoral de l'autre, les autorités locales devront porter le fait à la connaissance du Consul général, Consul, Vice-Consul ou Agent consulaire de la circonscription, et, à son défaut, à celle du Consul général, Consul, Vice-Consul ou Agent consulaire le plus voisin du lieu de l'accident.

"Toutes les opérations relatives au sauvetage des navires français, qui naufrageraient ou échoueraient dans les eaux territoriales de l'Italie, seront dirigées par les Consuls généraux, Consuls, Vice-Consuls ou Agents consulaires de France; reciproquement, toutes les opérations relatives au sauvetage des navires italiens, qui naufrageraient ou échoueraient dans les eaux territoriales de la France, seront dirigées par les Consuls généraux, Consuls, Vice-Consuls ou Agents consulaires de l'Italie.

"L'intervention des autorités locales n'aura lieu, dans les deux pays, que pour assister les Agents consulaires, maintenir l'ordre, garantir les intérêts des sauveteurs étrangers à l'équipage, assurer l'exécution des dispositions à observer pour l'entrée et la sortie des marchandises sauvées.

"En l'absence et jusqu'à l'arrivée des Consuls généraux, Consuls, Vice-Consuls et Agents consulaires, ou de la personne qu'ils délégueront à cet effet, les autorités locales devront prendre toutes les mesures nécessaires pour la protection des individus et la conservation des objets qui auront été sauvés du naufrage.

"L'intervention des autorités locales dans les différents cas ne donnera lieu à la perception de frais d'aucune espèce, hors ceux que nécessiteront les opéra-

CHAPTER VIII.

OF THE RECIPROCAL RECOGNITION OF PUBLIC MUNICIPAL LAW BY SEPARATE STATES.

1*st, Of the legislative capacity of the State.*
We have seen that recognition, whether we regard it from an absolute or a relative point of view, implies acceptance of the form of government established in the State, as adequate to

tions du sauvetage et la conservation des objets sauvés, ainsi que ceux auxquels seraient soumis, en pareil cas, les navires nationaux.

"En cas de doute sur la nationalité des navires naufragés, les dispositions mentionnées dans le présent article seront de la compétence exclusive de l'autorité locale.

"Les Hautes Parties contractantes conviennent, en outre, que les marchandises et effets sauvés ne seront sujets au payement d'aucun droit de douane, à moins qu'on ne les destine à la consommation intérieure.

"ART. 17.—Les Consuls généraux, Consuls, Vice-Consuls et Agents consulaires, ainsi que les Chanceliers, Secrétaires, Elèves ou attachés Consulaires, jouissent dans les deux pays de toutes les exemptions, prérogatives, indemnités et privilèges qui sont accordés ou seraient accordés aux Agents de même classe de la nation la plus favorisée.

"ART. 18.—La présente convention sera en vigueur pendant 12 années à dater du jour de l'échange des ratifications. Si aucune des Hautes Parties contractantes n'avait notifié à l'autre, une année avant l'expiration de ce terme, l'intention d'en faire cesser les effets, elle continuerait à rester en vigueur pendant une année encore, à partir du jour où l'une ou ·l'autre des Hautes Parties contractantes l'aura dénoncé.

"ART. 19.—Les stipulations qui précèdent sont exécutoires dans les deux États immédiatement après l'échange des ratifications.

"ART. 20.—La présente convention sera ratifiée et les ratifications en seront échangées à Paris, aussitôt que faire se pourra.

"En foi de quoi," &c.

express its rational and normal will. In recognising the State, we consequently recognise its legislative capacity; we accept its legislation, both statutory and consuetudinary, as defining the laws of its national existence sufficiently for international purposes.

2d, Of the distinction between legislation which has reference to public, and legislation which has reference to private, relations.

Between legislation which has reference to the public and to the private relations of the citizens of one State within the borders of another, there is this difference: Public relations, being dependent for their character on the character of the State itself, legislation which determines them is recognised as valid only within the legislating State; private or personal relations, on the other hand, being universal in their character, the legislation by which they are determined in the particular State is recognised as valid within the jurisdiction of other States. English law, for example, recognises the public status which the law of France assigns to an individual—that he is a citizen, a magistrate, an official, a member of a profession, or a political criminal, *only in France*. It does not assign to him any of these characters in England. As regards his private status, on the other hand—if French law says that he is major or minor, married or single, a debtor, a creditor, or a personal criminal, English law recognises these characteristics as adhering to him in England.

Though, in municipal jurisprudence, criminal law belongs to the *jus publicum*, the rule that public law is local, which results from the existence of separate political communities, finds, in international law a partial exception in the case of acts which, from their personal, and as such universal, character, States mutually regard as crimes. But this exception does not apply to crimes committed against the State itself. Political, as opposed to personal crimes, are local, and political criminals, who have taken refuge under a political organisation against which they have committed no offence, are exempted from extradition, whether at common law or by treaty. This rule, more especially if the offence be repeated in the protecting country, does not exclude the exercise, either of the jurisdiction of the locality in which the offender has taken refuge, or the exercise by the Government of the right of *renvoi*. Phillimore gives two instances of the prosecution of political offenders by the English Government,[1] and quotes a lucid judgment by Lord Lyndhurst, in which he lays down that "the offence of endeavouring to excite revolt against a neighbouring State is an offence against the law of nations; that the law of nations is part of the law of England; and, consequently, that this offence will be tried and punished in England, though only on such evidence as shall seem adequate to an English tribunal."[2]

In Roman Catholic countries international recognition will be given to the status of a priest; and the status of a graduate of a foreign university, for certain purposes, is recognised amongst ourselves.[3] To the rule, on the other hand, that private status and private rights and relations know

---

[1] Vol. i. p. 525 (2d ed.)   [2] As to extradition, *v. infra*, p. 333 *et seq.*
[3] I mean in Scotland; England being in this respect, I believe, a non-reciprocating country.

no political limits, there are important exceptions arising from divergent conceptions of natural law. These we shall consider when we come to private international law. Of the limitations implied in partial recognition we have already spoken.[1]

3d, Of the judicial capacity of the State.

Jurisdiction being merely legislation defined in relation to special cases, legislative capacity implies judicial capacity, and the recognition of the former implies the recognition of the latter. Without travelling into the *comitas gentium*, then, or any other *terra incognita* to jurisprudence in the strictest sense, we, without difficulty, trace back to the primary doctrine of recognition the rule which, with more or less strictness, has been acted upon by all civilised nations, and which Mr Dudley Field proposes to introduce into his International Code—viz., that "full faith and credit shall be given in each nation, to the public acts, records, and judicial proceedings, of the tribunals of every other nation."[2]

On this general rule the only conditions imposed by reason, and recognised by practice, seem to be the following:—

1st, The judgment must be pronounced by a tribunal which the State to which it belongs regards as competent to deal with the case.

2d, It must be a judgment between parties duly cited, and legally represented, or defaulting.

3d, It must not be inconsistent with the public law, or the conceptions of morality prevalent in the country in which it is sought to be enforced.

[1] *Ante*, p. 216 *et seq.*   [2] P. 445.

To these conditions some States add that of *reciprocity*, but in this country we have followed the more liberal practice of dispensing with this condition;[1] and in England, Scotland, and the United States, a judgment by the tribunal of a State, which does not itself give effect to the *exceptio rei judicatæ* in favour of foreign States, will receive execution. In adopting this rule, we act on the maxim of the free-trader, that it is no reason why we should do what is wrong and foolish, that others refuse to do what is right and reasonable.

As "no State allows a foreign judgment to be executed within its territory, except under the authority and by the order of its own tribunal,"[2] and as no tribunal will execute a judgment without inquiry, if not into its merits, at least into its validity in the country in which it was pronounced, a foreign judgment may be impeached on the grounds of fraud or collusion.[3] Short of such allegations, however, or of a plea that it is excluded by one of the three conditions already mentioned, no inquiry ought to be made into the character of a foreign judgment; and States like France, which allow every foreign judgment to be questioned on its merits, sin against the principle of recognition. It is important to observe that this dictum applies to prize courts as well as to courts of municipal jurisdiction. "Since the case of Bernardi against Motteux,"[4] says Phillimore,[5] "it has been the clearly recognised law of England, that the sentences of courts of competent jurisdiction to decide questions of prize, are received in England as conclusive evidence in actions upon policies of in-

[1] Phillimore, vol. iv. p. 730 (2d ed.)   [2] Phill., vol. iv. p. 728.
[3] Field, p. 446.   [4] 2 Douglas, Rep. 526.   [5] P. 747.

surance, and upon every subject immediately and properly within the jurisdiction of such foreign courts. The question in later cases has not been with reference to the conclusive nature of the sentence, but whether it was given upon the point in controversy."

4th, *Of the executive capacity of the State.*

Rational will necessarily translates itself into power.[1] In recognising the legislative and judicial capacity of a State, we consequently recognise its executive capacity. The recognised State has thus a perfect right to demand, and, apart from other considerations, to enforce, the execution of its judicial sentences by the recognising State. But international rights being conditioned by the fact of separate political existence, foreign judgments can receive execution only by the political organisation which governs the State within which they are executed. Within the sphere of the normal relations one State cannot execute its own judgment within the territories of another State. Whilst foreign judgments are interpreted according to the law of the State in which they are pronounced, it may consequently be stated as a rule without exception, that their execution follows the law of the State which executes them. " It seems a clear proposition, of reason and law, that the foreign judgment when recognised must be interpreted and considered, as to its effects, according to the law of the State in which it was pronounced. Savigny and Fœlix are in complete accordance upon this not unimportant point."[2] On the other hand, that " the form and manner of its execution are exclusively governed by the law of the State

[1] *Institutes of Law*, p. 427.   [2] Phill., vol. iv. p. 729 (2d ed.).

which recognises and executes the judgment, is a clear proposition of public as well as international law, and does not appear to have been even controverted."[1]

5th, *Of the* forum *of foreigners.*

The question of the *forum* to which legal relations belong, falls properly under the subject of private international law. All that it seems necessary here to say on the subject is, that the civil tribunals of each State are open to the citizens of every other[2] who, for the time being, may be resident within their jurisdiction; and this not only for the enforcement of rights which have been already judicially ascertained elsewhere, but for their ascertainment. In this country, and in the United States, no exception is in this respect made, though the suit be between two *undomiciled* foreigners, for the breach of an obligation contracted *abroad*. But the extreme liberality of this rule is still exceptional.[3] The defender's residence is his *forum*, to which the pursuer must follow him. The maxim, *actor sequitur forum rei*, holds good in international as in municipal jurisdiction. The *forum* of the defender, as regards execution, is that of fulfilment, whatever may be the law—that is to say, the municipal system, by which the relation may fall to be construed. Foreigners, whether litigating with foreigners or with natives, are consequently at liberty to employ advocates and agents, of whatever description, recognised by the local law; and in the enforcement of such rights

---

[1] Phill., vol. iv. p. 731 (2d ed.)

[2] In Scotland provision was made by statute for "acctiones of strangers of uther renlmes" so early as 1487, c. 105.—Mackay's *Practice of the Court of Session*, Introduction, p. 9.

[3] Phill., vol. iv. p. 706 (2d ed.) *et seq.* Wharton, *Conflict of Laws*, p. 4 (new ed.)

as fall within the local jurisdiction, they are entitled to call into play the whole resources of the executive at the command of the citizens of the State. The municipal law of every recognised State being thus, as it were, adopted by the municipal law of every recognising State, stands, in point of efficiency, in a very favourable position when contrasted with the public law of nations, which has, as yet, no local habitation, and consequently no executive anywhere.

6*th, Of the exceptional position of criminal judgments.*

At first sight it would appear as if these principles must apply almost à *fortiori* to the sentences of criminal courts. Criminal law, seen from a municipal point of view, is, as I have said, public law (*jus publicum*); and this, for the very obvious reason that a crime against a citizen is a crime against the State. All well-ordered States, with the partial and very unfortunate exception of England, have long been accustomed to prosecute and to punish crimes in their own behalf, as well as in behalf of the citizen more immediately injured. From the State character which thus belongs to it, criminal law partakes of the local character which adheres to other departments of State law. But in the case of ordinary offences against property and person, their public and local is subordinated to their personal and universal character; and as the prevention of such crimes is the very first effort of incipient civilisation, it does not seem an extravagant stretch of international confidence for recognising States to assume, as a rule, their reciprocal capacity to deal with them. I consequently regard them as bound by the principle of recognition, and consequently by the common law of nations, apart from all special treaties, to act on that assumption. To a certain extent they no doubt do so. Wherever there is plenary recognition, the recognising State credits the recognised State with this capacity, and the former intrusts its citizens resident within the borders of the latter to its criminal jurisdiction. Each State administers its own criminal laws within its territories to foreigners and natives alike; and from its sentences there is—and, in the absence of an international tribunal, there can be—no judicial appeal. Even diplomatic interference with the criminal sentence of a foreign State, or with its execution in cases in which the crime has been committed within its territories, would be a violation of the principle of recognition.

The normal duties of the recognising State, even to its own citizens resident within the recognised State, have been fulfilled when, through the intervention of its ambassadors and consuls, it has seen that the local law of the recognised State is fairly administered to them.

As regards the citizens of the recognised State, any interference with the action of the local law would be a positive breach of the law of nations. Even in the case of a partially recognised and partially protected State, such interference is forbidden. Lord Dufferin's interposition in behalf of Midhat Pasha (July 1881) was wholly unofficial in form, however peremptory it may have been in substance. When Lord Granville's attention was called to the persecution of the Jews in Russia, and the alleged apathy of the Russian Government, in the House of Lords (Feb. 9, 1882), he declined, with the approval of Lord Salisbury, to interfere officially; and

Lord Shaftesbury, the great humanitarian, went the length of saying that, "so far from calling upon her Majesty's Government to interfere diplomatically, he doubted whether it would be wise even to exercise their moral influence."

So far, then, each State accepts the criminal law of every other State. But it is not enough that States shall permit each other's criminal laws to take their course, reciprocally, in the case of citizens resident within them—and this even when these laws are at variance with those of the domicile of the individual who is subjected to them. In loyal obedience to the principle of recognition, they must, as I have said, go farther than this. Each State must make the other's case its own, and aid it in the administration of its criminal laws and the execution of its criminal judgments. This view received the sanction of the Institute of International Law, in its meeting at Oxford in 1880.[1] "It is not treaties only that make extradition an act in conformity with law, and it may take place in the absence of any contractual obligation." To assume the legislative and judicial capacity of a State, is to assume its right to legislate and adjudicate, because powers and capacities generate rights; and to assume its rights, and to decline the duty of aiding in their enforcement, is to set at naught the universal principles, that rights imply the conditions of their exercise, and that duties are coextensive with rights. It is neither more nor less than to break with ethics altogether as the basis of jurisprudence, and to leave it without any basis at all. Much confusion has been introduced

[1] Resolution III. *Annuaire de l'Institut de Droit International*, 1881-82, p. 127; or *infra*, p. 345 note.

into this, as into so many other subjects—that of the recognition of civil judgments included—by the false distinction which we have encountered so often between perfect and imperfect obligations.

"The extradition of fugitives from justice," we are told by Mr Wheaton, "is an imperfect obligation;" and Sir Robert Phillimore's otherwise excellent chapter on extradition contains the remark, that "the result of the whole consideration of this subject is, that the extradition of criminals is a matter of *comity*, not of right, except in the cases of special convention."[1] Neither Wheaton nor Phillimore here, or anywhere else, attempts to trace the doctrine of comity to any ultimate principle; but both give lists of the writers by whom it is rejected and accepted, and as the latter list is the longer one, they accept the preponderance of numbers as decisive! The element of quality, however, appears not unworthy of consideration, if it were on no other ground than that the minority is headed by Grotius, and that the list ends with Kent. Kent's dictum, which Phillimore quotes,[2] is very remarkable, as coming from an American writer more than half a century ago. "It is the *duty* of Government to surrender up fugitives on demand, after the civil magistrate shall have ascertained the existence of reasonable ground for the charge, and sufficient to put the accused on his trial. For the guilty party cannot be tried and punished

[1] Vol. i. p. 522 (3d ed.) See another curious instance of this in Phillimore, vol. iv. p. 728, where he says that "law and comity speak different languages," and where, in virtue of the distinction, he of course assumes that, whilst comity speaks the language of common-sense, law speaks nonsense!
[2] *Ib.*, p. 519.

by any other jurisdiction than the one whose laws have been violated; therefore the duty of surrendering him applies as well to the case of the subjects of the State surrendering, as to the case of the subjects of the Power demanding, the fugitive." After quoting this passage, Phillimore makes the following instructive remark: "It must be admitted," he says, "that the English courts, even before the treaties and statutes hereinafter mentioned, appear to have held the doctrine that international comity was sufficiently stringent to compel the surrender of the criminal;" and he proceeds to cite cases in proof of his assertion. Surely *comity* that is sufficiently *stringent* to *compel*, treads rather too hard upon the heels of the *jus strictum!*

I have elsewhere[1] stated very fully the grounds on which I repudiate this cherished distinction; and when we come to private international law, I shall give you some other instances, equally remarkable, of its misleading character.

The obligation, then, not only to permit, but to aid in the administration of each other's criminal law, is a *debitum justitiæ*, —an obligation which, like all other obligations, is perfect in principle, and results as clearly from the doctrine of recognition as the doctrine of recognition itself results from the fact of State-existence. Grotius's position, that it is an *obligatio disjunctiva*,[2] which the State may satisfy, either by punishing the criminal itself, or by giving him up to be punished, does not satisfy the demands of the doctrine of recognition. The punishment must be intrusted to the State in which the crime is committed, otherwise the legislative and judicial capacity of

---

[1] *Institutes of Law*, p. 281 et seq.   [2] Grotius, lib. ii. c. xxi., iv. 3.

that State is ignored; and when Kent applies this principle to "the case of the subjects of the State surrendering, as well as to the case of the subjects of the Power demanding, the fugitive," his logic is irrefragable, though the opposite be the rule which is generally followed in extradition treaties. This objection, however, would not apply to the same extent if it was in his own State that the fugitive took refuge, and if it administered the criminal law, or enforced the sentence of the State in which the crime was committed, not its own criminal law applicable to the crime,—and this may have been what Grotius intended. But his words are indefinite, and he merely says that the State into which the criminal has fled shall punish him *pro merito*.[1]

The following were the dicta of the Institute on this subject: "Between States whose criminal legislation rests on analogous bases and which have mutual confidence in their judicial institutions, the extradition of *natives* would be a means of insuring the good administration of penal justice, because it is desirable as much as possible to take advantage of the jurisdiction of the *forum delicti commissi*.

"Even in admitting the actual practice which withdraws natives from extradition, no account ought to be taken of a nationality which has been acquired since the perpetration of the crime for which extradition is claimed."[2]

[1] The words are: Cum vero non soleant civitates permittere ut civitas altera armata intra fines suos pœnæ expetendæ nomine veniat, neque id expediat, sequitur ut civitas, apud quam degit qui culpæ est compertus, alterum facere debeat, aut ut ipsa interpellata pro merito puniat nocentem, aut ut eum permittat arbitrio interpellantis: hoc enim illud est dedere quod in historiis sæpissime occurrit: . . . est enim disjunctiva obligatio.—*Ut sup.* 1 and 3.

[2] *Infra*, p. 345 note.

In principle, then, there is nothing connected with this obligation that is either obscure or exceptional; and the only question with reference to it is as to the manner in which it can best be fulfilled. Is it more convenient, with a view to the jural punishment of crime, that States should agree to administer each other's criminal laws, and enforce each other's criminal sentences, judicially, or that they should, diplomatically, hand over their criminals, whether strangers or citizens, to each other, in order that each State may administer and enforce its own? The response of experience, in the case of foreigners, has been in favour of the latter alternative. For this there are two obvious reasons, which, in the case of natives, seem scarcely less forcible.

(1st) *The diversity of punishments arising from the necessity of adapting them to the special conditions of each people, or to the opinions with reference to these conditions which locally prevail.* We have seen that in civil cases foreign judgments in general are interpreted and their effects determined according to the laws of the States in which they are pronounced. Like a foreign contract, a foreign judgment is construed by foreign law; but the methods of procedure employed for its enforcement are prescribed by the law of the place where it is enforced. Now it would be very inconvenient that a foreign State, in which capital punishment had been abolished, should be called upon to administer the law of a State in which it was maintained—*e.g.*, to condemn and hang an Englishman; or worse still, to condemn and hang one of its own citizens for a murder which he had committed, and for which he would have been hanged in England. On the other hand, if we were to depart from this rule and adopt the punishment imposed in the country in which the criminal was resident, a country which had abolished capital punishment would immediately become a receptacle for all the murderers who could contrive to escape from the countries in which that punishment was still retained. Then, if we pass from major to minor offences, how could the passport or tariff regulations of a Continental country be administered or observed by English law? These are delinquencies to which the rule, *de minimis prætor non curat*, may apply, and they are not generally covered by extradition treaties; but if there is to be a *prætor* at all, he must be the local *prætor*, and the law which he administers must be the local *jus prætorium*.

(2*d*) *The difficulty of throwing criminal courts open to foreign prosecutors, as civil courts are thrown open to civil pursuers.* Even in cases in which States that have adopted milder criminal codes than their neighbours, might be willing to give foreigners the benefit of what they conceive to be an advance in civilisation, the proceeding is rendered almost impossible by the difficulty of prosecuting crimes in other countries than those in which they have been committed,—a difficulty which arises from the necessity not only of discovering and transporting witnesses, but of examining localities. The laws of evidence too, which play so prominent a part in criminal prosecutions, as I have said, belong to the *lex fori*, and in many respects necessarily partake of a local character.[1]

7*th, Of extradition treaties.*

In these circumstances, with a view to prevent the mis-

---

[1] *Report of Royal Commission on Extradition*, 1868—Sect. II.

carriage of justice, extradition treaties have now been negotiated between almost all civilised States. Unless regulated by treaty, the Institute holds that the practice of extradition can never be certain and regular.[1] In virtue of these treaties, States surrender to each other those whom they mutually regard as criminals, on the demand of the executive, conveyed through the usual organs of diplomatic intercourse. In some States the intervention of the judicial element in the extraditing State is requisite, whilst in others the demand of the foreign State is accepted as a *prima facie* proof of guilt. In the opinion of the Institute, the former ought to be the universal rule.

On this subject the Institute says :—

" XVIII. It is desirable that in the countries of refuge, the magistrates should be called upon to judge of the demand for extradition after an open debate " (*après un débat contradictoire*).

" XIX. The State called upon ought not to make the extradition, if the competent judicial authority has decided that, in accordance with its public law, the demand ought not to be entertained." [2]

It is a point on which a wide division of opinion and practice still exists, whether the competent authority, judicial or other, should grant extradition on the production of a warrant of arrest for the imputed crime duly issued by the foreign magistrate, or should require that the commission of the crime should be so established as that the laws of the country where the fugitive, or person accused, is found, would

[1] *Infra*, p. 345 note. [2] *Ib.*, p. 347 note.

justify his apprehension and committal for trial, if the crime had been there committed. The former is the more usual system on the Continent, but the latter requirement is insisted on in England.

These treaties usually contain lists of all the ordinary crimes against person and property; and the special crime alleged to have been committed must, in general, be specified. It has been a disputed point whether a person extradited on one charge may be tried upon another embraced in the list; and the question is not quite settled even in the present day. The American Government maintained [1] that in the Treaty of 1842 between England and the United States, there is no provision that a criminal extradited shall not be tried for an offence other than that upon which he has been surrendered. The English Government, taking the contrary view, refused to surrender a person,[2] whose extradition was demanded by the United States, unless it were guaranteed that he should not be tried on any other charge than that upon which he was extradited. This position was maintained, chiefly on the very doubtful argument that the Act of Parliament of 1870 [3] had the power to give construction to the Treaty of 1842, and to effect a modification of its provisions. Since then, however, the opinion of the English lawyers has changed. The *Report of the Royal Commission on Extradition*,[4] presented to Parlia-

---

[1] Case of Lawrence, *State Papers* (1876), lxxxii.
[2] Case of Winslow, *State Papers* (1876), lxxxii. and lxxxviii.; also Brent, *Times*, June 20, 1876.
[3] 33 & 34 Vict. c. 52, sect. 19.
[4] *Report of Royal Commissioners on Extradition*, May 1878—Sections VII. and XIV.

ment in 1878, adopted the views maintained by the United States, and recommended new legislation and a new treaty, extending extradition to all crimes specially enumerated.

On this subject the views of the Institute are thus expressed:—

"XXII. The Government which has obtained an extradition for a definite offence is bound at common law, if there is no convention to the contrary, not to allow the prisoner to be tried or punished for any other offence.[1]

"XXIII. The Government which accords the extradition, may, however, consent that the prisoner shall be tried for other offences than those which led to his extradition, provided that these are offences which would have led to extradition."[2]

The only exceptions as regards ordinary crimes which this country and most others introduce, have reference to their own citizens and subjects who, as I have said, are reserved for the local courts. Foreign political offenders we do not ourselves treat as criminals; and in the adoption of the rule, which exempts them from extradition, most other countries have now followed our example and that of Switzerland.[3]

But the definition of a political offence is still a matter of some difficulty. This subject was keenly discussed at the meeting of the Institute in Oxford, in September 1880, as could not fail to be the case in an assembly in which democratic and despotic States were equally represented, and at a time when, from what had already occurred, the murder of the Emperor of Russia, which took place shortly afterwards,

---

[1] *Infra*, p. 347 note.   [2] *Ib.*, p. 347 note.
[3] See treaty between Germany and Italy, October 1876.

was no doubt regarded by M. de Martens, who was present, as a possible event. The following were the conclusions at which we arrived:—

" XIII. Extradition ought not to take place for political offences.

" XIV. The Government to which the requisition is made has the sovereign right of determining, according to the circumstances of the case, whether the facts, in virtue of which extradition is claimed, have or have not a political character. In appreciating these facts it ought to be inspired by the two following ideas:

" *a.* Facts which unite in themselves all the characteristics of crimes at common law (assassinations, fire-raisings, thefts, and the like) ought not to be excepted from extradition, on the sole ground that their authors had a political intention :

" *b.* Extradition for crimes having at once the character of political crimes and crimes at common law, ought not to be accorded, without receiving from the State demanding the extradition, the assurance that the prisoner will not be judged by an exceptional tribunal.

" XV. Extradition ought not to apply to desertion of soldiers or sailors belonging to the army or navy of the State demanding it, for purely military delinquencies. But the adoption of this rule ought not to be an obstacle to the giving up of sailors belonging to the navy or to the mercantile marine of the State, where the matter is regulated either by treaties or by mercantile usages."[1]

To prevent the escape of criminals, provision is now made

[1] *Infra*, p. 346 note.

for arrests being effected by telegraphic messages from one Government to another, the production of the requisite documents being afterwards made.

The expenses connected with extradition naturally fall upon the Government which demands it.

8*th, Of the* droit de renvoi.

There can be no question of the right of a State to refuse its hospitality to the citizens of any other State whose presence it regards as detrimental to its interests, or whose character is a subject of national abhorrence, though it may not be possible to prove that they have committed any crime for which they can be tried by the positive law of either country. We are no more bound to harbour blackguards within the borders of the State than to permit them to enter our doors. The right of expulsion, when exercised for purposes of police, and not with a view to prevent the competition of foreign skill or labour, has been universally recognised; and the Alien Acts, which were passed in 1792 and 1793, in consequence of the influx of foreigners caused by the French Revolution, and which have been unhappily again called for in Ireland, are declaratory of the common law of nations. Mr Field (§ 321, p. 165) very properly proposes to qualify the absolute terms in which the rule is commonly stated, by the condition that the cause of expulsion shall be explained to the nation the members of which are expelled. This right of expulsion, of course, ceases with naturalisation even in cases in which the original citizenship subsists; and, with the facilities for naturalisation which are now given, this becomes a consideration of importance. On the other hand, as regards the interests of the State to which the alien belongs, though the question of expulsion, like that of extradition, falls to be decided by the State in which the obnoxious individuals have taken refuge, and no free State can be called upon to give them up, it is an international duty to take precautions to prevent them, whilst residing within its boundaries, from injuring the State from which they have escaped. In the case of military refugees, this is done by "interning" them at a distance from the frontier; whilst civilians, at the request of the nation to which they belong, conveyed through its ambassador, will be placed under the surveillance of the police. Failure to adopt such measures of precaution gives rise to an international right,[1] on the part of the threatened State, to demand their expulsion.[2]

---

[1] Bluntschli, quoted by Hall, p. 177.

[2] The following are the Resolutions on the subject of "Extradition" above referred to :—

" I. L'extradition est un acte international, conforme à la justice et à l'intérêt des États, puisqu'il tend à prévenir et à réprimer efficacement les infractions à la loi pénale.

" II. L'extradition n'est pratiquée d'une manière sûre et régulière que s'il y a des traités, et il est à désirer que ceux-ci deviennent de plus en plus nombreux.

" III. Toutefois ce ne sont pas les traités seuls qui font de l'extradition un acte conforme au droit et elle peut s'opérer même en l'absence de tout lien contractuel.

" IV. Il est à désirer que, dans chaque pays, une loi règle la procédure de la matière, ainsi que les conditions auxquelles les individus réclamés comme malfaiteurs seront livrés aux gouvernements avec lesquels il n'existe pas de traité.

" V. La condition de la réciprocité, en cette matière, peut-être commandée par la politique ; elle n'est pas exigée par la justice.

" VI. Entre pays dont la législation criminelle reposerait sur des bases analogues et qui auraient confiance mutuelle dans leurs institutions judiciaires, l'extradition des nationaux serait un moyen d'assurer la bonne administration de la justice pénale, parce qu'on doit considérer comme désirable que la juridiction du *forum delicti commissi* soit, autant que possible, appelée à le juger.

" VII. En admettant même la pratique actuelle qui soustrait les nationaux à

In conclusion, it must be distinctly understood that the *droit de renvoi* extends to the citizens of a recognised State only as individuals. The expulsion or exclusion of the citizens of a recognised State, as such, would be a violation of the principle of recognition and a breach of the law of nations. Even in the case of a partially recognised State, like China, there can, I think, be no question that the withdrawal of the Chinese Embassy from Washington is the appropriate re-

l'extradition, on ne devrait pas tenir compte d'une nationalité acquise seulement depuis la perpétration du fait, pour lequel l'extradition est réclamée.

"VIII. La compétence de l'État requérant doit être justifiée par sa propre loi, et elle ne doit pas être en contradiction avec la loi du pays de refuge.

"IX. S'il y a plusieurs demandes d'extradition pour le même fait, la préférence devrait être donnée à l'État sur le territoire duquel l'infraction a été commise.

"X. Si le même individu est réclamé par plusieurs États à raison d'infractions différentes, on devrait avoir égard, en général, à la gravité relative de ces infractions.

"XI. En règle, on doit exiger que les faits, auxquels s'applique l'extradition, soient punis par la législation des deux pays, excepté dans les cas où, à cause des institutions particulières ou de la situation géographique du pays de refuge, les circonstances de fait qui constituent le délit ne peuvent s'y produire.

"XII. L'extradition, étant toujours une mesure grave, ne doit s'appliquer qu'aux infractions de quelque importance. Les traités doivent les énumérer avec précision ; leurs dispositions à ce sujet varient naturellement suivant la situation respective des pays contractants.

"XIII. L'extradition ne doit pas avoir lieu pour faits politiques.

"XIV. Le gouvernement requis apprécie souverainement, d'après les circonstances, si le fait à raison duquel l'extradition est réclamée a ou non un caractère politique. Dans cette appréciation, il doit s'inspirer des deux idées suivantes :

"(a) Les faits, qui réunissent tous les caractères de crimes de droit commun (assassinats, incendies, vols), ne doivent pas être exceptés de l'extradition à raison seulement de l'intention politique de leurs auteurs.

"(b) En tout cas, l'extradition pour crimes ayant tout à la fois le caractère de crime politique et de crime de droit commun ne devra être accordée que si l'État requérant donne l'assurance que l'extradé ne sera pas jugé par des tribunaux d'exception.

"XV. L'extradition ne doit pas s'appliquer à la désertion des militaires appartenant à l'armée de terre ou de mer, et aux délits purement militaires. L'adop-

sponse to the passing of the Chinese Exclusion Act by the Congress of the United States. Were the Irish to be similarly excluded, though they form but a very insignificant portion of the population of the British empire, there can, I imagine, be little question that the measure would be treated by this country as a *casus belli*; whilst, on the other hand, the expulsion of Fenians would be regarded as an exercise of the right of *renvoi*, of the propriety of which the United States was fully entitled to judge.

tion de cette règle ne fait pas obstacle à la livraison des matelots appartenant à la marine de l'État ou à la marine marchande, qui est réglée par les traités ou par les usages maritimes.

"XVI. Une loi ou un traité d'extradition peuvent s'appliquer à des faits commis antérieurement à leur mise en vigueur.

"XVII. L'extradition doit avoir lieu par la voie diplomatique.

"XVIII. Il est à désirer que, dans le pays de refuge, des magistrats soient appelés à apprécier la demande d'extradition après un débat contradictoire.

"XIX. L'État requis ne doit pas faire l'extradition si d'après son droit public l'autorité judiciaire a décidé que la demande ne doit pas être accueillie.

"XX. Le gouvernement qui a obtenu une extradition pour un fait déterminé est, de plein droit et sauf convention contraire, obligé de ne laisser juger ou punir l'extradé que pour ce fait.

"XXI. Le gouvernement qui a accordé une extradition peut ensuite consentir à ce que l'extradé soit jugé pour des faits autres que celui qui avait motivé sa remise, pourvu que ces faits peuvent donner lieu à l'extradition.

"XXII. Le gouvernement qui a un individu en son pouvoir par suite d'une extradition ne peut le livrer à un autre gouvernement sans le consentement de celui qui le lui a livré.

"XXIII. L'acte émané de l'autorité judiciaire qui déclare l'extradition admissible devra constater les circonstances dans lesquelles l'extradition a eu lieu et les faits pour lesquels elle a été accordée.

"XXIV. L'extradé devrait être admis à proposer comme exception préalable, devant le tribunal appelé à le juger définitivement, l'irrégularité des conditions dans lesquelles l'extradition a été accordée."

CHAPTER IX.

OF THE RECIPROCAL RECOGNITION OF PRIVATE MUNICIPAL LAW BY SEPARATE STATES.

1*st, Introductory remarks.*

We have seen that the local character which, from national and political causes, adheres to the rights and obligations of the citizen, does not circumscribe those of the individual. The relations in which human beings, considered simply as rational and responsible entities, stand to each other, are, in their nature, universal and independent of the communities to which these entities belong—they are *juris gentium*, not *juris gentis*. But in order that they may be realised as objects of positive law, these relations must be defined, not only in their universal and permanent, but in their local and temporal aspects; for it is in the colouring which it takes from the conditions of its manifestation that positive differs from natural law. It is here that the international element—the element, that is to say, which jurisprudence derives from the division of mankind into separate communities—comes into play. The right and duty of mutual confidence involved in the primary doctrine of recognition, implies the acceptance by the recognising State of the definitions which the recognised State may have imposed on these legal relations; and this, as a rule, even when these definitions differ from those which it imposes on the same legal relations when existing between its own citizens. It is to the doctrine which treats of this interchange of jural confidence that the term Private International Law is commonly applied.

This subject is often, indeed usually, treated as a separate branch of the science of jurisprudence, and is even cultivated by a separate class of international jurists. Though this arrangement may have given rise to some theoretical misconceptions, for practical purposes it is commendable. Private international law, as we shall see, has no claim to the character, which its cultivators have sometimes ascribed to it, of a separate system of positive law, ranking *pari passu* either with municipal systems or with the public law of nations. As Mr Hall has said, it is not even a part of international law proper,[1] which is confined to the relations of States to States; and the multitude of relations and consequent interests affected by its rules is so great as to render it scarcely possible that it should be satisfactorily studied otherwise than apart. On this ground, I should gladly have handed it over to the many eminent specialists, by whom it is at present cultivated. From this mode of treatment, however, I am precluded by the scheme of this treatise, in which my aim is to present the science of international law, not exhaustively but completely, by exhibiting the interdependence of its parts, and by tracing them up to their ultimate source in nature, and their proximate source in recognition, rather than down to their consequences in particular places and at given times. In dealing with this important and difficult subject, I shall consequently be con-

[1] Hall's *International Law*, p. 45.

tented if, by defining its limits and determining its international character so far as it goes, I can place the objects of the study clearly before my readers, and remove certain misconceptions that have prevailed very widely with reference to the foundations on which it rests.

Sect. I.—*Of the relation in which private international law stands to the doctrine of international recognition.*

The fact of recognition carries with it a presumption to the effect, not only of the recognised State having justly defined the legal relations which fall within its jurisdiction, but of its being able and willing to enforce its definitions. It is from this presumption that the right of every separate political entity arises, not only to administer its own municipal law, without interference within its own limits, but to have that law, in so far as it affects the interest of its citizens, recognised by every other separate political entity. The recognition of private legal relations, as defined by each separate State, thus follows as a corollary from the general doctrine of recognition. It appeals to no separate fact, and calls no alien principle into play. It is indeed merely the right of recognition seen on its private side; and if the fact of existence warrants recognition in the one direction, it warrants it in the other. For one State to deny the private rights of the citizens of another, or to withhold the presumption of its ability to define and enforce them, is, so far, to withdraw recognition. The narrower form of private recognition is, therefore, a *debitum justitiæ*, just as much as the wider form of public recognition; and without entering on special considerations at all, and resting simply on the general principles of our system, we thus get rid of the necessity for any exceptional basis for this branch of our science.

Nor is the primary presumption, springing from the general doctrine of recognition, invalidated by the fact that legal relations, nominally identical, may be differently defined by the recognised and the recognising State. In studying the character of positive law, we have seen that the form of a legal relation may, and very often does, depend on the local circumstances in which it arises, and those local circumstances must be locally determined. Cosmopolitan relations may be dealt with by cosmopolitan science; but each separate political entity must be credited with municipal insight peculiar to itself, and we shall consequently find, on analysing them, that the whole of the doctrines of private international law, as a separate branch of the science of jurisprudence, resolve themselves into the single doctrine of the localisation of legal relations. It was to the acute mind of Savigny that the subject first presented itself in this simple aspect; and though even he did not throw off the trammels of the previous teaching to the extent that the leading Continental and American jurists have now done, and his faithful friend and disciple, M. C. Brocher of Geneva, may sometimes be disposed to claim rather too much for him, there can be no doubt that the inadequacy of the *comitas gentium*, as a basis for this particular department of international law, was first pointed out in that eighth volume of his *System* which Mr Guthrie has so excellently translated and commented for our use.

Sect. II.—*Of the objects of private international law.*

Savigny says that the object of this branch of jurisprudence, whether it be brought into action by the collision of particular laws in the same State, or of the territorial laws of independent States, is "to ascertain for every legal relation that law to which, in its proper nature, it belongs or is subject."

To the words legal relation, as the literal rendering of the German phrase *Rechtsverhältniss*,[1] Mr Guthrie, here and elsewhere, appends, as an equivalent, the word "*case;*" and Mr Westlake, in his first edition, defines private international law, "That department of private jurisprudence which determines before the courts of what nation each suit should be brought, and by the law of what nation it should be decided." It will be obvious to you, however, that a legal relation does not by any means imply the existence either of a case or of a suit. Marriage, for example, and guardianship, are legal relations; but it would be very sad if all marriages gave rise to cases, or if all guardianships ended in suits. The primary object of jurisprudence is, so to influence the conduct of individuals by the knowledge or science of jural relations which it teaches, as to prevent such occurrences, not to deal with them when they occur; and by the medium of private international law, jurisprudence seeks to effect this object by assigning legal relations to the municipal or territorial law by which it assumes that they will be found to have been already determined. If that law requires to deal with them judicially, that is an accident, arising possibly from its imperfection as a system, but for which private international law, as a doctrine of jurisdiction, is not

---

[1] The *Rechtsverhältniss* or *legal relation* is the jural fact or phenomenon, in itself; the *case* is the statement of it as it exists, or is supposed to exist, in the particular instance; and the *suit* is the process by which its reality, if disputed, is inquired into and determined.

responsible. It is an error very characteristic of practical lawyers to imagine that legal relations are defined only for the purpose of facilitating litigation, whereas the effect of their perfect definition would be to prevent litigation altogether, except in so far as it arises out of questions of fact. As the empire of scientific jurisprudence extends, the sphere of litigation diminishes; and it is possibly an indistinct perception of this fact which renders practitioners, for the most part, so inimical to scientific jurisprudence.

Even when legal relations give occasion to cases or suits, the vast majority of them, of course, raise no questions of local law or local jurisdiction. Where both parties are resident in, and citizens of, the same country, and where the subject-matter of the controversy is likewise wholly within its boundaries, it is plain that the native law and the native courts must exclude all others. If foreign law is referred to at all, it can only be by way of illustration, or in order to aid counsel in arriving at an opinion, or the court in applying the native law by the light which may be shed on it by comparative jurisprudence. On the other hand, it is not necessary, in order to raise a question of law or of jurisdiction, that the parties should either be resident in a foreign country, or that they should be resident in, or citizens of, different countries. Suppose a man and a woman, both domiciled in Scotland, marry abroad, where the marriage law is different from ours, and that they immediately return to Scotland: the question of the validity of such a marriage in the country in which it was contracted may become a very important element in judging of its validity in Scotland; and the same may be true with reference to its effects, whether here or abroad. Or, without quitting the country at all, two Scotchmen may enter into a contract the validity of which may depend on foreign law. Suppose the one sells to the other an estate which he professes to have inherited in a foreign country—a sugar or a cotton plantation, in a Dutch or a Portuguese colony, we shall say—the laws of succession and of the transference of heritable property in Holland or in Portugal, or in their respective colonies, may have to be inquired into, and, if necessary, judicially determined in a Scotch court; and this even although the cause should finally be sent to Holland or to Portugal. And the same thing may occur though the estate be situated in one of our own colonies—*e.g.*, in the Mauritius or in British Guiana—if the French or Dutch law of succession has not been repealed by Act of Parliament. Even in so ordinary a transaction as the sale of moveables—wine at Bordeaux, or corn at Dantsic—a more or less clear indication of intention may raise the question whether the contract shall be governed by Scotch or by foreign law. Nor is it necessary, in order to give occasion to a question of jurisdiction, that there should be diversity of law; and consequently, the epithet of "the conflict of laws," which has been used to characterise this department of jurisprudence, is not a happy one. Systems which are foreign to each other are not necessarily conflicting systems; on the contrary, as regards all the leading relations of life, those of the different nations of Europe are far more frequently identical. Still, if the relation arose in a foreign country, this very fact of identity must be determined, and it may be necessary to ascertain the law of a foreign country before we can administer our own. A case of private international law may thus arise which involves no conflict. The change of *forum* alone, without any diversity of rule, may affect, or even reverse the decision, for the simple reason that the laws of evidence and procedure are those of the *forum*. The laws of succession, marriage, &c., being identical, the facts may admit of proof in one country and not in another.

But even where identity of rule does not exist, the very object of this branch of jurisprudence is, by referring the question to its *real forum*, to seek the true rule. There must, as we have seen, be such a rule, and there can be but one; and the fact of its existence renders the conflict merely apparent. The so-called conflict is simply the question to which, of two or more municipal systems, the relation belongs,—a question the answer to which is, for the most part, quite independent of the agreement or difference between the territorial laws. And as mere identity of rule does not prevent the existence of questions of private international law, so neither does mere disparity of rule produce conflict, provided there be no controversy as to the rule to be adopted, or of the municipal system which is to prevail. The only real conflict, as Bar [1] following Savigny has pointed out, arises where two municipal systems essentially distinct both claim to determine the same legal relation, and determine it differently; a state of matters which obviously can arise only from imperfection in this very branch of jurisprudence, or its imperfect recognition by the one system or the other.

Where two or more systems exist under the same legis-

[1] *Das Internationale Privat und Strafrecht*, p. 7.

lature, and there is a court of appeal which strives to bring them into accordance by a process of continual assimilation, there are quite sure to be divergent judgments, but there can be no true international conflicts. The conflicting judgments pronounced by the Court of Session and the House of Lords, even when they proceed from opposing national traditions, have no proper place in international jurisprudence. However the fact may stand, the theory is, that the House of Lords administers Scotch law, and that there is but one final judgment, which is Scotch. A conflict of systems would no doubt arise if the same question were tried and differently decided in the Court of Session, and in a court of law of co-ordinate jurisdiction in England; the question of legitimation *per subsequens matrimonium*, for example, in England and in Scotland. But even here it could scarcely be called an international conflict, so long as there was but one nation. In the valuable chapters on international law which Mr Fraser has given us, in his treatise on *Husband and Wife*,[2] he seems occasionally to assign an international character to cases in which the judgment of the Court of Session has merely been overruled by the House of Lords from the feeling, very just probably, that the reversal was actuated by English traditions. For an example of a true conflict, let me refer you to page 1300, where he says: "It has been decided by the French tribunals, that marriages contracted in a foreign country by the subjects of France, in contravention of the French Code, are void; while, on the other hand, the English courts have held them to be valid, disregarding the law of the domicile, and

[1] Pp. 1280 and 1288.

enforcing that of the place of the celebration. So, a marriage in London between two Portuguese persons, who were first cousins, was sustained by the English court, although by the law of the domicile in Portugal first cousins could not marry."

Sect. III — *Private international law being a doctrine of rights and duties, logically deducible from the doctrine of recognition, is a branch of the science of nature.*[1]

In directing your attention to a department of jurisprudence which the labours of practitioners, too often defective in scientific training, have almost entirely detached from the necessary basis on which we have seen the other departments of jurisprudence to rest, I feel that you will be disposed to ask me for a fuller explanation than I have yet given of the links which connect this subject with those which we have previously studied, and with their common roots.

To natural law those of you who have followed our previous discussions will readily understand that its relation must be the same with the other branches of positive law—it accepts its dicta, and it finds its function in defining the rights and duties which these impose on the relations with which it deals. So far there is no difficulty, and I do not believe that, at bottom, there is any conscious disagreement amongst writers, though here, as elsewhere, there is much inaccuracy of expression and confusion of thought relating to the character of natural law; and you will hear, as usual, of its being modified,

---

[1] So much progress has been made in this department of jurisprudence since I began to lecture, twenty years ago, that for Continental and American readers I should not have thought it necessary to retain this section. In England, however, it may still have its uses. The subject is excellently treated in the second edition of Wharton's *Conflict of Laws*.

adapted, limited, and the like. To these expressions you will know to attach the only meaning of which they are susceptible. In accordance with the principles which we have long ago established, they mean simply this: that natural laws, when realised in the concrete, yield different positive laws, not in consequence of the diversity of principles, but of the diversity of the circumstances in which the same principles are called into play. But the circumstances being given, they determine positive laws as absolutely in this as in any other department of jurisprudence. Private international relations are relations of right on the one hand and duty on the other, and cannot by possibility receive expression by means of laws which rest on an hypothesis either of a separation between rights and obligations, or of the one, or the other, or both, possessing a character short of the *strictum jus*. The old woman's fable of a sort of international civility called the *comitas gentium*, still in favour in this country, after being abandoned by almost all Continental and many American jurists, was accordingly at last formally repudiated by a unanimous vote of the Institute of International Law, at its first business meeting at Geneva in 1874.[1] It still enjoys favour, however, not with our practical lawyers alone, but with our practical diplomatists. It appears, as we have seen, in the celebrated "Slave Circular," which was issued not long ago by our Foreign Office. It often crops up in Parliament, and I occasionally find passages in the *Revue de Droit International*, and even in the documents issued by the Bureau of the Institute, which lead me to doubt whether all the members of that learned body were fully in

[1] See Bulletin, Session de la Haye, 1875, p. 34 of M. Mancini's very able *Rapport*.

possession of the grounds of their own resolution. For these reasons it may be well that we should bestow upon it a little more attention than it would otherwise have deserved.

The *comitas gentium*, then, is presented to us in two aspects, which, though often confounded, are essentially distinct. On the one hand, it is represented as a voluntary recognition of the absolute independence of States *de jure;* on the other, as a voluntary or self-imposed limitation of the right of national independence. In the first of these aspects it amounts to an entire surrender of the right to recognition in so far as it has reference to private municipal law. In the second aspect, though an inadequate expression, it can scarcely be regarded as a repudiation of that right. Though it fails to affirm the truth, it does not necessarily assert error, because duties do not cease to be duties when they are voluntarily performed, whatever Kant may have said to the contrary.

It is when it assumes the character of a voluntary recognition of the *un*limited jural independence of another State, and when the basis of the right to recognition of private municipal law is sought, not in the necessary limitation, but in the unlimited assertion of national independence, that a positive error is committed. The insecure basis even of comity is thus struck from the feet of private international law, and no standing ground, either voluntarily or involuntarily, either moral or legal, is left to it. Yet the fact that this is the position in which this branch of jurisprudence has, for the most part, been placed by its expositors, will be apparent if we analyse the fundamental propositions on which private international law is said to be founded. I shall translate them from Fœlix;[1] but they are in substance those of Huber which Story has adopted, and which indeed were almost unquestioned down to Savigny's time.

"1. Each State possesses and exercises alone and exclusively sovereignty and jurisdiction within the whole extent of its territory.

"2. No State can by its laws directly affect, bind, or dispose of objects beyond its territory; or affect or oblige persons who do not reside within it, whether or not they be subject to it by the fact of their birth."

The second of these propositions is manifestly implied in the first,—it is the same proposition in a negative form; and it would be so even if we were to strike out from the first the words "alone and exclusively," because the perfect sovereignty of one State necessarily excludes the perfect sovereignty of every other.

But these two propositions, Fœlix tells us, engender an important consequence,—corresponding to the third of Huber's propositions,—which comprehends the whole doctrine of private international law—viz., that *all the effects which foreign laws can produce within the territory of any nation depend absolutely on the consent of that nation, either express or tacit.* Here the *comitas gentium* comes in, for, apart from it, the third proposition is a mere restatement of the first and second propositions,—a reassertion of the doctrine of independent sovereignty.

It is upon this one doctrine, then, that the whole fabric is made to rest. But if this doctrine be true, if the laws of one

[1] *Traité de Droit International Privé.*

State can in no circumstances whatever have any jural claim to recognition by the laws of another State, the jural basis of international law is cut away. Its existence *ex debito justitiae* is denied. The link which connects it with jurisprudence is broken—for to say that one State may voluntarily consent to recognise the private rights of the citizens of another State, to a greater or less extent as it feels disposed, or finds convenient, is to found it on no appreciable principle at all. There is no limit to, and consequently no measure of, what a nation *may* consent to. It may consent not only to recognise foreign laws in circumstances in which to ignore them would be to rob private citizens—its own possibly—of their rights, but it may consent to adopt the whole of a foreign code and substitute it for its municipal law;—nay, in the exercise of that unlimited caprice which is involved in the idea of unlimited independence, it may abandon its public as well as its private law, it may throw its independence away, subject itself to a foreign rule, and commit national suicide. It is not many years since the ancient Duchy of Savoy dived under the waters of revolution as an Italian, and came up as a French province; and though the change of nationality was not so complete, its effect as regards this matter was the same when the separate Italian States became a single kingdom, and the smaller States of Northern Germany virtually became portions of Prussia. But the fullest assertion of the right to be complying is one thing, and the discovery of a principle in accordance with which compliance becomes a subjective duty corresponding to an objective right, is quite another thing. The first is given in the right of national independence when seen from the subjective side exclusively; but the problem is to get hold of the corresponding objective right: because, so far from laying the foundation for a system of private international law, the subjective independence of the State positively excludes it. If private international law is to have a place within the realm of jurisprudence at all, it must rest, not upon the right of the State which concedes it, but on that of the State to which it is conceded, a right which the conceding State recognises in the character of a duty.

Savigny saw the weakness of the position of his predecessors in this matter, and pointed it out with his usual acuteness. "Many authors," he says, "have attempted to resolve these questions (the questions relating to the foundation of private international law) by the principle of the independence of States,—the sovereignty,—and they take as their point of departure the two following rules: 1st, each State may exact, that within the whole extent of its territory no laws shall be recognised but its own; and, 2d, no State can extend the application of its laws beyond its limits. Far from demurring to the truth of these principles, I wish to push them to their last limits; but I do not think that they can aid us greatly in the solution of our problem. *The greatest extension of the independence of the State would lead us to refuse to strangers all legal capacity.* That doctrine was well known to the Romans, and if it did not receive a complete application, there was at least, as regarded legal capacity, a very wide difference between Romans and strangers. The constant tendency of modern law has been to establish on this point a complete assimilation between natives and strangers."[1] In a subsequent passage he says : " Compared to the strict law (of national independence), of which I spoke above, this assimilation may be regarded as a voluntary agreement between sovereign States, by which they admit laws, originally foreign, into the number of the sources from which their tribunals are to seek for judgments with reference to numerous legal relations. *We must be careful, however, not to see, in this arrangement, the effect of pure goodwill, the revocable act of an arbitrary volition, but far rather a proper development of law, following in its course the same direction with the rules which have been established with reference to collisions between the particular laws of the same State."* [2]

When one reads such passages as these, one cannot but regret that Savigny was so loyal an adherent to the historical school, for he has certainly brought us up to the very borders of a philosophical explanation of the principle on which private international law is entitled to a place in the science of jurisprudence.

That explanation, I believe, is to be found, not in the absolute and unlimited, but in the relative and limited character of the independent existence of the State as a fact, and consequently as a subject of international recognition. If the State were independent in fact, it would, on the principles of the *de facto* system of jurisprudence (which otherwise than by mistake I believe is the only system of jurisprudence), be independent in right; and other States would have no rights in relation to it. It would be entitled to ignore their existence,

[1] The corresponding passage will be found in Guthrie's translation, 2d ed., p. 68, to which all the references apply, though, in some cases, I have retained my previous translation.

[2] See Guthrie, p. 70.

and in ignoring their existence to ignore their laws. And if this independence belonged equally to all States, it is obvious that neither rights nor duties could subsist between them. There could be no *jus inter gentes*, either public or private. But States, like individuals, we have seen,[1] are not independent in fact, and consequently they are not independent in law. The right of independence is limited — not by convention or agreement, or anything of that sort, but in its own nature, and of necessity — to the assertion of that amount of free subjective action which corresponds to real subjective power, and which will really contribute to the life and development of the State. Carried beyond this point, which it can be only exceptionally and spasmodically, it defeats its own purpose,—it ceases to be a right, and becomes a wrong, not only to other States, but to the State itself. It amounts to a refusal to give or accept that mutual aid on which the exercise of State rights are dependent, and is thus suicidal and self-contradictory. The right to refuse to recognise foreign law, whether by carrying out foreign contracts and executing foreign decrees, or by negotiating extradition treaties, reaches just up to the point at which the refusal ceases to minister to the objects of State-existence on the part of the State refusing. At this point the obligation, the *debitum justitiæ* to recognise foreign law, takes the place of the right to repudiate it— the subjective duty begets the objective right. The right of judicial, like the right of physical self-assertion, is thus limited by necessity; for here, as everywhere else, nature abhors waste; superfluity is sin. The right of self-defence, and even

[1] *Ante,* pp. 2, 108, 140, &c.

of self-assertion by war, *if need be*, is a right which is included in the right of separate State-existence. But even when we enter the sphere of the abnormal relations, we shall find that the *right* of war *exists, only to the extent to which it is necessary;* or, in other words, justifies only such acts as are requisite for the vindication of its jural objects in the special circumstances in which it is carried on. From this limitation, not from without but from within, inherent in the right itself, and forming one of the necessary conditions of its exercise, have sprung the laws of civilised warfare; and even the rights of neutrality, intervention by peaceful means, guardianship, and the other relations which our imperfections force upon us, as we shall see afterwards, are similarly limited. Now, precisely in the same manner, the right of exclusive jurisdiction is absolute to the extent to which its exercise is necessary to protect the real interests of the State; but it does not go beyond this, and the moment this limit is reached, I again repeat that it does not merely come in contact with other rights which limit it practically by creating a conflict,—it is necessarily limited by itself, its exercise becomes contradictory, and as such impossible, because it has reached the point at which it is dependent on external aid. Beyond this point the *meum* can live only in and through the *tuum;* the law within the State can vindicate itself only by recognising the law without the State; municipal becomes dependent on international law.

It is on this principle of necessary self-limitation, forming, as it does, an element in the principle of national independence, that private international law is founded, and in virtue of which alone it enters the sphere of jurisprudence. It is not an exceptional or contradictory principle to the right of the State as a separate jural entity; it is the complementary or correlative duty which that right involves, and the recognition of which is inseparable from its existence,—its contradictory being its extension beyond the limits which its objects have set to it. International obligations, thus understood, hold the same relation to the principle of national independence that order holds to liberty, that objective hold to subjective rights, that the rights of neutrals hold to the rights of belligerents. In this view it falls within the sphere of duties on the part of those who recognise it, and of rights on the part of those who vindicate it; and whether recognised or not by positive law, takes its place, as I have said, within the sphere of the science of jurisprudence, and stands on the common field of nature.

A great deal of confusion with reference to the basis of private international law, as in so many other branches of jurisprudence, may be traced to the attempt to draw an absolute line of demarcation, resting upon principle, and constant in its practical operation, between what are called perfect and imperfect obligations. I have already[1] explained to you very fully the grounds on which I hold that no such distinction is known to natural law, and I shall not renew the discussion here otherwise than by reminding you of its results as they bear on the matter in hand. There are obligations relating to matters more or less important; there are obligations which are, and which are not, capable of being embodied in positive law; and there are obligations which do, and which do not, generally require to be so embodied. But the line by

[1] *Institutes of Law*, p. 281 *et seq.*

which these different classes are divided, is one which is traced sometimes indeed by physical necessity, but in the vast majority of cases by mere temporary expediency, and which consequently changes with time, place, and other circumstances.

The difference between the mode in which the doctrine of the *comitas gentium* is stated by most writers in the abstract and applied in the concrete, is an amusing instance of what you will very often observe in the literature of our profession —viz., that persons of good practical understanding, but unaccustomed to speculation, state quite erroneously doctrines which they apply quite correctly. In the present instance, whilst maintaining that international justice is an imperfect obligation, excluded by the principle of national independence from the category of rights and duties, they no sooner come to instances of its application than they tell us that it cannot be violated without injustice. "In many instances," says Mr Burge,[1] "its admission could not be refused without *flagrant injustice*. Thus, if instead of the law under which parties had entered into a contract, some other law which neither of them had contemplated were to be applied, either the one might incur an obligation not incident to it, or the other might be relieved from an obligation which he had incurred. If such a state of international law prevailed, there could be no confidence in the dealings between the subjects of different countries. In every other case in which there may be a conflict between the domestic and the foreign law, there would be the same danger of committing *injustice* if the recognition of the foreign law could not take place."

[1] *Commentary*, vol. i. p. 4.

Now, if the distinction between perfect and imperfect obligations were a sound one,—if the former fell within and the latter without the sphere of justice, and if private international law rested on an imperfect obligation,—the neglect of it might be ungenerous or impolitic, but it could not be *unjust*. In farther proof of the assertion that this distinction is continually abandoned in the concrete even by those who maintain it in the abstract, take this illustration: No imperfect obligation, it is said, can form a *casus belli*; and the *comitas gentium*, on which private international law rests, being an imperfect obligation, war cannot justly be undertaken in defence of the principles of private international law which result from it. But no sooner do we come upon a somewhat unusually strong instance of the actual or possible violation of these principles than we are immediately told that it would form a *casus belli*. "There is," says Sir Robert Phillimore, "no country, not only in Europe, but in the world, since the opening of China and Japan, in which there may not be foreigners both transient and resident. Being allowed to enter a State, of which they are not natives, they have a *strict right* to be secured from injury while therein; the ill-usage of them, whether by positive maltreatment or by a *denial of justice*, may and ought to be resented by the State of which they are members. A refusal of redress in such cases would be a justifiable *cause of war*. If by long usage and custom they have been allowed to enjoy certain rights, and these, though originally the fruit of free concession, are violently, suddenly, and without equitable notice, withdrawn from them, an injury is done to them for which it is the *duty* of their own State to obtain reparation, the denial of which *justifies* a course of reprisals, or *war according to the exigencies of the case*. But here the narrow province of international right ends, and the wide domain of international comity begins."[1] I confess that I am unable to see any line by which "the limits of the narrow province" are marked off from those of "the wide domain," except that which is traced in each particular instance "by the exigencies of the case." It is quite a sufficient line—it is all the line which distinguishes positive or concrete law from natural or abstract law; but it is a line which, shifting as it does with time and place, I object to hear spoken of as founded on a permanent distinction which no man ever has pointed out, or I think ever will point out. It is by ascribing permanence to what is naturally and properly mutable, that an air of mutability has been thrown over principles which are more stable than the hills, and that people go on repeating, with a sickly sentimentalism, and a total want of perception of the irony which lay under it, the celebrated saying of Pascal: "In the just and the unjust, we find hardly anything which does not change its character in changing its climate. Three degrees of an elevation of the pole reverse the whole of jurisprudence. A meridian is decisive of truth, and a few years of possession. Fundamental laws change. Right has its epochs. A pleasant justice which a river or a mountain limits. Truth on this side of the Pyrenees, error on the other."[2]

Such would, indeed, be a pretty accurate description of the

---

[1] Vol. iv. p. 2.
[2] *Pensées*, partie i. art. vi. § 8.—Sir W. Hamilton's, transl., *Lectures on Metaphysics*, vol. i. p. 86.

comitas gentium, and of any branch of positive law which was placed on such a basis. It is just as impossible to rest the law of nations on morality apart from justice, as it is to rest municipal law on justice apart from morality; and yet this double impossibility is continually being attempted, and attempted too by the very same individuals. A few practical lawyers of very high philosophical and general culture are altogether free from this reproach; but as regards the vast majority both of writers and speakers, I am guilty of no breach of charity in representing this irrational and untenable opinion as at once the popular and the professional doctrine.

From these observations it seems to result that private international law, being a consequence not of the right of national independence abstractly considered, but of the limits which nature has assigned to that right by the reciprocal duties involved in its exercise, the fundamental propositions of this branch of jurisprudence will be the following.

Sect. IV.—*The fundamental propositions of private international law.*

1*st*, The right to vindicate its own sovereignty, which is implied in the existence and guaranteed by the recognition of a separate State, involves the duty of recognising the sovereignty of other separate States.

2*d*, This recognition of the sovereignty of a separate State, as a whole, implies the recognition of the elements which constitute its sovereignty—viz., the rights of the private citizens of whom the State is composed; of the municipal laws by which these rights are defined; of the courts by which, if need be, they are ascertained; and of the executive arrangements by which they are enforced.

These propositions make no claim on any exceptional principle. The unphilosophical conception of a branch of jurisprudence at variance with the others thus disappears, and the necessary character, which belongs to jurisprudence as a whole, is vindicated for private international law.

Sect. V.—*Of the temporary and partial exclusion of recognition necessitated by conflicting interpretations of natural law, and the consequent call for assimilation of municipal systems.*

Having examined the ground on which private international law may claim admittance by the gate into the temple of justice, in place of climbing over the wall like a thief, or asking like a beggar for an alms at the gate, the next question which meets us is, Why should it claim admission at all? or, in other words, Why should it be necessary to administer the laws of one State within the borders of another? If it be true that the principles of natural law are universal and immutable, and that all positive laws alike seek to realise these immutable principles, why should positive laws differ? And if they do differ, in point of fact, why not assimilate them rather than perpetuate their differences by reciprocal recognition? Would not the simplest solution of the conflict of laws be to strike at the root of the matter, and to remove the conflict by identifying their provisions all the world over? Even if this cannot be accomplished at once, is it not assimilation rather than reciprocal recognition which we ought to assign to this department of jurisprudence as its invariable object?

Now this question can be answered only by attending to the different sources of these conflicts.

A conflict, or difference of rule between two legal systems, or between the special provisions of two legal systems with reference to the same relation, may arise from a disagreement as to the natural characteristics and consequent laws of the relation, or, in a single word, as to principle. The principles themselves, it is true, do not vary; but it is far otherwise with the interpretations which are put on them by fallible beings. Though there is always one road that is shorter than any other, it does not follow either that we should find it ourselves, or that the evidence of our neighbours with regard to it should be infallible. It is not with reference to the concrete factor of positive law alone that there is risk of error—we may miss the road, just as we may fail to find the means of locomotion. Whether the channel of revelation be subjective or objective, it is not only possible, but unhappily very usual, for nations as well as individuals to mistake its meaning.

A difference arising from this cause, of course, implies error, on one side or both; and it follows from the fact of separate national existence that each State is bound to assert the truth of the interpretation in which it believes, and to repudiate that of its neighbour as erroneous. A private law founded on such an erroneous interpretation of natural law, however formally enacted, is not a law at all in the sense which attaches to law as falling within the scope of the science of jurisprudence. It is a mere arbitrary human enactment,—what I have elsewhere characterised as a legislative blunder. Where the conflict arises from this cause, or where one of two free, and as such responsible, communities believes it to arise from this cause, there ought to be neither recognition nor compromise; for no State would be justified in recognising, even partially, a law which it believed to be founded on error. Here it is assimilation and not reciprocal recognition that we must aim at; and the entire removal of such conflicts must be intrusted to the future advancement of scientific jurisprudence. Ultimately, we must hope that there will be no differences between the laws of civilised nations where the only possible ground of difference is error. Conflicts arising from this cause create abnormal relations; and, as we shall see in the case of abnormal relations generally, can be recognised by jurisprudence only provisionally, and as vanishing quantities.

Sect. VI.—*Of the permanent exclusion of assimilation by diversity of circumstances, and the consequent call for the reciprocal recognition of conflicting municipal laws.*

A difference may arise, and most of the differences between legal systems of at all a developed kind do actually arise, not from disagreement as to principle, even in the cases in which that is loosely asserted of them, but to diversity in the circumstances in which the same principle is brought into play.

In this case the conflict has a foundation *in fact*, which, in general, does not admit of removal; for the circumstances of all nations are not alike, and cannot be made so. Diversities of climate, soil, geographical position, natural production, occupation, race, language, stage of intellectual and moral development, political institutions, historical antecedents, and a thousand other peculiarities in the earthly lot of nations, stamp themselves on their municipal systems, and keep them apart. God did not intend that all nations should be alike, or that they should ever become so; for though perfection, supposing it to be attainable, seems to shut out diversities in degree, there is no reason to suppose that it would exclude diversities in kind. Even "in our Father's house there are many mansions." It is when diversities in legal systems arise from this latter cause,—where both parties, judging from the points of view which circumstances have imposed, may be right,—that nations must "agree to differ;" and each nation being, *ex hypothesi*, the best judge of its own circumstances, every other nation is bound to accept its decision as the wisest, where it professes to be dictated by these circumstances exclusively.

A very simple example, which I have elsewhere[1] used for a similar purpose, will illustrate both of these classes of conflicts. You are aware that the fact of marriage,—the existence, that is to say, of the marriage - contract,—may be proved in Scotland either by promise *subsequente copula*, or by *habit* and *repute*. I purposely say *proved*, and not *constituted*, for the use of the latter word always leads to confusion between the ceremony which, whether lay or ecclesiastical, belongs to the proof, and the consent which is the essence of the contract, and alone constitutes it. Well, then: we in Scotland—adhering to what was the common law of Europe, England included, down to the Council of Trent—say that, as society exists amongst us, the facts, either of promise and *copula*, or habit and repute, occurring in conjunction, *prove* to *our* satisfaction the fact of marriage in Scotland. Our

[1] *Institutes of Law*, p. 233.

neighbours on the opposite side of the Border find that these facts have no such meaning amongst them; but they do not dispute our *construction* of them, arising as it does out of an estimate of the peculiar characteristics of Scottish society. They take our word for it that the facts mentioned do prove marriage with us; and they recognise the validity of a Scotch marriage thus proved, though the proof would not be sufficient in England. But in doing so, they do not, in my opinion, recognise any principle peculiar to our law, and alien to theirs,—as they themselves often suppose,[1]—for there is no question of principle at issue between us. Both parties are agreed that the foundation of the marriage is the

---

[1] An English friend, for whose opinion I have the greatest respect, tells me that, "by the law of England, after the consent has been most fully proved, there remains the concurrence of the public authority to be proved before a marriage can be asserted to have taken place—in other words, that a marriage is constituted by the two elements, of consent of the parties, and concurrence of the public authority, and not by either alone." But the concurrence of the public authority is not a *constituent* of the marriage, for the very simple reason, that when the consent of the parties is proved, it cannot be withheld. The public authority has no choice in the matter, either in England or anywhere else. He is bound by his office to ascertain and declare what *others* have done. In Scotland, as well as in England, it is the public authority who determines the tests by which the reality of matrimonial consent shall be ascertained in general, and applies them, judicially if need be, in the particular instance; but in so doing, he no more makes the consenting parties husband and wife, or contributes towards making them so, than he makes, or contributes towards making them, male and female. That they are male and female, is a fact which he may be called upon to ascertain as a condition of the reality of their matrimonial consent, and the consequent existence of the matrimonial relation between them—or, in other words, of the fact of matrimony; but the two facts are equally independent of *his* consent. The only difference between them is, that the one is a jural fact, and the other is a physical fact. Viewed as a farther guarantee for the reality of matrimonial consent, the value of the interposition of public authority is unquestionable, and the law of England, in my humble opinion, does wisely in exacting it.

consent of the parties, or rather that this IS *the marriage*, whatever may be the tests of its reality which any particular State may impose; and in giving effect to the difference between our law and theirs, they simply examine us as witnesses, so to speak, as to what facts, if established, will be sufficient to prove consent in Scotland; and we tell them that either promise *sub. cop.*, or *habit* and *repute*, will prove it. It is plain that if an English court wishes to get at the bottom of the *fact*, as to whether or not consent took place in Scotland, they are bound to settle the question of opinion somehow—they must determine what will prove the fact in the eyes of Scotchmen and Scotchwomen; and in accepting the answer which the *law* of Scotland gives to it, they are not only acting on the principles of reciprocity, but they are accepting the best evidence, and adopting the only course by which they could safely administer the law of England. They are simply administering their own law of contract. Such was unquestionably the meaning of Lord Mansfield when he said: "There can be no doubt that any action tried here must be tried by the law of England. But the law of England says that, in a variety of instances with regard to contracts legally made abroad, the laws of the country where the action rose should govern;"[1] and still more manifestly it was the meaning of Lord Stowell when, in the great case of Dalrymple *v.* Dalrymple, he laid down that "being entertained in an English court, it must be adjudicated according to the principles of English law applicable to such a case; but the only principle applicable to such a

[1] Coloper, 341—1 *Bell Com.*, 307.

case, by the law of England, is, that the validity of Miss Gordon's marriage-rights must be tried by reference to the law of the country where, if they exist at all, they had their origin. Having furnished this principle, the law of England withdraws altogether, and leaves the legal question to the exclusive judgment of the law of Scotland." In the opinion of both of these eminent judges, the law of England can vindicate *its own principles*, only by availing itself of the means by which a foreign system tells it that they can alone be vindicated *elsewhere*.

But put the opposite case, and suppose (an extravagant supposition, I allow, but one which will serve the purpose of illustration) either country—acting in contravention of the rule, *contrahentium voluntatem, potius quam verba, spectari*,[1] that the will of the contracting parties, rather than their words, is to be regarded—were to hold that the form of a marriage ceremony having been gone through was sufficient, though it were done in jest, or though the parties, or one of them, were incapable of consent, or the like. Here a conflict of the kind of which we first spoke would arise as to the principle which lies at the root, not of the contract of marriage alone, but of all contracts; and a country which adopted so absurd a rule would have no right to expect that it should be recognised by any other country.

Sect. VII.—*Diversity of circumstances does not always exclude assimilation of legal systems.*

But though conflicts, arising from diversity of circumstances, must as a rule be provided for by the doctrine

[1] *Digest*, 50, 16, 1, 219—Story, 361.

of reciprocity, it does not follow that they ought, in all cases, to be retained. For: 1st, The circumstances may have changed, and may be no longer diverse, in which case assimilation will be called for on the very same ground which formerly justified reciprocal recognition; or, 2d, the circumstances may yield to the law, and a law, at first erroneous or arbitrary, may afterwards become the true law for both nations alike; or, 3d, the diversity of circumstances may be so small that it can be ignored with less inconvenience to the two communities than that which is occasioned by the diversity of law resulting from its recognition; or, 4th, the diversity of circumstances may have been imaginary, and the different rules founded upon them may be a mere accident, the result of ignorance of each other's habits, in which case a little mutual explanation, and the application of the give-and-take principle, will suffice for their removal.

Savigny, in a note, gives a case in which the application of the principle of assimilation was surely the proper remedy. "Up to the 1st January 1840," he says, "there existed in the town of Breslau *five* particular laws of succession, and of the patrimonial rights of husband and wife, which constituted so many local jurisdictions. Often the law varied from house to house; sometimes even a single house, placed on the confines of two jurisdictions, was governed partly by the one and partly by the other."[1] Now there never could be such diversity of circumstances as to warrant such a diversity of codes as this; and even if the rule which was

[1] See Guthrie, p. 65.

adopted had been the worst of the five, its adoption must have been a relief to all parties.

But wherever the adoption of a new rule, even if it should be little more than an arbitrary rule of conducting business, must be imposed on a whole community, assimilation will in general be too dearly purchased, unless the inconveniences arising from disparity be very considerable. Certainty is the great end to be aimed at by legal machinery, and it will in general be better attained by a rule, or even by two rules, which are somewhat complicated and cumbersome, if they be familiar to all parties, than by one which, though simpler, and abstractly preferable, is new and strange to one or several of them. For these reasons, petty legal reforms, whether under the guise of assimilation or any other, whilst they are an annoyance to practical men, are improvements of a kind for which no true speculative lawyer will thank their authors. It is a question of degree, however; and a rule may be so cumbersome, so expensive, so easily evaded, or so easily rectified, as to render its change a very great boon to the community.

Sect. VIII. *The law-merchant.*

There is one department of private international law in which the interests involved being less affected by diversities of local circumstances than in any other, the principle of assimilation has been very extensively acted on, and in which something like an international code of private law has consequently been developed. I refer to what is known as the law-merchant.

The *law-merchant*, or *lex mercatoria*, is the body of usage which has grown up in consequence of the continual intercourse between the merchants of the civilised nations of the world during many ages, and which has been reasoned out and defined by the decisions of courts of law. M. Pardessus[1] has remarked on the great similarity of mercantile codes in all times and places; and in the historical portion of the course, I am accustomed to explain, that the history of the development of what we may almost regard as one system, was the history of the progress, not only of mercantile relations, but in a very great measure of civilisation.

The meaning usually attached to the term law-merchant, and that which I here adopt, is somewhat different from, and somewhat narrower than, that belonging to what at first sight might seem its synonym—viz., mercantile law. The great subject of mercantile law has been divided by an eminent foreign writer,[2] quite correctly, into three departments.

1*st*, The commercial legal relations between individuals,—private mercantile or commercial law (*Privathandelsrecht*).

2*d*, The commercial legal relations between the citizen and the State,—public commercial or mercantile law (*Oeffentlicheshandelsrecht.*

3*d*, Commercial legal relations between different States,—international mercantile or commercial law (*Handelsvolkesrecht*).

Now the first of these departments is that which is commonly spoken of as the law-merchant, but the third is that with which alone we can concern ourselves here, because the first, being purely municipal, falls scientifically beyond my province, whilst I have been relieved of the second by the somewhat unscientific division of labour which obtains

---

[1] *Us et Coutumes de la Mer*, p. 37. [2] Thöl., see PhilL, iv. 622, 623.

THE LAW-MERCHANT. 381

amongst us. It is of this department — viz., of *private international mercantile law*, that Mr Bell speaks in the Introduction to his *Commentaries*,[1] when he says, "The law-merchant is a part of the law of nations founded upon the principles of natural equity, as regulating the transactions of men who reside in different countries and carry on the intercourse of nations, independently of the local customs and municipal laws of particular States. For the illustration of this law, the decisions of courts, and the writings of lawyers in different countries, are as the recorded evidence of the application of the general principle; not *making the law*, but handing it down; not to be quoted as precedents or as authorities to be implicitly followed, but to be taken as guides towards the establishment of the pure principles of general jurisprudence."

These words show us how just was the appreciation which Mr Bell, the greatest of our text-writers after Lord Stair, had formed of the task of creating a system of private international mercantile law—a task to the accomplishment of which he was himself so important a contributor. The law was not to be *made* by judges or by writers, but they were to ascertain what it was as custom—*i.e.*, mercantile usage *at its most advanced point*—had made it; and this law they were to administer and transmit, with such criticisms and suggestions as might render it a more efficient means of vindicating the principles of natural law in ordinary mercantile transactions. Of the manner in which the formation of a more rational and more consistent system of consuetudinary law may be con-

[1] Introduction, p. 5.

sciously guided by a single eminent individual, the judicial career of Lord Mansfield forms the most famous instance. "There had gradually been accumulated a rich collection of materials," says Mr Bell in the same work from which I have just quoted, "when Lord Mansfield, in the middle of the last century, was appointed Lord Chief-Justice of the King's Bench. This eminent man, who has been called the father of the commercial law of England, devoted his splendid talents during an uninterrupted period of thirty years to the great duty of constructing, in a series of judicial determinations, a system of mercantile law. The spirit with which he proceeded has thus been stated by one who enjoyed much of his confidence,—Mr Justice Buller: 'Within thirty years the commercial law of this country has taken a very different turn from what it did before. Before that period we find that in courts of law all the evidence in mercantile cases was thrown together; they were left generally to a jury, and they produced no established principle. From that time, we all know, the great study has been to find some certain general principles which shall be known to all mankind, not only to rule the particular case then under consideration, but to serve as a guide for the future. Most of us have heard these principles stated, reasoned upon, enlarged and explained, till we have been lost in admiration at the strength and stretch of the human understanding.'"

It is to be feared that the method which Lord Mansfield pursued of guiding customs to the formation of rules more suited to effect the ends for which all rules exist—viz., the vindication of the principles of natural law—has not been very scrupulously adhered to by recent law reformers. The process of assimilation between the mercantile laws of England and Scotland, the ultimate success of which would probably have been secured by bringing to bear upon custom those influences by which it is guided in the ordinary course of historical development, has been attempted to be stimulated by artificial means. Royal Commissions have reported on the practicability of at once identifying the mercantile laws of the two kingdoms, and the Legislature has endeavoured partially to realise their suggestions. These proceedings, except in so far as they have had for their object to give statutory recognition to changes which custom had already introduced, or for which public opinion really called, must, I fear, be regarded as indications of a false conception of the function of legislation. To suppose that the Legislature can *make customary law* is not indeed *so* foolish as to suppose that it can unmake natural law, or "modify it, alter it, and adapt it," which, I think, are the fashionable phrases. Human customs, unlike God's laws, *are* under human control, and the Legislature forms a factor, and no insignificant factor, in human activity. That it is a factor which may very powerfully influence the formation of consuetude is unquestionable. But the question is, Ought it—consulting as it professes to do the ends of justice and the convenience of merchants—not rather to wait till the new customs which it wishes to introduce are so far formed as to be pretty loudly called for by public opinion ? If the new custom is really in process of formation by means of the action of public opinion, expressed through Chambers of Commerce and the like, it will itself become part of the common law without statutory aid at all; and the inconvenience occasioned by its being forced on a minority to whom it is distasteful, or unfamiliar, by a statute that it requires a whole series of decisions to construe, will be avoided by a very moderate expenditure of time and patience.[1]

Though the law-merchant, in the aspect in which we have just been considering it, forms unquestionably a branch of the law of nations, it has been declared, on very high authority, to form part also of the common law of England. Blackstone, in his *Commentaries*,[2] says that there is "a particular system of customs, used only among one set of the king's subjects, called the custom of merchants, or *lex mercatoria*, which, however different from the general rules of the common law, is yet engrafted into it and made part of it." To the same effect Mr Bell says: "This law-merchant is, in England, said to form part of the common law; and it is so much a part of that law that it requires not to be proved by witnesses, like matter of foreign regulation, but is noticed, judicially, by the court. The same precision in the laying down the legal doctrine is not to be found in Scotland; because, in our books, little attention has been given to the subject, and the dicta of our older judges have perished. But the same principle operates as in England, and our courts are daily in the habit of proceeding on this law-merchant as fully authoritative in Scotland, and of allowing the decisions of foreign courts and the writings of foreign lawyers to be cited in illustration of it."[3]

---

[1] "Le droit coutumier," says M. C. Brocher, "ne progresse que par une lutte intestine entre le présent et l'avenir."—*Cours de Droit International Privé*, p. 5.
[2] Introduction, § 3. [3] Vol. i. p. 6.

Much of this law has been embodied in statute since these words were written; and there is no portion of our whole municipal system which has been so nearly reduced to the form of a code as the portion of it which refers to maritime affairs. But the subject-matter of this code belongs to my colleague in the Chair of Scotch Municipal Law, and I shall consequently content myself with having thus attempted to mark the place which belongs to the law-merchant in a scientifically developed system of private international law.

Sect. IX.—*Private international law is not a separate system of positive law, and in this respect it differs both from public international law and from municipal law public and private.*

Every system of law, properly so called, fixes the legal relations of its subjects. Private municipal law determines what facts shall be held to constitute the relations of marriage, guardianship, and the like,—what shall be held to constitute sale, letting and hiring, service, and so forth, between private citizens. Public municipal law, or as we say constitutional law, fixes the relations between the State and the citizen, whilst public international law determines what shall amount to State existence, belligerency, blockade, and the like, between nation and nation. But private international law determines no legal relations whatever; it simply says by what system they shall be determined. It is a doctrine of jurisdiction, and nothing more.

I do not find that the difference between private international law, and public international law, more especially, is in general pointed out so clearly in this respect as it ought to be. Fœlix, for example, seems to hold that *mu-*

tatis mutandis their function is the same. "Public international law," he says (*jus gentium publicum*), "regulates the relations of nation to nation—in other words, it has for its object the conflicts of public law." Now, in public international law there ought no more to be a conflict than in a single municipal system, for the simple reason that the whole world is its *municipium*,—the whole world, that is to say, which it recognises as jurally existent. Even when, from the necessity of the case, this law is administered by the prize courts of a particular country, the decisions of which may conflict with those of another, its character is, professedly, altogether cosmopolitan.

Listen to the great Lord Stowell, whose words come in always like a ray of sunshine through the surrounding mystification. "It is to be recollected that this is a Court of the Law of Nations, though sitting here under the authority of the King of Great Britain. It belongs to other nations as well as to our own; and what foreigners have a right to demand from it is the administration of the law of nations simply, and *exclusively of the introduction of principles borrowed from our own municipal jurisprudence, to which, it is well known, they have at all times expressed no inconsiderable reluctance.*" [1] And in another case, the famous one of the Swedish convoy, he says:[2] "In forming my judgment, I trust that it has not for a moment escaped my anxious recollection what it is that the duty of my station calls for from me—namely, not to deliver occasional and shifting opinions to serve present pur-

---

[1] The Recovery, C. Robinson, p. 349.
[2] The Maria, 1 Robinson, p. 349.

poses of particular national interest, but to administer with indifference that justice which the law of nations holds out without distinction to independent States, some happening to be neutral and some belligerent. *The seat of judicial authority is indeed locally* HERE, *in the belligerent country, according to the known law and practice of nations; but the law itself has no locality,"* and consequently, he might have added, having no local limits, can raise none of the conflicts to which local limits give rise. But the very reverse of this is the case with private international law. With the exception of the law-merchant, of which I spoke in the last section, there is no system of private international law common to all the world. It is local law; and every question which arises under it falls to be settled by some local system or systems, *except the single question, " By what local system shall it be settled ? "* If a question of status arises, it is regulated by the law to which the person is subjected by birth, residence, citizenship, and the other circumstances which go to make up his domicile or his nationality; if the question has reference to property, a distinction is generally taken between that which is moveable and that which is immoveable, the localisation of the former being regulated by the *lex domicilii*, that of the latter by the *lex loci rei sitæ;* if it is a question of contract, its validity will be determined by the law of the land in which it was entered into; if it is a question of evidence, or of remedy, it will be governed by the *lex fori:* but each of these cases, and every analogous case you can imagine, will be governed by the municipal law of *a* particular country, and not by any general code which is common to several, or to them all. The laws of several, or of all the civilised countries of Europe, may be alike on the point—or they may be different—that is nothing to the purpose.

It is quite possible that the same case may fall to be governed by two or more municipal systems, on the ground that it involves two or more sets of relations. Of this the case of Don *v.* Lippman,[1] which occurred in our own courts, whether rightly decided or not,[2] is an excellent example. That case involved two questions,—one as to the validity of a contract, the other as to the nature of the remedy. The first question was decided in accordance with the law of France, the *locus contractus*—the second in accordance with the law of Scotland, the *lex fori;* but there was no question as to any other law but municipal law, except the question as to *which* municipal law.

In these remarks I have supposed that we start from the consideration of the legal relation, and have seen that in that case the only question with which the international lawyer has to deal is, What is the municipal system which governs this relation? But let us take the question, as Savigny has done, from the opposite starting-point; let us take the rule of law *first*, and ask what are the legal relations which that rule covers? In this case it is obvious that we are only looking at the same matter from the opposite side, and we are still occupied with the local limits, with the question of jurisdiction, with the domain of law, exclusively of its subject-matter. In the former case we were asking ourselves under what

---

[1] Jan. 20, 1836, 14 S. 241. Reversed as to prescription—2 S. and M'L., 682, May 26, 1837.

[2] Guthrie, p. 268.

municipal system the relation—the "case" that has been put before us—falls; in the present we are asking ourselves whether a system of municipal rule which has been put before us applies to such or such a case. When this simple view of the matter is presented to us, we feel at once the absurdity of regarding the subject of private international law as consisting in an enumeration of the collisions arising between different municipal systems, and an attempt to dispose of them by referring them to some separate system founded on comity which civilised States in general are willing to acknowledge. Though the existence of such collisions between municipal systems be unquestionably that which has given occasion to the formation of what may be called a system of rules of international jurisdiction, the rules are not intended for the removal of these collisions, and indeed cannot remove them. Even if we possessed an international legislature, it would decline to charge itself with such a task. If the collisions are to be removed at all, it must be by municipal and not by international legislation; for the assimilation of different municipal systems, even when effected by international treaty, demands the previous action of municipal legislation. The two States do not adopt a common international rule, but agree to change their municipal rules, or one of them, whilst the international portion of the transaction, the negotiation of the treaty, falls within the scope not of private but of public international law. Even the codification of the rules of private international law by international action, and their adoption by a treaty to which the whole civilised world should become parties, would not necessarily affect these municipal collisions in the slightest degree. All that it would do would be to fix the rules by which they were to be disposed of.[1] It is consequently with great reason that Savigny remarks, in his brief and abstract way, "Most authors who have written on this subject have occupied themselves with the collisions as the only problem which they had to resolve, and this to their great prejudice. The following is rather the natural filiation of ideas. With reference to the rules of law we demand, What are the relations of law which are subject to these rules? and with reference to the relations of law, To what rules are they subject? The question as to the empire of these rules, and as to the difficulties to which the demarcation of these limits may give rise, the so-called collisions or conflicts, are questions which, in their nature, are subordinate and subsidiary."[2]

Sect. X.—*The rules of private international law necessarily form part of every municipal system, and may consequently be enforced by the municipal executive.*

If the rules of private international law are more limited in their object than those of the public law of nations, and, as not determining the character of the legal relations which they recognise, do not rise to the dignity of a separate system, there is another direction in which they contrast with them

---

[1] It is difficult to bring out this point in language which shall be quite unequivocal, and I am not sure that the words used even by the Institute, though quite correct, may not lead to misapprehension. The task which the Institute professes to have set before it is to frame—"Régles générales qui pourraient être sanctionnées par des traités internationaux, en vue d'assurer la décision uniforme des conflits entre les diverses législations civiles et criminelles."— *Annuaire*, 1880-81, p. 8. The uniformity, of course, is to be in the definition of the local law, not in the local law defined.

[2] Guthrie, vol. viii. p. 7.

very favourably—they admit of being enforced. This advantage, however, they owe, for the present at all events, not to their international, but to their national character. The rules of jurisdiction to which the custom, or if we choose to use the word in this limited sense, the comity of nations, has communicated a partially international character, each State accepts, in the sense which its judges attach to them, as part and parcel of its local law, which, as a condition of its recognition by other States, it binds itself to recognise. The judgments of the local courts form a body of precedents which not only regulate their own future action, but when adequately supported by reasoning are quoted abroad as having international validity. An international tribunal possessing a continuous jural existence, the guardian of its own traditions, and capable of vindicating its decrees by an international executive, the absence of which renders public international law pretty nearly inoperative, is here no longer a desideratum. The construction of a foreign contract by foreign law is just as much within the competence of the Court of Session as the construction of a Scotch lease, or of the missives of sale of a house in Edinburgh. And the Scotch construction, if sound in Edinburgh, will be sound wherever a similar contract falls to be construed. Nor would this character be greatly affected even by the negotiation of international treaties by which rules of jurisdiction common to the whole civilised world should be adopted; because an international judicature which should apply these rules to all the relations in which questions of jurisdiction may arise, is scarcely a realisable conception, even as a court of appeal; whilst the practical difficulties in the way of an international executive for the vindication of private rights and obligations within the territories of separate States, seem altogether insurmountable.

Sect. XI.—*Of treaties for the adoption of uniform rules of private international law.*

But though the interpretation of such treaties must necessarily be intrusted, without appeal, to the local courts of each separate State, it by no means follows that they would be inoperative in promoting uniformity of action. Questions of private international law excite so little general interest, and appeal so little to national pride and passion, when compared with questions of public international law, that the sole object of each State, for the most part, is to decide them in accordance with international conceptions. All that the local courts desire to know is, by what law the relation is governed. That well-considered treaties would facilitate their labours in this direction is unquestionable, and with this view the Institute of International Law arrived unanimously at the following resolution :—

"The Institute recognises the evident utility, and even for certain matters the necessity of treaties, by which civilised States should adopt, by common accord, obligatory and uniform rules of private international law, by which public authorities, and especially the tribunals of the contracting States, should bind themselves to decide questions concerning persons, property, acts, successions, procedure, and foreign judgments."[1]

In accordance with this resolution, the Institute has under-

[1] Bulletin, Session de la Haye, 1875, 1st fascicule, p. 34.

taken the task of preparing drafts of such treaties, which will probably form one of the most fruitful branches of its labours.

Sect. XII.—*The determination of the temporal limits of rules of law belongs to municipal, not to international, jurisprudence.*

So much for the local, we must now turn to the temporal, limits of the rules of law.

In order to fix by what rule of law a certain legal relation falls to be determined, it is not sufficient to ascertain under what jurisdiction or legal domain it falls in point of space, we must determine, moreover, within what limits it falls in point of time; for positive law is continually changing, and unless we fix on the moment at which the rule, whatever it may be, is to be applied, we cannot tell what the rule is. Savigny's remarks to this effect are so acute, and in their application as indicating a ground of scientific subdivision in this department of law, I think so entirely original, that I shall translate them in full.

" To the question of the local limits of positive laws, there is a second question which attaches itself, and which, though quite separate, is analogous to the first. Up to this point we have considered the rules of law as fixed, without taking any account of the changes which time may operate in them. But it is an essential characteristic of positive law that it should not be stationary, but, on the contrary, should offer a continual succession of organic developments. When we characterise it, accordingly, we say that it *belongs to it* to vary with the time. Moreover, every judgment on an existing legal relation is necessarily based upon legal facts which belong to a past time, more or less distant. But inasmuch as in the interval which separates the origin of the legal relation from the present moment, the positive law may have undergone modifications, it is necessary to determine at what epoch we are to take the rule which governs the legal relation. We have here, then, limits of a new kind assigned to the empire of the rules of law, and we come in contact also with a new kind of possible collisions, not less difficult or less important than those relative to the other kind of limits. From the first point of view the rules of law appear to us simultaneous, fixed, and immovable; from the second point of view they appear as successive, and varied by a continual development. To put the matter shortly, I shall characterise this double point of view by the following expressions:—

" 1*st*, Local limits of the empire of the rules of law ;

" 2*d*, Temporal limits of that empire." [1]

Under these two heads, and, with something like ostentatious simplicity, Savigny has arranged his whole treatise on "the empire of the rules of law over legal relations." But the work, which does not profess to be devoted to private international law exclusively, though short in comparison with its ponderous predecessors, covers a larger scientific area than belongs to that branch of jurisprudence; and a moment's reflection will show you that the second chapter falls entirely beyond *our* limits, and re-enters those of municipal law. For, suppose the local limits to be fixed,—and the question, relating, we shall say, to the validity of a will, to be determined by the will being sent to Prussia, or Prussian law rather

[1] Guthrie, p. 49.

being invoked by our courts for its decision, on the ground that the testator was domiciled in Berlin at the time of his death, all questions as to whether the Prussian law of wills has been changed during the period which elapsed between the date of the will and the death of the testator, whether these changes affect the will retroactively, or whether their effect is limited to wills made subsequently to the period at which they were introduced,—all these questions, I say, which Savigny discusses with so much acuteness in the second chapter of his work, fall to be determined *by the municipal law of Prussia.* Even when the locality has changed its political connection and consequent municipal system, the question as to whether the system which now governs the locality differs from that which it has superseded, stands on precisely the same footing as when the change has resulted from the ordinary channels of legislation. Whether Alsace was governed by French or German law at a particular period, is a question just of the same kind as the question whether or not she recognised civil marriages. To the internationalist they are mere questions of fact, which he addresses to the municipal lawyer, and with reference to which he accepts his decision. They stand on precisely the same footing as the question whether or not a holograph will is valid in Prussia, or any other question of Prussian municipal law. They are questions of great interest, delicacy, and importance, which arise continually in our own municipal system, and which must force themselves with still greater urgency on the inhabitants of frontier districts which undergo perpetual changes of nationality.

Sect. XIII.—*Of the means of localising legal relations.*

The endlessly numerous and complicated questions which present themselves for solution in the branch of jurisprudence with which we are now engaged, when seen in their widest generality, resolve themselves, as I have explained to you, into *an inquiry into the local limits of the rules of law over legal relations;* or—stating the same question conversely,—into an inquiry into the legal relations which fall within the local limits of the various rules of law. It is in the latter form that the question has, in general, presented itself to the minds of lawyers; and it is in this form that it can be most conveniently dealt with for practical purposes, and with the smallest innovation on established modes of thinking.

(a) *Of the classification of legal relations.*

With a view to the systematic prosecution of this inquiry, these relations have been divided into various classes. Of these classes, the two most important are those which spring from, and centre in, the peculiar characteristics of persons, on the one hand, and of things, as opposed to persons, on the other: and here, consequently, though with a special object, you come in contact with the classification of the objects of law into persons, things, and actions, which is already well known to you in your study of municipal systems. Corresponding to the third class of rights, which are treated by the Romans under the head of *actions*, there is a class of legal relations called *mixed*, which, springing neither directly from persons nor from things, are not exclusively inherent in the distinctive characteristics of either, and arise from artificial arrangements, by which certain immaterial, and often indefinite, rights over persons or things are recognised as existing in persons. With relation to this classification, Ahrens has very truly remarked, that " law in all cases relates, in its origin and in its object, to persons; that it possesses a character essentially *personal;* and that, on this account, the division, which is ordinarily established into personal laws, real laws, and laws of obligations, as three co-ordinate parts, is not exact. All law is, in the first instance, and above all, personal. Law applies itself also undoubtedly to things, and to actions, inasmuch as they are physical conditions for the development of man; but the laws concerning things and actions are divisions which relate only to the objects of law, and have always reference, at the same time, to the person as its subject."[1] To the same effect, Savigny remarks that "all law exhibits itself, in the first instance, as power appertaining to the person; and that, seen from this primitive and direct point of view, we ought to consider legal relations, in general, as attributes of the person."[2]

This qualification being kept in view, it is quite possible to avail ourselves in this, as in other departments of law, of the classification I have mentioned.

This classification of legal relations, then, suggested as it no doubt was by the arrangements of the Roman law, was, at an early period—the earlier half of the fourteenth century—embodied by internationalists in the celebrated division of what are technically known as statutes, into *statuta personalia, realia, et mixta.*

In order that you may apprehend the peculiar meaning attached to the word "statute" by writers on this subject,

[1] *Droit Naturel,* p. 170.   [2] Vol. viii. p. 14.

and understand the manner in which the rules of law, by which it has been attempted to assign the different legal relations to their proper local domains, have developed themselves, it is necessary that I should interpolate a slight historical sketch, which my anxiety to preserve the doctrinal treatment of our subject unbroken will necessarily render exceedingly brief.

The more important provincial towns which fell under the dominion of Rome, as the empire extended itself gradually in all directions, though subjected to the subsequent legislation of the imperial city, were not entirely deprived of their own municipal laws. These were preserved *as special and exceptional legal systems;* and it was their existence which, in general, gave occasion to the Roman jurisconsults to treat of such subjects as jurisdiction and domicile, and not the existence of separate and entirely independent municipal systems, which their arrogant assumption of universal dominion naturally led them to ignore. These local laws stood out as what Savigny calls *particular* laws, in the midst of the surrounding common law of Rome,—greatly modified by it, no doubt, but still retaining peculiar characteristics of their own. At a subsequent period, when the incursion of the Germanic nations occurred, the peculiar privileges of the town populations were a second time spared; and they soon came to contrast with the Lombard and other Teutonic institutions far more strongly than they had formerly done with those of Rome. " The separate systems of laws, which in the middle ages formed themselves in almost all the towns of Italy," says Savigny, " were much more extensive and important than those which had existed under the empire."

They contrasted not only with the Roman law, but with the Lombard law, considering each of these as a common law. It was for the laws of these towns that was created the technical expression *statuta*, which was subsequently employed in other countries, and to which is attached the theory of *statuta personalia, realia, et mixta.*

In his work on the history of the Roman law in the middle ages, Savigny has given a fuller account of this matter; but I shall only quote to you a few sentences, which I do for the purpose of removing a misapprehension which might very possibly arise in your minds in consequence of a double meaning which has come to be attached to the terms personal rights and personal laws. "When the Goths, Burgundians, Franks, and Lombards, founded kingdoms in the countries formerly subject to the power of Rome, there were two different modes of treating the conquered race. They might be extirpated by destroying or enslaving the free men; or, the conquering nations, for the sake of increasing their own numbers, might transform the Romans into Germans, by forcing on them their manners, constitution, and laws. Neither mode, however, was followed; for though many Romans were slain, extirpated or enslaved, this was only the lot of individuals and not the systematic treatment of the nation." Amongst ourselves it would seem that the Romanised population almost entirely disappeared. But such was not the case in Continental countries. "Both races, on the contrary," Savigny continues, "lived together, and preserved their separate manners and laws. From this state of society arose that condition of civil rights denominated personal rights, or personal laws, in opposition to territorial laws."[1] In this passage the term personal laws is used very much in the sense which Savigny elsewhere attaches to the particular laws of the conquered nation in general—*i.e.*, whether personal or real; whereas in the division of legal relations on which the doctrine of the *statuta* is founded, personal laws refer to the rights assigned to the person, not as the *civis* of a particular city, but as an individual (*persona*), which is the Roman sense, and the sense in which, as opposed to real, we employ the term in modern legal phraseology. From the peculiar organisation of society at this period, however, it is easy to see that these essentially distinct meanings of the phrase would necessarily become, to a certain extent, coincident, and that all "particular rights," whether real or personal, would be called personal rights. The rights of the conquered, —even those which had no reference to what we call personal rights, being enjoyed irrespective of those territorial arrangements in accordance with which the soil was distributed in usufruct, in return for military services, amongst the warriors of the conquering tribe—were supposed to adhere to the *person*, whereas the rights which were dependent on these arrangements were supposed to cling to the *soil*. It was thus that there came to be personal rights belonging to the Germanic tribes which were successively conquered by each other, as well as to the previously existing Roman, or Romanised town populations. But in the position of these latter, there was a peculiarity which must have given this personal character to the systems of law which prevailed amongst them more

[1] Cathcart's translation, vol. i. p. 99.

decidedly than to those which one Germanic tribe retained under the dominion of another. When these conquests occurred, a very large portion of the Roman population took refuge in the towns; and the municipal laws which, under the Empire, were distinguished by the *absence*, now became distinguished by the presence in *excess*, of the Roman element. But the Roman law, as you know, sets out expressly from the *persona*, and in the *persona* it recognises all rights as centred; whereas the fundamental idea of feudalism is territorial,—not the feuer, but the feu. The laws of the town populations were thus personal, in a more peculiar sense than those of the inhabitants of the surrounding country; and as the town laws were also the type of peculiar laws, the identification between personal laws in the Roman and municipal sense, and personal laws in the medieval and international sense, becomes intelligible.

But there is another consideration which still farther explains this occurrence. Persons of Roman descent, or sprung from the races which the Romans had conquered, and who, as inhabitants of the towns, or connected with the town populations by origin, were entitled to claim their peculiar municipal privileges, came also frequently to be landholders in the surrounding country; or the process was reversed, and persons of Teutonic descent, whilst still holding their lands from their own feudal superiors, purchased or otherwise acquired town privileges. Persons in either position, it is obvious, would be subject to two sets of laws—the one the burgher law, which partook largely of the Roman element; the other the feudal law. By the first, not only their personal rights as to status, but the arrangements by which their movable property was acquired and held and transmitted, were mainly regulated,— because their movable property was chiefly situated in the towns; the other governed their land rights and everything which belonged to them, in their character of feudal vassals or superiors. Between the latter and the former class of rights there was, moreover, this essential distinction, that the former class of rights adhered to them wherever they went; whereas the latter, the land rights, belonged to them only so long as their connection with the particular landed possession out of which they had sprung continued uninterrupted. It is obvious, that without great inconvenience and injustice, not only to themselves but to others, those who were held to be of age, to be married, to be capable of contracting, and the like, could not be deprived of these qualities by taking up their abode in another State; whereas when separate nationalities began to develop themselves, a serious inroad on national independence would have been occasioned had they carried with them the rights or obligations with reference to landed property which existed in the place of their former abode—or had the land which they left behind them, and which they continued to possess, been tenable or transmissible in accordance with the rules of a foreign State. When these considerations are kept in view, we can see clearly the course of events by which personal rights in the medieval or exceptional sense came to be identified with personal rights in the Roman and in the modern sense of rights adhering to the person, and we get hold of the train of thinking which led to the technical distinction between real and personal statutes.

This distinction is ascribed by Savigny (vol. viii. p. 121) to

Bartolo or Bartolus, a famous Italian professor of law in the fourteenth century,—so famous as to be called the star and luminary of lawyers, the master of truth, the lantern of equity, and the guide of the blind. Bartolus belonged to the scholastic jurists, who succeeded the Glossers (*Glossatores*) of the school of Irnerius, whose activity began to decline after the great compilation of Accurtius, as has so often been the case when codification has taken the place of free scientific criticism and development. It has been truly said that in our day Bartolus, Baldus, and Accurtius are chiefly remembered as having been targets for the wit of Rabelais. In acquaintance with the text, the scholastic jurists were far inferior to their predecessors, the *Glossatores*, and this remark, which has been made with reference to them as a body, does not seem to have found an exception even in Bartolus, who with, and even beyond Baldus, was the great apostle of the sect. Gravina, in a passage which Hallam has quoted,[1] says of him, that "he was so fond of distinctions, that he does not divide his subject, but breaks it to pieces, so that the fragments are, as it were, dispersed to the winds. But whatever harm he might do to the just interpretation of the Roman law as a positive code, he was highly useful to the practical lawyer by the number of cases his fertile mind anticipated; for though many of these were unlikely to occur, yet his copiousness and subtlety of distinction is such that he seldom leaves those who consult him quite at a loss." In addition to his activity as a professor, Bartolus, during his comparatively short life (according to the common account he died at the age of forty-

[1] *Middle Ages*, vol. i. p. 67.

six) filled several judicial positions with repute, and enjoyed a great reputation in public law.[1] To these circumstances is probably owing the fact, to which even Savigny, who was disposed to disparage him, bears witness,—viz., that traces of independent thinking on legal topics are more conspicuous in his works than in those of his more learned predecessors. If the extent to which it has been adopted by practical lawyers be a test of the value of a distinction, few surely are entitled to rank higher than the distinction which led him to adopt the division of statutes with which we are here concerned.

(*b*) *Appreciation of the statutory theory.*

The account which Savigny gives of the classification itself, and which is in accordance with the passages from other jurists, of which you will find a pretty complete collection in Story, is the following :—

"Personal statutes are those laws which have for their object chiefly (*principaliter*) the person and his condition, even when they contain accessory dispositions relative to property. Real statutes are those laws which treat principally (*principaliter*) of things, that is to say, of immovables, even though persons should also be treated incidentally.

"Mixed statutes, according to some authors, are those laws which relate neither to persons nor to things, but to acts; according to others they are laws which relate both to persons and things. These two definitions," Savigny adds, "though apparently contradictory, enter notwithstanding into each

---

[1] *Bedeutung der römisch-deutschen Kaiserwürde. Vortrag* v. *Dr Carl Wilhelm* v. *Lancizolle.* Berlin, 1856,—p. 5.

other. The practical meaning of this distinction," he continues, "is this: Taking as our point of departure the question, What are the laws which are applicable, even beyond the States in which they have been issued? the following is the reply. The personal statutes apply to all the persons who have their domicile within the State of the legislator, even when these persons appear before a foreign judge. The real statutes apply to all immovables situated in the State of the legislator, whoever may be the judge called upon to decide with reference to them, whether native or stranger. Finally, the mixed statutes apply to all the acts which have taken place within the State of the legislator, whatever may be the country in which the decision is pronounced. Such is the system as a whole, but in the details we find a great divergence of opinion; for there is no agreement either as to the limits of these different classes, or as to their practical application."[1]

Savigny's estimate of the value of the distinction is too important to be omitted.

"We cannot reject this theory," he says, "as completely false; for it is susceptible of the most diverse interpretations and applications, amongst which one may come upon some which are entirely just. But as it is by no means complete, and gives occasion to a crowd of equivocations, we cannot accept it as the basis of the inquiry with which we are occupied.

"Some modern authors have pretended that this doctrine has been finally accepted as a general custom. That assertion is by no means proved, and it is scarcely possible that

[1] Guthrie, p. 141 et seq.

it can be true; for the opinions of authors, and the decisions of judicial tribunals, which more or less accord with them, are too divergent to be cited as testimonies of the existence of the custom. There is, nevertheless, this element of truth in the assertion, that down to the latest times, almost all the authors who have treated of our subject have employed the technical expressions of personal, real, and mixed statutes; but as they attach to these expressions rules and ideas altogether different, the element of truth is reduced to very narrow limits."[1]

With this somewhat disparaging view it is interesting to contrast the remarks of M. Mancini, the greatest living authority in Italy on private international law.

"Savigny well says that the statutory theory is neither entirely true nor entirely false, but that it contains a part of the truth. It has a primary merit—that, namely, of being a theory *à priori*, largely conceived so as to embrace the whole matter of conflict, laws, and statutes. Its second merit is that it recognises, in certain laws, in those which form the personal statute, an essential power of such a kind as to extend their action to countries beyond the territorial jurisdiction. When we consider that during the last two centuries, and up almost to our own day, in the midst of such a blaze of philosophical speculation, there was neither academy, nor tribunal, nor writer of repute who did not accept the empirical system of voluntary and reciprocal goodwill between nations (*comitas*) as the first and sole foundation for the efficacy of foreign laws within the territories of other nations, we are

[1] Guthrie, p. 142.

astounded to find our jurists of the thirteenth century already elevating themselves above this system, and preferring principles of a less variable kind. . . . But this is not all: when we approach the exposition of the fundamental theory which, according to our views, admits of being proposed for practical purposes "—he refers to the substitution of nationality for domicile—" we see that it reduces itself to a more correct expression of some of the same ideas which the statutory theory expressed in a confused and vicious manner; we learn how the statutory theory had anticipated the salient points of the truth ; we recognise a link of connection, and a relation more intimate than we imagined between the principle of nationality invoked by men of science in the full nineteenth century, and the doctrine of the personal statute invented by the Italian jurisconsults of the century rendered illustrious in the history of Italy by the Lombard League and the battle of Legnano. We may pause, then, with sympathy and respect before the venerable presence of those who were our second masters after the Roman jurisconsults; and although the statutory theory may seem to have fallen into desuetude since the introduction of the new code, we may endeavour, by making use of the great works which it inspired, to give it a new life, and to bring it into harmony with the philosophical tendencies of the modern spirit."[1]

(c) *Modern significance of the statutory theory.*

Without entering further, for the present at least, into discussions of which the statutory theory has been so fruitful, and passing over the question which has been so variously resolved

[1] *Bulletin de l'Institut*, 1875, p. 20.

by jurists, as to whether the relations which have been referred to the third class of mixed statutes, constitute really a distinct class at all, or whether they ought not rather to be referred to one or other of the two first classes, according as the real or personal element may seem to preponderate, we shall assume the soundness of the distinction, to the extent of admitting, that there are certain legal relations which, for practical purposes, may be conveniently regarded as adhering to persons, and others as adhering to things. And as, in order to become familiar with an object, it is often desirable to quit the point of view to which we have been accustomed, we shall here venture on a slight innovation on the order in which legal relations were contemplated by the authors of the statutory theory, and in which we ourselves are accustomed to contemplate them.

All legal relations being attributes of the person are, as we have said, fundamentally personal. There are no moral or legal relations between things, corresponding to the mathematical, numerical, chemical, and other physical relations which subsist between them. Persons alone have jural rights and duties, and it is the collective conception of these which we endeavour to convey when we speak of legal relations. It was the preponderance of this essential element which no doubt led to the precedence which has been given to personal statutes, for Bartolus and his contemporaries were not unmindful of the warning of the *Digest*, that it is for men alone that laws exist, *hominum causa omne jus constitutum sit.*[1]

L. i. v. 2—*De statu hominum.*

But as it is with the locality of legal relations, not with their character, that we are here directly concerned, we shall try whether a shorter road to the localisation of personal rights may not be found by beginning with those relations, the locality of which is in some measure determined by the stationary character of their objects.

(*d*) *Of the localisation of the rights and obligations which result to persons from the possession of immovables.*

Lands and houses never go from home. Their jural is dependent on their physical locality. It is here that the subtle element of human volition, which, in the localisation of movables, and still more of persons, we have so much difficulty in appreciating, disturbs us least. Even Mahomet had to go to the mountain. In the case of immovables, the *lex domicilii* if we may so speak, is inseparable from the *lex loci:* the two conceptions of jural and physical locality are identical. The law of the land, it is true, may be changed by legislation or revolution—even the sovereignty of the land may be changed by conquest or by cession; but the law of the land, as it is for the time being, governs the land, or, in other words, determines the rights and duties of those to whom the land belongs. In order to localise the relations which centre in an immovable object, then, all that at first sight seems requisite is that a geographical or topographical fact should be ascertained.

Further, domicile or homeness and nationality are here coincident; and if we choose to fix the jural locality of an immovable object from a political, rather than from a physical, point of view, the result will be the same. Nationality here, indeed, is only a collective name for those municipal rights and duties which begin and end at the frontiers of separate States.

But immovables do not in general belong to the State. The land is portioned out to private persons, whose rights and duties of a personal kind, as we shall see hereafter, are determined by the law of the land to which they are personally subject. Is this land, then, necessarily that in which their immovable possessions are locally situated? So long as the rule obtained that political naturalisation was indispensable for the tenure of immovable property, this question admitted of an affirmative answer, at least in so far as nationality was accepted as determining the rights and duties of the person. If only a native was allowed to be a proprietor of immovables, there was no difficulty in holding that every proprietor of immovables was subject to native law. But this rule, in almost all States, has been relaxed; and we ourselves, in our recent legislation, have altogether departed from it. By the Naturalisation Act of 1870 (33 Vict. c. 14) it is enacted :—

§ 2. " Real and personal property of every description may be taken, acquired, held, and disposed of by an alien in the same manner in all respects as by a natural-born British subject; and a title to real and personal property of every description may be derived through, from, or in succession to an alien, in the same manner in all respects as through, from, or in succession to a natural-born British subject."

Here then, even as regards immovable property, we find ourselves in presence of a question which cannot be determined physically or geographically. We have to determine the jural locality of the property of a person who, *ex hypothesi*, is not jurally in the place in which his immovable property is situated, and who, when he goes to his mountain, carries alien personal rights and duties along with him. Before considering the localisation of its proprietor in other respects, then, let us try to complete our conception of the jural locality of the property, and of the influence on the relations of the proprietor which result from its immovable character.

What are the personal rights and obligations, on the part of a proprietor, which centre in an immovable object, and which, even as an alien, he may enjoy, on the one hand, and, on the other, must accept? What do we mean when we say that immovables are governed by the *lex loci rei sitæ?* What rights and duties do the *statuta realia*, in their modern signification, determine? On this subject, Savigny says, "He who wishes to acquire, to have, to exercise a right to a thing, goes for that purpose to its locality, and voluntarily submits himself, as to this particular legal relation, to the local law that governs that region. When, therefore, it is said that real rights are to be judged by the law of the place where the thing is situated (*lex rei sitæ*), this assertion rests on the same ground as the application of the *lex domicilii* to the personal status. Both arise from voluntary submission."[1] When we come to the subject of movables, we shall see reason for hesitation in extending to them the local law. But the local law, even in the case of an alien proprietor, determines all questions relating to the acquisition of immovables, whether

[1] Guthrie, p. 174.

by sale or prescription, to feu-duties, to letting, and hiring, and mortgaging, working of mines and minerals, servitudes, and to all taxes and public burdens.

Public rights, on the other hand, being of a political character depend on nationality, and do not result to an alien from the possession of property, whether movable or immovable. He does not possess the suffrage, either municipal or parliamentary, and he cannot himself be elected to any office, either political or magisterial.

So far there is little difference of opinion amongst jurists. But the case is very different when we come to consider the jural capacity of the alien proprietor of immovables, in so far as it depends on his personal status: by what law, for example, the age at which he can acquire, alienate, or succeed to immovables is to be determined. Here the question arises, whether the general rule, as we shall find it to be, that status is governed by the law of domicile, or, on the new theory, of nationality, wherever the individual may be, and into whatever relation he may enter, finds an exception when these relations have reference to immovable property. This question has received both affirmative and negative answers, which, in many important respects, have led to opposite results. There are indeed three shades of opinion, which Sir Robert Phillimore has thus summarised:[1]—

"1. There are those, beginning with Huber and ending with Savigny, who hold that this capacity to acquire or alienate is governed by the law of the domicile of the acquirer or alienator.

[1] Vol. iv. p. 447.

"2. There are those who hold that this capacity does not belong to the qualities of the person, as such, but to the legal working or effect of these qualities; and therefore, that the *lex fori*, before which the matter is adjudicated, and not the law of the domicile, should be applied.

"3. Those who hold, with Story for their principal exponent, that, generally speaking, the law of the domicile should be applied, but not in the case of *immovables*. In this case, the *lex rei sitæ*, or the *statutum reale*, must govern,—a position emphatically condemned by Savigny."

Savigny's opinion, in this matter, is in accordance with his general contention that *status* is governed without exception by the law of domicile. "It is my opinion that every one is to be judged, as to his personal status, always by the law of his domicile, whether the judgment is at home or abroad, and whether the personal quality itself, or its legal effects, be the object of the judgment."[1] In the adoption of this opinion the Scotch courts have been guided by what has now come to be the almost universal doctrine in Continental countries,[2] as opposed to that which still prevails in England and America; and in so doing, I think they have acted in accordance with the fundamental principles of international law.

As "person" is merely a collective term for personal qualities, it seems to me, that if we recognise the person, or, in other words, the jural existence of a foreigner at all for municipal purposes, we must take him as we find him, and recognise in him the personal qualities—of majority or minority,

[1] Guthrie, p. 152.   [2] Fraser's *Parent and Child*, p. 577 *et seq.*

for example—which his own municipal law assigns to him. If, with reference to a certain class of legal relations, we redefine him according to our own notions, so as either to increase or diminish his jural capacities, we have made a different person of him, in a jural sense. The person whom we now recognise is not an alien, but a native to the extent to which he is thus redefined, and we have taken away from him characteristics which we affected to confer on him by the clause of the Naturalisation Act which I have quoted. For this reason I incline to Savigny's opinion (pp. 131 and 224 *et seq.*), and that which has obtained recognition in Germany, that the law of domicile ought to govern succession and all other rights dependent on *status*, even with regard to immovable property. Considering that immovable property must always be held and administered in accordance with the *lex loci*, I do not see that "the sovereignty which is vital to every independent State" need, as Phillimore says, be interfered with by a law which fixes majority with reference to land a year earlier or a year later, or even which sends land to one individual heir, or one set of heirs, more than to another. The compulsory subdivision of landed property, as in France, which the recognition of the French law of succession in immovables might occasionally introduce into this country, would no doubt be much at variance with our existing customs. But if its tendency, as Phillimore apprehends, would be subversive of our existing social institutions, or the political organisation which rests on them, it might be forbidden on public grounds. The doctrine of recognition, as we have already seen, does not bring within the category of international rights or duties any arrangements which are at variance with public law, as understood by the recognising State. On this ground, as on that of immorality, foreign contracts and relations of every kind may be declared invalid. In this principle, as it seems to me, we have a far more logical answer to anything which may be amiss in the laws of succession of other countries, than we can derive from a distinction between movable and immovable property. On these grounds, I believe that the Institute of International Law was right in laying down that, on the assumption that nationality was to be substituted for domicile, it should govern succession without exception (*quelle que soit la nature des biens*); and it was only the feeling that the innovation was one which would not be accepted either in this country or in America,[1] that induced me to join in the *reserve* drawn up by Sir Travers Twiss.[2]

But here we come on questions of *status*, and their patrimonial consequences, which will be better discussed under the head of the localisation of the person. I shall only add, as regards Scotland, that the rule which refers questions of *status* to the *lex domicilii* suffers no derogation where the exercise of his rights over immovable property by an alien minor is under consideration. "It would be arbitrary, and contrary to a rational interpretation of our law of minority as a whole," says Mr Fraser, "to apply some of its provisions relative to heritable property, while the minor's disabilities in other respects were left to a foreign law. This would do violence to the spirit and intention of the Scotch law of minority, while it would not enable the *lex domicilii* to provide con-

[1] Field's *International Code*, pp. 404, 405.   [2] *Revue*, 1881, p. 72.

sistently and completely for the protection of its minor subjects."[1]

(c) *Of the localisation of the personal rights and duties which result from the possession of movables.*

The localisation of immovables furnishes, so to speak, the type or ideal to which, in the localisation of movables, whether animate or inanimate, the law seeks to approximate. All law is a recognition of fact. It is the fact of locality which governs the law of locality; and as the fact becomes, if not less obvious less permanent, in consequence of its dependence on human will, the difficulties of our subject increase. Fixtures, though their removal be physically possible, are held to be jurally localised by the object their adherence to which, for the time being, localises them physically. The element of will, though not overruled by necessity, as in the case of immovable objects, is held to be interpreted by the element of physical fact. The door of a shooting-box on Ben Nevis, to all jural intents and purposes, is just as much in Scotland as Ben Nevis itself; and just as much, though it belonged to Prince Bismarck, as though it belonged to the Duke of Argyll. The fact that Prince Bismarck might carry off the door to Germany, and that he could not, by any appliances that we yet know, carry off Ben Nevis, makes no difference in the eye of the law. The presumption that, for his own sake, he will not do so, is accepted as a fact sufficiently stable to form the basis of a positive law in the one case, just as the physical impossibility was in the other. So far there is, and there ought to be, no difference of opinion. But the physical possibility of removal, though

[1] Fraser's *Parent and Child*, p. 587.

in the case of the door it was held to be overcome by the presumption against its exercise, was nevertheless a reality which circumstances might raise into the character of the determining fact in the question of jural locality. Suppose that, in place of the door of a shooting-box, the object which we seek jurally to localise is a tent which a foreigner has pitched for a night, a sketching umbrella which he has set up for a few hours, or a portmanteau which he has beside him on the top of a coach. Here questions of far greater difficulty arise; but they are still questions of fact, or rather of a fact, for the fact which we have to establish is always the same—viz., where is the tent, or the sketching umbrella, or the portmanteau, whilst it continues to belong to the same person, most likely to be found?—what is the normal *situs* of its existence in relation to him?—where, *as his*, is *it* at home?

This inquiry, always difficult and of doubtful issue, several of the most distinguished German jurists,[1]—Savigny himself being of the number[2]—have attempted to cut short by abolishing the distinction between movables and immovables, and holding both to be governed by the *lex rei sitæ*. The physical locality of a material object at a given time, they say, can always be ascertained; and as the municipal law of the State governs every part of the State, it must govern every object that comes within it, for however short a period. But an awkward alternative here arises. Either we must make this rule extend to persons, and govern such subjects as succession —which both in movables and immovables Savigny hands over to the *lex domicilii*—or else we must separate a man

[1] Phillimore, vol. iv. p. 449, note.   [2] Guthrie, p. 174 *et seq.*

from his luggage. The personal element in the relation, in short, has been overlooked, and it is the thing only, not the right to it, that we have localised.

Savigny has recognised this difficulty, and broken through his rule in the case of the portmanteau. "In such cases," he says,[1] "it is evident that no application can be made of the *lex rei sitæ*;" and he applies the same rule to mercantile goods *in transitu*. With reference to them he says, "We are rather obliged to seek, in thought, for some resting-place at which such things are destined to remain for a longer, perhaps an indefinite time; such a resting-place may perhaps be indicated beyond a doubt by the clearly demonstrated intention of the owner; in other cases it will coincide with the domicile of the owner."

But Savigny contends that there is another class of movables to which the *lex rei sitæ* may be safely applied. "This happens with the furniture of a house, with a library or collection of works of art, and the stocking (*inventar*) of a landed estate."[2]

A doctrine which rests on the distinction either between a portmanteau and a library, or between an inn and a hired house, seems scarcely worthy of such a mind as Savigny's. If the proprietor of the portmanteau hires a suite of apartments in a hotel for the winter, or builds a house for himself at Cannes, as Lord Brougham did—is the portmanteau then *in transitu* or at rest? Or, suppose the portmanteau is stuffed with books, or that its proprietor transports a considerable library in several portmanteaus to a foreign country, as both

[1] Guthrie, p. 180.   [2] *Ib.*

Savigny and Brougham must often have done—*quid juris?* Or again, if the character of the books be taken into account, what do you say to Murray's or Baedeker's hand-books, which exist for the very purpose of being packed into portmanteaus and carried in pockets? Then, if the rule is once broken through, the question comes to be, whether there is any use in carrying its application beyond fixtures—*i.e.*, beyond objects which cannot be removed without injury. Will anything be gained by attempting to draw a line between one kind of movables and another, by conjectures which we form as to the intentions of their owners, or by pretending to localise or domicile objects which are destitute of will independently, whilst we declare locality and domicile to depend on the manifestation of will? Is there any reason, in such circumstances, why we should not go over at once to the *lex domicilii* of the owner, and say that it shall govern his movable and personal property, just as the *lex rei sitæ* governs his real or immovable property? In cases in which human will determines the *situs*, is not the presumption that a man will choose to have his movable property about him, which has found expression in the phrase *mobilia sequuntur personam*, more likely to be in accordance with the fact of its jural *situs*, than the fact of its physical *situs* elsewhere, for the time being?

It is only in exceptional cases that the presumption will be called into play, for, as a rule, the physical *situs* will correspond to the domicile of the proprietor; and in the exceptional cases in which they are separated, the effect of the presumption is to bring the ephemeral fact back to the permanent fact by bringing the ephemeral will back to the permanent will.

Such, at all events, is the feeling which has hitherto prevailed amongst ourselves; and the rule that the *lex domicilii* governs movable and personal, just as the *lex rei sitæ* governs immovable property, may be held as established both in this country and in America. "The doctrine," says Field,[1] "is commonly stated substantially as follows: Personal property has no *situs;* and the title acquired to it, if good by the law of the domicile, is good everywhere, and will be recognised and enforced in every State unless it conflicts with its laws or the rights of its citizens."[2]

On the whole, I believe that the application of the law of domicile to movables is really the arrangement which will come nearest to the fact. But that the inconveniences attending it are no novelties, is plain from the vacillation which even our own courts have exhibited in the matter. The rule that *mobilia sequuntur personam* is not yet a hundred years old in our jurisprudence. It was established in 1788 by the Court of Session, in the case of Bruce *v.* Bruce,—a judgment which was affirmed by the House of Lords. By this case,—and still more expressly by Hog *v.* Lashley, in 1792; Ommanney *v.* Bingham, in 1796; and Somerville *v.* Somerville, in 1801,—the old rule that the actual should be likewise the legal site of inanimate movables was abandoned,

---

[1] *International Code*, p. 396; Phillimore, p. 433; Fœlix, *Droit Internationale Privé*, vol. i. p. 127.

[2] But doctors differ on this subject, it would seem, in America as elsewhere. See Wharton's *Conflict of Laws*, as quoted and commented on by Westlake, p. 161.

though it had the authority of our best jurists, Lord Stair included.

The impossibility of arriving at a rule which shall be thorough-going either way,—which Savigny confesses when he takes refuge in so weak an expedient as "circumstances,"[1] is brought home to us most strongly, perhaps, when we consider the case of animate movables,—horses, for example, or dogs. The horses which form part of the stocking of a farm we should not hesitate, with Savigny,[2] to consider as fixtures; whereas the horses which the Prince of Wales took with him to India were as clearly domiciled in England during his passage through Egypt as he was himself. And between these cases the shades are infinite; and the difficulties of each case, if taken apart from the question of personal domicile, would raise, often very needlessly, all the difficulties attendant on that difficult subject.

Are the Queen's horses and dogs, for example, English or Scotch, or have they two domiciles, on the assumption that that is her position? All that is certain is that their locality is fixed neither by the will of heaven, as in the case of a mountain—nor by their own will, as in the case of a person—but by the will of their owner; and the question of the localisation of animate as of inanimate movables, thus resolves itself into the question of the localisation of the person whom they follow.[3]

---

[1] Guthrie, p. 181.   [2] Ib., p. 180.
[3] The whole of this difficult subject is discussed with much acuteness by Mr Westlake, who was the first to draw attention, in England, to the distinction between movables as isolated, and when included in a universal assignment, on or by bankruptcy, marriage, or death.—Chap. vii. p. 154 et seq.

(*f*) *Of the localisation of the person.*

Whatever may be the relation between instinct and reason, it is of reason alone that jurisprudence takes cognisance as the source of will; and it is man alone whom, as the possessor of reason, jurisprudence credits with the possession of will. But rational will being, as we have elsewhere seen in the last analysis, coincident with power,[1] and power being the source both of rights and obligations, it is man alone who has either rights or obligations. Again, rights and obligations are what, collectively, we call legal relations; and thus it is that legal relations, in strictness, are confined to persons.

The physical relations which subsist between inanimate objects, and even the animal relations between animate beings, are, in the jural sense, involuntary, and for this reason are not convertible into rights and duties inherent in the objects. In so far, however, as these relations are subject to human will and power, they are convertible into rights and duties inherent in human beings. A horse or a dog can move physically, but he cannot move rationally, and consequently cannot jurally determine his own locality—he cannot localise himself. But a man can move not only physically but rationally—nay, he may move rationally, and consequently jurally, even when he cannot move physically. Moreover, he can take his horse and his dog along with him; and jurisprudence, assuming his actions to be guided by reason till the contrary be established, holds him entitled so to act. A man who is *sui juris* may consequently be jurally where he will, and act jurally where he is; and jurisprudence will recognise him as being and acting,

[1] *Institutes of Law*, p. 427 *et seq.*

wherever it can be shown that he really wills to be and to act. The element of will, which in the localisation of immovables sank to its lowest, here rises to its highest point.

But jural will, as we have said, must be real, or, in other words, it must be in accordance with the general tenor of the volitions of a sane person, not merely exceptional, ephemeral, or apparent. Now the difficulty in determining the question of personal localisation is to distinguish between real will and apparent will. Will is not always expressed in words, still less normal or real will. Even when words are used, it by no means follows that the words can be relied on. A man may, quite truthfully, express an intention of retaining or changing a locality or domicile, which he not only does not carry into action, but which the actions of his whole life prove to have been merely an expression of temporary and transient feeling. Even at the time there may have been others who knew that his will was not what he proclaimed it to be. In these circumstances the law falls back on his actions for a commentary on his words, or rather it accepts his words, whether oral or written, only as a contribution to the *res gestæ*, which, as the best index to his real will, it recognises as the motives of its ultimate decision. It is by keeping this consideration in view that we see the truth of Lord Loughborough's remark, that "domicile is a question of fact and not of law," or rather that it is a question of law which must be determined by fact. As Mr Westlake has very well said, "Domicile is the legal conception of residence."[1] It is the fact of *homeness*, as the

---

[1] First edition, p. 30.

law gathers it from the various indications of rational volition submitted to it. In principle it is the very same question on which the validity or the *locus solutionis* of a contract rests. But the determination of this fact in questions with reference to the localisation of the person has always been, and I fear will continue to be, a matter of exceptional difficulty, arising from the wide field which the *res gestæ* so frequently cover.

An attempt which has found favour with many jurists, and been admitted into several codes, has been made to obviate it by accepting the fact of nationality as conclusive of the reality of personal will; and holding the individual, with all the relations which municipal law ascribes to him, as jurally at home wherever he is politically nationalised. Of the value of this attempt I shall speak when we have considered the means by which the fact of homeness has been sought to be more directly determined.

In the Roman law there were two distinct grounds on which individuals might be subjected to specific local domains—viz., citizenship and residence—*origo* and *domicilium*. Savigny has expounded very fully the nature of these grounds, and has brought out with great clearness their dependence on the existing conditions of society, and the territorial arrangements of the Roman empire. As these arrangements were swept away by the Germanic conquests, and as the society of modern Europe exists under conditions altogether different, it need not surprise us to find that, though the terms which the Romans employed to designate the ties which bound the individual to his locality are still familiar to our ears, their modern should differ essentially from their ancient signification. The extent to which this change has taken place has been very different in the case of the one term and of the other. *Origo*, in the Roman sense, stating the matter very generally, signified the rights of citizenship acquired by an individual, and the burdens of citizenship imposed upon an individual by birth, adoption, emancipation,[1] or admission into one or more of the municipalities, which, like a legal network, covered the whole empire. With us, on the contrary, it signifies the fictitious domicile ascribed to the individual in the place in which his father, or, in the case of a natural child, his mother, was domiciled at the period of his birth—the place where he was actually born, in the case of his parents having no domicile, or where he was found, in the case of a foundling. In place of being a substantive ground on which an individual was subjected to a particular jurisdiction, *origo*, in the modern sense, is thus merely an element in determining the question of domicile,—one ground which, in the absence of others, or taken in conjunction with them, may lead us to assign him to one jurisdiction, or sphere of local law, in preference to another. In this view, Savigny remarks that the phrase *domicilium originis*, which has crept into modern use, would have had no meaning in the mouth of a Roman jurist, because the two terms, to him, represented two orders of ideas essentially distinct and independent of each other.[2] In the modern jurisprudence it signifies a domicile resulting, not from the choice, but the origin of the individual, and has thus a perfectly intelligible meaning.

The Roman sense of the term *domicilium* approached much

[1] Guthrie, p. 88 *et seq.*   [2] *Ib.*, p. 131.

more nearly to that in which we use it, though from the existence of *origo* as a separate ground of jurisdiction, its application was, of course, more limited than with us. The definition of *domicilium* which we find in the Code, consequently still retains its applicability, and is quoted in all modern books, not for historical or rhetorical, but for practical purposes.[1]

"It is not doubtful that every one has his domicile in that place which he has made the residence of his family and the chief seat of his fortunes; which he does not mean to leave unless he be called away; from which, when he is absent, he regards himself as being on a journey; and to which, when he returns, he regards his journey as ended."[2]

In the Roman law, the law of domicile came into play only where there was no original *forum*; and Savigny is clear that, where a conflict arose between them, the law of the municipality (the *origo*) would always prevail over that of the domicile;[3] though as regards jurisdiction, a person might be cited, not only in every town in which he had citizenship by *origo*, but also in every town in which he had a domicile.[4] The result at which Savigny arrives, then, with reference to the relation between the law of modern Europe and that of Rome, is that, whilst *origo* has altogether ceased to exist in the sense which the Romans attached to it, domicile has not

---

[1] Guthrie, p. 97.

[2] "In eodem loco singulos habere domicilium non ambigitur, ubi quis larem, rerumque ac fortunarum suarum summam constituit, unde rursus non sit discessurus, si nihil avocet: unde cum profectus est, peregrinari videtur: quod si rediit, peregrinari jam destitit."—*Cod.*, lib. 10, tit. 39, 7.

[3] Guthrie, p. 120. [4] *Ib.*, p 112.

only held its place as a ground of determining both jurisdiction and territorial law, but has become the only ground. "The line between what is and is not applicable in the whole teaching of the Romans on this subject will be made plainer by considering separately the three effects which Roman law attaches to domicile as well as to citizenship.

"1. Municipal burdens (*munera*) may here be put out of view altogether, as they related to exclusively Roman circumstances.

"2. Jurisdiction (*forum domicilii*).—This effect of domicile not only remains in modern law, but is still more important than it was among the Romans; for with them the *forum originis* very often coexisted with the *forum domicilii*, so that the plaintiff might choose between the two. With us, *origo* in the Roman sense has vanished; and thus the *forum domicilii* is now the only ordinary and regular *forum* of every man.

"But this jurisdiction, like domicile itself upon which it depends, has now a signification different from what it had in the Roman law. It no longer relates, as it did then universally and necessarily, to the judicial authority over municipal territory to which the domicile refers, but to a judicial territory and local jurisdiction which may have very various origins and limits, and may or may not coincide with the boundaries of a municipal territory.

"3. The particular territorial law, to which, as his personal law, every individual is subject. Here we repeat the observation which has been made with respect to jurisdiction. This effect of domicile has not only remained, but has become still more exclusively applicable, and therefore more important than it was among the Romans; but at the same time it has, like the *forum domicilii*, acquired with us a different meaning."[1]

In fixing the jural locality of a free man, the determining element is his own free will; and I very much doubt whether, as regards his private relations, any single test of volition will ever be found adequate to supersede the various considerations involved in the conception of domicile. Had Savigny lived to see the unification of Germany, it is possible that nationality and not domicile might have been the test which he would have applied to the determination of personal status.[2] But however this might have been, a scheme which has received legislative recognition in France and Italy and Belgium, and which the Institute of International Law, at its meeting at Oxford in September 1880, approved by a unanimous vote, demands our very respectful consideration. It is not alien to preconceived notions, for, as M. Brocher has shown,[3] it is substantially a proposal to revert in principle to the Roman *origo*, and to give to it exclusive, in place of co-ordinate or even primary, authority. Neither is it an objection to it that the outburst of national feeling which led to the formation of the new kingdom of Italy and to the new Italian school of jurisprudence, may have favoured the reception of a theory which seemed to counteract the idea of individualism which forms the basis of domicile, and which its disorganising tendencies in the family and in the State had discredited. So long as individual

---

[1] Guthrie, p. 124.

[2] Brocher, *Droit Internationale Privé*, p. 69 *et seq.*; Wharton's *Conflict of Laws*, p. 17, note; *Revue de Droit International*, 1881, No. I. p. 7.

[3] *Ut sup.*, p. 74.

freedom of action is preserved by declaring the acceptance or retention of nationality to depend on personal choice, nationality can scarcely be made to bind the citizen too closely to the State; and modern legislation, our own included, has been all in the direction of facilitating a change of nationality.

The question thus comes to be one purely of convenience. Is it by fixing the nationality or by fixing the domicile of the person that we shall most readily, most safely, and most economically ascertain the jural domain which covers his personal rights and obligations? The jural domain, we must not forget, is a fact already existent in the case of every citizen of a recognised State, and our problem is simply to determine by which of these two tests we shall best discover it. Now, of the greater facility and economy with which the test of nationality may be applied there can be no doubt, and on this ground the scheme has many obvious merits. It is scarcely conceivable that there should be a civilised man who does not belong to some nation, and the nation to which he belongs can be ascertained by bringing the facts of his present position in contact with some positive law, which is in general far more definite than any definition which we can possibly frame of the fact of domicile. If nationality would serve the same purpose as domicile, then, the superiority of its claims is incontestable, and its adoption would obviate some of the heaviest and most costly litigation that occupies the courts of law in all countries. But would the fact of nationality, if ascertained, serve the same purpose as the fact of domicile in all cases, or, indeed, in any case except where it had been conceded only on a previous proof of domicile? In the first place, its inapplicability to cases which fall under different legal systems within the same State is acknowledged. "It will be seen at once," says Mr Westlake, "that political nationality is inapplicable as a criterion between countries like England and Scotland, which belong to the same State though possessing different laws. Thus, to take an example from movable succession,—about which there is no question anywhere but that either domicile or political nationality must govern,—If a British subject, having more or less connection both with England and Scotland dies intestate, it is only by means of the former criterion that it is possible to determine whether his movable property shall go by English or Scotch law. To this extent domicile must be and is respected, even in a country like France or Italy, which draws its general rule from the political character."[1] Now, in such States as France and Italy, it is conceivable that the suggestion of the Institute, that they should bind themselves by treaty to the adoption of nationality as determining the law to be administered, *le plus tôt possible*, might be adopted. But when we bear in mind that the objection applies not only to England and Scotland, and to many of our colonies, but to many of the States of the American Union, progress in this direction, if progress it would be, must be relegated to a very distant future. It was to meet this difficulty that Mr Westlake offered the very ingenious suggestion that domicile should not be changed within the same nationality except by means of registration. "By depositing a written

---

[1] "Domicile or Political Nationality, and ascertainment of Domicile by Registration."—Paper read before the Social Science Association at Edinburgh, 7th October 1880.

declaration of his desire to change his domicile," he says, "the tedious and costly, and at best uncertain, inquiry into the intention of an individual would be put an end to, because no intention would be of any value which the testator or intestate had not expressed by an unambiguous declaration. It would remain impossible, as it should do, for a person to change the law to which his property was subject by a mere declaration, because the transfer of his residence would still be necessary to the transfer of his domicile, the declaration being an addition and not a substituted condition."[1] He further proposes that a year's residence should be exacted. Of the value of such registration as an adminicle of proof of change of domicile there can be no question; but to its adoption as the sole test of such a change, even as regards succession, there is, I think, much difficulty. At what *punctum temporis* is a man likely to have made up his mind to abandon the ties which bound him to the country of his origin? Mr Westlake gives the example of a Scotsman long resident in London; but no Scotsman ever makes up his mind, on any one particular occasion, that he is never to return to Scotland at all. The consequence is, either that he would never register, and that his formal might be at variance with his real character; or that, if he did, he would be acting on a momentary impulse, which would give no true indication of his permanent volition. As a palliative of the evils of the law of domicile, registration might, however, in many conceivable circumstances, be of great value.

But it is only between separate States, as we have seen,

[1] *Ib.*, p. 8.

that the test of nationality is contended for, and it is in this point of view that we must consider it. Does nationality, then, necessarily guarantee the entire jural locality of the person both as a man and as a citizen in every case, or in any case, indeed, in which it is not coincident with domicile? Will its separate proof determine the jural locality of the private rights and duties of the person whom it fixes down to a political domain? Is it not possible, that nationality and domicile may be separated in fact; and that whilst a man's rights and duties, as a citizen, bind him to one State, his rights and duties, as a private person, may bind him to another State? May not his nationality be individual, whilst his domicile has its roots in the family to which he belongs and the society in which he actually moves, or the converse?

Let us take a case which has actually occurred. A Dutch nobleman of Scotch descent, holding a high political office in Holland, where his family had been resident for three centuries, and where he possessed large estates, succeeded to a Scotch peerage. That both in his public and private relations he was localised in Holland is unquestionable; but that he or his son, with a view to taking his seat in the House of Lords, should comply with the requirements of our Naturalisation Act (§ 7) by residing not less than five years,[1] and renouncing his character as a Dutch citizen, while in his private relations he continued to be a Dutchman, was not only possible but very likely. Residence in any one country, on the part of persons of large means, is not very constant in any case; and if Baron Mackay, the father, who succeeded

[1] The practice of the Home Office, I understand, is to require eight years.

to the title, had purchased a house in the West End of London, and lived in it during the season, leaving servants in it the rest of the year, I do not see that English nationality could have been refused him on the ground that he spent the rest of his time at the Hague, more than if he spent it at Mentone, or on the Lake of Como. In fixing his nationality, just as in fixing his domicile, all the usual questions as to which was his principal residence, and where he preponderatingly resided, would have arisen. The Secretary of State could not have prevented him from holding property, and buying, selling, and bequeathing it, any more than he could prevent him from being born, from marrying, dying, and being buried in Holland. He could not even have demanded of him a declaration of intention with reference to these transactions in future; for he would probably have told him, with great truth, that the point was one as to which he had not made up his own mind.

Are our courts, then, to deal with a person in this position in all respects as an Englishman, or are the Dutch courts bound to recognise him as such? Suppose he marries his deceased wife's sister, she being an Englishwoman? If we make nationality the test of the locality of his private relations, how can we refuse to take him with his encumbrances; or if we repudiate the marriage, can we expect the courts of Holland to follow our example? We should thus have the law of domicile governing his private relations in Holland, quite irrespective of his change of nationality; and we should have the fact of his being a nationalised Englishman falling back into the character of an adminicle of proof or disproof of domicile, which I take to be its true character in questions of private international law. Whether political recognition should be granted to a foreigner on a proof of residence which falls short of a proof of domicile, is a question of public not of private law.[1]

But if the two be made coincident, and if a proof of domicile *de facto* be required for naturalisation, we are back again into all the difficulties of the law of domicile, with the additional disadvantage of their solution being laid on an executive, in place of a judicial officer. The practical result of such an arrangement would be, that the Secretary of State would grant naturalisation only on the ground of a judicial inquiry, in which he would always appear as defender, and the fact of domicile would have to be ascertained in a more cumbrous and expensive way. Nor would the case be one of unfrequent occurrence. If nationality may, as we have seen, run away and leave domicile behind it, the case in which the converse takes place is far more common. How often does it happen that our own countrymen, from motives of health, or pleasure, or business, take up a temporary residence in a foreign country which family and business connections formed abroad gradually make permanent, whilst politically they continue to be Englishmen? In the case of persons of high rank, or the representatives of historical families, a permanent change of nationality is scarcely in their option; and yet persons, even of this class, constantly become, to all private intents and purposes, voluntarily domiciled abroad. They are

---

[1] As to the greater inconveniences which would result to countries having mixed populations, see Wharton's *Conflict of Laws*, p. 17, § 7.

educated, live, marry, and die abroad. Others exercise various arts and follow various callings—they trade, contract, teach, and enter into every possible relation of private life which does not involve citizenship. And this may go on for generations, not only blamelessly, but with credit and advantage to all parties; for the loss of nationality by physical absence from one State, apart from its acquisition in another, is a mere arbitrary municipal arrangement, which may or may not correspond to fact. The son of a citizen is a citizen of the nation to which his father belongs, and can lose his citizenship only by indicating his own volition to that effect. Any inference in the case of his posterity which might arise from the mere lapse of time ought certainly to be counteracted by an unmistakable indication of contrary volition. By returning to England, taking the oath of allegiance, and occasionally voting at an election, sitting on a bench of justices of the peace, or drilling with the volunteers, a succession of persons who had been domiciled in a foreign country for centuries, provided they were not nationalised, might continue to be good Englishmen. The Mackays might have done so for the last three hundred years. Even without returning at all, the Naturalisation Act, by a very slight change on § 6, might make provision for the permanent retention of British nationality, by a declaration made before any diplomatic or consular officer in her Majesty's service abroad. Would it, in such circumstances, be just to such persons that their personal rights, or to others, that their personal obligations, should continue to be governed by the law of England? Would such an arrangement not be a separation of law from fact, and the recognition of an arbitrary and fictitious localisation of a far more flagrant kind than that which M. Mancini stigmatises as a possible result of minority and majority being made to depend on the law of domicile? "An individual," he says, "coming from a cold country where nature is languid and the development of the physical and moral faculties is slow, continues, with reason, by the laws of his country for a longer period in a position of minority and incapacity than he would do by the laws of a warm country. If an individual arrives in a southern country and there takes up his abode, will he have acquired instantly (*instantanément*), in consequence of this fact, the physical and moral qualities which he wanted, so that it would be suitable to apply to him the conditions of majority, established by the laws which governed the warm country?"[1] The answer, as it humbly seems to me, is, that domicile, so far from taking place instantaneously, is necessarily the result of a gradual process, by which law conforms itself to fact; whereas nationalisation may take place instantly, and, even in our own cautious country, requires the lapse only of five years. In addition to this, there is the difficulty of carrying the public arrangements of one State into the territories of another—a difficulty which carries us beyond the doctrine of recognition, as hitherto understood in international jurisprudence. The French Code, which says that the character of a Frenchman shall attach to a French citizen wherever he goes, or the Italian Code, which has borrowed its provision, may govern the relations of an absent Frenchman or an absent Italian in France or in Italy; but

[1] Bulletin de l'Institut de Droit International, Session 1875.

beyond France and Italy, its provisions with reference to citizenship are *brutum fulmen*. If a Frenchman or an Italian, whilst retaining his citizenship, has become a domiciled Englishman in point of fact, no arbitrary union between public and private rights and duties which French or Italian legislation may establish, can prevent us from holding him to be an Englishman, in point of law, as regards those private relations which in their nature cling to his person; and any treaty which we should enter into to the contrary would be a blunder in jurisprudence. For these reasons it seems to me that no law of naturalisation can save us from the necessity of ascertaining the fact of domicile as best we may, and accepting it as the criterion of personal as opposed to political localisation.[1] And this remark applies, as I have explained, even to the case in which naturalisation should be made dependent on domicile. Domicile, and not nationality, would still be the governing fact in the localisation of the person, and nothing would be gained by not accepting it as such directly, whereas a very serious impediment would be thrown in the way of the acquisition of new nationalities, and as a consequence of that liberalisation of international relations by which our recent legislation, with reference to naturalisation, has been distinguished. Our object must be to facilitate the acquisition of domicile by facilitating naturalisation,—not to tie them together, or to put the one in the place of the other. Let our doors be thrown hospitably open, but do not let us count as members of our family those who, by qualifying themselves for nationalisation by any

---

[1] Bar's *International Law*, Gillespie's translation, Note A, p. 110 *et seq.*

process short of the acquisition of domicile, have thrown in their lot with us only in a public capacity.[1]

(*g*) *Of the localisation of jural acts.*

The right to exist, as a person, involves the right to energise freely. The right of choosing his own sphere of existence, on the part of the person, involves the right of choosing his own sphere of action.

In determining the jural locality of an action by an individual, or of a transaction between individuals, just as in determining the locality of the persons who act or transact, the first question which we have to ask is the question of volition, —Where did the individual or individuals rationally— *i. e.*, really—wish to act or to transact? But the question of volition is a question of fact; and the whole subject consequently resolves itself into an analysis of the circumstances presented to us by means of the ordinary laws of evidence. Where the subject-matter of the transaction does not localise it, the inquiry must often be attended with difficulty.

Local jurisdiction, except in the case to be immediately mentioned, is coincident with territorial law; and the follow-

---

[1] I shall explain hereafter the grounds on which it appears to me that the simplest mode of relieving neutral States from responsibility for their private citizens would be to substitute for the unenforcible Foreign Enlistment Acts an international agreement, to the effect that every man should be held to be a citizen of the State under whose banner he fought, and of that State only. The status of neutral citizenship is incompatible with the belligerent character; and as foreign enlistment, though it may be forbidden, cannot be prevented, the maintenance of such citizenship during war must produce entanglements. On the other hand, however, if the belligerent were killed the first week, it would be very unfair to his family, or to his creditors, that his succession should be regulated by the law of the country in which he served. Belligerency is a public relation which ought to determine public status, *but public status only.*

ing are the conclusions, with reference to both subjects, at which Savigny has arrived, as the result of discussions, into which the character of this work does not permit us to follow him.

Jurisdiction will be founded, and the territorial law will emerge—

"1st, At the place which is specially fixed for the fulfilment of the obligation, whether it be so fixed by a verbal indication of intention, or because the act which is to be brought about by the obligation can possibly be performed only at a single place.

"2d, Failing the appointment of a place of fulfilment, this jurisdiction may be founded by the fact that the obligation arises out of the debtor's course of business, which is fixed at a particular place.

"3d, The jurisdiction may be fixed by the place where the obligation arises, if that coincides with the domicile of the debtor.

"4th, The place where the obligation arises may found jurisdiction, even if it be away from the domicile of the debtor, if the circumstances create an expectation that its fulfilment shall also be at the same place.

"5th, If none of these conditions exist, the *forum* of the obligation is at the domicile of the debtor.

"All these cases," Savigny adds, "however various they appear, and however accidental their connection may seem, yet admit of being reduced to a common principle. It is always *the place of fulfilment* that determines the jurisdiction, either that expressly fixed (No. 1), or that which depends upon a tacit expectation (Nos. 2-5). In both cases a voluntary submission of the defendant to this jurisdiction is to be assumed, unless an express declaration to the contrary excludes it."[1]

The application of the local law, even when ascertained, will of course be excluded where it is at variance with the public law, or the conceptions of morality which lie at the root of the private law in force at the place of the court which decides the question. A contract for the sale of a slave would not be enforcible in England, though England were at once the domicile of the seller and the stipulated *locus solutionis*. In the very important contract of marriage, this principle, of course, excludes in all Christian States the recognition of polygamous and incestuous marriages by citizens of the State, though celebrated in countries in which they are permitted. Under this latter head we, for the present, include a marriage with the sister of a deceased wife, though the prohibition has been removed, with the Queen's consent, in several of our own colonies; and it is doubtful whether the international conception of incest can be said to extend beyond brother and sister in the blood, so as to include even uncle and niece, if a Papal dispensation has been obtained. On similar grounds Roman Catholic countries repudiate divorce, and, as a consequence, the marriage of divorced persons, whether with their paramours or with others. But, as a general rule, the principle that the place of fulfilment determines the local law remains unshaken.

Whilst recognising the validity of marriage, as of every

[1] Guthrie, p. 209.

other contract the validity of which is recognised in the country in which it is contracted, the State in which the marriage is fulfilled reserves to itself the right of construction. The rights, duties, and obligations arising from a marriage are thus always determined by the lex domicilii. The validity of a marriage contracted in France, like the validity of any other contract, will thus be determined by the law of France (the *locus contractus*), whilst the matrimonial relation established between the spouses, and the patrimonial relations which may arise between them and their children, in the event of the father being a domiciled Englishman, will be determined by the law of England, the *lex domicilii*. This doctrine, from another point of view, results from the principle, which we have already considered, which assigns all questions of status to the *lex domicilii*.[1]

A point, apparently undecided in our law, has been thus determined, rightly according to Savigny, by the law of Prussia.

"The Prussian law, as a general rule, holds the local law of the domicile subsisting at the beginning of the marriage as decisive for its whole future endurance."[2] A more natural provision, one would say, would be to accept a change of domicile in fact as a change of domicile in law, to this as to all other effects, and to allow the actual domicile to govern matrimonial and patrimonial rights and duties.

(*h*) *Of the rule*, locus regit actum.

In determining the formal arrangements for carrying out transactions, regarding which the parties may be presumed to

---

[1] Guthrie, p. 148.   [2] *Ib.*, p. 297.

be indifferent, or to value only as means of fulfilling their intentions, the rule expressed in the maxim, *locus regit actum*, has been everywhere adopted.

"This rule," says Savigny, "means that the form of a juridical act shall be considered satisfactory, if it be in accordance with the law of the place where the act is done, even if another form is prescribed by the law of the place where the legal relation itself has its seat."[1] It is by this rule that the forms of all contracts are determined, from marriage down to the most trifling sale of movables; but its most important action is perhaps with reference to testaments made abroad. These, if made in accordance with the forms in use at the place in which the testator is resident, will be valid everywhere else. But in this, as in other applications of it, the rule is facultative, not imperative, and with us its action is excluded in succession to immovables. In a conveyance of property of all other kinds, the option of adopting the forms of his own domicile, or those of his residence, rests with the testator. A holograph will made by a Scotchman in Prussia, where testing is a judicial act, or in France, where the interposition of a notary is requisite, will be valid,—not in Scotland only, but in Prussia, or in France; whilst, conversely, a will made in accordance with Prussian or French form, will be valid in Scotland. Some writers hold that the same option exists with reference to the ceremonies of marriage, though the possibility of carrying out those of the domicile will be assumed to exist only in the persons of officials, and in localities which enjoy the rights of exterritoriality. A marriage, valid within the

[1] Guthrie, p. 319.

British dominions, can be celebrated, according to English formalities, at an English embassy or consulate, within the lines of an English army, or on board a British man-of-war. But though recognised by statute, the international validity of these marriages is doubtful, and an additional celebration, in accordance with the *lex loci*, is in all cases a safe precaution.[1]

(*i*) *Of the* lex fori.

The *forum* is a public institution of the State; and in approaching it we come again within the range of public municipal law. As the recognition of the state implies the recognition of its municipal law, it implies the recognition of the rules of judicial procedure, in accordance with which that law is administered. Moreover, as each State reserves to itself the right of determining what is true or false, it reserves to itself also the right of determining by what means truth and falsehood may be best ascertained. The laws governing the admissibility, and determining the value of evidence, are consequently the laws in force at the *forum* in which an action is raised.

The law of prescription appears, at first sight, to fall under the category of laws of evidence and procedure, and, as such, to be determined by the *lex fori*. Such was the view of it which was taken in the important case of Lippmann *v.* Don, as decided on appeal by the House of Lords. But Savigny contests this doctrine, and Bar and Westlake adopt his views. Savigny argues that the local law of the obligation itself, and not the law of the place at which it is sought to be enforced, ought to govern the term of prescription, on the ground that this term stands in connection with the substance of the obli-

[1] Fraser, vol. ii. p. 1312.

gation; and he contends that substantial justice requires that the option of selecting a *forum*, at which this term is longer or shorter than at another, should not be given either to the pursuer or to the defender.[1] The point is one of obvious difficulty, and has been ably discussed by Mr Guthrie in his note.[2]

These brief indications of the scope of the *lex fori* bring us, as I have said, again on the borders of public international law, and complete our sketch of the reciprocal recognition of private municipal law by separate States. The leading principle of the whole doctrine is the entire equality as regards jural capacity between the States to which it is applied. It does not transcend the limits of full jural recognition — what I have characterised as plenary recognition — by the law of nations. In whatever terms we may choose to speak of such semi-barbarous States as Turkey, China, Japan, and the like, they are not recognised States in this sense — their recognition is only partial — and in place of recognising their jurisdiction, and accepting their local law, the civilised States, as we have seen, maintain judges of their own to administer justice within their borders, whenever it is demanded by the interests of their own citizens. An honest contract made in China, or in Turkey, would no doubt be valid, and might be enforced in England; but its honesty would not be assumed in virtue of the judgment of a Chinese or a Turkish court, nor would it be determined in England by Chinese or Turkish law—the latter of which excludes the evidence of unbelievers. When civilisation comes in contact with barbar-

[1] Guthrie, p. 250. [2] Note B, p. 267 *et seq.*

ism, the principles of civilisation must be applied, and facts must be determined by civilised rules. But once determined, civilised men must be contented to weigh the facts in barbarous scales.[1] Life, property, and even virtue, have not the same value amongst savages and civilised men. The "Bulgarian atrocities" would have been ten times more atrocious had they been perpetrated in England. The responsibilities of savages diminish in proportion to their rights; and this is true not only of cruelty and immorality, but of such crimes as theft and perjury. My friends, who hold colonial judgeships, tell me that if they were to send to prison all witnesses who tell lies in their courts, there would very soon be no free negroes at all, and the beneficent objects of emancipation would be defeated.

CHAPTER X.

RELATIONS OF MUTUAL AID.

(A) *Pacific co-operation in behalf of freedom.*

The key-note of this work, from the first, has been the interdependence of States, as opposed to their independence, which is the leading thought in ·most treatises on international law. I have represented interdependence as the necessary condition at once of the continued coexistence of separate political entities, and of their progress towards that

[1] Lawrence's *Wheaton*, p. 223.

freedom of separate action on which their development, as ethical entities, depends. This law of the life of States I have traced back to the still wider law of the reciprocity of rights and duties—a law of relations which embraces the whole sphere of conscious existence. Wherever there is a conscious subject and a conscious object, they can live and grow only in and through each other.

As the soundness of this doctrine, which binds jurisprudence to ethics at every step, must be taken for granted at the present stage of our progress, it would be worse than superfluous that I should here enlarge on co-operation, either as a duty or as a right. The only question is as to the extent to which it can be regarded as a principle of action within the sphere of the normal relations. So long as no abnormal conditions of coexistence have arisen, can separate States do more for each other than to let each other alone? Does the relation of mutual confidence, which we have seen to be the normal attitude of recognised States, ever jurally admit of being converted into the attitude of mutual assistance?

From the adoption of the freedom of separate action as the object of international jurisprudence, it results that this question can receive an affirmative answer only to a limited extent, and for exceptional purposes. Recognised States are international persons who have attained majority—they are *sui juris*, and it is generally under conditions more or less abnormal that one grown man can aid another. A perpendicular wall needs no buttress, and he that is whole needs no physician. But, in States as in men, strength and health are only relative terms, and even in so ordinary a case as the enforcement of its own criminal law, we have seen, under the doctrine of extradition, the existence at common law of the right and the duty of mutual aid. It is thus not alone the presence of so formidable an element of disturbance as war which entitles one State to call in the aid of another; and, without attempting to exhaust a subject so largely dependent on circumstances, the following may be mentioned as directions in which recognising States are jurally bound to co-operate with each other.

1st, In framing and continually readjusting the positive laws by which their mutual relations are defined,—(international legislation).

2d, In applying these laws to special cases,—(international jurisdiction).

3d, In enforcing these laws in the event of resistance,—(international execution).

In an irregular form the European Concert, for the present, charges itself with these functions.

4th, In carrying out engineering operations of international importance, such as the construction of international roads, railways, canals, harbours of refuge, and the like.

5th, In protecting such works against the encroachments of separate States, or of exclusive interests.

6th, In vindicating international honesty by the liquidation of debts, whether incurred by one State to another, or by a State to the citizens of another State. The fact that individuals speculate in foreign funds merely with a view to their private gain, is no reason why the States which borrow from them should be permitted to lower the tone of international morality by swindling them with impunity.

7*th*, In preventing the spread of infection by quarantine regulations.

(*B*) *Warlike co-operation in behalf of freedom.*

Though war, as we shall see, is an abnormal relation both between belligerents *inter se* and between belligerents and neutrals, it is a normal relation, when jural at all, between allies. It is by the aid of this normal relation, indeed, that the abnormal relations with which we shall have to deal in the second part of the present work can, for the most part, be most easily and safely removed. By separate action nations may occasionally burst the bars of the prison-house to which their jealousies have consigned them, but it is by combination alone that the door can be opened. There is scarcely any object of international interest which might not be attained by an alliance similar to that by which the aggressive policy of the first Napoleon was arrested; and, had the alliance been more complete, and the allies more enlightened and more true to each other, the design which they originally entertained of guiding the revolution by pacific means might possibly have been accomplished. Yet it is strange how little progress internationalists have made in the use of this inestimable weapon since the Declaration of Pilnitz in 1791. Combined action, whether in Turkey or in Egypt, seems still impossible; whilst the mutual jealousy of Russia and England prevents both of them from effecting, either conjointly or severally, the common object which they have in view of establishing order and settled government in

Central Asia. In time of peace no attempt is made to devise a scheme of common action, and each warlike occurrence thus takes the States of Europe by surprise, just as if they were entering, for the first time, on the experiences of international life. All that they have to guide them is an unbroken narrative of failure, from which no inferences have been drawn and no lessons have been learnt. In presence of this neglect of the reasoned study of the public law of nations, the care and industry which is bestowed by our ablest jurists, not without success, on the development of private international law, seems pretty much as if a shepherd were to occupy himself in shooting rabbits and sparrows, whilst his flocks were being carried off by wolves and vultures.

END OF THE FIRST VOLUME.

PRINTED BY WILLIAM BLACKWOOD AND SONS.

THE INSTITUTES OF LAW:

A TREATISE OF THE PRINCIPLES OF JURISPRUDENCE AS DETERMINED BY NATURE.

By JAMES LORIMER,

Advocate, Regius Professor of Public Law and of the Law of Nature and Nations
in the University of Edinburgh.

New Edition, Revised throughout and much Enlarged.

Demy 8vo, 18s.

OPINIONS OF THE PRESS.

"For the variety of the topics which it embraces, and the fulness with which it discusses them, Professor Lorimer's new edition of his 'Institutes of Law' deserves a place on the shelves alike of the jurist, the historian, the civilian, and the canonist."—*Law Magazine.*

"It is the only complete treatise on the principles of jurisprudence which this country has for long produced.......It is an able exposition, and should succeed in awakening a revived interest in the study of the principles of our science."—*Journal of Jurisprudence.*

"'The Institutes of Law' is an earnest and powerful effort to place another system in the place of utilitarianism."—*Times.*

"Two qualities of Professor Lorimer's volume demand from us a special meed of praise. One is its literary style, so flexible and finished; always elegant and dignified, and rising smoothly and gracefully to the level of its subject-matter. ....The other is its erudite suggestiveness, introducing the reader, as it does, to the intellectual society of many of the foremost thinkers of the human race."—*Scotsman.*

"We recommend this volume to all lawyers who look on their craft in a large and philosophical spirit, as well as to every cultivated and thoughtful man. Its style is pure and is eminently attractive."—*Spectator.*

WILLIAM BLACKWOOD & SONS, EDINBURGH & LONDON.

STUDIES IN ROMAN LAW.
WITH COMPARATIVE VIEWS OF THE LAWS OF FRANCE, ENGLAND, AND SCOTLAND.

By LORD MACKENZIE,
One of the Judges of the Court of Session in Scotland.

Fifth Edition, Revised, Edited by JOHN KIRKPATRICK, Esq., M.A. Cantab.,
Dr Jur. Heidelb., LL.B. Edin.

Octavo, 12s.

OPINIONS ON THE FOURTH EDITION.

"A new edition of Lord Mackenzie's well-known book calls for little comment upon the bulk of the work. It is the accepted elementary text-book for students of comparative jurisprudence.......The contributions to the present edition are of three kinds. First, there is the addition of very numerous references to the original authorities of antiquity, in addition to the indirect method of referring to modern text-writers, mainly French and German, upon the different branches of the Corpus Juris. This is wholly good, and constitutes a distinct addition to the value of the book. Secondly, there is a large contribution of additional notes by the present editor, filling in to some extent the details of the original sketch. They are most numerous in that part of the work which deals with the law of civil procedure—a branch of Roman law upon the complex nature of which modern research and discovery have thrown much light."—*Pall Mall Gazette.*

"Contains a valuable addition furnished by the editor, Mr Kirkpatrick, in the shape of fuller references to the original authorities on Roman law."—*Saturday Review.*

"A thoroughly serviceable text-book on Roman law. Great praise is due to the accomplished and erudite editor of this fourth edition for the manner in which he has performed his task."—*Journal of Jurisprudence.*

"We feel sure that the student, or any one using the volume professionally, will not fail to be impressed with the accuracy and learning which Mr Kirkpatrick has displayed."—*Courant.*

"But now we have Mr Kirkpatrick coming to the rescue with all the appliances of modern research and criticism, and stamping the original volume with an entirely novel form and feature. To say that he has produced a new work would be misleading, for the text of Lord Mackenzie remains, and the same useful purpose it has served before may be again accomplished. But a valuable supplement has been added, drawing it within the category of scientific exposition, fitting it to serve as a manual to students, and as an aid to the exact as opposed to the mere general reader. In this respect it occupies a commanding position in comparison with all previous editions."—*Scotsman.*

WILLIAM BLACKWOOD & SONS, EDINBURGH AND LONDON.

Sir Archibald Alison, Bart.

SOME ACCOUNT OF MY LIFE AND WRITINGS. An
AUTOBIOGRAPHY. By the late SIR ARCHIBALD ALISON, BART., D.C.L. Edited by his Daughter-in-Law, LADY ALISON. Two Volumes, 8vo, with Portraits, 36s.

"Deserves to be read not for amusement merely, but instruction.......Affords a striking example of what perseverance and directness of purpose can accomplish."—*Athenæum.*

"There is much of fair-mindedness and old-fashioned courtesy scattered over these two volumes, which it is rather pleasant to come across, after the surfeit of 'Reminiscences' of a very different sort which we have recently had."—*Spectator.*

MEMOIR OF THE HONOURABLE
GEORGE KEITH ELPHINSTONE, K.B., VISCOUNT KEITH,
ADMIRAL OF THE RED. By ALEXANDER ALLARDYCE, Author of 'The City of Sunshine,' &c. 8vo, with Portrait, Illustrations, and Maps, 21s.

"In writing his life of Admiral Lord Keith, Mr Allardyce has done an excellent piece of literary work, and made a valuable contribution to our naval history.......We can recommend Mr Allardyce's book as most interesting reading, being full of varied and animated incident, while it contains much valuable historical information."—*Times.*

"As a careful study of a life-history which interweaved itself with many of the gravest historical events, the present volume may be warmly commended."—*Observer.*

"A valuable contribution to our stock of naval biography."—*Academy.*

ROUGH RECOLLECTIONS OF MILITARY SERVICE AND
SOCIETY. By LIEUT.-COLONEL BALCARRES D. WARDLAW RAMSAY. Two Volumes, post 8vo, 21s.

"The brace of laughable stories which we shall now quote will recall Charles Lever's merriest vein.......We can quote no more samples of Colonel Ramsay's strictly personal recollections, but must remark that they are all so uniformly good, that our selections can lay no claim to be in any sense the pick of his well-stocked basket."—*Spectator.*

"The volumes are charged with anecdotes, some of them truly delicious........ These amusing volumes are, as we have said, replete with authentic and excellent anecdotes of persons great and small."—*Saturday Review.*

A CRITICAL INQUIRY INTO THE SCOTTISH LANGUAGE.
With the view of Illustrating THE RISE AND PROGRESS OF CIVILISATION IN SCOTLAND. By FRANCISQUE-MICHEL, F.S.A., Lond. and Scot., Correspondant de l'Institut de France, &c. In One handsome Quarto Volume, printed on handmade paper, and appropriately bound in Roxburghe style, 66s.

"Assuredly only a most enthusiastic philologist and archæologist would have taken the pains which have borne their fruits in this very unique work.......We have seldom opened a book of the kind in which we found such interesting or even seductive reading. The style is light and lively, the facts are fresh, original, and piquant; and, in short, in striking into bypaths of archæological history, while collecting curiosities and eccentricities of philology, M. Michel has imparted to his chapters much of the animation of mediæval romance. For, after what we have said, we need hardly add that this is no mere scholarly disquisition on words and their synonyms. It came naturally within the scope of the author's inquiries to sketch the manners of the Scottish nation in early times, and to embrace, in a rapid but comprehensive glance, the progress of their arts, industries, and sciences."—*The Times.*

THE WORKS OF HORACE. TRANSLATED INTO ENGLISH VERSE. WITH A LIFE AND NOTES. By SIR THEODORE MARTIN, K.C.B. Two Volumes, post 8vo, printed on hand-made paper, 21s.

"Of the translation itself we can speak in terms of almost unqualified praise. Whether it be looked at from the point of view of the scholar or of the English reader it is alike excellent.......Sir Theodore Martin's chief characteristic as a translator is his consummate ease. One might read page after page without ever suspecting that the work was a translation; and yet, on comparing it with the Latin, it will be found that almost every shade of meaning is expressed or suggested with a fidelity which Conington himself has scarcely equalled."—*Saturday Review.*

MEMOIR OF ALEXANDER SETON, EARL OF DUNFERMLINE; President of the Court of Session, and Chancellor of Scotland. With an APPENDIX, embracing a List of the various PRESIDENTS OF THE COURT, and GENEALOGICAL TABLES of the four principal Legal Families of Scotland (ERSKINE, HOPE, DALRYMPLE, and DUNDAS). By GEORGE SETON, Advocate, M.A. Oxon. Small 4to, 21s.

"A piece of honest work was to be expected from the practised hand of Mr Seton, and on the whole the reader will not be disappointed.......The author has done his best to give a human interest to his narrative; he has aimed at showing that antiquarian biography need not be 'dry as a bone, hard as a stone, and cold as a cucumber.'"—*Athenæum.*

"We have here everything connected with the subject of the book that could interest the historical student, the herald, the genealogist, and the archæologist. The result is a book worthy of its author's high reputation."—*Notes and Queries.*

"The author has made good use of everything that could throw any light on the character of Chancellor Seton."—*Academy.*

A TOUR IN GREECE, 1880. By RICHARD RIDLEY FARRER. With Twenty-seven Full-page Illustrations, by LORD WINDSOR. Royal 8vo, with a Map, 21s.

"The most chaste and elegant book of the present season........Mr Farrer's narrative is well written and scholarly. It leaves nothing to be desired as a description of the Greece of the past as seen in the remains of it existing in the present day."—*Land and Water.*

"Mr Farrer's narrative is decidedly above the average: in many respects we should be inclined to give it rank as the best account of a pleasure tour in Greece.......Lord Windsor has shown both taste and judgment in the selection of scenes for his illustrations."—*St James's Gazette.*

THE REVOLT OF MAN. By WALTER BESANT. Sixth Edition. Crown 8vo, 3s. 6d.

"'The Revolt of Man' is decidedly clever.......It is a happy idea well worked out, and must rank amongst the best literary confections of its kind."—*Athenæum.*

"The romance contains a love-story carried on under conditions of freshness that will inspire envy in the heart of many a novelist."—*Globe.*

"The author of the satirical romance before us has achieved a very remarkable success.......The book, as a whole, ought to be read by everybody who has the wit to appreciate it, with a great deal of pleasure and amusement."—*Saturday Review.*

"A vivacious satire, sustained and wrought out with exceptional ingenuity and point."—*Scotsman.*

WILLIAM BLACKWOOD & SONS, EDINBURGH AND LONDON.

www.ingramcontent.com/pod-product-compliance
Lightning Source LLC
Chambersburg PA
CBHW022107300426
44117CB00007B/626